STATES AND THE ECONOMY

States and the Economy

POLICYMAKING AND DECENTRALIZATION

Robert H. Wilson

Westport, Connecticut
London

Library of Congress Cataloging-in-Publication Data

Wilson, Robert Hines.
   States and the economy : policymaking and decentralization /
Robert H. Wilson.
     p. cm.
   Includes bibliographical references and index.
   ISBN 0–275–94506–5 (alk. paper)
   1. United States—Economic conditions—1945–   2. Central-local
government relations—United States.   3. State governments—United
States.   4. United States—Economic policy.   I. Title.
HC106.5.W56   1993
338.973—dc20   92–33329

British Library Cataloguing in Publication Data is available.

Library of Congress Catalog Card Number: 92–33329
ISBN: 0–275–94506–5

First published in 1993

Praeger Publishers, 88 Post Road West, Westport, CT 06881
An imprint of Greenwood Publishing Group, Inc.

Printed in the United States of America

∞™

The paper used in this book complies with the Permanent Paper
Standard issued by the National Information Standards
Organization (Z39.48–1984).

10 9 8 7 6 5 4 3 2

For Rita and David

Contents

Illustrations

FIGURES

MAPS

APPENDICES

Acknowledgments

This book represents the culmination of several years of work, and much of the work was undertaken with others. My initial foray into state development policy occurred in a policy research project, in the L.B.J. School of Public Affairs, University of Texas at Austin, co-directed with my colleague Jurgen Schmandt. This collaboration proved very productive and we next examined state telecommunications policy with Frederick Williams, College of Communication, University of Texas at Austin, joining us as a co-director. Further studies of telecommunications policy followed and our team expanded to include Sharon Strover, also of the College of Communication. These projects involved research teams comprised of our graduate students, and much of the thinking presented in this book originated and was refined in these very rich and exciting projects. My debt to these colleagues and student researchers is substantial.

As my attention shifted to writing the book, others provided very important assistance. The empirical analysis of economic geography relied very heavily on the extraordinary computer programming talents of Starling Pullum, of the Population Research Center, University of Texas at Austin. Excellent research assistance was provided by former students, Marian Barber and Robert Stephens, and editorial assistance came from Alison Tartt. In the final phases of the project, I benefitted greatly from the close reading of the manuscript by Emmette Redford, a colleague at the L.B.J. School. Finally, Yayoi DiSanto provided tireless help, ranging from revising the manuscript, to bibliographical research, to developing tables and graphs. Her talents and hard work made my work much easier, and for this I am very grateful. Grants from the University Research Institute and the Policy Research Institute of the University of Texas at Austin proved crucial to the work.

1

Introduction

The longest period of post–World War II economic growth in the United States ended in 1991. The recession, however, was only one, and perhaps not the principal, source of concern about the country's economic future. The brutal deindustrialization of the late 1970s and early 1980s, the uncertain success of U.S. goods in the international market, the revolving regional recessions of the 1980s—first in the Southwest, then in the Northeast and Midwest—and the ever-expanding turmoil in financial markets created great uncertainty and concern. Various effects of increasing income inequality in the country became more apparent, confidence in the country's educational system eroded and the difficulty of the young in buying homes was very different from those of their parents a generation ago. These concerns further contributed to apprehension about the future.

For most of this century, the federal government has been the principal forum for addressing economic development issues. Although the development role of the federal government has remained central, federal policy has not responded to the recent development needs of states and regions. For both economic and political reasons, state government in the United States has been rejuvenated as an important public policy arena for effecting economic change. As during other important economic junctures in the country's history, those states that understand and take advantage of these changing circumstances will be in a better position to ensure their future prosperity.

Economic development policy is the most dramatic example of rejuvenated state government. Even though states have exercised important roles throughout the history of the country, they have not been perceived as leaders in development policy until recently. Their previous lack of initiative can be explained by a number of factors. Following World War II, the economies of many states created a stable set of demands on state government. A set of state institutions and investment patterns evolved that provided a stable environment for structurally stable economies. But in recent years, structural economic change has changed the nature of the economic environment faced by states. The traditional policies adopted by state governments in support of their economies are no longer consistent with the demands of the changing economy. The inadequacy of traditional education and training systems for the new economic reality is one dimension, and one that falls largely within state government responsibility. Research and development, technical and scientific labor, venture capital, technology diffusion, and telecommunications infrastructure are but a few of the other important elements of the new economy, and ones to which state governments are directing their attention.

This revival of state government was not sought by state officials. Rather, it has been the reaction of states to responsibilities thrust upon them by a fiscally stressed federal government as well as by economic and political decentralization. These changes have presented challenges to state governments, and these governments have responded in surprisingly innovative ways: they have improved their fiscal and technical capabilities; they have adopted a new range of policy initiatives; and they have adapted existing institutions to a new economic context.

Economic decentralization, referred to here in terms of the spatial distribution of economic activity and not to ownership or control of capital, has been one of the central features of recent structural change in the U.S. economy. This change can be characterized by two types of employment shifts. First, employment in traditional manufacturing industries declined in the 1970s, but during roughly the same period new and fast-growing advanced technology manufacturing firms have emerged. Technology and international competition have driven much of the change in the manufacturing sector. The net effect of this shift has been a dramatic decline in relative employment levels in manufacturing and a rapid expansion in the service industries—the second significant employment shift.

Restructuring of the U.S. economy, coupled with stiff international competition, has produced a series of ancillary problems. These include employment mismatches, both sectoral and spatial, in which workers in declining industries have not been trained adequately for employment in a growing sector nor located in regions where employment growth is occurring. Some have argued further that wage differentials in the declining and growing sectors have produced increasing wage and earnings inequality. Furthermore, cities and states were not well prepared to incorporate the infrastructure and fiscal implications of the rapid population shifts—largely from the North to the South and West—linked in part to structural economic change.

The spatial impact of structural economic change was not addressed by the federal government in any significant way during the 1980s. The types of federal policies that might have eased spatial adjustments, such as slowing the spatial mobility of capital, plant-closing programs, and retraining or employment programs in areas of high unemployment, were not adopted in Washington; in fact, some tools of potential help were dismantled. Rather, under federal policy, the marketplace became the arena in which adjustments were made. As the effects of these brutal adjustments took hold, the locus of policy initiative was transferred to state and local governments where, unlike Washington, pressure for action was acute and focused.

As structural change has worked its way through the economy, two long-term impacts have become clear. First, the technological advances initially identified with advanced technology products are being absorbed by all sectors of the economy. Anecdotal evidence of this technological diffusion can be found in the ubiquitous computer chip, which is no longer used only in computers but in everything from automobiles to refrigerators to toys. In addition, technological advances have permitted productivity increases in traditional manufacturing and in the service sector. The rather dismal productivity growth rate of recent decades should dramatically improve as these advances move throughout the economy.

A second impact of economic change, and one fundamental for the argument being made in this book, is that regional and state economies have become more structurally diversified. While this argument will be more fully developed in Chapter 2, diversification is the result of an increasingly spatially dispersed manufacturing sector. Even the pattern of the more spatially concentrated advanced technology manufacturing sector is unlike that of traditional manufacturing. Diversification is also influenced by the growing importance of a rapidly growing, spatially dispersed service sector. Much of the service sector employment is population dependent, and thus its rate of growth is strongly associated with population change. Key subsectors, however, such as producer and business services, are less dependent on local population and demand but are nevertheless also concentrated in major cities of all regions and contribute to the diversification of regional and state economies.

Diversification in regional and state economies can be conceived as decentralization in the national economy. States and regions which in an earlier period had highly specialized economies now have relatively larger shares of other sectors and thus have become more diversified. For most states diversification has not come easily. For the traditional manufacturing states in the Midwest, diversification has followed a dramatic downturn in the very sectors in which these states had previously held comparative advantages. Today, however, we see a thriving advanced technology robotics sector in the region, one that is supplying key inputs to most manufacturing sectors.

Industrialization in the South followed a distinct pattern, but one consistent with the decentralization argument. Historically, a region with low levels of manufacturing based on low-wage, low-skill production, the South now boasts extensive manufacturing, somewhat weighted to the lower end of manufacturing sectors, but also with a significant share of advanced technology manufacturing. Diversification meant relatively rapid growth in the South, but even here difficulties were encountered: uncontrolled growth placed excessive demands on infrastructure, and the inadequately trained labor force and ineffective school systems were incompatible with the demands of some of the growing sectors.

The emerging economy is displaying a structure and location pattern distinctly different from that of the past, but in addition this economy is based on a mix of factors unlike that of the past. For example, new firms and emerging sectors frequently cannot call upon traditional sources of financing, and therefore sources of high-risk financing—seed and venture capital—must be available. The education and skill requirements of the work force are also changing; the share of total employment that is low-skill labor is sharply declining while high-skill labor is increasing dramatically. Research and development (R&D) is becoming more critical to economic growth. Some view R&D as just one aspect of the new "information economy." Whether one agrees with this characterization or not, production and transmission of information is becoming a larger share of the national product, and telecommunications is the infrastructure critical to competitiveness in information-intensive business. Finally, the U.S. economy is more internationalized, which means that firms are more involved in export activities and competing abroad. To be successful, firms must not only supply good products but also have available a rather extensive export infrastructure, including transport facilities, marketing, and financing capabilities.

In the U.S. economy, the private sector is the primary actor in development. But for virtually all of the contemporary economic challenges listed here, the public sector also has a vital role to play if the economy is to reach its full potential. Hence, development policy is important, if not critical. But the public sector itself faces two challenges. The support traditionally provided to the economy by the public sector must be adapted to a new set of infrastructure and development needs. Furthermore, the roles and functions of federal and state governments are themselves being redefined.

Political decentralization, with its resulting shifts in intergovernmental relations, provides a second important context for state development policy. Political decentralization, a form of which was manifest in President Reagan's New Federalism, implies a strengthening of state and local government or, as some might argue, a restitution of the constitutional prerogatives and responsibilities of the states. Shifts in the relationship and relative power of federal and state governments have occurred throughout the country's history. The Constitution provided for strong state governments with considerable autonomy, and the states fully exercised this autonomy. The federal government exercised its constitutional powers at the time of the Civil War, delimiting potential actions by states, but states regained their relative position thereafter. In the early part of this century, the federal government began to expand its intervention in the economy to the detriment of state prerogatives. The requirements of an increasingly complex and interconnected economy led to federal involvement in a wide range of policy areas.

While some argue that an aggressive federal government was the source of that expansion of power, it is also apparent that states were not up to the task before them. In the 1930s, one scholar observed, "I do not predict that the states will go, but affirm that they have gone . . . gone because they were unable to deal even inefficiently with the imperative, the life and death tasks of the new national economy."[1] Several decades later, in a survey of state government, the former governor of North Carolina, Terry Sanford, again found states unable to meet the challenges before them.[2]

Purported intrusion of the federal government into areas of state responsibility has been one of the long-standing complaints of the Republican Party. During the four Republican presidencies of the last two decades various actions were taken to reestablish a more proper relationship between the federal government and the states. The contemporary debate on the intrusive nature of the federal government involves two issues. One concerns intergovernmental relations and the appropriate assignment of governmental responsibilities. The discussion frequently involves the normative question of what government *should* do, with the answer by some being that government in the United States, especially the federal government, is doing entirely too much. The second underlying concern has been the differing interests of Democratic and Republican party constituencies. Whatever the relative importance of these two issues, a third factor has effectively consolidated political decentralization. The Democrat-controlled Congress and Republican presidency have produced a stalemate in Washington, and a striking lack of federal consensus and initiative in many policy areas. With this immobilization at the federal level, states or local governments have represented the only venue available for many policy issues. The Clinton presidency ends, at least for the next several years, the period of divided government. However, the fiscal constraints resulting from the federal debt will not soon disappear and this will undoubtedly limit the range and extent of federal initiatives.

A set of forces, originating in the 1950s, prepared states for meeting the challenge that would befall them in the late 1970s. These included a set of institutional reforms in state government—resulting from constitutional reform, reapportionment, and expanded political franchise—and the state administration of federal initiatives. Even during periods of federal leadership in domestic policy and expanding federal expenditures, states frequently played major roles in implementation; as a result, they had to expand their human, financial, and technical capabilities. These factors produced steady progress in improving the competence and capability of state government, creating a foundation upon which a new set of active and progressive governors, Democratic and Republican, could reestablish a significant state role in public policy agenda setting.

State governments have become a principal arena for discussions of development policy but to fully understand their response two questions must be addressed. Do states have the policy instruments and resources available to address this issue effectively? And do the policies adopted represent a distinct break from past practice and, thus, represent innovation?

Until recently, state economic development policy was conceived fairly narrowly, generally consisting of programs to recruit manufacturing firms to a state through business assistance or incentives. Under these programs, businesses are directly benefitted and, consequently, there is direct intervention by state government in the marketplace. Such incentives are frequently offered to businesses contemplating the location of new production facilities. This form of state action, commonly called industrial recruitment, is of long standing. In 1936, Mississippi state government created the Balance Agriculture with Industry (BAWI) program with the objective of attracting manufacturing investment to this predominately rural and very poor state to diversify its economy.[3] The BAWI program set the pattern for the South's industrial development strategy, attempting to capture manufacturing firms decentralizing from the industrial heartland, and anticipated the forms of incentive packages that are now frequently extended by most states to firms: tax abatements, low-interest loans, subsidized training programs, and subsidized facilities.[4]

In the late 1970s and 1980s, the competition was no longer limited to low-wage manufacturing but broadened to include automotive manufacturing plants and electronic manufacturing, both domestic and foreign.[5] In 1978, Pennsylvania successfully outbid Ohio with an incentive package worth $71 million to attract the first foreign automotive manufacturing facility, a Volkswagen plant, to Westmoreland County, southeast of Pittsburgh.[6] In 1980, Tennessee attracted a Nissan plant with an incentive package that amounted to about $11,000 per job and in 1985 lured GM's Saturn plant with a package worth $26,000 per job. Kentucky gained a Toyota plant around the same time for $50,000 per job. In 1985, Illinois won over Diamond-Star Motors, a joint venture of Chrysler and Mitsubishi, and Indiana attracted a joint Fuji-Isuzu plant with packages worth $50,000 per job.

The airlines industry has been also subject to intense competition. Whether for manufacturing facilities, maintenance facilities, or hub services provided by airports, the airlines industry is viewed as very attractive and likely to be a solid industry in the future, even though many of the companies face financial difficulties in the short term.[7] McDonnell Douglas, in searching for a site for a major new plant, has asked for help from local and state governments in borrowing its $1.4 billion investment in facilities and equipment on an "off balance sheet" basis. The bonds must be held by someone other than McDonnell Douglas, most likely a government or quasi-government agency. Northwest Airlines struck a deal with the State of Minnesota that will likely be worth $800–$900 million dollars. In order to attract a United Airlines maintenance facility, Virginia passed special legislation for the negotiation, Oklahoma City voters approved a local tax increase, and Colorado offered a package worth $2,000 per employee-year for workers at the facility. Another proposal calls for America West Airlines to form a partnership with the state of Arizona or Nevada. Unlike the earlier attempts to industrialize the rural South, these states were competing for high-wage, advanced production technology firms and making very large financial commitments.

Similar competition among states, though not on the same scale, occurs in the advanced technology sector for research and development facilities. Intense competition for Microelectronics and Computer Technology Corporation (MCC) and Sematech, industry consortia in microelectronics research and development and in microelectronics production technology, drew large incentive packages from many communities before an Austin, Texas, location was chosen. Competition for federal research laboratories has also produced sizable incentive packages. In capturing a magnetism research laboratory, the University of Florida organized a consortium which included out-of-state competitors. Intense competition for the supercollider-superconducter research laboratory, a multibillion dollar research facility, drew bids from many states, but in the end a location in Waxahachie, Texas, was chosen. Even though the number of jobs created, as compared with that of automobile production plants, is relatively small, the facilities are nevertheless deemed highly desirable for the potential multiplier effect that research and development activities hold for commercialization of new products and production technology.

Several hypotheses have been developed to explain the involvement of states in these competitive struggles for investment.[8] According to one hypothesis, the intense economic distress of the late 1970s created a political demand, focused on state government, for policy initiatives. The interregional variation of this explanation was found in the second "war between the states," announced in 1976 by *Business Week* when the stark contrast in prospects between northern and sunbelt states became evident.[9] As structural change worked its way through the economy during the latter half of the 1980s, competition was found to be less focused on the North and South than between states within a single region and among cities or areas within a state. Given that even states with no economic distress participate in this competition, the distress hypothesis appears incomplete.

Another plausible hypothesis for this competition is the arms race scenario.[10] States adopt incentives in order not to fall behind other states. Policies are not adopted due to their demonstrated or potential effectiveness, but because other states have adopted similar programs. This explanation is consistent with the historical pattern in which innovation in one state is quickly adopted in other states. This strategy, however, may or may not produce sound public policy.

States are not the only participants in this competition, and it is important to reflect on the relative bargaining position of other actors. States are competing for investment, whereas firms, or the federal government, are searching for investment sites. In a single competition, there are many potential sites, or states, but only a single investor. States, consequently, can be played off against one another and the less attractive a state is for a particular investment, the greater the concessions that must be offered to attract the investment. Public incentives generally affect only a limited number of a firm's location factors, and these are not likely to be critical to a firm's location decision. However, with only a single buyer and many sellers, the buyer has a considerable advantage in negotiating with governments on incentive packages.[11]

The nature of the incentive package can affect firms not directly involved in the negotiation. When the package includes incentives for a specific firm rather than broad incentives (e.g., a tax abatement for an individual firm rather than lower tax rates for all firms), a question of fairness arises among firms that must compete with the firm being attracted.[12] In addition, taxpayers are affected parties. The benefits and costs from a taxpayer's perspective are often not fully considered in these bidding wars. In general, the more narrow the incentive package in terms of the intended beneficiary, the fewer the benefits to taxpayers.

Although the bargaining scenario may appear to place states at a disadvantage, some argue that benefits can accrue even to states that lose.[13] If a state carefully analyzes its economic strengths and weaknesses in developing a bid, this understanding may improve subsequent policymaking in the state. Furthermore, the bidding process may strengthen cooperation between the public sector and the private sector, which again may provide a better basis for developing policy in the future. Also, the losing states may capture external benefits. For example, although Austin won the Sematech competition, Sematech named several universities in other states as affiliated centers of excellence; Florida received $51 million worth of federal education grants as a direct result of its involvement in the competition.[14]

Although competition among states and communities for investment has certainly not diminished since the mid-1970s—it probably has actually increased—governments are more sophisticated in their understanding of the competition. As a result, they may require firms receiving incentive packages to meet performance standards that insure the development of resources in the community and state, and they may attempt a more realistic matching of firms' location requirements and attributes of the local economy. Even so, this type of competition generates a modern variation of the boosterism that has been characteristic of local and state governments since the founding of the country and, as such, remains subject to poor judgment and abuse.

State development policy is today certainly more than industrial recruitment, and even recruitment programs target advanced technology firms associated with the emerging sectors of the economy. This book defines state development policy even more broadly, to include state roles in infrastructure provision, economic regulation, technology development and diffusion, resource mobilization, and others. Some activities affect a state's economy directly, whereas others have an indirect effect. The historical analysis will show that these types of activities are by no means unique to recent state policy.

States supply various types of infrastructure, such as highways, which not only generate economic activity directly, through construction expenditures, but also indirectly by affecting the costs incurred by firms, such as transportation costs. States have played this type of role since the founding of the country, occasionally with dramatic effect. The construction of the Erie Canal forever changed the region's pattern of commerce and allowed New York to project its commercial presence throughout the Great Lakes area. State governments also participated in the enormous expansion of the railroad system during the last century[15] and highways in recent decades. In California, early state efforts in water development played a major role in establishing the conditions for economic growth. More recently, Arizona developed a successful water resource management system with the aim of facilitating growth. One may choose not to call these efforts innovative; nevertheless, state governments have frequently fulfilled their responsibilities for infrastructure provision quite well, and in many instances substantial development impacts have occurred.

Within the parameters of the U.S. Constitution and the exercise of national functions, states regulate businesses of various types, including utilities—electricity, natural gas, and telecommunications—financial institutions—banks, savings and loans, and insurance companies—professional occupations, and others. Some of these regulatory functions, as will be seen below, predate the U.S. Constitution, and many have evolved as the intergovernmental roles in regulatory federalism have changed. In addition, the rationale for regulation and the means by which firms are regulated vary among industries. Although the purpose of the regulatory function rarely includes economic development, its exercise nevertheless affects a state's economy.

In terms of social infrastructure, state governments make enormous contributions. States, in cooperation with localities, have established public and compulsory education in the United States. Education today constitutes the largest single expenditure for states, and the level of education and quality of the labor force represent important dimensions of a state's economy. Although the federal government provided the impetus at certain times—as in the Morrill Land Grant Act of 1862 and subsequent legislation intended to encourage states to establish colleges and universities and in compensatory and early childhood education of the 1960s—state governments, in cooperation with localities, have held principal responsibility for the provision of education. In addition, state governments have been major participants in the agricultural extension services, a form of technology transfer, which historically have contributed to the high standing of U.S. agriculture in the world economy.

Investments in transportation, water systems, education, and technology transfer are actions that affect the level of activity in a local economy indirectly; they usually affect the productivity of factors of production but are not themselves commodities and, consequently, are somewhat removed from the marketplace. Most of these activities require very substantial public funding and may not seem to most observers to be potential avenues for innovative behavior. Yet these activities can play an important role in contemporary economic change.

In spite of exercising significant functions throughout the history of the country, states have not been perceived as leaders in economic development policy. The apparent lack of development policy initiative on the part of state governments can be explained by a number of factors. During periods of economic stability, a stable set of demands are placed on state government, and a corresponding set of state institutions and investment patterns emerges. We find a good example of this behavior in Texas. The Texas Railroad Commission, established in the early part of this century, managed oil production in the state in a fashion that established stability in the market and protected independent oil producers, a highly significant political constituency. Low-level expenditures for such social programs as education were perfectly consistent with the needs of oil and agricultural industries in the state. A similar pattern was evident in most of the southern states.

The lack of the prominence of state involvement in economic matters can also be traced to a factor operating during the period of rapid industrialization at the turn of the century: the demands associated with the formation and control of a national market. The nationalization of the economy meant that barriers to interstate commerce, erected by states for various purposes, had to be removed. The regulatory activities of states, in railroads and electric power, for example, were to be subordinated to a federal regulatory policy which controlled interstate commerce. The federal government also promoted the settlement of the West, frequently motivated to act when states or territories were found not to have the resources required. The inadequacy of states was very evident during the Depression, when the federal government assumed a new development responsibility—the management of the national economy.

As we near the end of the twentieth century, state development policy faces a different economic environment. First, high rates of unemployment and permanent loss of manufacturing and other jobs have created significant pressure on state governments to take action after it has become clear that the federal government will not address spatial impacts of structural change. Second, the traditional policies, including economic and social infrastructure investments and economic development tools, adopted by state governments in support of their economies, are no longer consistent with the demands of the emerging economy. Research and development, technical and scientific labor, venture capital, and technology diffusion are but a few of the important factors for the emerging economy, and these received only limited attention from state governments in the past.

Structural economic change has created new sets of needs in the different industries and segments of the economy. Some of these economic requirements have been translated into political demands and these have become part of the state policymaking environment. It is not that these demands could not be met through federal actions—in many instances, as in the formation of industry research consortia, like MCC and Sematech, or in opening overseas markets to U.S. producers, action by the federal government is essential—but, in general, the federal government has not been responsive to regional and urban economic problems resulting from economic change. Despite little experience in innovative development policy, most states have attempted to respond to new economic needs.

Economic change and the demands of the new economy are strong forces, but state policy will be unlikely determined solely by the technical demands of a changing economy. Specific strategies and programs adopted in states are the outcomes of political processes. Severe and depressed economic conditions force governors and legislatures to take action, but sustaining these actions over the long term requires support after the crisis has passed. Political leaders must be persuaded that new economic development efforts are worthwhile. Organized constituencies, such as business organizations or labor groups, are more likely to be persuasive than unorganized constituencies. But the changing economy is itself affecting the shape and strength of economic constituencies with the possible eclipse of important traditional industries by new constituencies formed in rapidly growing sectors. This process will result in the adaptation of state policies and institutions to the evolving needs of state economies. The outcomes of this political process will be more critical to the future prosperity of state economies than at any time in recent history.

The argument of this book is that economic decentralization and political decentralization are forcing state governments to adjust and even reform a wide range of their functions and programs, including economic development functions that are the main focus of this book. These two processes have thrust state governments to center stage for many policy issues. The specific reaction of states, however, is not predetermined; rather, the reaction will be conditioned by the economic and political structure in a state and by the innovative capacity of state institutions. In fact, it is safe to assume that some states will be more successful than others in taking advantage of their own internal resources and preparing for the future.

The structure of this book is designed to develop these arguments. First, economic and political decentralization will be examined in Chapters 2 and 3, respectively. A framework for considering the role of states in their economy will be established in Chapter 4 and a number of the roles—strategic planning, tax policy, regulation, labor laws, and state–local governmental relations—are discussed in some detail. Case studies of three critical policy areas—development and technology policy, telecommunications policy, and education and training—will then be presented in the following three chapters. Economic development and technology policy generally involves targeted assistance to particular economic sectors, and the state serves as a program provider. Telecommunications policy involves a state regulatory role which has traditionally been a question of establishing a rate structure for monopolies that is fair for consumers and insures the economic viability of the service providers. In the contemporary setting, telecommunications policy has become much more complex and states are being forced to address questions of economic development. Education and training, long a principal responsibility of state government, represent a social infrastructure argued by some to be the most important factor in determining the long-term prospects for a state's economy. While these three roles are quite different—state as economic development program provider; state as economic regulator; state as social infrastructure provider—each is of great importance to the emerging economy.

These three policy areas will be contrasted in several ways in the final chapter in order to draw conclusions concerning the significance and importance of state governments in contemporary economic change. First, the stakes that states face in the restructuring of economic geography are reconsidered. The contrast of agenda setting in the intergovernmental system for each of the three policy areas demonstrates the complexity of policymaking but also the remarkable flexibility of the country's governmental structure to respond to new economic and political challenges. The effect of increasing participation of diverse interest groups and a more competent state apparatus on the quality of economic development policymaking is discussed. The inadequate response of the intergovernmental system, and of states in particular, to certain issues establishes the constraints under which state policymaking continues to operate. Finally, the importance of state policy in this period of economic change is assessed.

NOTES

1. L. H. Gulick, "Reorganization of the States," *Civil Engineering* (August 1933): 421.

2. Terry Sanford, *Storm Over the States* (New York: McGraw-Hill, 1967).

3. James C. Cobb, *The Selling of the South: The Southern Crusade for Industrial Development, 1936–1980* (Baton Rouge, LA: Louisiana State University Press, 1982): Chapter 1.

4. John E. Moes, "The Subsidization of Industry by Local Communities in the South," *Southern Economic Journal* (October 1961): 187–193; Bruce J. Schulman, *Federal Policy, Economic Development, and Transformation of the South, 1938–1980* (New York: Oxford, 1991): 47–49.

5. Michael R. Gordon, "With Foreign Investment at Stake, It's One State Against the Others," *National Journal* (October 18, 1980): 1744–1748.

6. William Fulton, "VW in Pennsylvania: The Tale of the Rabbit That Got Away," *Governing* (November 1988): 32–39. A casualty in the restructured automobile industry, this plant was closed in 1988.

7. "Airwars, Financing Planes, and Airlines," *State Policy Reports*, vol. 9, no. 15 (August 1991): 2–4.

8. Dennis O. Grady, "State Economic Development Incentives: Why Do States Compete?" *State and Local Government Review* (Fall 1987): 86–94; Advisory Commission on Intergovernmental Relations (ACIR), *Interjurisdictional Tax and Policy Competition: Good or Bad for the Federal System* M–177 (Washington, D.C., April 1991): Chapter 2.

9. "The Second War Between the States," *Business Week* (May 17, 1976): 92–111.

10. Paul Peretz, "The Marks for Incentives: Where Angels Fear to Tread?" *Policy Studies Review*, vol. 5, no. 3 (1986): 624–633; Grady, "State Economic Development Incentives," pp. 91–92.

11. Larry C. Ledebur and William W. Hamilton, "The Great Tax-Break Sweepstakes," *State Legislatures* (September 1986): 12–15.

12. Ledebur and Hamilton, "The Great Tax-Break Sweepstakes," p. 14.

13. Gregory Harrison, "The Sematech Project: The States' Perspective," *Site Selection and Industrial Development*, vol. 34, no. 4 (August 1989): 7–9.

14. Harrison, "The Sematech Project," p. 7.

15. Elmer E. Smead, *Governmental Promotion and Regulation of Business* (New York, NY: Appleton-Century-Crofts, 1969): 201–202.

2

Structural Economic Change and the States

By the late 1970s, the dramatic effect of technological change and intense international competition had transformed the structure of the U.S. economy. Although the process of change dated from the 1960s, its effect had become especially visible by the start of the 1980s. Sometimes characterized as a new industrial revolution, this phenomenon involved a broad range of new technological products and processes which affected economic structure and labor markets. This revolution occurred on a worldwide basis, facilitating international trade and the further integration of the world economy. Countries and regions were now competing in world markets for many, if not most, types of goods. The international division of labor brought forth by these developments resulted in severe structural adjustments in the United States.

Structural change in the U.S. economy has restructured the economic geography of the country. For most of this century the industrial heartland was located in land extending from New England through the Middle Atlantic regions and to the Midwest. Today the manufacturing sector follows a much more decentralized pattern. Although the degree of decentralization varies among sectors—e.g., the retail trade sector is more spatially disperse than the petrochemical industry—the overall pattern has been one of diminishing geographical specialization among sectors. In turn, decentralization has led to diversification in the economic structure of states and regions. States tend to have a broader range of economic activities than before and this creates opportunities for innovative development policies. The distinguishing characteristics of state economies have become less dependent of levels of manufacturing and more on certain service sectors and on occupational structure.

The effect of these structural adjustments on state and regional economies will be examined in this chapter. Economic change in the national economy will first be discussed. Special attention will be devoted to telecommunications, an increasingly important infrastructure for the new economy. The second section examines the spatial impact of structural economic change. This involves consideration of the location patterns of the various industrial sectors and the subsequent effect on state economic structure.

STRUCTURAL CHANGE IN THE U.S. ECONOMY

Two principal forces have led to structural economic change in the U.S. economy during recent decades. The first is technological change. Just as in early phases of great technological change—e.g., the emergence of iron making and the steam engine in the eighteenth century or of steel, the internal combustion engine, and electricity at the end of the last century—the development of computer and communications-based technologies are creating fundamental change in the economy. These new technologies have been the basis for new rapidly expanding industries and have contributed to restructuring of traditional industries. The second force at work has been international competition. The effect of imports on the national economy and the problems of U.S. goods competing in the international marketplace are well known. The U.S. share of world imports increased from 12.9 percent to 17.5 percent between 1970 and 1986, whereas its share of world exports fell from 13.8 percent to 10.3 percent during the same period.[1] Foreign investment in the United States is large and growing, and in several key sectors, such as the automotive sector, foreign imports are being replaced by domestic production in foreign-owned facilities, most notably by the Japanese firms Toyota, Honda, and Mazda. These forces have led to fundamental change in the U.S. economy.

Economic structure is a complex concept and no single measure adequately describes it. As a result, a number of measures of structure will be presented here. The economy is first divided into a number of industrial sectors or categories. Each sector can be measured by a number of variables, including employment or value of production.[2] Although employment and value of production are closely related, they are not perfectly correlated. Differences in the two measures result from differences in productivity among sectors which is, in turn, related to levels of capitalization. Technological innovation, particularly in production technology, can produce significant increases in productivity in some sectors. For example, manufacturing sectors can increase levels of output without corresponding increases in employment if more productive technology, such as flexible production systems or industrial robots, are adopted.

Employment and Gross Domestic Product

For purposes of this study, the national economy is divided into fourteen industrial categories (see Table 2.1). The five manufacturing categories attempt to capture significant sectoral distinctions in manufacturing. Metallurgy, machinery, and transportation sectors are capital-intensive and high-wage sectors. Petroleum and petrochemical are very capital-intensive and high-wage, but relatively small and with a location pattern unlike that of the other manufacturing sectors. Nondurable and miscellaneous durable manufacturing consist of a wide range of very labor-intensive manufacturing and produce consumer goods. The advanced technology category includes the so-called high-technology industries, including electronics, instruments, some chemicals, and others.

The service sector is disaggregated into seven subsectors (numbered 8 through 14 in Table 2.1), using a modified version of a categorization proposed by Stanback et al.[3] The intent of this categorization is to group services that respond to similar types of demand. For example, the distributive services—including transportation and public utilities—provide intermediate inputs to businesses and service final demand of residential customers. Producer services, consisting of financial, insurance and real estate, legal accounting, business services, and others, are those services that are largely provided to businesses. Likewise, consumer services comprise those types of services provided principally as final demand to residential consumers.

The changes in the share of employment in the various sectors have been quite substantial in recent decades (see Table 2.2). Over the period 1967 through 1988, the manufacturing sectors' share of total employment declined by nine percentage points to 19.2 percent, while the service sectors increased by about ten percentage points, ending at 71.8 percent of total employment. Substantial variation among the subsectors of manufacturing and services, however, exists. The most dramatic decline among the manufacturing sectors occurred in metallurgy, machinery, and transportation followed by significant declines in nondurable and miscellaneous durable sectors. After an initial decline of relative shares in advanced technology, following the end of the Viet Nam War, the sector increased its relative share through the mid- to late 1970s, stabilized in the early 1980s, and then declined somewhat toward the end of the 1980s.

The unprecedented decline in the manufacturing employment share led to enormous social distress, especially in the highly industrialized states, and to a debate on deindustrialization.[4] The fear was that the manufacturing core of the economy was being lost to foreign competition in both international and domestic markets. Contributing to the loss of competitive position of U.S. firms was a trade policy that maintained an overvalued dollar.[5] Even though the resurgence of manufacturing in the latter half of the 1980s lends cre-

Table 2.1
Industrial Sector Definitions*

1. Agricultural, forestry, fisheries mining (010–050)

2. Construction (060)

3. Nondurable, nonchemical manufacturing: food and kindred products (100–130);
    textile mill products and apparel (132–152); paper and allied products (160–162);
    printing, publishing and allied products (171–172); leather and leather products
    (220–222)

4. Chemicals, petrochemicals, and plastics: chemicals and allied products (180–192
    except 181, 192); petroleum, coal, rubber and plastics (200–212)

5. Machinery (except electrical), metal, and transportation equipment: metal industries
    (270–301); machinery, except electrical (310–332, except 321, 322); transportation
    equipment (351–370 except 352, 362)

6. Miscellaneous durable goods: lumber, wood products, stone, glass, clay, and concrete
    (230–262); electrical machinery except high-tech (340–350 except 341 and 342);
    miscellaneous (390–392)

7. Advanced technology sectors: drugs (181); organic and inorganic and miscellaneous
    chemicals (192); office and computing equipment (321+322); radio TV and
    communication equipment (341); electrical machinery, equipment and supplies (342);
    aircraft and parts (352); guided missles and space vehicles (362); instruments
    (371-382)**

8. Distributive services (400–472): includes transportation, communications, public
    utilities

9. Wholesale trade (500–571)

10. Retail trade (580–691)

11. Producer services: finance, insurance, real estate, business and professional services
    (700–742, 881–892)

12. Consumer services: repair, household and personal services, social services (750–802,
    862–880)

13. Private sector health and education (812–861)

14. Public administration (900–932)

*Census codes in parentheses are taken from Bureau of the Census, Census of Population
and Housing: 1980; Public Use Microdata Samples -- Technical Documentation (Washington,
D.C., March 1983), Appendix H, pp. 142-148.

**Advanced technology sectors are based on the third definition of high-tech sectors, those
that both use technology-oriented workers and that have high research and development
expenditures, developed in Richard Riche et al., "High Technology Today and Tomorrow:
A Slice of the Employment Pie," Monthly Labor Review (November 1983), p. 52.

dence to this argument and foreign manufacturing firms are increasingly in-
vesting in the United States,[6] manufacturing sectors will not recapture the
relative employment levels of past decades. In other words, the change in
the relative share of manufacturing employment has been a structural, not a
cyclical, phenomenon.

The very sizable increase in service sector employment was not evenly distributed among the subsectors. Distributive services and wholesale trade actually declined slightly in their relative shares or total employment. The employment share for consumer services declined somewhat but by the end of the 1980s regained its 1967 level while the share for public administration remained constant. Retail trade and health and education each grew by about three percentage points. The greatest growth occurred in producer services, which almost doubled its share of total employment.

One theme of the deindustrialization debate was that the service sector employment replacing industrial employment was inferior with respect to skill and wage levels and the levels of productivity were low. As a result, the service sector could never become a dynamic, leading sector for national growth. In fact, service sector employment was seen as entirely dependent on manufacturing employment and if the manufacturing sector was weak, so would be the service sector. This argument is perhaps applicable to certain segments of services, such as consumer services and retail trade, but producer services and health and education can serve as key growth sectors and provide an export function in a local or regional economy.

The deindustrialization debate has been superseded. It is now understood that certain service subsectors, especially producer services and telecommunications activities, are tightly linked to manufacturing, but also essential to the success of manufacturing.[7] Relying on 1982 data, it was estimated that about one-half of the output of service industries consisted of inputs to production of goods and structures in the nonresidential business sector of the economy.[8] For example, business services—a significant component of producer services including engineering, accounting, advertising, and others—represent inputs for many types of manufacturing and are capable of improving the success of the manufacturing sector. Given competition in the international marketplace, new ways of developing, producing, and marketing goods must be devised; this process is more information-intensive than in the past, and business services represent a strategic component of the process.

The pace of structural change has not remained constant during the two-decade period. In terms of the shifts in manufacturing and service sector employment, 80 percent of the total change had been registered by 1982. By the mid-1980s the most dramatic impact of structural change had worked its way through the industrial structure and by the end of the decade the general structure of the new economy was in place. This is not to say that further change will not occur, for economies are always changing. Rather the point is that a new, relatively stable employment structure was consolidated by the end of the 1980s, and after the temporary turbulence resulting from the recession of the 1990s, relative stability should again return.

A second means of characterizing economic structure is through the use of production measures. Gross domestic product figures are estimated by the Bureau of Economic Analysis (see Table 2.3). Although these estimates cannot be

Table 2.2

Industrial Structure of Employment in the U.S. Economy: 1967–1988

Year	AGRI-CULTURE	CONST-RUCTION	MANUFACTURING					Total
			Non-durable	Misc. Durable	Petro-chemical	Machinery	Advanced Technology	
A. Employment Shares								
1967	4.0	5.8	9.8	3.7	1.3	8.0	6.0	28.8
1968	3.7	5.7	9.8	3.6	1.3	8.1	6.1	28.9
1969	3.4	6.0	9.3	3.7	1.3	8.3	5.9	28.5
1970	3.4	6.0	8.6	3.4	1.7	7.8	5.3	26.8
1971	3.4	6.4	8.6	3.4	1.6	7.3	4.9	25.8
1972	3.3	6.1	8.5	3.3	1.6	7.5	4.8	25.7
1973	3.3	6.3	8.1	3.2	1.8	7.6	4.9	25.6
1974	3.3	6.3	7.9	3.3	1.7	7.4	4.7	25.0
1975	3.3	5.7	7.4	3.0	1.5	7.3	4.7	23.9
1976	3.4	5.7	7.7	3.0	1.5	7.0	4.6	23.8
1977	3.2	5.8	7.4	3.0	1.5	6.8	4.8	23.5
1978	3.0	6.0	7.0	3.0	1.6	7.1	5.1	23.8
1979	3.0	6.1	6.9	2.8	1.5	7.1	5.2	23.5
1980	3.1	5.8	6.9	2.7	1.5	6.8	5.2	23.1
1981	3.3	5.8	6.8	2.6	1.4	6.4	5.1	22.3
1982	3.5	5.7	6.6	2.4	1.4	6.0	5.0	21.4
1983	3.3	6.1	6.6	2.4	1.4	5.4	4.8	20.6
1984	3.2	6.2	6.5	2.5	1.3	5.3	5.0	20.6
1985	3.1	6.1	6.1	2.5	1.2	5.3	5.0	20.1
1986	3.0	6.2	6.1	2.4	1.2	5.0	4.9	19.6
1987	2.8	6.0	6.0	2.5	1.2	4.7	4.9	19.3
1988	2.8	6.1	6.0	2.4	1.3	4.8	4.7	19.2
B. Earnings Ratio[1]								
1976	0.71	1.12	0.96	1.00	1.32	1.41	1.42	1.21
1988	0.76	1.06	0.97	1.00	1.28	1.33	1.52	1.22

Source: U.S. Department of Commerce, Bureau of the Census, Current Population Survey,
March, various years. Extracted from computer tape.

[1]Defined as average earnings in a sector divided by average earnings for all sectors,
that is, the national average.

					SERVICES		
Distri- butive	Wholesale Trade	Producer	Retail Trade	Consumer	Health and Education	Public Admini- stration	Total
7.9	4.0	6.9	14.7	8.9	14.1	4.9	61.4
7.7	3.9	7.0	14.6	8.8	14.8	5.0	61.8
7.6	3.9	7.4	14.8	8.4	15.0	5.0	62.1
7.7	3.9	8.2	15.8	8.5	14.9	4.8	63.8
7.8	3.8	8.5	16.1	8.1	15.4	4.6	64.3
7.3	4.2	8.5	16.2	7.9	15.7	4.9	64.7
7.4	3.9	8.8	16.4	7.8	15.7	4.7	64.7
7.0	4.0	9.1	16.4	7.8	16.2	4.9	65.4
7.2	4.1	8.9	16.8	7.8	16.9	5.3	67.0
7.0	4.1	9.1	17.0	7.9	16.8	5.2	67.1
7.1	4.1	9.5	17.0	7.9	16.6	5.2	67.4
7.0	3.9	9.8	17.0	7.8	16.5	5.1	67.1
7.0	4.0	9.8	16.7	7.5	17.1	5.2	67.3
7.1	4.1	10.2	16.6	7.8	16.9	5.4	68.1
7.0	4.5	10.5	16.8	7.7	17.0	5.1	68.6
6.8	4.2	10.7	17.0	8.4	17.3	4.9	69.3
7.0	4.1	11.0	17.4	8.5	17.3	4.8	70.1
6.9	4.0	11.5	17.3	8.7	16.7	4.8	69.9
6.9	4.0	11.8	17.6	8.8	16.7	4.9	70.7
6.7	4.0	12.1	17.7	8.7	17.0	4.9	71.3
7.0	3.9	12.7	17.7	8.8	16.8	5.0	71.9
6.8	3.7	12.8	17.6	8.7	17.1	5.0	71.8
1.39	1.29	1.09	0.64	0.55	0.92	1.28	0.93
1.37	1.23	1.17	0.60	0.58	1.00	1.24	0.94

Table 2.3
Sectoral Composition of Gross Domestic Product: 1967–1988

Year	AGRICULTURE (and Mining)	CONSTRUCTION	MANUFACTURING		
			Durable	Nondurable	Total
1967	4.9	4.9	16.5	11.0	27.5
1968	4.7	4.9	16.5	11.0	27.3
1969	4.8	5.1	16.0	10.7	26.7
1970	4.8	5.1	14.5	10.5	25.0
1971	4.7	5.2	14.1	10.3	24.4
1972	4.8	5.2	14.3	10.0	24.3
1973	5.9	5.2	14.5	9.7	24.2
1974	6.3	5.1	13.9	9.4	23.3
1975	6.2	4.8	13.1	9.6	22.7
1976	5.8	4.9	13.6	9.7	23.3
1977	5.6	5.0	14.1	9.6	23.7
1978	5.7	5.2	14.3	9.1	23.4
1979	6.3	5.3	14.0	8.8	22.8
1980	6.9	5.1	13.1	8.6	21.7
1981	7.9	4.6	12.9	8.6	21.5
1982	7.1	4.5	11.6	8.7	20.3
1983	5.8	4.5	11.5	8.9	20.4
1984	5.7	4.6	12.1	8.6	20.7
1985	5.2	4.7	11.5	8.3	19.8
1986	4.0	4.9	11.4	8.4	19.8
1987	3.9	4.8	11.0	8.4	19.4
1988	3.7	4.8	10.9	8.6	19.5

Source: Economic Report of the President (Transmitted to the Congress)
(Washington, D.C., February 1991), Table B-10.

		SERVICES			
Transportation and Public Utitlities	Wholesale and Retail	Finance, Insurance and Real Estate	Services	Government	Total
8.7	16.4	14.3	11.2	12.1	62.7
8.6	16.6	14.1	11.2	12.5	63.0
8.6	16.6	14.2	11.5	12.6	63.5
8.8	16.7	14.4	11.9	13.3	65.1
8.9	16.8	14.8	11.9	13.4	65.8
9.0	16.8	14.5	12.0	13.3	65.6
8.8	16.7	14.1	12.1	12.8	64.5
8.9	16.9	14.2	12.3	13.0	65.3
9.0	17.3	14.0	12.7	13.3	66.3
9.1	17.0	14.0	12.8	13.1	66.0
9.1	16.9	14.3	12.9	12.6	65.8
9.0	16.8	14.7	13.0	12.2	65.7
8.8	16.9	14.7	13.3	11.9	65.6
9.0	16.4	14.9	14.0	12.0	66.3
9.0	16.1	15.0	14.1	11.9	66.1
9.3	16.3	15.3	14.9	12.3	68.1
9.5	16.2	16.0	15.4	12.3	69.4
9.5	16.5	15.4	15.6	11.9	68.9
9.4	16.5	16.1	16.3	12.0	70.3
9.4	16.3	16.5	17.1	12.0	71.3
9.2	16.1	17.0	17.6	11.9	71.9
9.1	16.1	17.1	18.0	11.7	72.0

Table 2.4
Occupational Sector Definitions

		Occupational Codes - U.S. Census
1	Management	003–037
2	Professional	043–199
3	Technical	203–235
4	Sales	243–285 (except 276, cashiers, moved to Clerical)
5	Clerical	276, 303–389
6	Service	403–469
7	Farming	473–499
8	Crafts	503–699
9	Operative	703–889

disaggregated into the same sectoral categories used above for employment, the categories of total manufacturing and total service product are comparable, and the trends in these categories are similar to the ones identified for employment. Manufacturing's share of gross domestic product demonstrated a long-term decline, but stabilized in the mid-1980s, reflecting the rebound of U.S. manufacturing during the middle of the decade. In services, the share of gross domestic product remained fairly constant during the 1970s and then increased significantly in the 1980s. The increase in the share of service sector employment, noted above, was fairly constant during the entire period, suggesting an improvement in the sector's productivity during the 1980s. In contrast, the agriculture and mining sectors have had a larger share of gross domestic product than they have had of total employment, reflecting the sectors' relatively high levels of productivity and capital intensity.

In addition to shifts in the industrial structure of the economy, changes in the types of jobs generated in the economy have occurred. A substantial increase in the high-paying management, professional, and technical occupations is observed (see Table 2.4 for definitions of categories and Table 2.5 for shares). Crafts and operative occupations, which include blue-collar manufacturing jobs, accounted for a decline of seven and one-half percentage points. A slight increase occurred in the low-paying clerical occupations and in the better-paying sales category. In contrast to the relative stability found in the shares of employment by industry, changes in shares by occupation continued through the 1980s, especially in management and operative occupations.

These changes in occupational structure and the relative wages hold profound implications for social well-being and public policy. Three large sectors—clerical, services, and operative—consist of low-wage, low-skill employment and constitute 49.4 percent of total employment. On the other hand, the high-wage, high-skill sectors—management, professional, and technical—are growing substantially and in 1988 represented 27.9 percent of total employment. The prospects for economic mobility are very dependent upon the occupational sector that an individual enters. The high-wage occupational sectors are all ones that require high levels of education for entry. Education, as will be discussed in Chapter 7, clearly has become a significant factor in employment prospects.

Productivity

The low rate of U.S. productivity[9] growth since the 1970s, especially compared to the historical patterns in the United States or to current levels of productivity improvement among international competitors, has come to be considered a major problem facing the economy.[10] Many have attributed slow productivity growth to be the result of the growing importance of the service sector, which has demonstrated particularly low productivity increases.[11] Manufacturing productivity performed quite well in the mid-1980s, but service sector productivity dragged down the national rate of increase.

This widely held view has been criticized on a number of grounds, several of which relate to the issue of technological change. A very forceful critique argues that productivity has substantially been underestimated because of the difficulties in incorporating changes in the quality of inputs, particularly computers, and in the quality of outputs. The rapid improvement in computer technology has made quite substantial improvements in the quality of computers used as inputs in the economy. If methods to account for change in quality are incorporated, a significant proportion of the productivity differential between manufacturing and nonmanufacturing disappear.[12] Change in quality of outputs, also linked to technological improvements, are no easier to incorporate and have likely led to underestimating productivity change.[13]

Irrespective of these measurement problems, international competition has produced great pressure on U.S. firms to increase productivity, and many of the new technologies provided the means for achieving productivity gains. The advanced technology products—computers, electronic chips, and telecommunications technology—are being incorporated in all sectors of the economy and are affecting productivity.

The diffusion of these recent advances repeats the diffusion of technological innovation found in earlier industrial revolutions. Joseph Schumpeter, in a well-known book,[14] discussed the process by which technological innovation will render some traditional products and production processes obsolete. But the

Table 2.5
Occupational Structure of the U.S. Economy: 1970–1988

Year	Management %	Management Wage Ratio	Professional %	Professional Wage Ratio	Technical %	Technical Wage Ratio	Sales %	Sales Wage Ratio
1970	7.6	1.83	10.3	1.43	2.5	1.32	8.4	1.15
1971	7.4	1.85	10.2	1.41	2.4	1.31	8.3	1.16
1972	7.7	1.83	10.6	1.38	2.2	1.29	8.2	1.18
1973	7.9	1.82	10.5	1.42	2.3	1.24	8.5	1.14
1974	7.8	1.82	10.8	1.39	2.5	1.28	8.1	1.18
1975	8.2	1.76	11.4	1.41	2.7	1.21	8.3	1.14
1976	8.4	1.77	11.2	1.41	2.5	1.17	8.3	1.12
1977	8.5	1.75	11.1	1.41	2.6	1.20	8.5	1.14
1978	8.5	1.74	11.5	1.38	2.7	1.18	8.4	1.12
1979	8.7	1.70	11.5	1.39	2.8	1.18	8.3	1.14
1980	9.2	1.65	11.5	1.39	2.9	1.22	8.5	1.16
1981	9.1	1.67	11.8	1.42	2.9	1.25	8.6	1.19
1982	9.7	1.77	12.2	1.45	3.1	1.18	8.5	1.13
1983	10.2	1.77	12.4	1.44	3.1	1.23	8.7	1.11
1984	10.5	1.78	12.1	1.44	3.1	1.21	8.8	1.10
1985	10.5	1.75	12.2	1.42	3.1	1.20	9.1	1.12
1986	10.8	1.74	12.6	1.47	3.0	1.21	9.1	1.13
1987	11.3	1.72	12.5	1.47	3.2	1.18	9.2	1.13
1988	11.9	1.69	12.9	1.45	3.1	1.21	9.2	1.12

Source: See Source for Table 2.2

Clerical		Services		Farming		Crafts		Operative	
%	Wage Ratio	%	Wage Ratio	%	Wage Ratio	%	Wage Ratio	%	Wage Ratio
18.4	0.77	14.5	0.50	3.1	0.34	13.5	1.29	21.9	0.86
18.4	0.76	14.5	0.49	3.1	0.36	14.0	1.28	21.5	0.87
18.3	0.75	14.3	0.50	2.9	0.43	14.4	1.26	21.3	0.86
18.3	0.74	14.3	0.49	2.9	0.41	14.3	1.27	21.1	0.87
18.6	0.74	14.4	0.50	2.9	0.40	14.0	1.27	20.9	0.87
18.6	0.76	14.6	0.50	2.9	0.43	13.7	1.26	19.7	0.87
18.6	0.75	15.0	0.50	2.9	0.42	13.5	1.27	19.7	0.88
18.5	0.75	14.9	0.48	2.7	0.42	13.6	1.26	19.7	0.89
19.0	0.74	14.5	0.49	2.4	0.46	13.7	1.26	19.3	0.89
19.4	0.73	14.4	0.49	2.4	0.43	13.8	1.27	18.8	0.90
19.5	0.74	14.3	0.49	2.4	0.43	13.6	1.25	18.1	0.88
19.1	0.74	14.7	0.47	2.5	0.41	13.4	1.25	17.9	0.87
19.4	0.74	14.8	0.47	2.6	0.41	11.8	1.24	17.9	0.84
19.3	0.74	14.8	0.49	2.7	0.40	11.6	1.20	17.2	0.83
19.6	0.74	14.7	0.48	2.4	0.41	11.8	1.19	17.0	0.82
19.6	0.73	14.6	0.49	2.4	0.41	11.8	1.19	16.7	0.83
19.5	0.70	14.4	0.49	2.4	0.40	11.5	1.17	16.7	0.81
19.4	0.71	14.2	0.46	2.3	0.42	11.3	1.16	16.6	0.81
19.0	0.69	14.0	0.50	2.2	0.43	11.4	1.16	16.4	0.80

innovation, historically, created new products and improved productivity in traditional sectors. In the contemporary context, this process has been accelerated by international competition. Advanced technological inputs and advanced production technology have improved the ability of firms to compete.

The various new technologies have contributed to the expansion of the advanced technology manufacturing sector. Many have had profound effects in traditional manufacturing.[15] Advanced production technologies, such as flexible manufacturing, are used to improve the manufacturing process, thereby improving productivity and competitiveness. An example is found in textile production in North Carolina. Textiles, historically a major employment sector in the state, had been very adversely affected by international competition. The industry reinvested and incorporated technologically advanced production processes,[16] and now the state is again able to compete internationally in a market that had grown to be dominated by production in Third World countries. In a similar fashion, the U.S. automotive industry has adopted advanced production technology such as computer-controlled robots. In addition, automobiles themselves have incorporated the advanced technology products; automobiles are increasingly controlled by computer chips. Many traditional products such as refrigerators, gas pumps, watches, and others incorporate chip-based technologies.

A distinction made between high-tech and low-tech manufacturing industries in the early 1980s, based on the technological sophistication of the product and production process, no longer holds. The difference is disappearing as a result of maturation of the so-called high-tech sectors and the adoption of advanced technology in traditional sectors. Furthermore, if firms and sectors do not improve productivity, they will not survive in the international marketplace.

The evidence of productivity improvement in services is scarce, perhaps the result of the measurement problems described above. High levels of productivity growth have been found in communications and wholesale trade in the 1980s, but most other service sectors demonstrate quite slow improvement.[17] The banking industry has incorporated a broad range of new technologies, but its productivity increase, as measured for the national industry, has been low. The effect of this technology may be obscured by the rapid expansion of branch banking and the resulting employment increase in relatively inefficient branch locations.[18] If true, the current consolidation and down-sizing in the banking industry to eliminate excess capacity should reveal productivity gains at least partially attributable to technological innovation.

Information and Telecommunications

The need for telecommunications services in the contemporary economy derives directly from the economy's dependence on information and, more specifically, on the need to communicate information. The extraordinary expansion in the role of information in the economy was noted in the pioneering work of

Harold Innis that appeared in the early 1950s.[19] In the early 1960s, Fritz Machlup assessed the importance of information resources in the economy, particularly in terms of efforts to create new, socially useful knowledge and to disseminate information to the uninformed.[20] Machlup estimated that in 1958 approximately $135 billion was spent on the production and distribution of knowledge, which represented 29 percent of gross national product. He also established a distinction between investment in information (research and development) and consumption of it, and tied future increases in productivity to the investment component. Marc Porat estimated that the information activity component of the U.S. economy in 1967 was around 46 percent of GNP and that so-called information jobs accounted for 53 percent of labor income.[21] A conceptual recognition of the increasing importance of information in advanced societies was advanced by Daniel Bell.[22] Beniger gives the "information economy" a history by arguing that the control function requirements of increasingly complex industrial organizations are of long standing, and the contemporary advances in telecommunications are simply the most recent form of control innovation.[23]

Whether one adopts the tenets of Porat's "information economy" or Bell's "postindustrial" society, there is little doubt that the information needs of the economy have increased dramatically in recent decades. Given its importance in transporting information, telecommunications infrastructure has become a central component in both the U.S. and international economies. In addition, many of the technological breakthroughs of recent decades have had direct and far-reaching effects on communications. The critical breakthrough has been the merging of computers and communications. Computers now talk to each other and transmit data over telephone systems, and the telecommunications networks are themselves computer-intensive. The intelligence of telephone systems, the switch, is a computer. The switching and transmission capacities of communications systems have increased enormously in recent years, and further progress is foreseen.

Using Porat's work, we can identify industrial sectors that purchase a relatively high share of inputs from the telecommunications sector (Standard Industrial Classification code, 48).[24] The telecommunications-intensive sectors are service subsectors (see Table 2.6). With the exception of wholesale and retail trade, they are growing more rapidly than total service sector employment. The telecommunications requirements of businesses in these sectors are leading to a concentration of superior telecommunications infrastructure in areas where these firms locate, particularly in large cities like Atlanta, Chicago, Los Angeles, and New York.[25]

Telecommunications allows firms to change the way they operate; the functions remain the same, but the methods of interacting with clients and customers have changed.[26] In addition, telecommunications advances have created markets for new firms whose sole purpose is to provide information through telecommunications systems.[27] The processing, storage, and retrieval of information with computers can easily be linked with telecommunications systems.[28] Providers of

Table 2.6
Employment Growth in Telecommunications-Intensive Sectors: 1970–1988
(percent per year)

	1970–1980	1980–1988	1970–1988
Telecommunications Intensive Users[1]			
Finance and Insurance	3.94	2.96	4.02
Business Services	5.65	8.39	8.98
Computer/Data Processing	n/a	15.48	n/a
Real Estate	4.30	3.76	4.77
Wholesale and Retail Trade	3.41	2.79	3.56
Hotels	3.79	3.44	4.21
Telecommunications Service Providers			
Communications Services	2.01	0.87	1.58
TOTAL SERVICES	3.97	2.91	4.01
TOTAL EMPLOYMENT[2]	3.04	1.98	2.84

Source: U.S. Department of Commerce, Bureau of the Census, County Business Patterns,
          United States (No. 1) (Washington, D.C., various years).

[1]These sectors were identified through the U.S. national input model, as reported in Marc
Uri Porat, The Information Economy: The Technology Matrices (1967) (Washington, D.C.:
Department of Commerce, 1977), Table I. Each group makes relatively large purchases from
the communication sector SIC 48. Petroleum Refining and Plastics and Rubber sectors are
also telecommunications intensive, but are small manufacturing sectors and are excluded
from this table. Finance and Insurance includes SIC 60 Banking, 61 Credit, 62
Commodities, 63 Insurance Carriers, 64 Insurance Agents; Business Services includes SIC 731
Advertising, 731 Credit Reporting, 81 Legal Services, 891 Engineering and Architecture, 893
Accounting and Auditing, 7392 Business Management and Consulting (with 1987 SIC code
definition, 874), 7394 Leasing and Rental (with 1987 SIC code definition, 7353, 7359, and
7840), 7399 Business Services n.e.c.; Computer/Data Processing; Real Estate includes SIC 65
Real Estate; Wholesale and Retail Trade; Hotels includes SIC 70 Hotel, 75 Repair Services;
Communications Services is SIC 48.

[2]Includes government, services, manufacturing, and construction employment.

information, including firms that provide credit checks, financial information,
or news, frequently use telecommunications systems to deliver their product.

Even in manufacturing, one discovers an increased need for telecommunications.[29] Flexible manufacturing systems and multilocational firms require more
extensive coordination and control, especially between headquarters and dispersed production sites.[30] Large companies like General Motors and Boeing have
effectively developed internally owned and operated telecommunications companies. Even within single plants control systems in automated production facilities, such as those that use robotic technologies, must incorporate a
telecommunications system.

The effects of new telecommunications capabilities on rural economic development are becoming visible. As predicted by classical location theory, reducing the costs of transporting goods or information—the effect of better communication systems—should produce a more spatially dispersed location pattern. Indeed, numerous examples of telecommunications-intensive firms moving to small towns and rural areas, such as telemarketing firms locating in small towns in Nebraska and elsewhere, have been observed.[31] The so-called back-office activities of major firms have relocated to mid-size and small towns and even overseas. Even though many types of service activities require the face-to-face interaction with suppliers and clients, and telecommunications may produce more centralized control systems for some services,[32] many activities do not require location in major cities, and telecommunications technologies permit these to be located outside metropolitan areas.

The technological breakthroughs in telecommunications have produced substantial increases in productivity. Employment in communications services (SIC 48) actually grew slowly in the 1980s even though the industry dramatically expanded (Table 2.6).[33] One factor that confounds the analysis of the size and growth of telecommunications providers, however, is the increase in internal provision of telecommunications by users themselves. As described above, many firms have chosen to bypass, totally or partially, public networks by developing their own communications systems.[34] Major banks, airline companies, and others have established very large and advanced private systems. Under some circumstances, the excess capacity in these private systems can be sold to other businesses, thus placing these firms in the business of providing telecommunications services.

The expansion in telecommunications markets has also affected equipment markets. In 1990, the value of shipment from U.S. communications systems and equipment and telephone and telegraph equipment firms was around $33 billion.[35] The expansion of these markets has also produced employment growth in these manufacturing sectors substantially above the growth in total manufacturing employment (see Table 2.7).

Telecommunications is a particularly interesting aspect of the current process of technological innovation, and it embodies much of contemporary technological change. The information-handling capabilities of the new technologies—both computers and telecommunications—hold great promise for improved productivity, especially for the service sectors.[36] Telecommunications, however, is affecting virtually all sectors of the economy and will not only affect productivity of many sectors but will also affect economic geography. There are significant policy issues concerning telecommunications, especially for state governments, and these will be examined in Chapter 6.

THE RESTRUCTURING OF ECONOMIC GEOGRAPHY

At this point, the effect of structural economic change on the country's geography will be assessed. Economic activities locate in some physical setting,

Table 2.7

Employment Growth for Telecommunications Equipment[1] Providers: 1970–1986 (percent per year)

	1970–1980	1980–1986	1970–1986
Telecommunications Equipment	2.01	1.17	1.78
Electrical Computing Equipment	9.78	1.11	6.94
Radio and TV Receiving Equipment	-2.62	-5.33	-3.11
Communications Equipment	1.49	2.81	2.14
Electrical Components and Accessories	3.82	1.60	3.22
TOTAL MANUFACTURING	0.70	-1.58	0.19
TOTAL EMPLOYMENT	3.04	1.65	2.71

Source: U.S. Department of Commerce, Bureau of the Census, County Business Patterns, United States (No. 1) (Washington, D.C., various years).

[1]Telecommunications Equipment includes SIC 3573, Electrical Computing Equipment; SIC 365, Radio and TV Receiving Equipment; SIC 366, Communications Equipment; SIC 367, Electrical Components and Accessories.

giving rise to economic geography. Location patterns of similar types of economic activities, for example, of firms in the same industry, have been studied for many decades and the factors that contribute for the variation among location patterns of different industries identified. Although these patterns are of interest in themselves, our broader concern is the relationship of these location patterns and the regional economic structure that they produce.

Striking differences in the economies of the country's regions have existed since the time of the formation of the country. Regional differences were initially generated by differences in agricultural products and the level of sophistication in artisan activities in the various regions. During later periods of mineral extraction and industrialization, distinctions among regions become even sharper. Regions with valuable raw materials—lumber or mineral-rich ores, for example—became the site of extractive industries, thereby giving the regional economies a relative specialization. Manufacturing emerged first along the Middle Atlantic and North East regions, but expanded steadily through the Midwest and created what would later be called the industrial heartland of the country. These economies were based on a specialization in manufacturing while other regions of the country, including the South, the Plains states, the Mountain states, and the West Coast, had economies based largely on agricultural and resource extraction activities. The process of regional economic change never ends; as old industries mature and new industries emerge, new location patterns are established, and regional economies, as a result, change.

Changes in the location patterns of the 14 industrial sectors will first be determined. The underlying variable used in examining location patterns will be the share of employment in a particular industrial sector in a particular state. For example, the share of retail trade employment in California is calculated by dividing employment in retail trade in California by total employment in California. These employment shares are similar to those calculated for the nation as a whole, in the previous section, but in this section they are calculated for states. If the employment share for a particular industry is roughly the same in all states, this industry is considered decentralized or spatially dispersed. If, however, the employment share is much higher in one or a few states than in the other states, the industry is considered spatially concentrated. Of particular importance is the extent to which the pattern of concentration/dispersion changes as a result of structural economic change.

With the 14 industry sectors and 50 states, the possible combinations for specialization are enormous. To understand these complex patterns, an index to measure the degree of specialization in location patterns will be employed. The Theil index serves this purpose well due to its strong decomposition properties (see Appendix 2.1 for a discussion of this measure). The Theil index is derived from information theory and is a powerful tool for studying differences in structure. The smaller the value of the Theil index, the less the difference in structure. If employment shares in all sectors in all states were of the same size, the Theil index would have a value of zero. The greater the value, the greater the inequality or dissimilarity. The national Theil index of industrial structure provides a single aggregate measure of the similarity/dissimilarity reflecting the location patterns of all industries combined. This national index can be decomposed, and a similar index calculated for each individual sector and the contribution of each sector to the overall national pattern can also be determined. The analysis will also include maps for selected industrial sectors in order to provide a visual image of these complex changes.

Spatial Patterns of Industries and Occupations

Between 1976 and 1988, relatively modest change occurred in the overall location pattern of the 14 industries; the national index followed a cyclical pattern with a modest downward trend, indicating less specialization (see national index in section A of Table 2.8). There were, however, quite significant differences among the location patterns of individual industries and significant change over time in particular industries.

Manufacturing sectors tend to have higher index values than do the service sectors, indicating a higher degree of spatial concentration among manufacturing employment. This result confirms the historical pattern in the United States and other countries that manufacturing production tends to be concentrated in relatively few areas, as a result of the location of raw materials and interindustry linkages that lend to the formation of manufacturing complexes. In contrast the service sectors tend to be population-based, and as a result the relative shares

Table 2.8
Spatial Structure of Industry: 1976–1988

Year	NATIONAL[1]	AGRI-CULTURE	CONST-RUCTION	MANUFACTURING					
				Non-durable	Misc. Durable	Petro-chemical	Machinery	Advanced Technology	Total[2]
A. Index of Structure Inequality-Theil Index									
1976	0.427	0.298	0.304	0.432	0.387	0.572	0.664	0.632	0.454
1977	0.432	0.287	0.332	0.430	0.402	0.608	0.640	0.609	0.451
1978	0.428	0.303	0.323	0.428	0.396	0.532	0.657	0.639	0.465
1979	0.420	0.296	0.328	0.426	0.354	0.521	0.629	0.625	0.457
1980	0.423	0.334	0.337	0.427	0.331	0.560	0.619	0.593	0.447
1981	0.427	0.366	0.351	0.433	0.356	0.529	0.622	0.591	0.444
1982	0.425	0.375	0.352	0.439	0.372	0.552	0.609	0.661	0.459
1983	0.421	0.347	0.372	0.438	0.364	0.513	0.600	0.661	0.443
1984	0.418	0.384	0.385	0.419	0.389	0.582	0.553	0.648	0.439
1985	0.424	0.384	0.377	0.403	0.361	0.544	0.594	0.654	0.440
1986	0.429	0.369	0.385	0.428	0.361	0.508	0.615	0.661	0.448
1987	0.428	0.367	0.390	0.419	0.387	0.561	0.588	0.645	0.441
1988	0.419	0.365	0.399	0.426	0.383	0.523	0.531	0.581	0.420
B. Share of Total Structure Inequality (Share of National Within Group Theil, Using 14									
1976	100.0	2.4	4.0	7.8	2.7	2.1	10.9	6.8	30.3
1977	100.0	2.1	4.5	7.3	2.8	2.1	10.1	6.7	29.0
1978	100.0	2.1	4.5	7.0	2.8	2.0	10.9	7.6	30.3
1979	100.0	2.1	4.8	7.0	2.4	1.9	10.6	7.7	29.6
1980	100.0	2.4	4.7	7.0	2.1	2.0	9.9	7.4	28.4
1981	100.0	2.8	4.8	6.9	2.2	1.8	9.3	7.0	27.2
1982	100.0	3.1	4.8	6.8	2.1	1.8	8.6	7.9	27.2
1983	100.0	2.7	5.4	6.8	2.1	1.7	7.7	7.6	25.9
1984	100.0	2.9	5.7	6.5	2.3	1.8	7.1	7.8	25.5
1985	100.0	2.8	5.5	5.9	2.1	1.6	7.4	7.7	24.7
1986	100.0	2.6	5.6	6.1	2.1	1.4	7.2	7.6	24.4
1987	100.0	2.4	5.5	5.9	2.3	1.6	6.5	7.3	23.6
1988	100.0	2.4	5.8	6.1	2.2	1.6	6.1	6.5	22.5

Source: See source for Table 2.2

[1]National within group Theil using 14 industrial sectors. Other Theil measures are the national Theil calculated for individual industries. See Appendix 2.1 for explanations.

[2]National Theil for combined manufacturing in Section A; share in Section B is sum of shares of individual manufacturing sectors.

[3]National Theil for combined services in Section A; share in Section B is sum of shares of individual service sectors.

				SERVICES			
Distri- butive	Wholesale Trade	Producer	Retail Trade	Consumer	Health and Education	Public Admini- stration	Total[3]
0.385	0.414	0.502	0.374	0.405	0.377	0.419	0.392
0.403	0.415	0.506	0.392	0.403	0.384	0.402	0.398
0.397	0.405	0.486	0.378	0.389	0.387	0.398	0.390
0.374	0.425	0.485	0.375	0.385	0.373	0.402	0.384
0.376	0.423	0.490	0.386	0.407	0.366	0.395	0.390
0.387	0.427	0.519	0.379	0.407	0.373	0.386	0.394
0.394	0.405	0.496	0.381	0.368	0.381	0.356	0.386
0.397	0.425	0.513	0.369	0.368	0.363	0.389	0.384
0.382	0.383	0.509	0.360	0.375	0.366	0.394	0.380
0.386	0.399	0.498	0.397	0.392	0.373	0.398	0.390
0.395	0.422	0.501	0.378	0.406	0.367	0.421	0.394
0.405	0.380	0.505	0.383	0.401	0.374	0.402	0.396
0.396	0.388	0.500	0.379	0.376	0.389	0.395	0.392

Sectors, in %)

6.3	4.0	14.9	14.9	7.5	14.8	5.0	63.2
6.6	3.9	15.4	15.4	7.4	14.8	4.9	64.2
6.5	3.7	14.9	14.9	7.1	14.9	4.7	62.9
6.3	4.1	14.9	14.9	6.8	15.2	5.0	63.6
6.3	4.1	15.2	15.2	7.5	14.6	5.0	64.6
6.3	4.5	14.9	14.9	7.3	14.8	4.6	65.2
6.3	4.0	15.2	15.2	7.2	15.6	4.1	64.9
6.6	4.1	15.2	15.2	7.4	14.9	4.4	66.0
6.3	3.6	14.9	14.9	7.8	14.6	4.6	65.8
6.3	3.8	15.7	15.7	8.1	14.7	4.6	67.1
6.2	3.9	15.6	15.6	8.2	14.5	4.8	67.4
6.6	3.5	15.8	15.8	8.2	14.7	4.7	68.5
6.5	3.5	15.9	15.9	7.8	15.4	4.7	69.1

of service sector employment would not vary much among states and thus be more spatially dispersed.

A closer examination of Table 2.8, however, reveals a number of quite significant changes, especially for the manufacturing sectors. The Theil index for total manufacturing declined from 0.454 in 1976 to 0.420 in 1988. This implies that manufacturing employment, as a whole, became more decentralized (see Map 2.1). In 1976, states in the heartland—Pennsylvania, Ohio, Indiana, Wisconsin, and Michigan—were all among the states with the highest high shares of manufacturing employment. By 1988, Pennsylvania, Ohio, and Indiana no longer had such relatively high levels and were replaced by South Carolina, Alabama and Rhode Island. A number of other states, outside the traditional heartland, demonstrated relatively higher levels and thus decentralization in the location of manufacturing employment.

Such a decentralizing trend has been explained, theoretically, as a spatial filtering process. As certain industries mature, especially the assembly production of consumer goods, they decentralize from their seed-bed region (usually in the industrial heartland) to peripheral regions in order to take advantage of transportation and labor cost differentials.[37] While the manufacturing categories used in Table 2.8 are too aggregated to capture the filtering process of individual industries, the relative decentralization of lower-order nondurable and miscellaneous manufacturing sectors is clear. In addition to following a more decentralized pattern, the national decline in the relative size of manufacturing employment, identified in Table 2.1, meant that manufacturing's contribution to the overall pattern significantly declined; the manufacturing sectors accounted for 30 percent of the national index in 1976 but only 22.5 percent in 1988 (see Table 2.8, section B).

The two key manufacturing subsectors, in terms of size, wage levels, and the overall location pattern of manufacturing, are machinery, metallurgy, and transportation equipment, and advanced technology. The machinery, metallurgy, and transportation sector was quite centralized in 1976 (Theil index of 0.664) but became much more decentralized by 1988 (see Map 2.2). While Wisconsin, Michigan, Illinois, Indiana, Ohio, and Pennsylvania remain the core area for this sector, increases in relative shares occurred in a number of states in the South. But given its declining relative size, this sector has a diminished impact on the overall pattern of industry.

The advanced technology manufacturing sector also demonstrates a high level of spatial concentration, one that has changed little between 1976 and 1988 but one that differs quite substantially from traditional manufacturing (see Map 2.3). In 1988, not a single state with the highest share of machinery, metallurgy, and transportation employment also had a high share of advanced technology employment. States with high employment shares included most of the New England states, Colorado, and California. Relatively high levels were also found in Arizona, Texas, and New York. As has been well documented, the industries in this sector tend to be research-

Map 2.1
Employment Share of All Manufacturing Sectors by State: 1976 and 1988

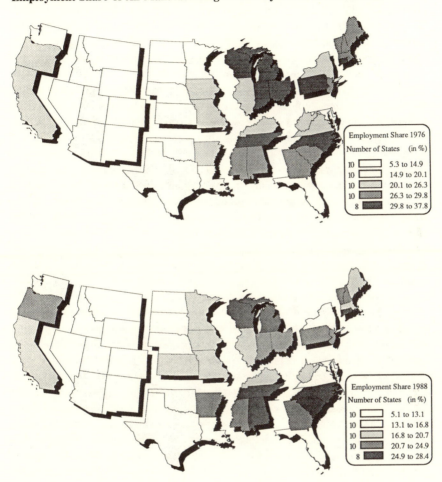

Source: See source for Table 2.2.

intensive and were strongly supported by military research funds following World War II.[38] Research funds were decisive in generating the advance technology research/industry complexes, closely linked to major research universities, in Boston and the Silicon Valley.

Service sector activities have traditionally been population-serving and, consequently, closely related to the spatial distribution of the population and its purchasing power.[39] As a result, economies of various regions have been found to have similar levels of employment in services. Some sectors are

Map 2.2
Employment Share of Machinery, Metallurgy, and Transportation Equipment
Sectors by State: 1976 and 1988

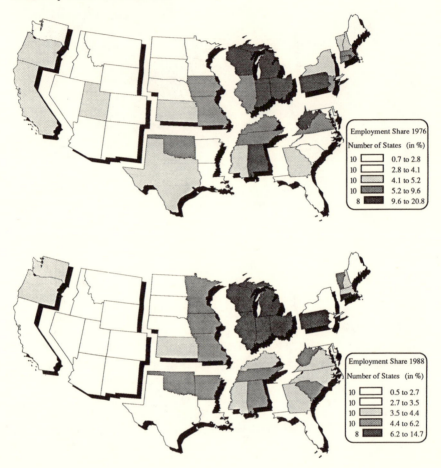

Source: See source for Table 2.2.

clearly linked to local demand, such as retail trade, and their share of employment will not vary dramatically among regions. However, some subsectors, such as health and education and, especially, producer services, can
function as export sectors.

The service sectors are found to be spatially dispersed, and little change has
occurred in the value of the index for individual sectors, but because of their
increasing employment share, these sectors explained a larger share of the overall
pattern. The retail trade and consumer services sectors, for example, have low

Map 2.3
Employment Share of Advanced Technology Sectors by State: 1976 and 1988

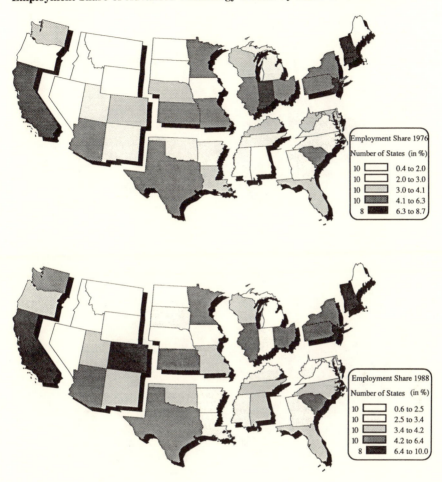

Source: See source for Table 2.2.

Theil values, indicating spatial dispersion. However, the service sectors are quite diverse. Producer services are substantially more spatially concentrated than other services, and although the degree of concentration did not increase over the 1976–1988 period, because of substantial growth throughout the nation, its contribution to the overall spatial pattern has increased significantly (see Map 2.4).

The Theil measure can be used in a similar fashion to determine the degree of concentration or dispersion of various occupations. Unlike the spatial distribution of employment by industry, the national Theil index for occupa-

Map 2.4
Employment Share of Producer Services by State: 1976 and 1988

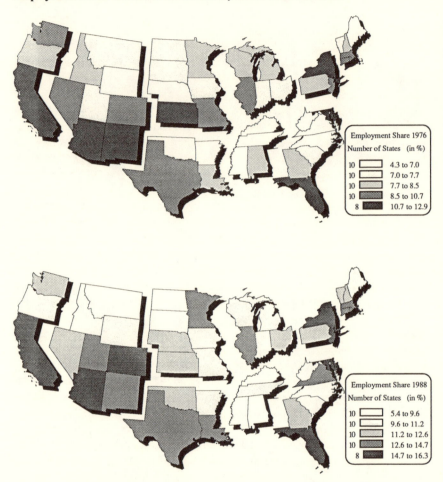

Source: See source for Table 2.2.

tional structure increased slightly during the period, indicating a slight increase in spatial specialization with respect to occupations (see Table 2.9).
This slight increase, however, is the result of two countervailing trends. The
high-paying occupations—management, professional, technical, and sales—
have become more spatially concentrated and are accounting for a larger
share of the overall pattern. Crafts, a high-paying occupation, has not
changed its degree of spatial decentralization, but it has grown relatively
smaller and become less important in the national pattern. The lower-paying

clerical, services, and operative occupations were more spatially dispersed at the end of the period.

Economic Structure of States and Regions

In this phase of the analysis attention shifts from the location patterns of industries to the economic structure of states and regions. The geographical location of industries and occupations gives rise to this economic structure. If a state has a relatively large share of employment in a particular industry, as compared to the share for the sector in the national economy, it likely exports the product of the industry to other states or countries. The reasons that an individual state would have such specialization in a particular industry depends on many factors, including natural resource endowment, human resource endowment, transportation, economic structure, and a host of others. This analysis will not attempt to identify the underlying comparative advantages of various states and their subsequent specialization, but rather it attempts to demonstrate that significant change has occurred in the economic structure of states and that this change relates to the spatial impact of structural change in the national economy.

While this analysis is ultimately concerned with states, and calculation of various indices use individual states as the unit of analysis, to simplify this presentation, states have been aggregated into the nine census regions (see Appendix 2.2 for a definition of region). This is not to suggest that all states within a region have the same economic structure, but patterns of change will be more easily identified by considering 9 regions rather than 48 states (Hawaii and Alaska are excluded).

A complex pattern of change in economic structure of the nine census regions is revealed in Table 2.10. In 1976, the New England, Middle Atlantic, and East North Central regions were all substantially specialized in manufacturing employment, but by 1988 the extent of this specialization declined[40] (and even disappeared in the Middle Atlantic region) and its composition in New England and the Middle Atlantic regions became more heavily weighted toward the advanced technology sector (see Table 2.10 and Map 2.1). Of these regions, only the East North Central region maintained an employment share in machinery, metallurgy, and transportation equipment above the national average in 1988. The region with the highest level of specialization in manufacturing in 1988, however, was the East South Central, which relied especially on nondurable and miscellaneous durable and machinery, metallurgy, and transportation equipment (see Map 2.1). Four regions—South Atlantic, West South Central, Mountain, and Pacific—not specialized in manufacturing in 1988, nevertheless demonstrated significant increases in the share of the advanced technology manufacturing sector.

An increasingly important source of regional specialization has been producer services. The Middle Atlantic and Pacific regions, and to a lesser extent New

Table 2.9
Spatial Structure of Occupations: 1976–1988

A. Index of Structure Inequality—Theil Index

	National[1]	Management	Professional	Technical	Sales	Clerical	Services	Farming	Crafts	Operative
1976	0.392	0.418	0.412	0.408	0.389	0.437	0.374	0.309	0.375	0.365
1977	0.398	0.427	0.432	0.414	0.420	0.437	0.372	0.306	0.375	0.365
1978	0.397	0.427	0.415	0.424	0.409	0.438	0.367	0.335	0.372	0.372
1979	0.388	0.426	0.407	0.407	0.385	0.425	0.366	0.306	0.370	0.360
1980	0.391	0.423	0.403	0.414	0.408	0.430	0.371	0.326	0.366	0.356
1981	0.396	0.438	0.403	0.411	0.411	0.429	0.369	0.348	0.377	0.370
1982	0.393	0.441	0.405	0.434	0.404	0.427	0.362	0.328	0.356	0.368
1983	0.388	0.459	0.394	0.420	0.406	0.420	0.356	0.318	0.350	0.355
1984	0.388	0.437	0.414	0.406	0.396	0.407	0.364	0.352	0.362	0.354
1985	0.395	0.456	0.418	0.421	0.408	0.414	0.365	0.313	0.370	0.361
1986	0.400	0.446	0.424	0.394	0.408	0.419	0.379	0.358	0.388	0.359
1987	0.402	0.461	0.432	0.422	0.416	0.420	0.365	0.368	0.376	0.358
1988	0.397	0.463	0.425	0.421	0.420	0.401	0.366	0.362	0.376	0.349

B. Share of Total Structure Inequality (Share of National Within Group Theil, %)

	National[1]	Management	Professional	Technical	Sales	Clerical	Services	Farming	Crafts	Operative
1976	100.0	9.0	11.8	2.6	8.2	20.7	14.3	2.3	12.9	18.4
1977	100.0	9.1	12.1	2.7	8.9	20.3	13.9	2.0	12.8	18.1
1978	100.0	9.2	12.1	2.9	8.7	20.9	13.3	2.0	12.8	18.1
1979	100.0	9.6	12.1	2.9	8.2	21.2	13.6	1.9	13.1	17.4
1980	100.0	10.0	11.9	3.1	8.8	21.4	13.6	2.0	12.8	16.5
1981	100.0	10.1	12.0	3.0	8.9	20.7	13.7	2.2	12.8	16.8
1982	100.0	10.8	12.6	3.4	8.7	21.1	13.7	2.2	10.7	16.8
1983	100.0	12.0	12.9	3.3	9.1	20.9	13.6	2.2	10.5	15.7
1984	100.0	11.8	12.9	3.3	9.0	20.5	13.8	2.2	11.0	15.6
1985	100.0	12.2	13.3	3.3	9.4	20.5	13.5	1.9	11.0	15.3
1986	100.0	12.0	13.3	2.9	9.3	20.4	13.7	2.1	11.2	15.0
1987	100.0	13.0	13.4	3.4	9.5	20.3	12.9	2.1	10.6	14.8
1988	100.0	13.9	13.8	3.3	9.7	19.2	12.9	2.0	10.8	14.5

Source: See source for Table 2.2.

[1] National within group Theil. Other Theil measures are the national Theil calculated for individual industries. See Appendix 2.1 for explanations.

England, have large shares of these services. In addition, regions like the South Atlantic, West South Central, and Mountain, with low levels of such services in 1976, had substantially increased their shares by 1988 (Map 2.4 indicates that certain states within these regions accounted for most of the producer services employment in these regions). Three regions—New England, Middle Atlantic, and the West North Central—have relied on private health and education employment for a degree of economic specialization. Some regions, such as New England, have demonstrated relative specialization in several of the key sectors, and this structure has been able to capture gains in the national economy. Other regions, such as the East North Central, have been less well positioned by their economic structure to take advantage of national trends.

The variation in the level of construction employment among regions is notable in Table 2.10. The construction sector was becoming more spatially concentrated, as reflected by the increase in its Theil index in Table 2.8, and the sector was accounting for an increasing share of the overall pattern of spatial economic structure. Table 2.10 demonstrates this same pattern. A few regions, such as the East South Central and South Atlantic, had relatively large shares of construction employment. The high levels of construction employment occurred in regions where employment and population had grown at levels above the national rate (see Map 2.5).[41] In other words, the uneven regional growth in employment led to a more spatially concentrated construction sector, and this in turn contributed to the differences in economic structure among regions.

The complex set of changes in economic structure of individual states can be captured with the Theil index, using individual states, rather than individual industrial sectors as above, as the unit of analysis. A decrease in the index means less variation among the economic structures of states, whereas an increase in the index means that differences in structure increased. The Theil index indicates that differences in the economic structure of states declined between 1976 and 1978, but after 1980 showed a fairly steady increase (Table 2.11). That is to say, during the 1980s, economic structures of states became increasingly differentiated. The fashion in which state economies become more diversified, however, varied substantially among regions, as we just saw.

Differences in structure contribute to differences in economic prospects. The types of jobs and wage levels in a state are related to the state's economic structure. Crude evidence of this assertion is seen in Table 2.11 where increasing differences in average state earnings, that is, salaries plus wages, occur after 1981 as increasing differences in economic structure emerge. The spatial distribution of types of jobs and their corresponding salary and wage levels are producing increasing differences in earnings among states after 1981 (see Figure 2.1). The Middle Atlantic and Pacific have maintained their high relative standing in terms of earnings, while New England has dramatically improved its position, ending the period with the highest regional average earnings. These regions have relatively large shares of dynamic, high-wage industries. The East North Central experienced a substantial decline, undoubtedly related to the relative decline of

Table 2.10
Employment Structure by Regions: 1976–1988

Region	AGRI-CULTURE	CONSTRUC-TION	MANUFACTURING						Total
			Non-durable	Misc. Durable	Petro-chemical	Machinery	Advanced Technology	
New England								
1976	1.4	4.9	9.1	3.6	1.8	6.7	7.7	28.9
1988	1.3	6.6	5.5	2.6	1.0	4.8	8.6	22.5
Mid Atlantic								
1976	1.3	4.3	8.4	3.0	1.6	7.6	5.9	26.5
1988	1.3	5.8	6.1	1.8	1.6	4.2	5.2	18.9
E N Central								
1976	2.3	4.8	5.9	2.9	2.1	14.0	4.9	29.8
1988	1.9	5.3	5.5	2.5	1.7	9.8	3.8	23.3
W N Central								
1976	4.5	6.7	7.3	2.0	1.2	5.2	4.0	19.7
1988	3.9	5.0	5.7	2.0	1.2	4.8	3.9	17.6
S Atlantic								
1976	3.4	6.4	11.4	2.8	1.2	3.9	3.1	22.4
1988	2.5	7.2	8.1	2.4	1.1	3.3	3.3	18.2
E S Central								
1976	4.5	6.4	11.0	5.0	2.3	6.7	2.5	27.5
1988	3.4	6.5	9.1	4.9	1.8	5.2	3.5	24.5
W S Central								
1976	6.6	7.8	5.4	2.5	1.4	4.6	3.6	17.5
1988	5.5	6.9	4.7	1.6	1.3	3.5	4.2	15.3
Mountain								
1976	6.1	7.5	4.5	2.5	0.7	2.6	3.1	13.4
1988	4.7	5.9	3.7	1.8	0.8	1.7	4.9	12.9
Pacific								
1976	3.8	5.0	6.0	3.4	1.1	4.4	5.8	20.7
1988	3.2	5.9	5.1	2.9	1.0	3.2	6.4	18.6
National								
1976	3.4	5.7	7.7	3.0	1.5	7.0	4.6	23.8
1988	2.8	6.1	6.0	2.4	1.3	4.8	4.7	19.2

Source: See source for Table 2.2.

44

			SERVICES					
Distri- butive	Wholesale Trade	Producer	Retail Trade	Consumer	Health and Education	Public Admini- stration	Total	Share of Workers
6.3	3.1	9.3	16.3	7.3	18.4	4.1	64.8	5.8
6.3	3.5	13.5	16.0	7.0	19.2	4.0	69.5	5.9
7.9	4.1	11.0	15.5	7.6	16.7	5.1	67.9	17.0
7.3	3.8	14.8	16.0	8.2	19.1	4.9	74.1	15.3
6.3	4.1	8.3	16.8	7.0	16.4	4.1	63.0	19.5
6.6	3.7	11.6	18.6	8.3	16.4	4.2	69.4	17.4
7.8	4.2	8.6	17.1	7.9	19.5	3.9	69.0	8.0
7.5	4.3	11.3	17.7	8.9	19.6	4.2	73.5	7.3
6.7	3.9	8.8	17.7	8.2	15.7	6.7	67.7	16.1
7.0	3.5	12.6	17.7	8.6	16.5	6.4	72.3	17.5
7.2	3.7	6.8	15.5	7.5	16.0	4.8	61.5	6.3
6.4	3.5	8.9	17.9	8.8	16.1	4.1	65.7	5.8
6.9	4.6	8.1	18.3	8.5	17.2	4.6	68.2	9.4
7.0	4.3	12.4	18.6	9.4	15.7	4.9	72.3	10.7
7.4	4.2	8.9	18.9	9.4	16.9	7.3	73.0	4.8
6.9	3.7	13.5	18.7	11.3	16.9	5.6	76.6	5.4
7.0	4.4	10.5	17.7	8.6	16.5	5.9	70.6	13.2
6.5	3.7	14.6	17.3	9.2	16.1	4.9	72.3	14.6
7.0	4.1	9.1	17.0	7.9	16.8	5.2	67.1	100.0
6.8	3.7	12.8	17.6	8.7	17.1	5.0	71.8	100.0

Map 2.5
Population Growth by State: 1970–1990

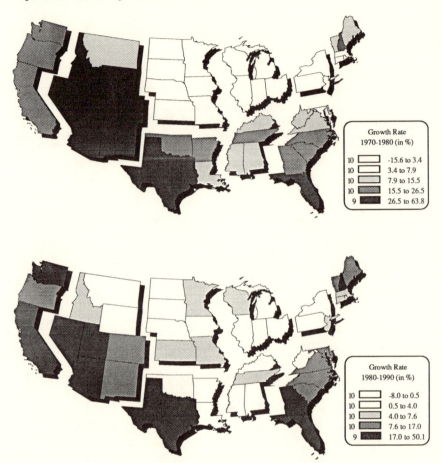

Source: U.S. Department of Commerce, Bureau of the Census, *Statistical Abstract of the United States, 1991* (Washington, D.C., 1991), p. 21.

its high-wage manufacturing sector, and the East South Central and West South Central, after a modest improvement, ended the period in lower earnings, likely the result of being positioned with large shares of low-wage industries.

For most of this century differences in per capita income among states has diminished.[42] Differences among states in terms of average earnings also decreased between 1950 and 1980, but at the same time inequality in earnings within states was increasing.[43] The results here, however, suggest that in the early 1980s the increasing differences in economic structure were reversing the long-term trend and that wage and salary inequality among states was also on the increase, a finding consistent with the increasing spatial concentration of the

Table 2.11
Economic Structure[1] of States and Mean Earnings: 1976–1988

	National Theil Index of State Structure	Mean State Earnings ($)	Coefficient of Variation Mean State Earnings
1976	0.225	8,394	13.3
1977	0.224	9,017	13.0
1978	0.221	9,902	12.5
1979	0.225	10,828	12.2
1980	0.223	11,778	11.7
1981	0.227	12,767	11.1
1982	0.238	13,435	11.8
1983	0.248	14,078	12.0
1984	0.244	15,092	12.5
1985	0.248	15,846	13.4
1986	0.255	16,566	13.4
1987	0.258	17,271	13.7
1988	0.257	18,174	14.3

Source: See source for Table 2.2.

[1]Defined by employment in 14 industrial categories.

high-wage occupations noted above. In other words, the specific changes in economic structure of states, which have been produced by structural change in the national economy, are generating differences in economic prospects among states. Some states with economies better positioned to take advantage of opportunities produced economic change.

CONCLUSIONS

Structural economic change in the U.S. economy has created more diverse state and regional economies. Manufacturing remains important to the national and regional economies, but the composition of manufacturing has changed dramatically, as has its spatial location. The rapidly growing service sector is more spatially diverse than manufacturing, and undoubtedly related to the spatial

Figure 2.1
Average Regional Earnings: 1976–1988

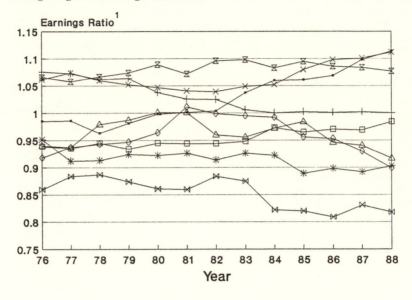

— New England   ＊ Middle Atlantic ┼ East North Central
＊ West North Central   ⊟ South Atlantic   ⋈ East South Central
◆ West South Central   △ Mountain   ✳ Pacific

Source: See source for Table 2.2.

[1]Earnings ratio is defined as average regional earnings divided by
average national earnings.

distribution of population, but key subsectors, such as producer services and
health and education, are becoming important contributors to state and regional
economic specialization. Important to all of these changes is telecommunications.
The national and world economies are becoming more information-intensive,
and telecommunications is a principal infrastructure for transmitting information.
This provision of information incorporates many of the electronics-related technological breakthroughs of recent decades. This creates the potential for increasing productivity in the creation, provision, and exchange of information and,
consequently, for improving the productivity of firms and the economy. In
addition, this new infrastructure has profound implications for the location of
economic activities. Although control functions of economic activity, say in a
large corporation, can be centralized through new telecommunications systems,

they also permit economic activities to be more spatially dispersed than did earlier communications technologies.

The changes in the country's spatial economy have profound implications for state governments. First, changes in a state's economy have a direct effect on the fiscal capabilities of states. A state's fiscal status is affected by growth, or lack thereof, in the state's economy. In addition, the changing structure of a state's economy may render a state's revenue structure ineffective. For example, if a state's revenue structure does not tap the income produced by the service sector, its fiscal capabilities will not match the strength of its economy. But economic change creates further challenges. States have important responsibilities in infrastructure provision. As seen here, telecommunications are vital. Also, as the occupational requirements of the economy change, educational systems must adapt, which, again, places pressure on state government. To be successful, state economic development strategies must be attentive to these changing demands of an evolving economy.

Appendix 2.1
The Theil Index

The Theil index, developed by Henri Theil, was derived from information theory.[44] Its purpose, similar to that of the coefficient of variation, the Gini coefficient, and others is to measure inequality in distributions.[45] The Theil index has most frequently been used to describe inequality in income distributions, but is well suited to describe inequality, or dissimilarity, in economic structures.

The Theil index is:

$$T = 1/n \ \Sigma(Y_i/u_y) \ \ln(Y_i/u_y) \tag{1}$$
$$= 1/n \left[\frac{\Sigma(Y_i \ \ln Y_i) - u_y \ \ln u_y}{u_y} \right]$$

where

n = the number of employment sectors
Y_i = employment in sector i
u_y = mean of Y
$\ln$ = natural logarithm

The second of the expressions clarifies that T is the dispersion of $Y_i \ \ln Y_i$ around its mean, standardized by the mean. T is bounded from below by zero, when all employment sectors have the same level of employment. At the other extreme, when all workers are found in a single employment sector, the upper bound is $\ln (n)$.

Aside from simplicity of calculation, another advantage of Theil's T is that it can be readily decomposed into terms representing variation among groups and variation within groups. For any number of mutually exclusive and exhaustive groups:

$$T = \Sigma(p_j\, u_j/u_y) \ln (u_j/u_y) + \Sigma(p_j u_j/u_y)\, t_j \qquad (2)$$

where p_j is the proportion of workers in the jth group, u_j is the mean number of workers for the jth group, u_y is the overall mean, and T_j is Theil's T for the jth group. The first term on the right is among-group variation and increases with the dispersion of mean employment size u_j around the overall mean u_y. Given that the variable Y is defined in terms of employment in sector i, the first term of expression (2) reflects changes over time resulting from differing growth rates of sectors (or states). The second term is the within-group variation, a function of T_j's suitably weighted; it captures the extent to which the spatial structure of an individual sector (or economic structure of a state) is specialized. When properly weighted and summed, the national within-group Theil index provides the summary measure for the degree of spatial specialization in the national economy. It is given in Section A of Tables 2.8 and 2.9, and in Table 2.10. This term can also be expanded to show the contribution of individual groups—for example, of specific sectors—to the overall index. These shares are reported in Section B of Tables 2.8 and 2.9.

Appendix 2.2
The Census Regions

New England
> Maine
> New Hampshire; Vermont*
> Massachusetts
> Rhode Island; Connecticut*

Middle Atlantic
> New York
> New Jersey
> Pennsylvania

East North Central
> Ohio
> Indiana
> Illinois
> Michigan
> Wisconsin

West North Central
> Minnesota
> Iowa
> Missouri
> North Dakota
> South Dakota
> Nebraska
> Kansas

South Atlantic

    Delaware; Maryland; Washington, D.C.*

    Virginia

    West Virginia

    North Carolina

    South Carolina

    Georgia

    Florida

East South Central

    Kentucky

    Tennessee

    Alabama

    Mississippi

West South Central

    Arkansas

    Louisiana

    Oklahoma

    Texas

Mountain

    Montana

    Idaho

    Wyoming

    Colorado

    New Mexico

    Arizona

    Utah

    Nevada

Pacific

    Washington

    Oregon

    California

    Alaska

*States were combined because of few number cases available in a state in the Current Population Survey.

NOTES

1. Martin Tolchin, "Competitive Edge Held Lost by U.S. Industry," *New York Times* (Nov. 14, 1991): C2.

2. The principal focus of this analysis will be placed on employment for two reasons. Data on employment are more reliable than data required for other measures, and employment levels are one of the crucial elements in the political dynamics of state development policy.

3. Thomas M. Stanback, Jr., Peter J. Bearse, Thierry J. Noyelle, and Robert A. Karasek, *Services: The New Economy* (Totowa, NJ: Rowman & Allanheld, 1981).

4. Barry Bluestone and Bennett Harrison, *The Deindustrialization of America: Plant Closings, Abandonment, and the Dismantling of Basic Industry* (New York: Basic Books, 1982).

5. Ann R. Markusen and Virginia Carlson, "Deindustrialization in the American Midwest: Causes and Responses," in *Deindustrialization and Regional Economic Transformation: The Experience of the United States*, Lloyd Rodwin and Hidehiko Sazanami, eds. (Boston: Unwin Hyman, 1989): 37–41.

6. Norman Glickman and Douglas Woodward, *The New Competitors: How Foreign Investors Are Changing the U.S. Economy* (New York: Basic Books, 1989).

7. Stephen S. Cohen and John Zysman, *Manufacturing Matters: The Myth of the Post-Industrial Economy* (New York: Basic Books, 1987).

8. Edward F. Denison, *Estimates of Productivity Change by Industry: An Evaluation and an Alternative* (Washington, D.C.: The Brookings Institution, 1989): 13–14.

9. Productivity is measured by physical output per unit of input. A general measure of productivity is output per hour of work; multifactor productivity uses a weighted average of various inputs—hours of work and quantities of capital, inventories and land—in the denominator. Although simple in concept, very difficult empirical problems arise in estimating productivity.

10. William Baumol, Sue Anne Batey Blackman, and Edward N. Wolff, *Productivity and American Leadership: The Long View* (Boston: MIT Press, 1989).

11. Edward F. Denison, *Estimates of Productivity Change by Industry: An Evaluation and an Alternative* (Washington, D.C.: The Brookings Institution, 1989): 40.

12. Ibid., Chapter 2.

13. James K. Galbraith, "A New Picture of the American Economy," *The American Prospect* (Fall 1991): 27–29.

14. Joseph A. Schumpeter, *Capitalism, Socialism, and Democracy* (New York: Harper & Row, 1962): Chapter VII, "The Process of Creative Destruction."

15. Cohen and Zysman, *Manufacturing Matters*, Chapter 10.

16. U.S. Department of Labor, Bureau of Labor Statistics Bulletin 2228, *The Impact of Technology on Labor in Four Industries: Textiles/Paper and Paperboard/Steel/Motor Vehicles* (Washington, D.C., May 1985): 4–5.

17. Denison, *Estimates of Productivity Change by Industry*, p. 40.

18. U.S. Department of Labor, Bureau of Labor Statistics Bulletin 2242, *Technology and Its Impact on Labor in Four Industries: Tires/Aluminum/Aerospace/Banking* (Washington, D.C., May 1986): 40–41.

19. Harold Innis, *Empire and Communication* (Toronto: University of Toronto Press, 1950); *The Bias of Information* (Toronto: University of Toronto Press, 1951).

20. Fritz Machlup, *The Production and Distribution of Knowledge in the U.S.* (Princeton, NJ: Princeton University Press, 1962).

21. U.S. Department of Commerce, The Office of Telecommunications, *The Information Economy: Definition and Measurement*, Special Report 77–12(1), by Marc Uri Porat (Washington, D.C., 1977). For the share of information workers from 1800 to 1980, see Mark Hepworth, *Geography of the Information Economy* (New York: The Guildford Press, 1990): 14.

22. Daniel Bell, *The Coming of the Post-Industrial Society* (New York: Basic Books, 1973).

23. J. Beniger, *The Control Revolution: Technological and Economic Origins of the Information Economy* (Cambridge, MA: Harvard University Press, 1986). For a discussion of the various conceptual contributions to the information society concept, see Hepworth, *Geography of the Information Economy*, Chapter 1.

24. Sectors were considered telecommunications-intensive if they purchase more than 10 percent of their inputs from the communication sector (SIC 48). This was done by examining the technology matrices in Marc Uri Porat, *The Information Economy: The Technology Matrices (1967)* (Washington, D.C.: Department of Commerce, 1977): Table 1.

25. Jurgen Schmandt, Frederick Williams, Robert H. Wilson, and Sharon Strover, eds., *The New Urban Infrastructure: Cities and Telecommunications* (New York: Praeger, 1990).

26. Thierry Noyelle, ed., *New York's Financial Markets: The Challenges of Globalization* (Boulder, CO: Westview Press, 1989); Hepworth, *Geography of the Information Economy*, Chapter 7; Wilson Dizard, *The Coming Information Age: An Overview of Technology, Economics, and Politics*, 2nd ed. (New York: Longman, 1985): 93–94.

27. Nicol argues that one important feature of the recent evolution of an information economy is the emergence of a highly diversified market for information services, and this creates further demands for telecommunications services. See Lionel Nicol, "Communications Technology: Economic and Spatial Impacts," in *High Technology, Space and Society*, edited by Manual Castells (Beverly Hills, CA: Sage, 1985): 192–193.

28. P. W. Huber, *The Geodesic Network: 1987 Report on Competition in the Telephone Industry* (Washington, D.C.: U.S. Department of Justice): 1.23–1.26.

29. Cohen and Zysman, *Manufacturing Matters*, Chapter 11.

30. Hepworth reviews the literature on spatial trends and information needs related to flexible manufacturing, *Geography of the Information Economy*, Chapter 6.

31. Martin Bernal, Joan Stuller, and Liching Sung, "Doing Business in Rural America," in *Telecommunications and Rural Development: A Study of Private and Public Sector Innovation*, edited by Jurgen Schmandt et al. (New York: Praeger, 1991): 18–58.

32. Lester Thurow argues that the centralization effect of telecommunications advances dominates the decentralizing tendencies at least in the service sectors. See Lester Thurow, "Regional Transformation and the Service Sectors," in *Deindustrialization*, edited by Rodwin and Sazanami, pp. 182–187.

33. Productivity in the telecommunications industry is discussed in Chapter 6.

34. Nicol, "Communications Technology," pp. 206–207.

35. U.S. Department of Commerce, International Trade Administration, *1991 Industrial Outlook* (Washington, D.C., January 1991): 30–1 and 31–1.

36. Thierry Noyelle and Penny Pease, *The Information Industries: New York's New*

Export Base (New York: Conservation of Human Resources, Columbia University, November 1988).

37. Luis Suarez-Villa, *The Evolution of Regional Economies: Entrepreneurship and Macroeconomic Change* (New York: Praeger, 1989): 86–88. For its application to Sunbelt–Snowbelt growth patterns, see R. D. Norton and J. Rees, "The Product Cycle and the Spatial Decentralization of American Manufacturing," *Regional Studies*, vol. 13 (1979): 141–151.

38. For a detailed study of the spatial impact of defense spending, see Ann Markusen, Peter Hall, Scott Campbell, and Sabina Dietrick, *The Rise of the Sunbelt: The Military Remapping of Industrial America* (New York: Oxford University Press, 1991).

39. This view is clearly articulated in the so-called economic base model. This model distinguishes between basic, or export, employment and nonbasic employment. The latter is largely service sector activity, serving local demand, and its size is determined by the success of an area's export activities. See Charles Tiebout, "The Community Economic Base Study," Supplementary paper no. 16 (Washington, D.C.: Committee for Economic Development, December 1962).

40. For purposes of this discussion, specialization in a region is defined by the region's share of employment exceeding the industry's share in the national economy. For example, manufacturing employment in New England in 1988 was 22.5 percent, whereas manufacturing represented 19.2 percent of national employment. Hence, New England had a relative specialization in manufacturing.

41. The last column of Table 2.10 gives the share of workers in each region. If a region's employment grew at the same rate as national employment, its share of workers would not change in the two years. An increase in a region's share of national employment would indicate that the region grew more rapidly than the nation as a whole.

42. Advisory Commission on Intergovernmental Relations (ACIR), *Regional Growth* A–74 (Washington, D.C., 1980).

43. W. Norton Grubb and Robert H. Wilson, "Sources of Increasing Inequality in Wages and Salaries, 1960–1980," *Monthly Labor Review*, vol. 112, no. 4 (April 1989): 3–13.

44. Henri Theil, *Economics and Information Theory* (Amsterdam: North-Holland, 1967); *Statistical Decomposition Analysis* (Amsterdam: North-Holland, 1972).

45. See Paul Allison, "Measures of Inequality," *American Sociological Review* (December 1978): 865–880.

3

Policymaking and the States

The regional impacts of structural change in the U.S. economy, identified in Chapter 2, created significant, if not overwhelming, challenges to state governments. These challenges included not only the economic welfare of state residents but the fiscal health of states themselves. Renewed activism of state government during the last decade can be understood as a political response to the distress and anxiety of populations faced with economic uncertainty. But the scope of action and effectiveness of the states depends on several factors.

In the first section of this chapter, the evolution of intergovernmental relations is examined, particularly in terms of two elements of the policy development process: the locus of policy initiative and the means by which policy is implemented. The complexity of these relations in no small part results from the extensive historical variations in the relationship of policy initiative and implementation in the intergovernmental framework. To foreshadow the finding of this discussion, decentralization of the type argued during the Eisenhower, Nixon, and Carter administrations was largely one of administrative decentralization, that is, of implementation of public policy. The Reagan and, to a lesser extent, the Bush administrations further endorsed decentralization of policy initiative. These two strands have in distinct ways contributed to state activism. The section concludes by considering how the recent shift in intergovernmental relations is affecting the states' policy agenda and fiscal situation.

When the country was formed, state governments had quite broad powers and extensively exercised these powers in promoting economic welfare. By the beginning of the twentieth century, the increasing dominance of federal action in economic matters and other policy arenas can be noted. Some factors contributing to the emergence of a strong federal role were the requirements of a unified national market and the development of an industrial economy. The significance of states, in the economy, certainly diminished with respect to the federal government, but the state presence has not disappeared. In the second section of this chapter, the various roles that state government play in economic development, including infrastructure provision, regulation, technology transfer, and promotions, are examined in a historical context. This history, which varies significantly by role examined, is a rich and complex one.

The intergovernmental system creates part of the context in which states operate. A second set of factors—institutional, fiscal and technical capacities—also affects state policymaking. The ability of state governments to respond to challenges depends on the capabilities of state legislatures and executive branches in formulating and implementing innovative policies. Recent innovation by states is the result of strong gubernatorial leadership in many cases, but also responsible are reformed and assertive state legislatures, technically upgraded state bureaucracies, and a much more diverse and aggressive array of interest groups. These interest groups include new business groups associated with the emerging and rapidly growing sectors of the economy. These factors, the topic of the third section of this chapter, have dramatically affected contemporary state policymaking.

Changes in intergovernmental relations and in state policymaking capabilities are producing a more prominent role for state governments in development policy. As structural economic change has affected regions and states, shifts in intergovernmental relations have been affecting the need for and capability of state action. This decentralization of policymaking, however, has not produced less government, as hoped by some who have argued for a New Federalism. State policymaking, however, does involve a broader range of actors, and thus is perceived by some to be more participatory, if not democratic, than federal policymaking. The substantial improvement in the capabilities of state governments and broader participation of the public in state policy have established an environment in which the opportunities for state policy innovation and initiative are greater than at any point since the turn of the century.

POLICY INITIATIVE AND IMPLEMENTATION IN THE FEDERALIST SYSTEM

The relationship between the federal government and the states has been a topic of debate and scrutiny throughout the history of the country. The debate revolves around the appropriate division of responsibilities and the relative autonomy of each level. A central issue during the Constitutional Convention was the supremacy of the national government, which was required, some argued, to have a nation. Others saw the enhanced responsiveness to citizens of a decentralized system as a more important quality for the proposed governmental structure. The search for an appropriate balance between federal and state powers did not end with the Constitutional Convention but has continued for the last 200 years.[1] The "middle ground" solution has in fact evolved over time, although for most of this century to the advantage of the federal government.

The evolution of intergovernmental relations has been the subject of extensive scholarly scrutiny. The various characterizations of these relations depend on the period being studied and the policy issue of concern. The relation has been described as dual federalism,[2] cooperative federalism,[3] and technocratic federalism.[4] Others have identified historical phases according to the nature of intergovernmental relations—dual federalism (1787–1913), cooperative federalism (1913–1964), centralized federalism (1964–1980), new federalism (1981–   )— with the general trend being toward increased federal dominance, at least until the last phase.[5] Still others have described intergovernmental relations as a layer cake, with distinct division of functions among levels of government, and as a marble cake, with responsibilities for various functions shared in varying proportions by different levels of government.[6]

Given that responsibilities for governmental action in most policy areas have been shared by state and federal governments, a number of questions become of interest to this discussion. At what level of government does the initiative for a particular type of action lie? What are the legal and resource bases for initiatives? What level or levels of government are responsible for administration of the initiative? The answers to these questions have changed over time, thus requiring a historical account, although special attention will be given to the recent debates concerning federalism.

The supremacy of the union was demonstrated during the Civil War when the ultimate limits of independent state action were established. After a short-lived period of federal leadership during Reconstruction, however, the relative autonomy of state action, exercised since the founding of the country, was again the pattern. Toward the end of the past century and in the early decades of the twentieth century an irregular pattern emerged. In economic issues, aggressive regulatory postures were assumed by states, resulting from the Granger and Progressive movements, in banking, railroads, and other areas. Although Theodore Roosevelt's presidential administration expanded the federal role in resource management and development and economic regulation, in other policy arenas, such as social welfare, workmen's compensation, vocational education, minimum wage, and administrative efficiency, state governments were the leaders in reform.[7] Certainly not all states were progressive and innovative, but a number were. Writing in 1932, Supreme Court Justice Louis D. Brandeis wrote, "It is one of the happy incidents of the federal system that a single courageous state may, if its citizens choose, serve as a laboratory, and try novel social and economic experiments. . . ."[8]

By the 1920s, however, policy innovation in state government had become rare.[9] The trend toward increased federal action in the economy, building on an irregular pattern in regulation of railroad, banks, utilities, and other industries and based on the interstate commerce, financial, and general welfare clauses of the U.S. Constitution,[10] reached new heights during the Great Depression. States, suffering from debt and deficit spending in the 1920s, were overwhelmed and unable to cope with the deterioration of the economy.[11] The inability of the Hoover administration to deal effectively and coherently with the economic crash, along with bankrupt state governments, severe cuts in state budgets, intraparty factionalism, and general disarray in state legislatures, set the stage for the public acceptance of a strong federal presence.[12] Under the New Deal, in addition to further expansion of economic regulation, the federal government assumed responsibility for macroeconomic management. The expansionary fiscal policy was effected through direct federal expenditures and an impressive range of public works investment—in public buildings, urban infrastructure, water resources, electrification, soil conservations and other projects. Although federal resources had been mobilized earlier, as in homestead legislation and in the completion of the transcontinental railroad system, the New Deal initiatives represented a substantial increase in scope. In addition, a vast array of social welfare measures was introduced, frequently patterned on earlier efforts of state governments.

Spheres of influence and autonomy of the federal and state governments have frequently been reviewed by the courts. The notion of dual federalism, in particular, rested in part on a judicially supported division of responsibilities between the two levels.[13] A turning point occurred in 1937 as the expansive federal initiatives were upheld by the courts. Decisions first protected states' powers, but after 1937, for the most part the courts found in favor of federal prerogatives.[14]

The dramatic change in the scope and influence of federal action during the New Deal resulted both from technical and resource capabilities of state and federal governments and political factors.[15] States lacked the policy instruments and resources to address the problems of the Depression, but many federal programs were implemented through state agencies.[16] The Federal Emergency Relief Administration (FERA), established in the early days of the first Roosevelt administration, provided quite substantial levels of federal funds to states for distribution, but with the requirement that states show proof of adequate supervision.[17] In order to qualify for federal funds, most states moved quickly to establish relief agencies. States were also required to match federal funds. To this requirement states responded with different levels of funding, laying the foundation for the disparity in levels of per capita welfare payments found among states even to this day. In later New Deal legislation pertaining to Social Security and unemployment compensation, states again were given significant roles in administration, funding, and eligibility determination. Roosevelt's approval of and encouragement for state experimentation can be found in the Social Security law. In these cases, federal actions led to new forms of federal–state cooperation, the expansion of state activity in several policy areas, modernization of state bureaucracies,[18] and higher state revenues. The redistributional effects of the state efforts, however, were reduced by the fairly regressive way in which states generated revenues.

Some New Deal programs bypassed state governments altogether. The Works Progress Administration (WPA), Public Works Administration (PWA), Federal Housing Administration, and Farm Security Administration were all implemented through newly formed federal agencies with little, if any, participation of state agencies. Although the pressing need for quick action justified the creation of new, centralized action-oriented agencies, a political factor was also present. In a pragmatic response to circumstance but also achieving a realignment of political forces, Roosevelt's urban and rural policies frequently bypassed state governmental and political structures in order to develop new urban and rural constituencies.[19] Whether Roosevelt was entirely successful in this attempt is debatable. One source of resistance to the New Deal efforts, which started to become effective toward the end of the thirties, was state governments. In addition, the highly decentralized political party system in the United States provided constraints, a phenomenon that continues to limit nationalization of public policy through federal initiatives.[20]

Although the leadership for most policies remained in Washington during the late 1940s and 1950s, a shift in implementation philosophy and structure from the New Deal to the Fair Deal can be noted. The Eisenhower administration was much concerned with an imbalance in federal–state relations and attempted to reinforce state authority through the implementation of federal policy, following the pattern found in the 1916 Highway Act,[21] which established the categorical grants-in-aid implementation strategy. States had increased their involvement in road construction prior to the act in response to the rapidly expanding use of automobiles and trucks and postal service's offer of free rural mail delivery. Congress recognized a national purpose in an integrated national highway system and passed the 1916 Highway Act. Federal funds were matched by state funds, and although the federal government had to preapprove state plans, construction of the roads was the responsibility of the states. The National Interstate and Defense Highway Act of 1956 and the Highway Revenue Act of 1956 utilized this same approach. The Eisenhower administration also adopted a decentralization strategy in the Housing Act of 1954 which shifted the implementation responsibility of urban renewal from federal agencies to local governments and business organizations.[22]

It was not until the 1960s that extensive federal activism again emerged.[23] Expansion of federal initiative in the 1960s was impressive both in terms of the range of policy areas and the level of federal resources allocated to these efforts. New federal policies on civil rights, education, welfare, health, environment, crime, regional development, elimination of poverty, indeed most areas of domestic policy, were legislated. In addition, there were substantial federal expenditures in cities to address poverty. Unlike the states' laboratories-of-democracy contribution to New Deal strategies, states did not offer model policies in the formation of Great Society legislation. Federal departments and agencies and intellectual policy elites external to government were heavily represented in task forces and other groups that developed policies.[24] The adaptation of policy to traditional state roles, however, was an important element of these new efforts. States' resistance had to be overridden in some areas, such as in civil rights and voting legislation. However, the instrument of implementation for much of the legislation was existing machinery in state and local government.

For the wide range of new federal policy initiatives of the 1960s, a variety of implementation strategies were used, but the most well-known mechanism was federal grants-in-aid to state and local governments. The use of this well-established mechanism was dramatically expanded during the Great Society.[25] More than 200 new grants-in-aid programs were introduced during the Johnson presidency, and federal aid increased from $8.6 billion to $19.1 billion at the end of the Johnson administration.[26] Many of the Great Society programs were directed to social welfare, and the composition of federal aid reflected this shift in federal priorities.[27] Federal legislation attempted to elicit the cooperation of other governments in the achievement of these national welfare goals; to a greater extent than in the earlier phase of cooperative federalism, the broader use of categorical grants-in-aid meant that policymaking was more clearly nationalized and states served principally administrative roles.[28]

The implementation strategies of the Great Society were not limited to categorical grants-in-aid. Small block grant programs for health and crime were also adopted.[29] Consolidating categorical grants-in-aid into block grants provided a means to give state and local officials the discretion denied under categorical grants-in-aid programs, a practice greatly expanded during the Nixon and Reagan administrations. Great Society implementation strategies also had political objectives; the Office of Economic Opportunity, for example, actively encouraged the participation of segments of the population, through community action agencies, previously disenfranchised and bypassed local governmental structures.[30]

President Richard Nixon, in the early 1970s, took steps toward implementing a more decentralized administrative structure to improve administrative efficiency.[31] By the mid-1970s, federal aid in the form of categorical grants-in-aid was 75 percent of total federal aid as compared to 98 percent in 1968. General revenue sharing and block grants became important vehicles for distributing federal aid.[32] As in the categorical grants-in-aid implementation strategy, states and local governments were key institutions for achieving federal goals, but under block grants and general revenue sharing, administration was further decentralized, providing local officials with greater discretion.

One curious effect of expanded federal policy during the 1960s, which continued through the 1970s, was the growth of state government. Federal transfers to state and local governments increased, and as a result of an expanded role in implementing federal policy, state governments expanded their expenditures and increased their employment (Table 3.1). Although policy initiative resided largely in Washington, D.C., the levels of federal funding and means of implementing policy, including federal mandates, had a significant impact on increasing the size of state government.[33]

Another effect on the increase in federal transfers was that state governments

Table 3.1
Federal, State, and Local Government Revenue, Expenditures, and Employment: 1952-1989

Year	GNP ($000)	Federal Outlays Share GNP	Federal Debt-Share GNP	Revenues (% of Personal Income) Federal Total	Revenues State Total	Revenues State Own Source	Revenues Local Total	Revenues Local Own Source	Expenditure (% of Personal Income) Federal Total	Expenditure Federal Inter-Govt.	Expenditure State Total	Expenditure State Inter-Govt.	Expenditure Local Total	Total Public Sector (000)	Public Employment Distribution (%) Federal (civilian)	Distribution State	Distribution Local
1952	351.6	19.3%	62.7	26.2	6.1	5.2	7.1	5.2	26.1	0.9	5.8	1.8	7.4	7,105	36.4	14.9	48.7
1957	451.0	17.0	49.8	24.4	6.9	5.8	8.1	6.0	23.0	1.1	6.8	2.1	8.7	8,047	30.3	16.2	53.5
1962	574.6	18.6	44.5	23.5	8.3	6.6	9.5	7.0	25.0	1.7	8.0	2.4	10.0	9,388	27.0	17.9	55.0
1967	816.4	19.3	33.6	25.0	9.5	7.3	10.0	6.9	25.9	2.3	9.1	3.0	10.3	11,867	25.2	19.7	55.1
1972	1,212.8	19.0	28.0	22.8	11.4	8.6	11.7	7.7	24.7	3.4	11.1	3.7	12.1	13,759	20.3	21.5	58.2
1973	1,359.3	18.1	26.6	23.0	11.8	8.8	11.7	7.4	24.8	3.7	10.8	3.7	11.6	14,139	19.7	21.3	59.0
1974	1,472.8	18.3	24.3	23.8	11.6	8.9	11.8	7.3	24.4	3.5	10.9	3.8	11.6	14,628	19.6	21.6	58.8
1975	1,598.4	20.8	25.9	23.1	12.0	9.1	12.2	7.4	26.0	3.8	12.1	4.0	12.4	14,973	19.3	21.8	58.9
1976	1,782.8	20.8	28.1	22.4	12.7	9.6	12.3	7.5	26.9	4.8	12.5	4.0	12.5	15,012	18.9	22.3	58.8
1977	1,990.5	20.6	28.4	23.9	12.7	9.7	12.2	7.4	27.0	4.6	11.9	3.9	12.2	15,459	18.4	22.6	59.0
1978	2,249.7	20.4	28.0	23.8	12.4	9.5	11.8	7.2	26.4	4.4	11.2	3.7	11.6	15,628	18.5	22.6	58.9
1979	2,508.2	20.1	26.1	24.6	12.1	9.3	11.5	6.9	26.4	4.2	11.0	3.7	11.5	15,971	18.0	23.2	58.9
1980	2,732.0	21.6	26.6	25.0	12.3	9.4	11.4	6.9	27.3	4.0	11.4	3.7	11.5	16,213	17.9	23.1	59.0
1981	3,052.6	22.2	26.3	26.2	12.3	9.5	11.4	7.0	28.5	3.8	11.6	3.7	11.4	15,968	17.9	23.3	58.7
1982	3,166.0	23.5	29.3	25.7	12.4	9.8	11.8	7.4	29.8	3.2	11.6	3.7	11.7	15,861	18.0	23.7	58.3
1983	3,405.7	23.7	34.0	23.9	12.6	10.0	11.9	7.7	30.8	3.1	11.8	3.6	11.8	16,034	17.9	23.8	58.3
1984	3,772.2	22.6	35.3	24.3	12.8	10.2	11.8	7.7	29.9	3.2	11.3	3.5	11.6	16,436	17.9	23.7	58.4
1985	4,014.9	23.6	37.9	24.3	13.2	10.5	12.1	8.0	31.0	3.2	11.8	3.7	11.8	16,690	18.1	23.9	58.0
1986	4,231.6	23.7	41.5	24.0	13.6	10.9	12.3	8.2	31.1	3.3	12.0	3.7	12.1	16,933	17.8	24.0	58.1
1987	4,515.6	22.2	42.6	25.2	13.7	11.0	12.4	8.3	30.4	3.0	12.1	3.7	12.3	17,281	17.9	23.8	58.3
1988	4,873.7	21.8	42.9	24.9	13.3	10.7	12.2	8.2	29.9	2.9	11.9	3.7	12.2	17,588	17.7	24.1	58.2
1989	5,200.8	22.0	42.7	24.9	13.4	10.7	12.1	8.1	29.0	2.9	12.0	3.8	12.2	17,859	17.4	24.4	58.2

Source: Advisory Commission on Intergovernmental Relations (ACIR), Significant Features of Fiscal Federalism: Revenues and Expenditures, vol. 2, M-176-11 (Washington, D.C., October 1991), Tables 6, 20, 40, 43, 117; ACIR, Significant Features, 1980-1981, Table 45; ACIR, Significant Features, 1984, Table 81.

and cities became more active participants in discussions and decisions on fiscal federalism. States generally supported increased discretion for state and local decision-making, but to the extent that the dollars being discussed were federal dollars, federal spending priorities affected state priorities.[34] Responding to these new circumstances, states became adept at influencing federal funding decisions through national lobbying organizations.[35]

Federal–state roles in welfare policy reflect the enduring political tension in redistributive policies. As mentioned above, the federal welfare efforts in the first several decades of this century frequently utilized program models first introduced at the state level. Unemployment insurance programs, minimum-wage laws, and mothers' pensions introduced in a number of states at the beginning of the century later served as models for federal legislation during the Depression.[36] The fact that the deleterious effects of industrialization were addressed in only a few states suggests that political culture varied among states and that most states chose not to engage in welfare policy, an implication that will be examined later in the contemporary context. A second implication, borne out later in the century, is that policies of redistribution can be effectively addressed only at the federal level. One normative explanation argues that politically weak groups (distressed individuals or localities) are more likely to find a responsive policy environment in a forum where decision-making addresses the broadest range of issues, that is, at the federal level.[37] A less polite characterization of this problem, and one that justified nationalization of policy during the Great Society era, is the Alabama syndrome. During the formulation of the Economic Opportunity Act, the question was raised whether the governor of Alabama, George Wallace, could be trusted to pursue the legislative intent of the act. The implementation of the act entirely bypassed governors.[38]

Competition among states for business investment and population growth creates resistance in states to "get out of line" in redistributive policy. State welfare policies that are too generous are believed to make a state less attractive to new investment. In addition, attitudes toward welfare vary greatly among states. This combination of factors has produced a welfare system in which the federal and state governments each have major roles. In particular, states have some discretion in establishing benefit levels and are largely responsible for administering welfare programs, subject to various federal requirements and mandates. States supplement federal welfare expenditures, and in spite of federal efforts to equalize spending, substantial variation among state welfare spending still exists (see Appendix 3.1).

Judicial decisions in the 1960s and 1970s, which applied the due process and equal protection clauses of the Fourteenth Amendment in the protection of individual rights, curtailed state policies.[39] Federal protection of the voting franchise has also received judicial support. Combined action by the judiciary and federal agencies has also reduced state and local scope of action in areas such as education, abortion, welfare, and labor standards.

In the field of environmental regulation, yet a different history of federal–

state relations in implementation is found. In 1967 federal air quality legislation, Congress endorsed a federal role for research and technical assistance, but it attempted to induce states to control air pollution. This attempt was unsuccessful, and in the 1970 Clean Air Act, greater federal leadership was adopted, including the establishment of national standards.[40] The state role was largely one of enforcement, and for this role federal funding was provided.[41] As this policy issue has evolved, a consensus has formed on the local and regional nature of many pressing environmental issues, such as toxic waste sites, water quality and ground water contamination, implying a need for local and regional strategies to deal with the problems. Taken in conjunction with the Reagan administration's policy of delegating environmental regulation programs, states are faced with increasing responsibilities for the environment.[42]

The Recent Debate

The supremacy of federal law over state law has repeatedly prevailed in a wide variety of policy areas. Writing in the 1950s, one scholar concluded that "The future of state rests not on constitutional protection but on political and administrative decisions."[43] Scholarly opinion in the 1970s confirmed the conclusion.[44] In *Garcia v. San Antonio Metropolitan Transit Authority* in 1985, the Supreme Court found that states are not constitutionally protected from intrusive federal legislation, but rather the structure of government and the political process are the vehicles available to states for redress from onerous federal legislation.[45] In 1987, in *South Carolina v. Baker*, the Supreme Court concurred in the reaffirmation of *Garcia v. San Antonio* but with a 5–4 vote.[46] With the Supreme Court dominated by appointees of Presidents Reagan and Bush, issues of federal supremacy are likely to be revisited in the 1990s; the decisions of this court to date, however, suggest that the legal framework of intergovernmental powers will not likely change to a significant extent.[47] Increased assertiveness and leadership of states in public policy matters must continue to rely on political and administrative acts and not on constitutional provisions.

An active federal government in the 1930s and again in the 1960s called on states to perform many different roles, producing an extraordinarily complex and cumbersome system. Reform of the intergovernmental system has been called for on administrative, political, and philosophical grounds. Some political theorists of administrative systems argue that the federal system has become inefficient. Redress of states' rights and prerogatives and local autonomy have been important issues, particularly for political conservatives. Others argue that in order to promote democratic participation of the population, government and policy decisions should be decentralized to the greatest extent possible.

The debate on intergovernmental relations began in earnest in the 1950s. The Council of State Governments, after undertaking a study of the federal grants-in-aid system at the request of former President Herbert Hoover, called for a return of dual federalism.[48] The Kestnbaum Commission and the Joint Federal–

State Action Committee, established by President Eisenhower, explored ways to shift public policymaking and implementation back to the states.[49] During the 1960s, however, further expansion of federal power was realized, even though this centralization meant a larger role for state government in implementation of federal policy. The Nixon administration pursued even more aggressively a decentralized implementation strategy that relied heavily on states.

While implementation of federal policy was being decentralized in certain respects in the 1970s, the federal government expanded its use of regulatory strategies to induce the cooperation of state and local governments in implementing its policy.[50] In the 1960s, the federal government had increasingly used regulation to achieve its policy objectives in fields such as environmental protection, education, and health and safety. But in the 1970s, the federal government expanded its use of forms of regulation such as partial preemption, crosscutting, cross-over requirements, and direct orders in order to involve state and local governments in the regulatory process.[51]

Under preemption, federal standards are issued for the country but states have some discretion in the manner in which they participate in achieving a national objective. In the Water Quality Act of 1985, for example, if a state fails to act, the federal government will implement the federal legislation. Under crosscutting requirements, the federal government imposes restrictions, such as antidiscrimination restrictions, on a broad range of programs, supplementing the earlier practice of restrictions on individual categorical grant programs. The cross-over sanction permits funds to be held for one program if states fail to meet the objectives of another program. This method was used in the Emergency Highway Conservation Act of 1974 to encourage states to adopt 55-mph speed limits.

These forms of federal regulation frequently placed financial burdens on state and local governments and have, consequently, severely strained intergovernmental relations.[52] These imaginative federal mechanisms for controlling state behavior, however, suggest that the decentralization of federal policy is far from complete and, in fact, has become more centralized in some regards, thus insuring that most policy areas will continue to involve federal and state, if not local, government action.

Under the Reagan administration, decentralization of decision-making and reductions in intergovernmental transfers were pursued with a vengeance. In sharp departure from the administrative decentralization and efficiency concerns of the Nixon period, Reagan's stated purpose was to reduce the size and scope of government intervention at all levels.[53] It was argued that this retrenched system of government would improve the relative position of states because their resources would be reduced less than those of the federal government.

Although a proposed restructuring of block grants for the purpose of reshuffling certain functions among levels of government (replacing the "marble cake" with a "layer cake" in certain policy areas) was not accepted by Congress,[54] the Reagan administration was successful in constraining the growth in federal aid.

Explicit and substantial reductions in federal aid in a wide variety of policy areas were enacted, producing an abrupt decline in the share of federal expenditures represented by aid in the early 1980s (see Table 3.1). Although the rate of growth was reduced, by 1984 the value of federal aid, $99 billion, had surpassed the 1982 level of $86 billion.[55]

The Reagan administration was successful in shifting principal responsibilities for administering federal aid programs to the states, to the detriment of local governments. All new block grant programs were federal–state in nature, and the share of federal aid bypassing states and going directly to local governments declined from 24.2 percent to 14.5 percent.[56] Although the Reagan administration's proposals for reductions in the role of the federal government were curtailed by congressional actions, in many areas—health, economic development, water development, environmental policy, telecommunications, and others—the federal government ended its leadership role in policy development and funding.[57]

A federal presence in state and local government has not, however, materially changed. The use of matching aid programs is still widely used, and federal mandates for local action as well as federal preemption and standards still greatly influence decisions by state and local governments.[58] As a consequence of these aid reductions, on one hand, and federal mandates, on the other, state and local governments were forced to increase their own source revenue (see Table 3.1).[59] The changes in intergovernmental relations of the 1980s can be characterized as less an orderly decentralization of responsibilities—some call it noncentralization of responsibility—than one of new responsibilities, especially in terms of the share of fiscal burdens being thrust on state and local governments. Some have characterized this situation as permissive federalism; the basic structure of intergovernmental relations remains centered on the federal government, particularly in terms of intrusive and expansive federal regulation and supportive judicial decisions, but states, nevertheless, have opportunities to seize the initiative in various policy areas.[60]

The dramatic decline of federal leadership and initiative in certain policy areas is the result of a number of factors. The growing national debt has sharply curtailed resources that might be used for policy initiatives (see Table 3.1). In addition, the Republican-controlled presidency with a Democrat-controlled Congress has found progress on major policy issues extremely difficult. In fact, in many policy areas a stalemate has been the result. Changes in direction of policy advanced by the executive branch have by and large been resisted by Congress, which itself has produced few new policies and little leadership. Even with the election of Bill Clinton and an end to divided government, new initiatives are unlikely to be forthcoming at the federal level in the foreseeable future as a result of the federal budget deficit. The national budgetary priorities are many and the discretionary share of the budget small. States and localities will unlikely find much help for their problems in Washington, D.C.

Intergovernmental relations have provided a very important context for state policymaking. The trend in this century has been toward a federal dominance in this relationship. The inability of states to respond to the tasks at hand, especially during the 1930s, contributed to these trends. In constitutional terms, the matter has been largely resolved in favor of the federal government: federal policy supersedes state initiatives. In addition to exercising control through aid, the federal government also exercises control through regulatory means. However, the relationship is not a one-sided one. A close reading of this relationship shows that for virtually all governmental functions, responsibilities are shared by the federal, state, and local governments. This is true not only for contemporary America, but has been true throughout history.

The expansiveness of federal initiative has frequently led to increased responsibilities of states in implementing federal policy. Following the New Deal and Great Society, actions were taken that reinforced a state role in implementation. Although this was a subordinate role, enhancement of state government capabilities resulted. Employment and budgets of state government grew as a result of administrative decentralization. In addition, federal initiative has been on the wane—by default in the 1970s and by political stalemate and fiscal bankruptcy during the 1980s and 1990s.

In the 1980s, the debate on the appropriate division of responsibilities and relative autonomy of states began to be overshadowed by the growing federal debt. The rapid pace of increase in federal expenditures and the inability to increase federal revenue, in no small part the result of the federal tax reduction in 1981, meant that severe constraints on federal revenue began to affect levels and composition of federal aid to state and local governments. Fiscal conditions of states will be discussed below, but it is important to note here that federal decisions on aid were not only subject to strong forces encouraging administrative decentralization but also to grim fiscal conditions. The effect was to limit intergovernmental transfers to states and localities, and, as a result, new pressures were placed on state and local policymaking. However, early administrative decentralization helped prepare states for the demands that decentralization of policymaking has placed on them.

DEVELOPMENT POLICY AND INTERGOVERNMENTAL RELATIONS: A HISTORICAL PERSPECTIVE

State innovation may have been the exception for much of this century, but states have nevertheless played an important role in economic development in the country since the colonial period. Recent innovative state development roles are found to have clear precedents. These state roles and a changing economy frequently produce change in intergovernmental relations. The purpose of this section is to identify the historical roles states have played in the economy and the origins of the intergovernmental development policy framework found in contemporary America.

Nation Building

The involvement of state and local government in the economy—establishing property and contractual rights, promoting and regulating business through franchising of local firms and licensing, regulation of common carriers, duties on imported goods, control of usury and currency, construction of transport facilities—predates the U.S. Constitution.[61] These functions originated and were defined in English common law and transplanted to the New World during the colonial period. In the early decades of nation-building, state governments assumed broad development roles, including internal improvements and provision of land grants.[62]

The Articles of Confederation permitted states to institute tariff duties and prohibitions on interstate trade. Restricting the ability of state governments to interfere with commerce was among the various commercial concerns evident as the first tentative steps toward forming a nation were taken. As Emmette Redford has noted, the Annapolis Convention in 1786 was called in order to consider whether a "uniform system in their commercial regulations . . . might be necessary to the common interest and permanent harmony."[63] Redford further makes a compelling case for the importance of the Constitution in establishing institutions necessary for the formation of a common national market. Interstate citizenship, interstate enforcement of commercial contracts, the centralization of the power to coin money, regulation of interstate and foreign commerce, and the power to supply facilities of commerce were later to become significant factors in forming the national economy. The federal government did not fully exercise many of these powers until the second half of the eighteenth century; they nevertheless demonstrate the concern for economic matters embedded in the U.S. Constitution.

After the ratification of the Constitution states fully exercised their powers in promoting their economies. The range of activities was extensive: licenses, regulation of prices and standards, protecting labor, creating money, regulating corporations, banks and insurance institutions, and direct public participation in the ownership of corporations.[64] The levels of funding for internal improvements in the early decades of the nation were also impressive. In terms of canal and railroad construction until the time of the Civil War, state governments had committed more than $300 million, local governments $125 million, and the federal government $7 million.[65]

Many elements found in contemporary efforts for economic development were present in state-supported internal improvements of the nineteenth century. First, government undertook very sizable investments for purposes of development, and some of these had profound and long-term impacts. Second, issues over principles such as state autonomy (the Jacksonian position of limiting the federal role in internal improvements), strict separation of private and public interests, and limitations on the power of corporations generally gave way to pragmatic action for promoting development. Third, intense competition among jurisdictions prompted these investments, and a substantial number proved to be major failures, establishing an early record of governments pursuing untimely or ill-conceived projects. Local boosterism found in contemporary efforts has its antecedents in the history of internal improvements by state governments.

The construction of the Erie Canal, completed in 1825, represents a classic and extremely successful case of a publicly backed development effort. Prior to its construction, commodities from the Great Lakes and Ohio River Valley were shipped through New Orleans. The western expansion of economic activity diminished the relative position of the East Coast. Recognizing that loss in comparative advantage, New York undertook the massive and technically difficult canal construction project. With its completion, production from western expansion could be shipped to the East Coast through the Erie Canal more economically than through New Orleans. This recaptured the comparative advantage for New York and reasserted its early dominance as a trade center in the U.S. economy.

Public sector participation in the construction of transportation systems in the United States was not a practice inherited from the English.[66] Infrastructure investments were made largely by the private sector in England. The need for a governmental role in the United States was obvious. The cost of building the canal, for example, greatly exceeded the capital available in the private sector; capital was mobilized by the public sector. Public sector participation also provided legitimacy to the investment, even if substantial profits were generated for private firms. This financing system, however, was not without its critics; Andrew Jackson prohibited the use of federal aid to such enterprise as " . . . unconstitutional expenditure for the purpose of corrupt influence."[67]

Nevertheless, with the success of the Erie Canal, many states and localities undertook similar efforts, frequently with the participation of private firms. In Massachusetts, for example, early pike construction in the western part of the state provided the precedent for state involvement for canal construction. However, in Massachusetts, competition between canal and railroad proposals, complaints of unfair private gains from public goods, and the proliferation of local interests arguing for one mode of transportation and for a favorable route substantially delayed state action and in the end led to an inefficient proliferation of railroad lines.[68] In canal construction, no other states proved as successful as New York. Many projects were financial fiascos, exceeding the funding capabilities of the governments, which were often unable to find markets to support the completed projects.[69]

The story of early railroad construction is similar. Until the time of the Civil War, railroad construction frequently relied on, sometimes extensively, funding, financing, or land grants from state and local governments.[70] In Missouri, reluctance to expand the role of government was overcome by the sense of urgency in the 1830s derived from economic progress being made in Ohio, Indiana, and Illinois.[71] Strong opposition to federal involvement in the state was relaxed in two instances: (1) when the state urged the federal government to extend the

Cumberland Trail through the state and (2) when it accepted a federal land grant to the state that could be used to support railroad expansion. By the 1850s, the state even provided substantial aid for railroad construction, as did counties and municipalities; the federal government contributed in the form of land grants. Care with the location of projects was required, however, to overcome localism and regional factionalism. Unlike the Eastern states, broad support of state-sponsored internal improvements came slowly in Missouri, in part the result of a poor economy and opposition to taxation in a predominately agricultural state. However, economic progress in adjacent states and the realization that private railroad companies could not mobilize capital through private sources eventually justified an active state government for development purposes.

Caution on the part of the public for internal improvements was certainly not unjustified. Abuse of monopoly franchise and land grants by railroad companies and poor decisions on the location of investments were common.[72] In Massachusetts, the practice of providing franchises by the Commonwealth, frequently with special privileges, was justified in the post-Revolution period as a means to mobilize resources for development. But these state activities created conflict. In Pennsylvania, the conflict over competitive advantage placed Philadelphia merchants in conflict with economic interests of Pittsburgh over the location of railroad lines.[73] By the mid-nineteenth century the practice of monopoly franchise had been sharply curtailed as a response to businesses, artisans, and rural interests hurt by such franchises.[74] Opposition to public grants for internal improvements also emerged as artisans and others believed railroad and merchant interests benefitted too heavily from the practice. Through state government politics and policy reforms were made.[75]

The performance of state government during the period of railroad expansion was mixed. Some states made wise decisions and successfully established not only competitive economic advantages, but also strategic advantages. The well-developed railroad network in the North proved a great economic boon both during and following the Civil War, whereas the underdeveloped railroad network in the South contributed to its defeat.[76] Even following the war, after a short period of state railroad investment by Reconstruction governments, there was little support in the South for further investment—little support could be rallied for any form of government action—and in the West low population densities prohibited large investments. As a result the federal government substantially expanded its support for developing the national railroad system, using principally land grants for Western expansion.[77]

Regulation and Business: The Intergovernmental Context

Industrialization of the country proceeded at a rapid pace following the Civil War. The formation of a national market and the growth of large industrial and financial concerns created a demand for government regulation of business from many sectors of the society. The sources of demand for regulation were several:

consumers and small businesses, especially farmers, concerned with the rapid growth of large and powerful enterprise. In addition, the need for the rational provision of natural monopolies, especially for services in the growing cities, became apparent. In some instances, the business sector itself looked for regulation to rationalize markets. Frequently, a tension between the regulatory objectives of states and federal government occurred. By the end of the 1930s, intergovernmental regulatory frameworks were well established, but the dynamics of the formation of these various frameworks revealed the impact of industrialization and the politics of state policymaking. Five examples of regulated industries will be discussed in some detail: railroads, banking, insurance, electric power, and telecommunications.

States and the federal government provided support for the construction of railroad networks, but as this industry grew, a new role was required. The growth of the railroad industry following the Civil War and into the early decades of the twentieth century was a tumultuous one. An extremely profitable industry involving enormous amounts of capital and a huge number of workers, it affected most economic interests in the nation including banking, oil, shippers, farmers, artisans, and others. There was a multitude of railroad companies and intense, if not chaotic, competition.[78] Railroad companies engaged in various strategies to create order in the industry, including pools and consolidations, and encouraged governmental regulation. The dominance of the railroad industry as an economic force produced a popular reaction, especially from the Grange and populist movements.[79] This reaction found expression at the state level through the establishment of regulatory commissions with substantial powers. Many railroad companies served multistate, if not national, markets and had to deal with a different set of regulations, generally onerous regulations they argued, in each state.[80] With support of the railroad industry, the Interstate Commerce Act of 1887 was passed and regulation of interstate rates become the responsibility of the Interstate Commerce Commission (ICC).[81] The ICC held relatively weak powers, a result of legislative intent and judicial rulings, until the Hepburn Act of 1906 and further judicial rulings that confirmed its power to set rates. By the 1920s, federal dominance in regulating the industry, to the detriment of state authority, was undisputed.[82]

Regulation of banking has a quite different history, particularly with respect to the intergovernmental framework.[83] Banking was a significant issue when the country was formed, and a dual banking system, with a national bank and bank chartering by states, existed almost continuously until 1836. The closing of the Second Bank of the United States eliminated the federal role in banking, and the era of so-called "free banking" continued until 1863.[84] It is, however, interesting to note the popular support for state banks in the Western states during the pre–Civil War period.[85] Settlers in the West looked to state government to resolve the problems of adequate currency and development capital, and publicly owned state banks were established.[86]

In legislation responding to the financial burden of the Civil War, nationally chartered banks were again introduced.[87] This legislation embodied dual banking but with several unique characteristics. First, an individual bank could choose whether to be chartered by the federal government or a state government. Each regulatory system had significantly different policies, and this in itself drove later change in banking regulation. The supremacy of federal law over state law with respect to national banks was established in 1819.[88] Although states could not intervene in national banks located in their territory, they had authority to charter and regulate state banks.[89] The dual system created competition, among the state banking systems and between the state and federal systems, for gaining banks as members, and both systems tended to liberalize their policies in response to these competitive pressures. But as a result of the Civil War legislation, the Federal Reserve System (1913) regulation, and mandatory membership in the Federal Deposit Insurance Corporation (1933), state banking had been "encircled," to use Redford's term, in order to establish a uniform national policy. He further argued that the constitutional basis for the supremacy of federal initiative had not been in doubt, but "in banking, as in many other fields of legislation, what characterizes congressional choices is not encroachment on state power but nonexercise of national power."[90] Hence, the locus for policy initiative is less one of constitutional prerogative than of national politics and performance of different regulatory regimes. (In Chapter 4, banking and savings and loan regulation will again be discussed in the context of the recent crisis.)

The regulation of a second financial industry, insurance, provides an interesting contrast in that state governments have held principal responsibility for regulation throughout the country's history. During the colonial period, insurance was generally written in England. By the mid-1700s, domestic insurance firms started to appear, especially for property and casualty.[91] The industry's tax revenue–generating capacity attracted the attention of state governments. The cash-rich industry represented a highly visible tax base, and in order to protect this source states provided special protection to local insurance companies. This protection was provided by a discriminatory insurance tax—a tax imposed on "foreign" insurance companies—that was not declared unconstitutional until 1985.[92]

A second justification for state regulation was the need to insure solvency of insurance companies. In order to fulfill contractual obligations to policyholders, insurance companies must make wise use of premiums over a long period of time; that is to say, when a policy comes due, the company must have adequate financial resources available. The ability of a policyholder to monitor a company's management of premiums and its funds in general is very limited. By the mid-1800s, abuses of some early insurance companies had prompted state governments to start regulating firms through evaluating solvency. Some companies threatened to leave states with strict regulations and others attempted to transfer regulatory authority to the federal government, where more lenient treatment was expected. In a unique ruling of the Supreme Court following the Civil War, the insurance business was declared not to be commerce and consequently not subject to the interstate commerce clause of the U.S. Constitution.[93] As a result, a federal presence was not deemed appropriate and regulatory authority was to be exercised by states.

The regulatory impetus of the progressive period was also felt in the insurance industry. The Armstrong Committee investigation of major life insurance companies in 1906, and the Merritt Committee investigation of fire insurance following the San Francisco earthquake produced more aggressive, stringent regulation of the industry by states. A threat to the state role occurred in 1944, when the Supreme Court recognized an earlier error in *Paul v. Virginia* and redefined insurance as commerce,[94] but the McCarran–Ferguson Act of 1945 reinstated the regulatory authority of states. In this act, antitrust provisions of national laws were suspended for the insurance industries in states that adopted appropriate enabling legislation. The details of application of this law have been established in the courts as a result of extensive litigation. Unlike most other areas of economic regulation, with supporting judicial decisions and federal legislation states were able to initiate and sustain the regulatory framework for the insurance industry. In recent years, however, this industry has been subject to change and stress, and the demands on regulatory bodies have been substantial. (In the next chapter, the recent history of insurance regulation will be discussed.)

Regulation of telecommunications presents another interesting case in terms of the intergovernmental response, but in this case the emergence of a new and important technology and its integration into the economy adds a significant dimension to the regulatory history. The first telephone system was introduced in Boston and connected the city with one of its suburbs, Somerville.[95] Following a brief period of competition between Bell Telephone Company and Western Union, a patent dispute was resolved in Bell's favor in 1879, and the company licensed the telephone in various cities.[96] When the patent expired in 1884, many other companies were formed, and the Bell Company lost its control. However, the Bell Company started providing long-distance services through connecting companies in cities and gained substantial leverage in the emerging industry.

The expansion of the telephone system created a series of public policy issues. First, should telephone service be considered a natural monopoly? If so, how is the monopoly to be organized? Should private companies be given local franchises or should a publicly owned utility be created? The industry had developed as one of many small companies serving local markets, and the regulatory questions were faced for the most part by local governments. Two types of spillover effects, however, could not adequately be addressed by localities. With many local franchises, who insures technical interconnectivity among them, a goal that will benefit everyone on the network? Standards, to which all companies would adhere, had to be established. In addition, how would service be provided to high-cost areas, such as in rural areas? Given that positive externalities are achieved by maximizing the number of customers on the telephone network, the answer to this question became problematic, especially when regulation, to the extent it existed, was exercised only over local franchises.

The framework eventually adopted—that of a single, predominant regulated monopoly provider, a position argued by the president of AT&T, Theodore Vail—was established in the Communications Act of 1934.[97] It created the Federal Communications Commission, which replaced the Interstate Commerce Commission as the responsible federal agency. Federal responsibility would involve regulating interstate telephone service, while local service would be regulated by state governments. Embodied in the act and regulatory framework was a commitment by the dominant carrier, AT&T, to achieve universal service. Local service rates would be kept low, even in remote, low-density, high-cost areas, through cross subsidization from profitable, long-distance traffic.[98] This regulatory system proved very effective in achieving a high telephone penetration through the country. (Changes to this regulatory system in the 1980s are the subject of Chapter 6.)

The common law form of regulation of public monopolies proved to be inefficient when applied to the growing electrical power companies. Under pressure from electric power companies and a number of progressive governors, states started to respond in 1907 when New York and Wisconsin established public utility commissions.[99] With these commissions, regulation of the industry moved from local government and the judicial system to a full-time state agency which employed technically competent specialists to develop analyses used in regulating the firms. The legislative delegation of this regulatory function to a specialized agency is interesting for two reasons. That full-time technical specialists in the utility commissions were required to exercise satisfactorily the regulatory function suggests that the technical issues, especially the engineering and accounting issues of electric power companies, were beyond the competence of legislatures. In addition, the nature of utility regulation—setting rates that would insure viability of the power companies but at the same time protect consumers—is a redistributive task and not one that legislatures are well prepared or inclined to pursue.[100] But growth of electrical power companies and transmission of electric power across state boundaries created problems for state-level regulation. In the 1920s and especially the 1930s, federal legislation introduced a federal regulatory presence based on the state models, again relying on the interstate commerce clause as a basis. States, however, remained responsible for regulating intrastate service.

Resource Mobilization

Although states effectively mobilized resources for development as the nation was being formed, as discussed above, the federal government became increasingly important in this role as the nation continued to expand westward after the Civil War. In particular, the federal government supported the western extension of the national railroad system, where either states had not been created or states themselves were unable to mobilize resources. Other forms of federal resource mobilization initiated during this period included land grants for settlement of the West through the Homestead Act (1862) and subsequent land acts.[101] The

Morrill Act (1862),[102] establishing land-grant colleges for education and research, and the Hatch Act (1887), providing assistance for state agricultural extension activities, represented a new role for an aggressive federal government. These acts established a new form of federal–state cooperation and created an effective model of technology transfer that would prove enormously successful in agricultural and rural development.

At the turn of the century resource development became a concern of the federal government. President Theodore Roosevelt encouraged resource conservation and development and in the 1910s and 1920s federal support of resource surveys, research, and planning was important.[103] The development of many resources—such as water and soil or electrical power[104]—requires substantial investments, and states frequently were unable to undertake such investments unassisted. Although some major federal projects were initiated before the 1930s—for example, a dam on the Tennessee River—it was during the presidency of Franklin Roosevelt that hydroelectric and water development investment greatly expanded.[105] These investments not only mobilized resources for development but were labor-intensive, thus achieving another objective of New Deal policy. Although states maintained a role in resource development, it was generally one of managing resources, not of developing them.[106]

Other Federal Roles

The question of national industrial standards became increasingly important as interregional trade expanded at the turn of the century. From such simple matters as establishing the voltage for electric power systems to complex matters such as standards for industrial materials and chemicals, interindustry trade and national markets required that standards be set. In the early decades of the twentieth century, the federal government played a central role in establishing these standards. The role consisted of encouraging the development of measures by trade groups and then formally adopting the measures.[107] During the administration of Secretary of Commerce Herbert Hoover, standards were established that affected more than 500 trade groups and 7,000 firms.

A new extension of federal initiative during the New Deal was in the area of macroeconomic management. If management of the national economy was to occur, it obviously had to be undertaken by the federal government; there would be little room for a state role. Several key elements of the national planning system proposed by the Roosevelt administration were eliminated as a result of judicial review or the conservative backlash prior to World War II. Nevertheless, the federal government assumed a new responsibility, formally recognized in the Employment Act of 1946, for macroeconomic policy that it continues to exercise.

The federal government was again active in a broad range of policy areas in the 1960s, as earlier discussed, and several were concerned with economic development. In particular, through the Appalachian Regional Council, Area

Redevelopment Administration, Economic Development Administration, the Manpower and Training Act, and Office of Economic Opportunity, the Kennedy and Johnson administrations attempted to target distressed communities. State and local governments were not perceived to be adequately addressing questions of distress and poverty, and the administration of federal programs frequently bypassed state and local governments. New federal and regional agencies were established to implement programs. With the passage of time, many of these agencies either reduced their scope of action or were dismantled. With few exceptions, federal attention to distressed communities greatly diminished by the 1980s.

Summary

State governments have participated in economic development activities since the founding of the nation. This participation has included infrastructure development, business development, regulation of business, resource mobilization, and others. States confront, however, several types of limitations in fulfilling a development role. At times the nature of the problem, such as the formation of a national market or management of the national economy, exceeds the scope of action available to states. States simply do not have the policy instruments to address such problems; hence, a federal presence is required. Redford argues that this type of limitation is first found in the U.S. Constitution itself, where important features of a national market are established. During industrialization, other federal roles in the areas of national standards, scientific and technical research, and especially macroeconomic management are required.

Limitations, however, on the scope of action have by no means diminished the long-standing concern of states with development nor have forms of state action been few. At times acting in response to competition from other states, at times in response to individual businesses or industries in a state, state governments have acted in a promotional capacity, providing infrastructure investments, or creating favorable conditions for local firms through tax and regulatory structures. The abuse of such actions and abuse associated with certain industries, especially the railroad and banking industries at the end of the last century, has also led to state actions of another sort.

Changes in intergovernmental relations have coincided with structural economic change. Following the Civil War, the economy regained its earlier growth trajectory and became increasingly dominated by manufacturing growth. High growth rates were accompanied by the emergence of the great industrial corporations, violent business cycles, and great social dislocations. Economic regulation, of railroads and other industries, occurred first at the state level. The decentralized political and administrative system began to give way to federal initiative and federal presence in the regulation of interstate commerce.

The federal government played a very important role in Western expansion, performing functions assumed by states in the East, beyond the resources available to states and territories in the West. An altogether new function—natural resource surveys and technology transfer for agriculture—is assumed, with participation of states. During this period of economic change, an expansive role in regulation by the federal government occurred. In banking and railroads, federal government action was perceived to be required to deal with problems of a national economy in formation, though in both cases there was state participation and sometimes the adoption of regulatory approaches introduced by states. By the second decade of the twentieth century, the role of federal regulation and its relationship to state regulatory power, had become better defined. The expansion of regulatory powers in securities, antitrust, banking insurance, labor laws, and other issues became the subject of federal concern and legislation.[108]

Overlaying the politics of early economic regulation was the context of industrialization and formation of a national market. The demands generated by a growing industrial economy and an increasingly complex society could not be met by the actions of state government. For example, the increasing integration of state economies into regional and national economies created various forms of externalities, or "spillovers" from one political jurisdiction to another, and states and local governments did not cooperate in order to control these negative consequences.[109] In other words, nationalization of the economy required nationalization of economic policy, hence a strong federal presence in the economy.

This examination of the role of state government in the economy reveals a prominent characteristic of the U.S. federal system; multiple points of access to policymaking and policy implementation exist. The fact that most policy areas involve roles for federal, state, and local government means that affected constituencies have several avenues for attempting to influence policy. In several examples in this discussion, an interest group unhappy with a particular regulatory regime could turn to another level or branch of government. Citizens prevailed on state governments to regulate various types of industries. Railroads supported federal regulation when early state regulation appeared to be onerous. Firms frequently turned to the courts for redress of regulation they perceived to be harmful. Multiple points of access to the government is a fundamental aspect of the system established in the U.S. Constitution. In the history of the states' role in the economy, this access has been fully utilized by many groups and has contributed significantly to the complexity in the U.S. intergovernmental system.

Even though the long-term trend of development policy found here represented an increasing federal dominance, states maintained important roles that reinforced state responsibility for economic conditions and activities within a state. Federal action was often the result of the inability of states to act. It is the capability of contemporary state policymaking to which we now turn.

INSTITUTIONAL REFORM AND POLITICS IN THE STATES

Local control of government was a central concern at the time of the writing of the U.S. Constitution, but powers of states have suffered erosion especially

Figure 3.1
Federal and State per Capita Expenditures: 1952–1989 (Constant 1982 Dollars)

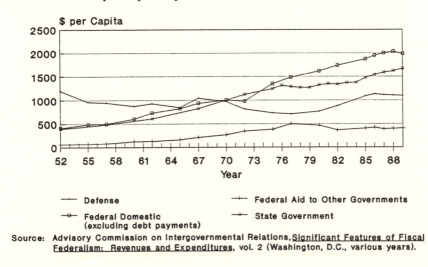

Source: Advisory Commission on Intergovernmental Relations, Significant Features of Fiscal Federalism: Revenues and Expenditures, vol. 2 (Washington, D.C., various years).

during this century. The formal powers of federal and state government are not the only factors, and perhaps not the most important ones, in determining the ability of the political system to respond to demands expressed by the society. In the system of largely shared responsibilities, described above, the fiscal, institutional, and political capabilities of different levels of government are critical in understanding the responsiveness of government.

Fiscal Conditions of the States

Federal leadership in most policy areas in the post–World War II period can be seen in the fairly steady increase in federal per capita expenditures (see Figure 3.1). Federal domestic spending (excluding defense spending and interest on the federal debt) increased fairly steadily from the 1950s through 1988. Defense spending declined following the end of the Viet Nam War, but experienced a modest increase in the Carter years and a rapid increase with Reagan until 1987, when a decline in real spending occurred. Federal aid—to states and localities—increased steadily until 1977. The moderate decline in the late 1970s was followed by a more substantial decline in 1982 followed by a fairly steady level of aid the following years. Real expenditures by state governments increased steadily until the mid-1970s, at which point spending stabilized. Around 1984, real state spending increased substantially, although the rate of increase declined in later years. Given that federal aid changed little during the decade, states were funding these increasing expenditures through their own source revenue (see Table 3.1).

States increased their own source revenue in the 1980s, but they did so under the shadow of a citizen tax revolt. After the success of Proposition 13 in California in 1978, the tax revolt spread to other states; eighteen states enacted limitations measures between 1978 and 1982.[110] Although the specific concern of the tax revolt varied among states, the focus tended to be on property tax rates.[111] By the end of the decade, limits on property tax rates were found in 30 states and on property tax revenues in 15 states.[112] Property taxes are used principally by local governments—municipalities, counties, school districts, and others—and to the extent that property tax limitations were established, the revenue-generating powers of local governments, not states, were affected. However, local governments are "creatures" of states, and states and localities have shared responsibilities for many policy areas. As a result, limitations on local government revenue led to pressures on states. In addition, in 22 states limitations were also placed on taxes and the spending of state government.[113]

The dramatic effect of tax limitations on local governments can be seen in the reduction of tax revenues, per $100 of personal income, between 1977 and 1982 (see Table 3.2). Local governments increased their tax revenues later in the decade, but never reaching the levels of the 1970s. State tax revenues also declined between 1978 and 1983, but not to nearly the same extent. By the end of the 1980s, however, state revenues were again at the levels of the 1970s. States also increased intergovernmental transfers during the 1980s to local governments (see Figure 4.1 in the next chapter).

Decline in federal aid, a hostile tax climate, and the recession of 1982 created enormous challenges for state fiscal policy. Helped by the long period of economic growth, most states were fiscally sound at the end of the 1980s. Fiscal health, however, was short-lived and the fiscal effects of federal mandates on states, particularly health services,[114] and the national recession of the early 1990s, wreaked havoc with many state budgets.[115] State revenues were not reaching projected levels and states were forced to reduce spending. The ability of states to provide aid to urban areas and local government decreased, creating yet another set of severe fiscal conditions. Even in the 1980s, however, there were instances in which states with clear objectives and funding needs were able to raise taxes and increase revenues. The fiscal pressures increased to the point that in the early 1990s, many states were seeking tax increases.[116] The tax revolt, though muted, had not disappeared and taxes remained an important electoral issue.[117] For the foreseeable future, states and localities will face severe fiscal constraints, and the federal government appears not to be an alternative source of funds.

Education and social services comprise the bulk of total state expenditures, that is, direct plus intergovernmental expenditures (see Table 3.3). Expenditures on education include very substantial aid to local school districts, and this level has increased somewhat between 1975 and 1988. In most states aid is to some extent equalized to provide equity in education expenditures among school districts with differing revenue generating abilities. In addition to this major role in public education, shared with local school districts, states also invest heavily in higher education (the state role in education is the subject of Chapter 7). In

Table 3.2
State and Local Tax Revenue per $100 of Personal Income: 1970–1990

				State				
Fiscal Year	Total	Local	State	General Sales	Personal Income	Corporation Income	Severance	Other
1970	$11.32	$5.07	$6.29	$1.86	$1.20	$0.49	$0.09	$2.65
1971	11.50	5.26	6.27	1.88	1.24	0.42	0.09	2.64
1972	12.24	5.51	6.77	1.99	1.47	0.50	0.09	2.72
1973	12.41	5.43	7.01	2.04	1.60	0.56	0.09	2.72
1974	11.93	5.16	6.81	2.07	1.57	0.55	0.11	2.51
1975	11.74	5.09	6.68	2.07	1.57	0.55	0.15	2.34
1976	11.98	5.17	6.85	2.10	1.65	0.56	0.16	2.38
1977	12.15	5.17	7.02	2.14	1.77	0.64	0.15	2.32
1978	12.08	5.01	7.10	2.21	1.82	0.67	0.16	2.23
1979	11.37	4.46	6.94	2.19	1.81	0.67	0.16	2.11
1980	11.02	4.26	6.78	2.14	1.84	0.66	0.21	1.93
1981	10.85	4.20	6.67	2.07	1.82	0.63	0.28	1.87
1982	10.59	4.12	6.49	2.01	1.82	0.56	0.31	1.79
1983	10.68	4.25	6.46	2.02	1.88	0.50	0.28	1.78
1984	11.30	4.35	6.96	2.21	2.09	0.55	0.26	1.85
1985	11.28	4.34	6.97	2.25	2.06	0.57	0.23	1.86
1986	11.24	4.37	6.90	2.26	2.04	0.55	0.19	1.85
1987	11.51	4.50	7.04	2.27	2.17	0.59	0.12	1.89
1988	11.60	4.57	7.06	2.33	2.14	0.58	0.12	1.88
1989	11.55	4.55	7.02	2.31	2.19	0.59	0.10	1.83
1990[1]	11.37	4.55	6.84	2.28	2.18	0.50	NA	NA

Source: Scott R. Mackey, "Recent Changes in State, Local, and State-Local Tax Levels," Legislative Finance Papers, no. 75 (Denver, CO: National Conference of State Legislatures, 1991), p. 7.

[1]Preliminary data.

the area of social services, the single largest component, and one that is steadily growing, is public welfare. For welfare programs, the states share funding and implementing responsibilities with the federal government and with local governments, and the growing burdens have forced a number of states to consider funding cutbacks. States also invest heavily in highways, though these expenditures have declined in recent years.

States share responsibility with federal and local governments in the provision of several types of infrastructure (see Table 3.4). The importance of education and highways for state government reappears in the intergovernmental structure

Table 3.3
Total State Expenditures by Function: 1975, 1980, 1985, 1988 (in percent)

	1975–1976	1980–1981	1985–1986	1988–1989
Education	38.8	38.2	39.2	38.9
Higher Education (direct)			13.4	12.8
Aid	22.2	22.6	22.9	23.3
Social Services	27.5	29.3	29.5	29.8
Public Welfare	19.3	20.3	20.3	20.6
Social Insurance	1.0	0.9	0.8	0.7
Health and Hospitals	7.2	8.1	8.4	8.5
Transportation				
Highways	11.8	10.0	10.3	9.9
Air Transportation	0.2	0.2	0.2	0.2
Natural Resources	2.5	2.0	2.0	2.0
Housing/Urban Renewal	0.3	0.3	0.5	0.6
Interest or Debt	2.7	3.1	4.7	4.7
Other	16.1	17.0	19.0	19.2
Public Safety			5.7	6.0
Sewage			0.3	0.3
Parks			0.6	0.6
Governmental Administration			3.5	3.7
Unallocable			8.9	8.6

Source: U.S. Department of Commerce, Bureau of the Census, Government Finance
(Washington, D.C., various years).

of expenditures. In only one area, natural resources, has the federal share of expenditures substantially increased between 1975 and 1987. The federal role in highways has remained constant while in housing and urban renewal increased through 1980, but diminished thereafter. In education and air transportation, the share of federal expenditures has diminished.

Institutional Reform

Following World War II, state governments faced several institutional issues which were to be addressed in the following decades. One problem, identified by the Kestnbaum Commission in 1955, was that "many state constitutions restrict the scope, effectiveness and adaptability of state and local action. These self-imposed constitutional limitations make it difficult for many states to perform all of the services their citizens require."[118] Endorsed by a broad range of organizations, new constitutions were adopted in 12 states by the end of the 1970s, and a number of other states considered constitutional reform.[119] Reform tended to strengthen state legislatures, through lengthening legislative sessions and reforming compensation, and to expand gubernatorial control over state bureaucracies and the legislative process. Reform, however, did not come to all

Table 3.4
Federal, State, and Local Expenditures in Areas of Shared Responsibility—
Infrastructure: 1975, 1980, 1987 (in percent)

	1975–1976			1980–1981			1987–1988		
	Federal	State	Local	Federal	State	Local	Federal	State	Local
Education	12.2	39.8	48.0	10.9	42.4	46.6	9.1	42.9	48.1
Highways	19.4	53.7	27.0	19.5	52.0	28.5	18.7	52.9	28.4
Air Transportation	57.6	9.9	32.4	62.3	5.7	32.1	47.3	6.3	46.4
Natural Resources	73.0	21.3	5.7	85.9	10.9	3.2	88.5	9.0	2.6
Housing/Urban Renewal	60.4	5.5	34.1	63.5	3.4	33.1	62.2	6.6	31.1

Source: U.S. Department of Commerce, Bureau of the Census, <u>Government Finances</u>
(Washington, D.C., various years).

states, because traditional distrust of state legislatures and governors remained intact in some states.

A second important institutional issue was malapportionment in state legislatures. The Supreme Court in the famous *Baker v. Carr* and subsequent decisions on reapportionment forced states to revise electoral systems.[120] These decisions produced direct effects, such as a relative decline of rural representation and thus greater attention to urban issues, and indirect effects on a range of state government activities that will be discussed below.[121]

The civil rights movement of the 1950s and 1960s contributed to the urgency of instituting change in state government.[122] The Voting Rights Act of 1965 and the Twenty-sixth Amendment to the U.S. Constitution in 1971 further affected suffrage and liberalized state election systems. State constitutional reform incorporated suffrage and election provisions, consistent with federal legislation, and enhanced protection of civil rights.[123] Though these reforms were thrust upon states by federal courts and Congress, they helped create the conditions for renewed state activism in the 1980s and 1990s.

Gubernatorial Leadership and the Executive Branch

Institutional reform, especially constitutional reform, tended to strengthen the executive branch of state government. Reform of state administrative structure and budgeting procedures has enhanced the governors' ability and authority in managing state affairs.[124] Expanded gubernatorial powers cannot, however, explain the rather extraordinary increase in strong, active governors coming to office in the 1970s and 1980s (these included James Blanchard in Michigan, Michael Dukakis in Massachusetts, Bruce Babbitt in Arizona, Bill Clinton in Arkansas, Jerry Brown in California, Richard Thornburgh in Pennsylvania, Thomas Kean in New Jersey, and William Winter in Mississippi). At any point in time, a number of governors will be perceived as dynamic, but in the 1970s and the 1980s there was an unusually large number of very active governors who provided leadership for initiatives in economic development, education reform, and welfare reform.[125]

In the 1980s, the direction of the national political parties and that of the governors began to diverge. The lack of attention to concerns of gubernatorial candidates by the national parties led to the formation of the Democratic Leadership Council and the Republican Governors Association.[126] Osborne hypothesizes that the traditional alignment of the Republican and Democratic parties was no longer adequate for the real needs faced by governors and states and that a new political paradigm had emerged. Issues were not being adequately addressed and, as the most visible politician at the state level, governors frequently faced great pressure to act. With expanded constitutional powers and strong leadership abilities, these governors seized the initiative in several policy areas.

Another expression of governors' assertiveness was in the strengthening of the National Governors' Association (NGA). Formed in 1906 as the Governors' Conference, the nonpartisan NGA had not been a significant forum for policy discussions and actions until the mid-1970s.[127] At that time the policy analysis capabilities of NGA were strengthened and the governors started using the organization as a vehicle to place state issues on the national agenda. Its headquarters location, in Washington, D.C., attests to the continuing importance of the federal government to states.

Gubernatorial leadership was a central element of state revival, but governors were able to call on a more capable executive branch for developing and implementing policy. A target of institutional reform, the executive branch of state government had been affected by other factors during the last two decades. As noted earlier, the number of state employees has grown fairly steadily since the 1960s (see Table 3.1), in part the result of administration of federal programs, as described above. Although slowing in the early 1980s, the growth in the number of employees regained former rates in the mid-1980s, roughly matching the changes in fiscal conditions of states described earlier. But the increase in state employment is not the central point. State bureaucracies were being directed by better-prepared individuals, and the improved level of training and expertise of state employees produced a more technically competent work force. Professionalization of state employees increased as a result.[128]

The Legislature

Institutional change on state legislatures, especially as a result of *Baker v. Carr* and expansion of the voting franchise, has produced several effects. First, a more diverse, by race and by gender, representation is found in state legislatures. From 1969 through 1990, the percentage of women serving in state legislatures increased from 4 to 20 percent.[129] In 1990, 5.6 percent of state legislators were African-American, but only 1.72 percent were of Hispanic origin (5 percent in California, 6.25 percent in Florida, 13.26 percent in Texas, and 32 percent in New Mexico).[130] The average age of legislators is declining in most states.[131] With the relative decline in the number of attorneys and farmers in state legislatures, a greater range of occupations are represented.[132] There has also been an increase in not only the share of full-time legislators but also in the salaries of legislators as their responsibilities have expanded.[133] Although professionalization of state legislatures is not universally endorsed, because it undermines the notion of citizen-legislators, it nevertheless affects the capabilities of legislatures and certainly reflects the increasing demands placed on state government.

Performance of state legislatures can be measured on several other variables.[134] In recent decades there has been wider adoption of annual legislative sessions. In 1960, only 18 states conducted annual sessions, whereas in 1990 the number was 43.[135] In addition, support provided to legislators and the legislative process in the form of legislative staff has substantially expanded and been upgraded. In the early 1980s, 16,000 full-time legislative staff positions existed in the 50 states.[136] The adoption of sunset laws and legislative audits demonstrate legislatures' commitment to oversight.[137] Legislatures have also developed their planning and budgeting capabilities.

Rejuvenated and strengthened state legislatures, however, do not necessarily imply that state policymaking has improved. Similarly, the enhanced competencies and powers of governors do not necessarily mean better state policymaking. Governors and state legislatures mutually determine the nature and quality of state policy. Some argue that these more capable and certainly more assertive state legislatures have infringed on gubernatorial prerogatives. Partisan politics can also complicate policymaking, particularly if the gubernatorial party does not control the legislature. Certainly, legislative fragmentation—the varied interests that influence individual legislatures as contrasted with the unity of purpose found in governorships—has been compounded by the increasing diversity found in legislatures.[138] Whether conflict or cooperation characterizes the interaction of governors and legislatures depends on many different factors.[139] Although governors to tend to hold some advantage in state agenda setting, legislatures have the capabilities and frequently the inclination to be active partners in state policymaking.

Politics, Political Culture, and State Policymaking

In areas of public policy where states have significant discretion in decision-making, the choices made by states vary widely. The factors contributing to the great variation include political culture, level of economic and educational development, extent of interparty competition, gubernatorial–legislative competition, fiscal conditions, professionalization of state legislatures, and others. The scholarship on the relative importance of these factors in policy outcomes is far from conclusive.

The study of state governments and political culture has a long history. In a very important contribution to this literature, Key elaborated the notion of state political culture and identified the importance of national politics and parties to state policymaking. Writing in the 1950s, Key noted that as the federal government and national parties became increasingly significant during and following the New Deal, state parties and policy were affected.[140] State politics became less autonomous, but remained heavily tied to traditions of political culture within a state. The concept of political culture was further elaborated by Elazar.[141] To describe political culture he developed categories of individualistic, traditionalistic, and moralistic cultures. The presence of one or some combination of these within a state could explain state policy choices, according to Elazar.

Traditionalistic culture tends to dominate Southern states, and the corresponding policy outcomes are low levels of taxation and government expenditures, particularly for welfare expenditures. Moralistic cultures, more common in the north of the country, are more open to innovation and tend to have higher levels of public services, especially in social policy areas, and higher levels of taxation. Individualistic cultures produce relatively moderate levels of governmental programs, but give emphasis to programs promoting individual success rather than the programs favoring the public good found in the moralistic culture. The variation in policy decision among states is thus argued to be associated with differences in political culture.[142]

Interparty competition has also been considered as a determinant of state policy outcomes.[143] Some have argued that the presence of significant competition would produce outcomes favorable to less-represented groups and would produce higher levels of spending for educational efforts as the two parties attempted to compete for the middle of the political spectrum. After identifying various types of competition, only in the rare case of interparty differences that are issue-based does competition appear to have an effect on policy outcomes.[144] Others have argued that attention to party competition missed the underlying factors of socioeconomic status of states; prosperous states provided higher levels of governmental services, especially for welfare programs. Variation among states on this factor provided the principal explanation for variation in policy choices.[145]

This literature, though inconclusive, is nevertheless helpful in understanding the complexities of state policymaking. The factors found to be important are themselves changing. Whereas interparty competition at the state level is becoming more prominent, especially in the traditionally Democratic South, party identification has declined throughout the country. On many policy issues, state political leaders do not look to the national party for direction or for aid in promoting their agendas. In the 1986 elections, as the Republicans lost control of the Senate, largely as a result of running on a Reagan platform, Republicans, running as pragmatic problem-solvers, gained several additional governorships. In some respects, it was difficult to distinguish Democratic from Republican governors.

Interest Group Politics

Interest group politics has changed substantially during the last two decades. The existence of conflicting factions, as they were called in Federalist Paper number 10, particularly minority interests, was a key concern in the constitutional convention, and the decentralized nature of U.S. governance has encouraged the formation of interest groups. During the last two decades, however, the nature of interest group politics has changed dramatically, particularly in terms of the proliferation of such groups.[146] New communications and information technology has permitted more actors to gain access to information critical to public policymaking and to mobilize affected constituents.

Business groups have proliferated as a result of the increasing complexity and diversity in the economy. Although there are a number of broad national business interest group representatives, such as the U.S. Chamber of Commerce and the National Association of Manufacturers, there are scores of other organizations representing industries, small businesses, major corporations, public utilities, minority businesses, and others. The emergence of new economic sectors, market segmentation, and expansion of international markets have diversified the economic interests of firms. Occupational groups—teachers, public sector employees, unions, medical, and healthcare workers—have formed interest groups, some of which are very influential. Public interest groups have multiplied; there were 2,500 in 1986, with supporting memberships of 40 million and budgets that totaled more than $4 billion.[147] Citizen groups, environmental groups, and single-issue groups have become adept at forming coalitions and are now significant actors in policymaking.[148]

The proliferation of groups has occurred at the state level as well. In 1973, the 46 states that required lobbyists to register reported 12,188 individuals and organizations registered; in 1991, the 50 states reported more than 29,000 individuals and organizations.[149] National interest groups will frequently have state affiliates.[150] State-level business organizations have specialized and proliferated.[151] Interest groups have become increasingly professional as the old-boy method of state lobbying has faded. The increasing sophistication of state legislators and state executive officers along with the legal restrictions placed on lobbying activity have required increasing competence on the part of lobbyists. Although business interest groups have always had the resources to develop and present technical and empirical data to bolster their recommendations, other interest groups have also developed this capacity, frequently drawing on national organizations or groups in other states.

The increased number of interest groups and their active participation in politics have occurred as the influence of the two major political parties has declined. Neither party has been entirely successful in capturing fully the interests and political expressions of minorities, women, taxpayers, environmentalists, consumers, community groups, and others.[152] These various publics are aggressively exercising their preferences, frequently outside of the party structure and even outside the legislative process, as seen in the increased use of initiative and referendum.

A concern with the influence of factions in government dates from Madison and has been revisited throughout the country's history.[153] The recent proliferation of interest groups, especially in Washington, D.C., is broadly criticized.

Some argue that the large number of groups makes it difficult to build consensus and reach policy compromises, gives minority interests (that is single-issue groups) too much power, and consequently undermines political parties and the policymaking process. In addition, if policymaking is heavily influenced by interest groups, those groups in society unable to organize and express themselves politically will not be part of the political process. One solution is to create surrogates, such as an office of public counsel in state regulatory commissions. Also citizens groups, such as the Consumers Union and the American Association of Retired Persons (AARP), may assume positions that reflect the interests of low-income constituents. Elements of the business community have also participated in policy discussions concerning the social programs, particularly education.[154]

One argument for the superiority of federal policy over state or local policy on issues of redistribution to low-income individuals and communities is that the interests of weakly organized groups will most likely be addressed in the policymaking body with the broadest representation—that is, in Congress. Historically, Congress has taken the lead in targeting distressed communities, to some extent during the New Deal but particularly during the Kennedy and Johnson years. Such federal action was sharply curtailed during the Reagan period, and the response of states to this policy vacuum has been mixed.[155] Most states target distressed communities and individuals to some extent as the result of their participation in federal programs—such as AFDC and health programs— that provide incentives for such targeting, and virtually all states equalize aid to school districts.

CONCLUSIONS

The performance of state governments has varied markedly during the nation's history. The factors affecting performance are many, and their interaction adds further complexity. To a large extent the evolution of state government activities is defined by the context of intergovernmental relations and is particularly affected by the level of federal government activism. The long-term trend, especially since the Civil War, is toward nationalization of public policy. However, certain episodes of marked federal activism, the New Deal and the Great Society, are followed by retrenchment or curtailment of federal leadership. States have experienced periods of activism, particularly at the turn of the century when state governments grappled with certain economic and social consequences of rapid industrialization and the growth of large corporations, but even in these instances, the federal government eventually became the principal arena for addressing these policy concerns.

The formation of a national market—a process that starts with the U.S. Constitution—and industrialization, particularly after the Civil War, account in part for the expansion of federal initiative and the long-term shift from state to federal predominance in intergovernmental relations. The basic institutions and policies responsive to the national market—monetary management, interstate commerce regulation, regulation of capital markets, industrial standards, national infrastructure systems, basic research, labor, health, environmental standards, and others—are predominately institutions of the federal government, even though states frequently share responsibilities for them.

Although states have been overshadowed in the intergovernmental system, they have by no means lost their enthusiasm for economic promotion and development noted in the earliest decades of the nation. These early roles—of infrastructure provision, regulation, and promotion—are the same roles performed by states today. Although the contemporary economy is much more characterized by interregional and international trade than in the early nineteenth century, states have retained important roles in their economy. The division between interstate and intrastate commerce, a division that has evolved and been frequently reinterpreted, still places responsibility on state government.

One salient characteristic of the American political system is the multiple points of access and influence in the system. This characteristic, a basic feature of federal systems in general, is of particular importance in the United States. As seen above, policy initiative shifts from one level of government to another for a variety of reasons. But the one that stands out in this discussion is that when one level of government seems unable or unwilling to respond to policy demands, another level of government is sought. Businesses, frustrated with the regulatory actions of state governments, turned to federal government. In the 1960s, state governments did not address questions of poverty and economic distress satisfactorily, and the federal government took the initiative. A similar tension can be found between state and local governments.

The recent history of the United States is one in which the federal government has not provided leadership in many policy areas. A confluence of political factors, represented by a Republican president and an increasingly uncooperative Democratic Congress, as well as a weakened federal fiscal position produced economic development policy by default; that is, let the "market" provide the framework for development. Unable to find a responsive government in the nation's capital, development concerns were expressed at the level of state government. For entirely independent reasons—including reapportionment, constitution reform, and expanded franchise—state governments were surprisingly well prepared to respond to these new demands. State governments had continued to perform important functions, even during the periods in which they were subordinated, but as a result of institutional reform they had been improving their policymaking capabilities. Strong governors and executive offices, increasingly assertive state legislators, and an expanding array of forceful interest groups created the environment in which response to economic change could be formulated. However, expanded participation also implies more complex, contentious decision-making. Fiscal constraints and public agenda-setting through initiatives and referenda appear to be permanent features of the policy environment for the foreseeable future.

States are demonstrating these newfound capabilities, but they remain imbedded in a federal system in which the federal government will remain an extremely significant actor. Within this system of intergovernmental relations related to the economy, considerable space is open to state initiative. It is the state response to these opportunities that we examine in the following chapters.

Appendix 3.1
Welfare Spending per $100 of Personal Income by State: 1987

State	State-Local Total Welfare	Cash Assistance	Medicaid	Average AFDC Benefit
New England	$2.65	$.53	$1.37	$164
Connecticut	1.90	.45	0.99	170
Maine	3.38	.64	1.85	129
Massachusetts	2.89	.62	1.42	198
New Hampshire	1.66	.16	0.59	157
Rhode Island	3.46	.68	2.07	162
Vermont	2.63	.61	1.31	166
Middle Atlantic	2.92	.50	1.06	127
Delaware	1.46	.27	0.32	103
Maryland	1.87	.40	1.07	119
New Jersey	1.89	.37	1.04	122
New York	3.76	.86	1.90	176
Pennsylvania	2.61	.62	0.98	116
Great Lakes	2.72	.71	1.32	122
Illinois	2.17	.69	0.90	101
Indiana	1.95	.25	1.28	92
Michigan	3.14	1.01	1.24	159
Ohio	2.82	.70	1.45	104
Wisconsin	3.52	.88	1.72	156
Plains	2.15	.35	1.14	118
Iowa	2.25	.45	0.99	124
Kansas	1.47	.25	0.68	115
Minnesota	3.22	.68	1.69	172
Missouri	1.59	.30	0.83	88
Nebraska	1.89	.30	0.89	110
North Dakota	2.79	.18	1.92	126
South Dakota	1.85	.26	1.01	94
Southeast	1.84	.32	1.10	70
Alabama	1.40	.26	0.82	39
Arkansas	2.07	.27	1.31	65
Florida	1.20	.20	0.69	86
Georgia	1.59	.29	1.11	88
Kentucky	2.40	.34	1.52	77
Louisiana	2.09	.35	1.25	56
Mississippi	2.18	.31	1.48	39
North Carolina	1.60	.40	0.82	94
South Carolina	1.63	.28	0.84	65
Tennessee	2.11	.24	1.40	56
Virginia	1.25	.30	0.62	97
West Virginia	2.52	.55	1.38	80

Appendix 3.1 (continued)

State	State-Local Total Welfare	Cash Assistance	Medicaid	Average AFDC Benefit
Southwest	1.71	.30	0.94	81
Arizona	1.62	.24	0.96	92
New Mexico	1.95	.34	0.90	79
Oklahoma	2.09	.38	1.22	97
Texas	1.18	.24	0.68	56
Rocky Mountain	1.96	.33	0.98	111
Colorado	1.85	.39	0.76	110
Idaho	1.51	.22	0.76	93
Montana	2.56	.40	1.38	122
Utah	2.15	.35	1.19	117
Wyoming	1.75	.29	0.80	115
Far West	2.06	.57	0.85	161
Alaska	3.07	.84	0.91	230
California	2.48	.96	0.96	198
Hawaii	1.95	.57	1.02	154
Nevada	1.10	.11	0.54	98
Oregon	1.61	.34	0.61	127
Washington	2.13	.61	1.06	158
U.S. Average	$2.26	$.56	$1.11	$127

Source: Steven D. Gold and Judy A. Zelio, State-Local Fiscal Indicators
               (Washington, D.C.: National Conference of State Legislatures, January
               1990), Tables C-4, C-5, pp. 42 and 44.

NOTES

1. Martha Derthick, "American Federalism: Madison's Middle Ground in the 1980s," *Public Administration Review* (January/February 1987): 66–74.

2. Edward S. Corwin, "The Passing of Dual Federalism," *Virginia Law Review*, vol. 36 (February 1950): 1–24.

3. Jane Perry Clark, *The Rise of a New Federalism: Federal State Cooperation in the United States* (New York: Russell, 1938).

4. Samuel H. Beer, "The Modernization of American Federalism," *Publius: The Journal of Federalism*, vol. 3, no. 2 (Fall 1973): 53–91.

5. Dennis L. Dresang and James J. Gosling, *Politics, Policy, and Management in the American States* (New York: Longman, 1989): 26–28; Emmette Redford, "Centralized and Decentralized Political Impacts on a Developing Economy: Interpretations of American Experience," in *Spatial Dimensions of Development Administration*, edited by James J. Heaphey (Durham, NC: Duke University Press, 1971): 121; Thomas R. Dye, *Politics in States and Communities* (Englewood Cliffs, NJ: Prentice-Hall, 1969): Chapter 3; Daniel J. Elazar, *The American Partnership: Intergovernmental Relations in Nineteenth-Century American Federalism* (Chicago: University of Chicago Press, 1962). The use of "new" in describing the post–1981 period is problematic in that Clark used "new federalism"

in the title of her 1938 book to describe what eventually became known as cooperative federalism. It was also used during the Nixon administration.

6. Morton Grodzins, "Centralization and Decentralization in the American Federal System," in *A Nation of States*, edited by Robert A. Goldwin (Chicago: Public Affairs Conference Center, 1964): 1–24.

7. David B. Robertson and Dennis R. Judd, *The Development of American Public Policy: The Structure of Policy Restraint* (Glenview, IL: Scott, Foresman, 1989): 35–53.

8. *New York State Ice Co. v. Liebman*, 285 U.S. 262 (1932).

9. James T. Patterson, *The New Deal and the States: Federalism in Transition* (Princeton, NJ: Princeton University Press, 1969): Chapter 1.

10. Elmer E. Smead, *Governmental Promotion and Regulation of Business* (New York: Appleton-Century-Crofts, 1969): 7–9.

11. Patterson, *The New Deal and the States*, p. 26.

12. Ibid., pp. 43–49.

13. Deil Wright, *Understanding Intergovernmental Relations*, 2nd ed. (Monterey, CA: Brooks/Cole Publishing Co., 1982): 468–469.

14. Advisory Commission on Intergovernmental Relations (ACIR), "The Question of Federalism: Key Problems," in *State Politics and the New Federalism*, edited by Marilyn Gittell (New York: Longman, 1986): 48–49.

15. Patterson, *The New Deal and the States*, Chapter 2.

16. V. O. Key, Jr., *The Administration of Federal Grants to States* (Chicago, IL: Public Administration Service, 1937).

17. Patterson, *The New Deal and the States*, Chapter 3.

18. As the result of the Ramspeck Act of 1939, these states without civil service merit systems were required to establish such systems for employees that would be supported by federal funds. See Dresang and Gosling, *Politics, Policy, and Management in the American States*, pp. 339–340.

19. John Mollenkopf, *The Contested City* (Princeton, NJ: Princeton University Press, 1983): Chapter 2.

20. Patterson, *The New Deal and the States*, pp. 200–202; Grodzins, "Centralization and Decentralization," pp. 7–9.

21. Commission on Intergovernmental Relations (CIR), *A Report to the President for Transmittal to the Congress* (Washington, D.C., 1955): 212–213; Key, *The Administration of Federal Grants to States*, pp. 11–13 and 34–42.

22. Mollenkopf, *The Contested City*, pp. 116–122; CIR, *A Report to the President*, Chapters 11 and 12.

23. David M. Welborn and Jesse Burkhead, *Intergovernmental Relations in the American Administrative State: The Johnson Presidency* (Austin, TX: University of Texas Press, 1989): Chapter 2.

24. Beer, "Modernization of American Federalism," p. 80.

25. Welborn and Burkhead, *Intergovernmental Relations*, pp. 7–10; Timothy Conlan, *New Federalism: Intergovernmental Reform from Nixon to Reagan* (Washington, D.C.: Brookings Institution, 1988): 5–8.

26. Dresang and Gosling, *Politics, Policy, and Management*, pp. 29–31.

27. Claude E. Barfield, *Rethinking Federalism: Block Grants and Federal, State, and Local Responsibilities* (Washington, D.C.: American Enterprise Institute for Public Policy Research, 1981): 15.

28. Thomas J. Anton, "Intergovernmental Change in the United States: An Assessment of the Literature," in *Public Sector Performance: A Conceptual Turning Point*, edited by Trudi Miller (Baltimore: Johns Hopkins Press, 1984): 24.

29. Welborn and Burkhead, *Intergovernmental Relations*, Chapter 6.

30. Mollenkopf, *The Contested City*, pp. 87–93; Barfield, *Rethinking Federalism*, p. 16.

31. Timothy Conlan, *New Federalism: Intergovernmental Reform from Nixon to Reagan* (Washington, D.C.: Brookings Institution, 1988): Part I.

32. Barfield, *Rethinking Federalism*, p. 5.

33. Grodzin, "Centralization and Decentralization," pp. 17–23.

34. Anton, "Intergovernmental Change in the United States," pp. 25–27.

35. Derthick, "American Federalism," p. 70.

36. H. L. Wilensky and C. N. Lebeaux, *Industrial Society and Social Welfare* (New York: Free Press, 1965).

37. Sara F. Liebschutz, "Targeting by the State: The Basic Issues," *Publius: The Journal of Federalism*, vol. 19 (Spring 1989): 12.

38. James Sundquist, *Making Federalism Work: A Study of Program Coordination at the Community Level* (Washington, D.C.: Brookings Institution, 1969): 271; Ira Sharkansky, *The Maligned States: Policy Accomplishments, Problems and Opportunities*, 2nd ed. (New York: McGraw-Hill, 1978): 7.

39. Derthick, "American Federalism," pp. 70–71.

40. Alan D. Jones, "State Roles in Protecting the Environment: A Decade of Growing Responsibilities," Background Papers of the 1988 Woodlands Conference, "New State Roles: Environment, Resources and the Economy" sponsored by the Center for Growth Studies, Houston Area Research Center, Woodlands, Texas, November 13–16, 1988.

41. Mavis Mann Reeves, "Galloping Intergovernmentalization as a Factor in State Management," *State Government*, vol. 54, no. 3 (1981): 104.

42. Jones, "State Roles in Protecting the Environment"; Jurgen Schmandt, "Regional Roles in the Scientific State," in *Growth Policy in the Age of High Technology: The Role of Regions and States*, edited by Jurgen Schmandt and Robert Wilson (London: Unwin Hyman, 1990): 34–35.

43. Leonard D. White, *The States and Nations* (Baton Rouge, LA: Louisiana State University Press, 1953): 4.

44. ACIR, "The Key Questions of Federalism: Key Problems," pp. 48–49.

45. 105 S. Ct. 1005 (1985); ACIR, *The Transformation in American Politics: Implications for Federalism* (Washington, D.C., 1986): 7.

46. 108 S. Ct. 1355 (1988). For a discussion, see John Kincaid, "The State of American Federalism, 1987," *Publius: The Journal of Federalism*, vol. 18 (Summer 1988): 2–5.

47. David B. Walker, "American Federalism from Johnson to Bush," *Publius: The Journal of Federalism*, vol. 21 (Winter 1991): 114–117.

48. Council of State Governments, *Federal Grants-in-Aid: Report of the Committee on Federal Grants-in-Aid* (Chicago, 1949).

49. CIR, *A Report to the President*; Joint Federal–State Action Committee, *Final Report of the Joint Federal–State Action Committee to the President of the United States and to the Chairman of the Governor's Conference* (Washington, D.C.: Government Printing Office, 1960).

50. ACIR, *Regulatory Federalism: Policy, Process, Impact and Reform* (Washington, D.C., 1984): Chapters 1 and 3.

51. Derthick, "American Federalism," p. 67.

52. ACIR, *Regulatory Federalism*, Chapter 5.

53. Conlan, *New Federalism*, pp. 12–13 and Part 2.

54. Barfield, *Rethinking Federalism*, Chapters 3, 5 and 6.

55. ACIR, *Significant Features of Fiscal Federalism*, vol. 2 (Washington, D.C., 1990), p. 76.

56. Walker, "American Federalism from Johnson to Bush," p. 112.

57. Although there is disagreement over the success of the Reagan administration to implement its "new federalism" project, there is little disagreement that the federal government has diminished its participation, in terms of initiative and funding, in a wide number of domestic policy issues. See Michael A. Pagano and Ann O'M. Bowman, "The State of American Federalism: 1988–1989," *Publius: The Journal of Federalism*, vol. 19 (Summer 1989): 1–2.

58. Some of the regulatory measures were even supported by the Reagan administration, especially in instances where other policy goals conflicted with state and local autonomy. See Conlan, *New Federalism*, pp. 211–218.

59. Total federal–state–local spending represented 30.6 percent of GNP in 1979 and 34.5 percent in 1988. Walker, "American Federalism from Johnson to Bush," p. 113.

60. Ibid., pp. 118–119; Daniel J. Elazar, *Exploring Federalism* (Tuscaloosa, AL: University of Alabama Press, 1987): Chapter 6.

61. Smead, *Government Promotion and Regulation of Business*, pp. 3–9; Louis Hartz, *Economic Policy and Democratic Thought: Pennsylvania, 1776–1860* (Cambridge, MA: Harvard University Press, 1948): 4–8; Jonathan R. T. Hughes, *The Governmental Habit: Economic Controls from Colonial Times to the Present* (New York: Basic Books, 1977): Chapter 1.

62. Oscar Handlin and Mary Flug Handlin, *Commonwealth, A Study of the Role of Government in the American Economy: Massachusetts, 1774–1861* (New York: New York University Press, 1947): Chapter 3; Hartz, *Economic Policy and Democratic Thought*, Chapter 1.

63. Redford, "Centralized and Decentralized Political Impacts," p. 94.

64. Ibid., pp. 98–99; Hartz, *Economic Policy and Democratic Thought*, Chapter 3.

65. Carter Goodrich, *Government Promotion of American Canals and Railroads: 1800–1890* (New York: Columbia University Press, 1960): 268; Redford, "Centralized and Decentralized Political Impacts," p. 101.

66. Hughes, *The Governmental Habit*, pp. 67–68.

67. Ibid., p. 67.

68. Handlin and Handlin, *Commonwealth, Massachusetts, 1774–1861*, pp. 184–194.

69. For the case of Pennsylvania, see Hartz, *Economic Policy and Democratic Thought*, p. 10; Hughes, *The Governmental Habit*, pp. 70–71.

70. Hughes states that more than 25 percent of total railroad capital stock of a billion dollars came from public sources, predominately state and local government in the antebellum period; *The Governmental Habit*, p. 72. In Pennsylvania, equity investments were made by the state and, especially, by cities and counties for a period of time. See Hartz, *Economic Policy and Democratic Thought*, pp. 86–88; Smead, *Governmental Regulation and Promotion of Business*, p. 203.

71. Primm, *Economic Policy in Missouri*, p. 84.

72. See Ross M. Robertson, *History of the American Economy* (New York: Harcourt Brace Jovanovich, Inc., 1973): 144–145, and Goodrich, *Government Promotion*; on the abuse of franchises, see Handlin and Handlin, *Commonwealth, Massachusetts 1774– 1861*, Chapters 6 and 7. In Pennsylvania, public investments in pikes, canals, and railroads produced quite low return and investments in bridges fared somewhat better. See Hartz, *Economic Policy and Democratic Thought*, pp. 92–93, 149–152.

73. Hartz, *Economic Policy and Democratic Thought*, pp. 10–14; state government provided an arena in which sectional interests were expressed and reconciled; pp. 42– 51.

74. In Pennsylvania, a significant anticharter movement emerged where the privileges afforded to incorporated businesses were criticized. See Hartz, *Economic Policy and Democratic Thought*, pp. 69–79.

75. Handlin and Handlin, *Commonwealth, Massachusetts 1774–1861*, Chapters 8 and 9.

76. Eric Foner, *Reconstruction: America's Unfinished Business, 1863–1877* (New York: Harper & Row, 1988): 18–20, Chapter 8.

77. Robertson, *History of the American Economy*, pp. 270–281.

78. Gabriel Kolko, *Railroads and Regulation, 1877–1916* (Princeton, NJ: Princeton University Press, 1965): Chapters 1, 2, and 3.

79. Lawrence Goodwyn, *Democratic Promise: The Populist Moment* (New York: Oxford, 1976): pp. 113–120; Hughes, *The Governmental Habit*, Chapter 4.

80. Kolko, *Railroads and Regulation*, pp. 164–169.

81. Smead, *Governmental Promotion and Regulation of Business*, p. 204. The constitutionality of federal regulation of interstate commerce was ratified in *Wabash Railroad v. Illinois* in 1886. Kolko, *Railroads and Regulation*, p. 33.

82. Kolko, *Railroads and Regulation*, pp. 89–90. Reagan notes that concern with the growing power of large businesses and price fixing also produced state antitrust laws in the 1880s, and the same coalition that produced the state legislation also supported the Sherman Antitrust Act of 1890; see Michael D. Reagan, *Regulation the Politics of Policy* (Boston: Little, Brown and Co., 1987): 21; Hughes, *The Governmental Habit*, pp. 120–128. Similar to the pattern in the railroad industry, antitrust legislation and, especially enforcement in the late 1930s, became increasingly a federal concern. See Robertson, *History of the American Economy*, pp. 461 and 622–623.

83. Emmette S. Redford, "Dual Banking: A Case Study in Federalism," *Law and Contemporary Problems*, vol. 31, no. 4 (Autumn 1966): 749–773; ACIR, *State Regulation of Banks in an Era of Deregulation* (Washington, D.C., September 1988): Chapter 1.

84. Robertson, *History of the American Economy*, pp. 187–193.

85. In an account of Missouri, state government responsibility for economic promotion and development is also found in its chartering of corporations, especially in utility companies, railroads, and mineral extraction firms. See James Neal Primm, *Economic Policy in the Development of a Western State: Missouri, 1820–1860* (Cambridge, MA: Harvard University Press, 1954): Chapter 3.

86. Ibid., Chapter 2.

87. Foner, *Reconstruction*, pp. 22–23.

88. *McCulloch v. Maryland*, 17 U.S. 4 Wheat 316 (1819).

89. For example, permission to allow branch banking by state chartered banks was a prerogative of state government.

90. Redford, "Dual Banking," p. 754.

91. Kenneth J. Meier, *The Political Economy of Regulation: The Case of Insurance* (Albany, NY: State University of New York Press, 1988): 49–52.

92. *Metropolitan v. Ward*, 105 S. Ct. 1676 (1985).

93. *Paul v. Virginia*, 75 U.S. 168 (1968).

94. *U.S. v. South-Eastern Underwriters Association*, 322 U.S. 533 (1944).

95. I. Pool, ed., *The Social Impact of the Telephone* (Cambridge, MA: MIT Press, 1977).

96. John Brooks, *Telephone: The First Hundred Years* (New York: Harper & Row, 1975): Chapters 3, 4, and 5.

97. Smead, *Governmental Promotion and Regulation of Business*, pp. 357–360.

98. Ibid., Chapter 17.

99. Douglas D. Anderson, *Regulatory Politics and Electric Utilities: A Case Study in Political Economy* (Boston: Auburn House, 1981): Chapter 2.

100. William T. Gormley, Jr., *The Politics of Public Utility Regulation* (Pittsburgh, PA: University of Pittsburgh Press, 1983): 24–26.

101. Robertson, *History of the American Economy*, pp. 293–296.

102. Ibid., p. 317.

103. Smead, *Governmental Promotion and Regulation of Business*, Chapter 23.

104. Ibid., pp. 449–451.

105. Ibid., pp. 5–6.

106. Of the Western states, the State of California was exceptional in that it was very aggressive in a wide range of promotional and regulatory activities. As a resource-rich state and with a rapidly growing population, it was better able than most states to undertake its own development activities. See Gerald D. Nash, *State Government and Economic Development: A History of Administrative Policies in California, 1849–1933* (Berkeley: Institute of Governmental Studies, 1964).

107. Robert Reich, *The Next American Frontier* (New York: Times Book, 1983): 88–90, 97–98.

108. Redford, "Centralized and Decentralized Political Impacts," pp. 111–112.

109. Beer, "Modernization of American Federalism," pp. 65–69.

110. David O. Sears and Jack Citrin, *Tax Revolt: Something for Nothing in California* (Cambridge, MA: Harvard University Press, 1982): Chapter 11; Steven D. Gold, "Recent Development in State Finances," in *State Politics*, edited by Gittell, p. 318.

111. Sears and Citrin, *Tax Revolt*, Chapters 3 through 6 provide an excellent analysis of factors contributing to the tax revolt in California. For a summary table of tax reduction measures in 32 states for the years 1978, 1979, and 1980, see Gold, "Recent Developments in State Finances," p. 323.

112. ACIR, *Significant Features of Fiscal Federalism*, vol. 1 (Washington, D.C., February 1991): 18.

113. Ibid., pp. 14–17. One form of citizen tax concern was the advocacy of earmarked taxes. New revenues generated from specific sources are dedicated to specific activities. Highway taxes have historically been the most common form of earmarked taxes. Although responding to citizens' concerns for controls on fiscal policy, such taxes are viewed by many as placing an unnecessary and inappropriate constraint on the legislative responsibilities of establishing spending priorities. In any event, recent work suggests that the use of earmarked taxes has stabilized—around 23 percent of state tax collections are earmarked—but nevertheless it remains an instrument for citizen tax limitation efforts.

Ronald K. Snell, "Earmarking State Tax Revenue," *Intergovernmental Perspective*, vol. 14, no. 4 (Fall 1990): 12–16.

114. In 1970, state expenditures for Medicaid accounted for 4 percent of state budgets. In 1990, they accounted for 13 percent, and are expected to raise to 16 percent by 1994. Ann O'M. Bowman and Michael A. Pagano, "The State of American Federalism: 1990–1991," *Publius: The Journal of Federalism*, vol. 20 (Summer 1990): 7.

115. Ronald K. Snell, "Deep Weeds: Dismal Outlook for 1991," *State Legislatures* (February 1991): 15–18; Christopher Zimmerman, "New Federal Budget Means a Bigger Bill for States," *State Legislatures* (November/December 1990): 12–13; "The Sad State of the States: Monster Deficits Are Cutting Local Services and Delaying Recovery," *Business Week* (April 22, 1991): 24–26.

116. Louis Uchitelle, "States and Cities Are Pushing Hard for Higher Taxes," *New York Times* (March 25, 1991): A1.

117. Michael de Courcy Hinds with Erik Eckholm, "'80s Leave States and Cities in Need," *New York Times* (December 30, 1990): 1.

118. CIR, *A Report to the President*, p. 37.

119. ACIR, *The Question of State Government Capability* (Washington, D.C., January 1985): 28–29, 40–60; Albert L. Strum, "The Development of American State Constitutions," *Publius: The Journal of Federalism*, vol. 12 (Winter 1982): 242–243.

120. *Baker v. Carr*, 369 U.S. 186, 82 S. Ct. 691, 7 Ed. 2d 663 (1962); Dresang and Gosling, *Politics, Policy, and Management in American States*, pp. 99–101.

121. Alan Rosenthal, *Governors and Legislatures: Contending Powers* (Washington, D.C.: Congressional Quarterly Press, 1990): 42–43.

122. Strum, "The Development of American State Constitutions," pp. 242–243. Strum indicates that significant reform in state constitutions had occurred in the first decades of the twentieth century, led by Governors Charles Evan Hughes, Robert M. LaFollette, and Woodrow Wilson, but following that period, little reform occurred until the mid-1950s.

123. ACIR, *The Question of State Government Capability*, pp. 24–43.

124. Ibid., Chapters 6 and 7.

125. David Osborne, *Laboratories of Democracy* (Boston: Harvard Business School Press, 1988); Larry Sabato, *Goodbye to Goodtime Charlie: The American Governship Transformed*, 2nd ed. (Washington, D.C.: CQ Press, 1983); Thad L. Boyle, "The Governor As Innovator in the Federal System," *Publius: The Journal of Federalism*, vol. 18 (Summer 1988): 131–153; Marshall Kaplan and Sue O'Brian, *The Governors and the New Federalism* (Boulder, CO: Westview Press, 1991).

126. Osborne, *Laboratories of Democracy*, Chapter 10.

127. Sabato, *Goodbye to Goodtime Charlie*, pp. 170–175.

128. ACIR, *The Question of State Government Capability*, pp. 157–172.

129. Center for the American Women and Politics, Rutgers University, as reported in the *New York Times* (February 25, 1991): 6.

130. Tables entitled "Black Legislators Following the November 1990 Elections" and "Hispanic Legislators Following the November 1990 Election," National Conference of State Legislatures (Denver, CO), January 1991.

131. Alan Rosenthal, *Legislative Life: People, Process and Performance in the States* (New York: Harper & Row, 1981): 31.

132. National Conference of State Legislatures, *State Legislators' Occupations: A Decade of Change* (Denver, CO, 1986); also see Rosenthal, *Legislative Life*, pp. 57–60.

133. Dresang and Gosling, *Politics, Policy, and Management in the American States*, pp. 112–113.

134. ACIR, *The Question of State Government Capability*, Chapter 4.

135. Rosenthal, *Governors and Legislatures*, p. 44.

136. Dresang and Gosling, *Politics, Policy, and Management in the American States*, pp. 113–132; Rosenthal, *Legislative Life*, Chapter 10; Rosenthal, *Governors and Legislatures*, p. 46.

137. Rosenthal, *Legislative Life*, Chapter 14.

138. Ibid., pp. 55–61.

139. Ibid., Chapter 8; for an examination of this relationship in budgeting, see Edward J. Clynch and Thomas P. Lauth, eds., *Governors, Legislatures, and Budgets: Diversity Across the American States* (New York: Greenwood Press, 1991).

140. V. O. Key, Jr., *American State Politics: An Introduction* (New York: Alfred A. Knopf, 1956): Chapter 2.

141. Daniel J. Elazar, *American Federalism: A View from the States* (New York: Thomas Crowell Co., 1966): Chapters 7–9.

142. For a discussion of the research literature testing these concepts, see Thomas J. Anton, *American Federalism and Public Policy* (Philadelphia, PA: Temple University Press, 1989): 50–60.

143. Thomas R. Dye, *Politics, Economics, and the Public: Policy Outcomes in the American States* (Chicago: Rand McNally & Co., 1966): 54–58.

144. Thomas R. Dye, *American Federalism: Competition Among Governments* (Lexington, MA: Lexington Books, 1990): 124–132.

145. Dye, *Politics, Economics, and the Public*, Chapters 9, 10, and 11.

146. Allan J. Ciglet and Burdett A. Loomis, eds., *Interest Group Politics*, 3rd ed. (Washington, D.C.: CQ Press, 1991): ACIR, *The Transformation in American Politics*, Chapter 6. For a discussion of the effect of the historical desire of self-governing communities to contemporary America, see John Kincaid, "Federalism and Community in the American Context," *Publius: The Journal of Federalism*, vol. 20 (Spring 1990): 69–87.

147. Ronald G. Shaiko, "More Bang for the Buck: The New Era of Full-Service Public Interest Organizations," in *Interest Group Politics*, edited by Cigler and Loomis, pp. 109–110.

148. Anton argues that the control of federal policymaking by the iron triangle—an alliance among Congressional subcommittees, federal agencies and affected clients groups—has been weakened as these new actors participate in coalitions to affect policy outcomes; see Anton, *American Federalism*, pp. 90–99.

149. Andrew Mollison, "State-Level Lobbyists Doubled Since '73," *Austin American-Statesman* (October 27, 1991): A11; drawn from the November 1991 issue of *Lobbying and Influence Alert*.

150. Clive S. Thomas and Ronald J. Hrebenar, "Nationalization of Interest Groups and Lobbying in the States," in *Interest Group Politics*, edited by Cigler and Loomis, pp. 63–80; ACIR, *The Transformation in American Politics*, pp. 238–241.

151. John Herbers, "It's the New Activism as Business Primes the Government's Pump," *Governing*, vol. 1, no. 10 (July 1988): 32–38.

152. John Holcomb, "State and Local Politics During the Reagan Era: Citizen Group Responses," in *State Politics*, edited by Gittell, pp. 120–138.

153. ACIR, *The Transformation in American Politics*, pp. 208–221.
154. Herbers, "It's the New Activism," p. 35.
155. ACIR, *The States and Distressed Communities* (Washington, D.C., 1985).
156. Liebschutz, "Targeting by the States," pp. 1–16.

4

The State Role in Economic Development

The public policy response to structural economic change began to appear in state capitals at the end of the 1970s. Severe manufacturing restructuring created extremely difficult challenges to the northern industrial states. The booming South did not face economic distress, but it nevertheless faced challenges resulting from its comparative disadvantage on many of the location factors important to its rapidly growing industries, such as inadequate numbers of highly skilled workers. The federal government did not adopt any significant adjustment policies and was beginning to limit, if not reduce, aid to state and local governments. States, however, had developed their policymaking capabilities, and were surprisingly able to respond to the challenge of economic change.

In response to these changes, states competed with each other for investment and jobs. Contributing to the competitive atmosphere were the widely publicized studies of state business climates. Indicators of a state's business climate were developed to rank states. Presumably, states with the highest ranking were the most attractive for investment and economic growth. These rankings received great attention but were widely disputed, particularly by states that ranked low. The rankings, nevertheless, may have induced states to take action to improve their business climate.

The first widely publicized attempt to rank states according to business climate was conducted by Fantus Co. in 1975.[1] This study, commissioned by the Illinois Manufacturers' Association, was part of an effort to revise certain state policies perceived to be detrimental to the state's manufacturing sector.[2] The specific concern was that the state's unemployment compensation system produced premiums much higher than those found in other states, and consequently, reduced the state's attractiveness to manufacturing investment. The loss of 155,000 manufacturing jobs between the mid-1960s and mid-1970s helped place this issue on the state's political agenda. The Fantus study used a variety of factors to measure business climate, though most were related to taxation, unemployment compensation, and labor laws.

In the late 1970s, Alexander Grant, a Chicago-based accounting and management consulting firm, started ranking states, with financial support of the National Conference of State Manufacturers Association, and in the early 1980s *Inc.* magazine started publishing its own annual ranking in its October issue. The Corporation for Enterprise Development, a nonprofit research organization, publishes its ranking in "Making the Grade: The Development Report Card for the States." The proliferation of studies—each with a distinct methodology involving differences in underlying theory, variables, and data—has produced distinct, if not conflicting, rankings of states.[3] The early rankings tended to emphasize tax-related indicators and measures of labor and energy costs and were more useful for firms seeking areas of cheap, low-skilled labor and low taxes. More recent studies have further expanded the range of indicators to include quality of life, development strategies, economic performance, capacity measures, and other factors.

The exercise of developing a broad-based indicator of business climate will never be entirely successful for several reasons. For one, a single measure of business climate will never reflect the investment factors for all industries, as seen in the distinct industry location patterns found in Chapter 2. The locational needs, for example, of a telecommunications firm and of an automobile assembly plant cannot be captured in the same indicator of business climate. Second, these measures are developed with an eye toward public policy and are consequently weighted toward those factors that can be affected by policy. The early indicators were heavily weighted toward business tax rates and factor costs, and in order to improve its business climate according to these indicators, a state had to reduce tax rates. If, however, revenues are used effectively, higher taxes may produce conditions that actually lower the cost of operating a business in a state.

In sum, a single measure of business climate appropriate for all economic sectors and appropriate for determining state policy is not likely to be found, especially in light of the diversity and change occurring in the U.S. economy observed in Chapter 2. Nevertheless, states continued to search for ways to create a competitive advantage over other states in order to capture new investment or retain existing investment. With the problem formulated in this fashion, the issue for states has been to identify policy options that could create such advantages. A close examination of the functions of state government reveals that states can and do affect their economies in many ways, thus creating the possibility of competition on many fronts. This chapter establishes a framework for analyzing the range of state functions available for creating a competitive edge. Specific elements of the framework—including taxation policy, regulation of utilities and financial institutions, labor laws, and relations with local government—will be discussed with attention on policy formulation and implementation in an environment of economic and intergovernmental change. In the next three chapters specific elements of the framework will be examined in detail.

THE FUNCTIONS OF STATE GOVERNMENT AND ECONOMIC DEVELOPMENT

State government affects local economies in many ways. The economy of a state is directly taxed through business taxes and indirectly taxed through taxes levied on individuals. These revenues are expended on a wide range of state functions that may also affect the operations of firms. Businesses may benefit from the expenditures on transportation systems or on education and training received by the labor force. State expenditures may lower factor costs or improve the productivity of resources in a state. Other types of public expenditures are deemed necessary by the society, such as those for criminal justice and law enforcement or for public welfare, but may have a limited impact on the economy of the state. Beyond fiscal policy and pattern of expenditures, states affect their economies through a variety of regulatory functions in such areas as public utilities, labor laws, and environmental standards. In addition, various types of state action are undertaken in conjunction with other levels of government; states establish the powers of local governments and also administer a variety of federal programs, as discussed in Chapter 3, which can affect a state's economy.

The purpose of this section is to establish a framework for considering the range of state functions affecting a state's economy (see Table 4.1). One dimension of the framework establishes the nature of the policy objective for a particular function. This dimension distinguishes between (1) activities that have a direct and explicit development concern, (2) activities for which development is a secondary priority, and (3) activities that rarely have development objectives but nevertheless affect the economy of a state.

The second dimension of the framework indicates the intergovernmental framework and the form of the intervention. For each state activity, the form of intervention—substantial expenditures or regulatory—and the role, if any, of the federal government is identified. The allocation of responsibility between the federal and state governments varies substantially among the various functions, and a number of federal activities that affect economic development involve a state administrative role. Table 4.1 confirms the complex system of intergovernmental relations that pertain to economic development.

States engage in many policy areas in which economic development is an explicit objective. Some of these policy areas also involve activities on the part of the federal government. The level of the federal funding and the extent to which states and federal government cooperate will be one important element of determining the relative influence of state policy and the degree of independence that states have in developing policy. In the areas of economic infrastructure

Table 4.1
State Development Activities: The Intergovernmental Framework

	STATE GOVERNMENT		FEDERAL GOVERNMENT		
	Funding	Regulatory Role	Funding — State Administration	Funding — No State Administration	Regulatory Role
Primary Development Objective[1]					
Planning/Institutional Mobilization (Chap. 4)	x				
Development Programs (Chap. 5)	x		x (CDBG)[2]	x (SBA)[4]	
Technology Programs (Chap. 5)	x			x	
Training Programs (Chap. 7)	x		x (JTPA)[3]		
Tax Incentive Programs (Chap. 4)	x				
Physical Infrastructure (Chap. 3)					
Water/Waste Water	x		x		x
Roads/Highway/Airports	x				x
Secondary Development Objective					
Public Education (Chap. 7)	x	x	x		x
Higher Education (Chap. 7)	x	x	x		x
Aid to Cities (Chap. 4)	x		x		
Labor Policy (Chap. 4)		x		x	x
Public Utilities (Chaps. 4 and 6)		x			x
Financial Institutions (Chap. 4)		x			x
Natural Resource Management (Chap. 3)		x			x
Transportation (Regulation of) (Chap. 3)		x			x
Potential Development Impact					
Tax Policy (Chap. 4)	x				
Powers of Local Government (Chap. 4)		x			
Environmental Protection (Chap. 3)		x	x		x

1 In parentheses is the number of the chapter in which the activity is discussed.
2 Community Development Block Grants.
3 Job Training Partnership Act.
4 Small Business Administration.

shared responsibilities among the federal, state and local governments prevail, although the federal role diminished somewhat in the 1980s (see Table 3.4).

State activities with secondary development objectives fall into two categories, public education and regulatory activities. States bear a major financial responsibility for public education, along with local government; the federal government's role is limited. In the area of regulation the intergovernmental regulatory system, described historically in Chapter 3, creates an important, though subordinate, role for state government. The intergovernmental regulatory system was subject to great turmoil in the 1980s, particularly with regard to financial institutions, and the federal deregulatory initiatives during the period had a significant effect on state regulation.

This framework will organize our discussion of states and economic development. Several questions will be investigated. How is policymaking and policy implementation conducted for the specific activity? To the extent that state policy for the specific activity is changing, what are the economic and political forces at work? Finally, to what extent can activities that affect a state's economy be used for development objectives? Are those programs with an explicit economic development objective likely to succeed in promoting development? Can those activities with secondary economic development objectives be used to promote development without compromising their other policy objectives?

In the remainder of this chapter and the next three chapters, various elements of this framework will be studied (indicated in parentheses in Table 4.1). Short studies of strategic planning, taxation and development, utility regulation, state regulation of financial institutions, labor laws, and state–local government relations will be investigated in this chapter. The next three chapters will present case studies of technology and development programs, telecommunications regulation, and education policy. This range of studies provides diverse examples of the form of state action and level of state expenditures and will provide the empirical base for testing our hypotheses concerning economic change and state policymaking.

STRATEGIC PLANNING

The challenges of economic distress and interstate competition were met in many states by the formation of a task force or a blue ribbon commission to study the state's economy and to develop a strategy for promoting development. These planning efforts were interesting because they mobilized nongovernmental resources and brought together representatives from various sectors of a state to think about the future; the state role was one of a catalyst. During a time of change, this approach has been especially helpful.

In the late 1970s, Governor Jerry Brown established the California Commission on Industrial Innovation (CCII) to investigate what was perceived to be a deterioration in the state's competitive position.[4] The membership of CCII was broad-based, including representatives from business (Steven Jobs and David

Packard among others), labor, higher education, and government. CCII identified the need to promote innovation not only in high-technology industries but also in the traditional industries of the state. State government in California had played a major role in earlier decades[5] in agriculture innovation through its support of university research and in water development, and consequently the concept of state leadership in development innovation was familiar.

The recommendations of CCII were of three types: public and private sector investment strategy, education and job training efforts, and improvement in the productivity of management and labor. Most of the strategies, however, relied on federal action rather than on state action. CCII identified international competition as the threat to state industry and found that the appropriate response to competition—to reverse the decline of schools and university research—required federal action. Although its diagnosis of the state economy proved to be accurate, CCII's recommendations did not become part of the state's legislative agenda. Governor Brown was defeated and his successor, Governor Deukmajian, adopted a quite different attitude toward state development policy. Deukmajian did not concur with the targeting of key industries, as implied in the CCII recommendations, but rather felt industries should rise and fall according to their ability to compete in the market. Government policy could help create an environment in which innovation was encouraged, but should not become involved in attempting to pick "winners." Although the CII recommendations were not directly adopted, the work of the commission did focus public discourse on the problems of economic change and provided a basis for later legislative deliberations.[6]

Faced with severe economic challenges and fiscal distress in state government, Minnesota responded in several innovative and unique ways. Building on a long tradition of active civic participation of business leaders and a cooperative spirit among various sectors of the state, in 1981 state leaders established Wellspring, a nongovernmental, nonprofit alliance of business, labor, government, education, and agriculture whose purpose was to strengthen the economy of the state through public policy and through public—private cooperation.[7] These groups were represented on the 40-member board of Wellspring. Balance was also addressed through co-chairs; the original co-chairs were Raymond Plank, chairman and chief executive officer of the Apache Corporation, and David Roe, president of the Minnesota AFL-CIO. Although Wellspring was nongovernmental, the governor served as honorary chairman, and grants were obtained from the State Planning Board. Wellspring served as a very useful vehicle for bringing a diverse set of leaders together to study problems faced by the state and for informing citizens of the state about these issues. The recommendations of Wellspring have had a significant impact on state policy, but the alliance has also had limitations. For example, Wellspring was unable to take a position on tax reform in 1985 for fear of dividing its membership.[8]

Another strategic planning activity was conducted during this same period under governmental auspices. The commissioner of the Department of Economic

Development established the Task Force on Technology Intensive Industries.[9] This task force included representatives from the state's high-technology industries, which had been quite active in various areas of state policymaking, and from the University of Minnesota's Institute of Technology. Although the task force was more narrowly focused on high-technology than similar bodies in other states, its 1981 report emphasized the need for coordination among the various elements of the state, including state government, educational institutions, tax policies, regulatory policies, and business and labor leaders, in order to insure that the state's industries could compete with those from other states.[10] The message in the report was conveyed in an urgent tone, and the work of the task force influenced the broad state development programs subsequently adopted.

The involvement of the State of New York in technology and development policy dates from the 1960s.[11] The New York State Science and Technology Foundation was established in 1963 during the governorship of Nelson Rockefeller. Under Governor Hugh Carey, the Economic Development Board was established in 1975. In 1978, the High Technology Opportunities Council was established, but met only once. The New York Assembly advanced its own ideas on technology policy and instituted the Legislative Commission on Science and Technology in 1980. These disjointed efforts were largely unsuccessful. In 1981, however, coordination and consolidation were achieved when the assembly established the Task Force on University–Industry Cooperation and the Promotion of High-Technology Industries, and the New York State Science and Technology Foundation was reconstituted as an authority responsible to the legislature.

One of the first actions of the new foundation board was to contract with the Batelle Columbus Laboratories for a study that would provide the basis for a state technology policy. The Batelle study identified strengths in the New York economy and related those to projections of rapidly growing high-technology sectors.[12] Those industries in New York with the potential to grow rapidly and bring substantial benefits, broadly defined, to the state, were identified. This study had a substantial impact on the policies and programs adopted by the state and will be discussed in the following chapter. What is important to note here is that the strategic planning process called for industry targeting and utilized the services of an outside consulting firm. In this respect strategic planning in New York was quite different from that found in most other states.

Like New York, North Carolina has had a long-standing involvement in development and technology policy.[13] State government, although providing no direct funding, helped provide infrastructure for Research Triangle Park when it was established in the late 1950s. In addition, Governor Terry Sanford encouraged the state to support science and engineering in order to promote economic and technical development in the state. This led to the formation of the North Carolina Board of Science and Technology in 1962. The efforts of this board and state government were substantially expanded in the 1980s. In 1982, Governor James Hunt appointed a Task Force on Science and Technology to determine the means by which the state could further utilize its scientific and technical resources in promoting development. The 15-member task force, which included representatives from financial institutions, labor, business, and the state assembly, worked closely with the Board of Science and Technology. Examining technology transfer, education, training, agriculture and other topics, the task force conducted forums throughout the state. As in the case of New York, the recommendations from this task force were largely adopted in state legislation.

Republican Governor Bill Clements in 1981 formed a blue ribbon commission, Texas 2000, to examine the future of that state's economy. Clements, an oilman, recognized that the economy of the state was undergoing fundamental change and hoped that the Texas 2000 Commission would focus public attention on the future of the state. Although the original agenda emphasized natural resources, science and technology emerged as a central element of the commission's work.[14] The final report emphasized economic change and identified issues related to advanced technology development.[15] Although the Clements administration did not introduce any significant legislation derived from the Texas 2000 effort, the commission placed economic diversification on the policy agenda of the state. It also introduced a new set of actors, related to the rapidly growing electronics and communications industries, to the state policymaking arena and encouraged new thinking about the role of higher education in the economy of the state. During the legislative session of the mid-1980s, technology development policy became a major issue.

The Greenhouse Compact, the plan produced by the Strategic Development Commission (SDC) in Rhode Island, was perhaps the most comprehensive attempt to elaborate and promote a state development policy.[16] Established in 1982, SDC members were appointed by the governor from the ranks of leaders in the state's business and financial communities, organized labor, higher education, public service, and the state legislature. After undertaking an extensive study of the state's economy, it proposed a $750 million economic development plan in 1983. The strategies advocated by the Compact included the targeting of industries in which the state had competitive advantages, support of export-oriented industries, shoring up of old-line industries in the state, nurturing research and development in new firms and industries (the greenhouse notion), and improving the state's infrastructure. The legislative package was not subject to modification or amendment. The Compact was voted down in 1984 in a state election by a four-to-one margin. Public opposition had several sources. Although the SDC had broad representation, it was perceived as elitist and operated virtually in secret. For example, the rank-and-file of organized labor opposed the plan even though union leadership was represented on the SDC. The distribution of costs and benefits of the Compact were not sufficiently articulated to satisfy skeptical citizens. In addition, industries not targeted objected to the special treatment given to those targeted. Business people appeared opposed to the degree of governmental intervention in the proposal.[17] The defeat of the Compact also ushered in a return of Republican control, and state development returned to earlier strategies such as improving the business climate through reduction in tax rates, reducing labor strike benefits, and using pension funds for small businesses.[18]

Governor Richard Thornburgh was elected in 1979 and immediately started to fulfill a campaign promise of revitalizing Pennsylvania's State Planning Board.[19] At that time, Pennsylvania's economic development strategies and programs had originated in the 1950s and 1960s and it was obvious that these programs and institutions were not capable of responding effectively to the economic distress in the state. The rejuvenated State Planning Board, with representatives from the state legislature, executive branch, local governments, organized labor, and civic leaders, produced a final report in 1981 entitled *Choices for Pennsylvania*. A second organization, the MILRITE Council, also played a significant role in the debate on state economic policy. Formed in 1978 by the Pennsylvania General Assembly, the MILRITE Council was composed of leaders from business, labor, and government. The broad mandate of this body included the development of industrial revitalization plans and the responsibility to encourage the participation of business, labor, and government in cooperative efforts. The MILRITE Council's activities, the State Planning Board's report, and, in 1982, the governor's "Advanced Technology Policies for the Commonwealth of Pennsylvania" established a broad consensus on development policy that was reflected in the Ben Franklin Partnership legislation of 1982. In a clear shift from the development policy of earlier years, the Ben Franklin Partnership favored small business and entrepreneurial policy over "smokestack" chasing.

Michigan was adversely affected in the late 1970s by structural economic change and foreign competition. With an economy heavily weighted toward durable manufacturing production, especially the automative industry, Michigan suffered a dramatic deterioration in its high-wage economy as it entered the 1980s. At the urging of the chairman of Dow Chemical and the president of the University of Michigan, Governor William Miliken appointed the High-Technology Task Force in 1981, drawing its membership from academia, finance, and advanced technology firms.[20] In 1982, Michigan's new governor, James Blanchard, continued the emphasis on economic development, but with a somewhat different substantive and operational focus. He established the Commission on Jobs and Economic Development, drawing more on the traditional manufacturing core than did Miliken's High-Technology Task Force; Chrysler President Lee Iacocca and United Auto Workers President Douglas Fraser were co-chairs. The commission's purpose was advisory, to review proposals. The Governor's Entrepreneurial and Small Business Commission provided a similar advisory function for representatives of small businesses. New policy initiatives originated in the Governor's Cabinet Council for Jobs and Economic Development, which consisted of several department heads and other development officials, and the Task Force for a Long-Term Economic Development Strategy. This latter group, consisting largely of academics, undertook an analysis of the Michigan economy and devised various development strategies. Its report, "The Path to Prosperity,"[21] emphasized technological innovation over industrial recruitment and had a significant effect on the policies adopted by the Blanchard administration.

State strategic planning exercises were particularly appropriate for defining the policy agenda to address economic change. Economic change was both rendering traditional manufacturing vulnerable and providing new opportunities for growth, though, as we saw in Chapter 2, the specific effects of change varied substantially among regions and states. With the federal government's lack of leadership in addressing economic change, state strategic planning was well suited for bringing together diverse interests to discuss the economic future and state policy for development. Economic distress may have been the primary impetus to these exercises, but they nevertheless provided a forum to examine how economic change was affecting a state and to identify the strengths and weaknesses of state given the requirements of change. Governors have extensively and effectively used this mechanism—the blue-ribbon commission or task force—to set the state's policy agenda.[22]

The strategic planning exercises were, however, not without problems. Expectations for advanced technology manufacturing development were oversold. Little attention was generally given to infrastructure, particularly telecommunications infrastructure, or to human resource development. Technological innovation in traditional industries was another topic frequently overlooked, and issues of community distress, rural development, and poverty were seldom part of the agenda. And many plans were never either implemented fully or even partially. Strategic planning, however, did have a lasting effect on agenda-setting for development efforts and helped clarify issues faced by the states.

TAX POLICY AND ECONOMIC GROWTH

Tax policy has been an important feature of state development policy for two principal reasons. In the mid-1970s, citizen tax revolts, discussed in Chapter 3, severely limited the ability of states and local governments to raise revenue. Although the intensity of the tax revolt has diminished, quite serious political constraints on taxation remain, and these significantly affect the ability of state and local governments to fulfill their responsibilities. Combined with the reductions in federal transfers to state and local governments and increased earmarking of revenues, the range of options available to state governments for revenue generation is constrained.

The second reason for examining tax policy is that it holds substantial potential for directly affecting economic development in a state through its impact on investment decisions and employment growth. Tax policy is, consequently, a potentially powerful instrument of economic development policy and one that has frequently been studied by strategic planning commissions and state legislatures. Though the share of state and local taxes that fall initially on businesses has declined during recent decades, differentials among states still exist and interstate tax competition is intense.[23] These differences in tax policies and tax rates give rise to the possibility of a state acquiring a competitive advantage over other states.[24]

During the Sunbelt–Snowbelt controversy of the late 1970s, high tax rates and relatively high welfare benefits of states in the traditional industrial heartland were perceived to be significant factors in the relative deterioration of their economies. This led to a reexamination of tax rates and the actual reduction in rates in a number of states.[25] In Massachusetts, for example, known as Taxachusetts, many attributed the economic distress of the state in the 1960s and especially in the 1970s to the high tax rates which made the state unattractive to business and placed an excessive burden on citizens. After extensive public discussion, including a citizen tax revolt, Proposition 2½ was adopted and property tax rates declined. Although this action was not taken to make the state more attractive to investment, business groups were supportive of Proposition 2½, and later these groups worked in the legislature for further tax reform.[26] Although these changes contributed to the state's rapid economic growth later in the 1980s, other, more powerful factors were largely responsible for the recovery.[27]

Determining the effects of tax rates and structures on economic growth involves quite complex methodological issues. Tax rates and structures have undergone substantial change in recent decades, and past patterns of regional economic growth have been ruptured by structural change and the growth of service sector employment. To relate tax policy and economic growth as both are changing is indeed difficult, and the literature on the effect of state taxation on economic growth, though extensive, is inconclusive.[28] Earlier studies generally concluded that state differentials in tax rates, though significant, probably did not have much effect on rates of economic growth. Contributing to this conclusion were the observations that (1) state taxes were just one of many costs incurred by firms, and for many firms other factors, such as availability of labor and labor costs, were much more important, and (2) high state taxes may have lowered the cost factors for individual firms through the provision of high-quality services, such as education or infrastructure.

More recent studies, with better specified models and databases, are detecting some effect of tax policy on growth.[29] Impacts on capital-intensive industries are stronger than those on labor-intensive industries, and property taxes are more significant than other types of taxes. This confirms an earlier finding that state taxes have little impact on interstate growth differentials but local taxes, especially property taxes, significantly affect intrastate location. In a sector-specific study, Wasylenko and McGuire found that although the level of tax rate was not significant, an increase in tax effort had an adverse effect on employment growth.[30] Improved definitions of state tax rates[31] and sector-specific studies[32] suggest that further research is warranted and may help unravel this quite complex topic.

Several recent studies have attempted to incorporate state expenditures in estimating the effect of tax rates on economic growth. If the revenues from relatively high tax rates are effectively used for education and training or for transportation infrastructure, factor costs of firms may be reduced, thus making the state attractive for investment. One study confirms this hypothesis for some public expenditure; expenditures on education, highways, and public health were found to increase economic growth; expenditures on transfer payments were found to retard growth.[33]

Taxes play a role in economic development, but the role is complex and not well understood. The relationship between tax rates and state growth rates, however, appears weak. Tax rate differentials among states do exist and interstate tax competition shows no signs of abating, whether or not taxes are significant in affecting rates of growth. The complexity of the relationship results from the varying influence of taxes on different industries—a function of relative capital intensity and the incidence of taxes, the level and types of governmental services received by businesses and their employees, and the adequacy of state fiscal structures. The effects of structural economic change, including the rapid growth of service sectors, changes in capital intensity, and in the occupational requirements of firms are further complicating our understanding of the relationship between taxation and growth.

The literature suggests that the wisest course of action for states is to insure that tax structures are efficient and adequate given changes in economic structure. Reliance on a particular tax, such as property taxes or oil severance taxes, produces a vulnerable tax system. In addition, as noted above, the greatest expansion in employment in recent decades has occurred and will continue to occur in the service sectors. Services are relatively undertaxed because many services, particularly business and professional services, are exempt from state sales tax and are not capital-intensive and thus do not incur high property taxes. Much attention has been focused on incorporating service sectors into the tax base. In Florida, the attempt to expand the tax base by taxing the advertising industry was unsuccessful when the industry threatened to leave the state. Although this solution was not accepted in Florida, states will likely attempt to design tax structures more closely tied to those sectors with above-average employment growth. Corporate and personal income taxes, for example, meet this requirement.

In addition to attention given to general tax rates many, if not all, states design development incentives to attract or retain businesses. One frequently used incentive involves state or locally levied taxes. Tax incentives can include property tax exemption or tax moratorium on land, capital improvements, inventory, and equipment; exemption or reduction of sales taxes; or tax credits for such items as investment or research and development (see Table 4.2). Tax incentives or abatements are, in essence, tax expenditures. These types of incentives, frequently used in conjunction with other business incentives, are forms of state action distinct from the changes in general tax structure, described above, in that they are targeted to certain firms or industries.

Tax incentives attempt to attract new businesses or retain existing business

Table 4.2
State Tax Incentives for Business: 1974–1990 (Number of States)

	1974	1979	1980	1981	1982	1983	1984	1985	1986	1987	1988	1989	1990
Corporate Income Tax Exemption	19	23	25	25	25	25	27	31	33	33	31	32	34
Personal Income Tax Exemption	19	18	20	20	20	20	21	24	26	27	28	32	32
Excise Tax Exemption	10	13	15	14	16	16	15	16	18	19	19	21	22
Tax Exemption on Land, Capital Improvement	18	25	29	29	29	30	33	34	34	34	35	35	35
Tax Exemption on Equipment, Machinery	26	28	31	31	33	34	32	34	35	35	39	41	41
Inventory Tax Exemption on Goods in Transit	38	44	45	46	46	45	45	47	47	48	48	48	49
Industrial Tax Exemption	32	39	42	43	43	44	42	43	44	44	44	45	45
Sales/Use Tax Exemption on New Equipment	31	35	36	36	38	38	39	42	42	44	44	45	46
Tax Exemption on Raw Materials	43	46	46	46	47	47	46	45	45	45	45	47	48
Tax Incentive for R&D	7	11	12	11	11	12	17	22	24	25	25	27	28
Accelerated Depreciation of Industrial Equipment	20	26	28	28	30	32	35	34	34	35	35	36	39
Tax Incentive for Job Creation	n/a	n/a	12	14	16	18	24	30	31	32	33	39	40
Tax Incentive for Industrial Investment	n/a	n/a	12	15	20	23	23	29	29	30	32	33	35

Source: Site Selection Handbook (Norcross, GA: Conway Data, Inc.), various years.

by lowering a firm's direct costs; that is, by lowering the tax liabilities of a firm in a specific location, the location may become the lowest cost site for the firm. There are other methods of achieving this same objective—provision of loans, training programs, below-market rents for buildings and land, among others— but all provide a subsidy, at public expense, to a firm.

Although the effectiveness and fairness of state and local tax incentives are widely disputed, enthusiasm of state government for these programs abound, and virtually all states now use tax incentives of some sort.[34] The size of the concessions has grown rapidly. The 1985 Illinois offer to attract Chrysler–Mitsubishi, mentioned earlier, included $100 million in tax breaks.[35] Under the threat of the loss of a major business, ConAgra, the state of Nebraska provided a set of tax incentives valued at $9 million in order to retain the headquarters of the firm.[36]

Tax incentive programs received a good deal of attention in the 1960s as less-developed states adopted them in an attempt to attract manufacturing investment.[37] The empirical evidence of the effectiveness of tax incentive programs is weak.[38] There are several relevant questions. Do these programs effectively attract firms that would have located elsewhere? Do the benefits of the programs exceed their costs? Do the programs significantly affect the rate of economic growth? The answer to the first question has, in part, been answered in the discussion of tax structures; because taxes are a relatively minor part of the total cost structure of firms, they are unlikely to be a critical factor in location decisions. This conclusion constrains the potential effectiveness of tax incentives to those instances where two or more states, or two locales in a particular region, have approximately the same cost structure for a firm. A large tax incentive may be decisive. Southern states have been attractive to firms decentralizing from northern states because of the prevailing low wages throughout the South. A tax incentive, in Mississippi, however, might make the state more attractive than Alabama. The very large incentive packages offered by the winning states in the automobile manufacturing sweepstakes, discussed above, appear to have been significant. The literature, however, suggests that tax incentives are most likely to affect subregional location decisions of firms.

Whether the state benefits from acquiring a firm through a tax incentive program, however, is not altogether certain. The forgone revenues of the tax incentive programs represent a cost to state government, and the additional tax revenue generated by the firm attracted to the state may or may not exceed the state's tax expenditure. At the same time, it is almost certain that these programs will not have a perceptible impact on the rate of economic growth in a state, simply because such programs affect a very small number of firms. Some argue that tax incentives targeted to firms in advanced technology sectors or for research and development might have a significant impact, but this has yet to be demonstrated empirically.

Tax incentive programs, in addition, are criticized on the grounds of equity, by firms not benefiting from the program and by taxpayers who suffer the tax

Table 4.3
Categories of State Regulatory Activities

Economic regulation

      Financial institutions—regulation of state-chartered banks, insurance companies, etc.
      Public utilities, especially setting of rates and bond rating of the companies.
      Natural resource regulation—extraction of resources.
      Transportation—regulation of intrastate trucking.

Social or "horizontal" regulation

      Health, safety, enviornmental, consumer, labor laws.

Source: Leigh Boske, ed., Regulation in Texas: Its Impact, Process, and Institutions,
          Policy Research Project Series, no. 76 (Austin, TX: LBJ School of Public Affairs,
          University of Texas at Austin, 1986).

expenditures. Also, these programs are highly criticized for placing states in competition in a zero-sum game. Tax incentive programs appear to have at best very little effect on a state's economy, may not be cost effective and are perceived by some to be inequitable; nevertheless, they are one of the most commonly used state economic development tools.[39]

REGULATION

State governments undertake a broad range of regulatory activities that affect businesses and individuals. The nature and purpose of state regulation varies substantially among the areas of regulation; for example, the purpose of licensing is quite different from that of regulating financial institutions. Our task will be made easier by limiting the analysis to forms of economic regulation only (see Table 4.3). Though state efforts in economic regulation are constrained by federal regulatory authority, as seen in Chapter 3, states have substantial authority and a variety of mechanisms to regulate economic activities within their boundaries.[40] In this section the objectives, the politics, and the potential effects of state regulation on the economy of a state will be discussed. An assessment is made of the potential role that regulation, or deregulation, might play in a state's economic development strategy. Studies of state regulation of energy and financial institutions will be presented.

Many forms of state regulatory activity preceded the ratification of the U.S. Constitution, and states continued to exercise this role during the early decades of the country (see Chapter 3). By the middle of the last century, however, licensing and franchising were undertaken systematically for classes of firms rather than on the firm-specific basis of earlier years. Toward the end of the last century, fear of large corporations, particularly in the railroad industry, which placed rural interests and small business interests at a severe disadvantage, resulted in new regulatory measures.[41] At the turn of the century, states and localities became involved in utility regulation.[42] The economic abuse argument was not the only justification for increased state activity.[43] "Cut-throat" competition resulted in some support from business and industrial interests for the regulation of markets. Regulation in the oil and gas industry during much of this century was frequently advocated by "independent" oil producers who wanted stability in the price of oil.[44]

Although the specific justification for and means of regulation vary among different industries and markets, the general rationale for regulation is that an unfettered market produces unsatisfactory outcomes. Such outcomes occur, for example, when individual consumers pay inappropriately high or discriminatory prices as a result of monopoly control in the industry (the perception concerning railroad and utility rates at the turn of the century); prices fluctuate to such an extent that producers cannot sustain their operations; segments of markets remain unserved; and a competitive market places certain types of firms in jeopardy (such as banks and insurance companies). The specific form of regulation to overcome these unsatisfactory outcomes varies, but the company or companies regulated are constrained in their operations (in terms of prices they can ask, types of investments they can make, or markets they must serve), though they are also protected from excessive competition. Firms may be given exclusive franchises—areas in which no other companies can compete—as is common for local service areas of utility companies. Or the entry of new firms in a market (for example, banks, savings and loans, or transportation companies) may be constrained to protect the viability of existing firms.

The goal of regulation is to produce economically viable companies with fairly priced goods serving all consumers, but there is extensive disagreement on the effectiveness of regulation in achieving this goal. Some argue that rectifying economic abuse of powerful firms can best be remedied by promoting competition, not restricting competition as in regulated markets. Furthermore, regulated markets may be captured, some argue, by the very companies being regulated. Regardless of the merits of the various arguments, deregulation and regulatory reform have been very much part of the national agenda for the last decade, especially in the fields of transportation and communications.[45]

Overturning decades-old regulation in the airline industry, deregulatory policies in the late 1970s were based on the premise that allocation of airline routes should be undertaken by markets, that entry of new airline companies would encourage competition and, consequently, this would produce a better outcome for consumers and force airlines to be efficient. Similarly, the long-distance component of the telephone business was believed to be better served by competition, resulting in the divestiture of AT&T (discussed further in Chapter 6). Federal efforts in deregulation have rested largely on grounds of economic efficiency: regulation distorts the true price of goods and produces inefficiencies in the market. Deregulation philosophy prevailed at the federal level, affecting economic activities throughout the country and affecting states in their regulatory functions. The principal change in state-level regulation, however, has been in terms of reform rather than deregulation,[46] with deregulation of occupational licensing providing the only exception.

Beyond the pressures of federal deregulation of the 1980s, states face other challenges in performing their regulatory function. State regulatory agencies must incorporate the implications of technological change for the regulated industries. For example, technological change has created the possibility of competition in markets that were formerly considered natural monopolies. Competitors may attempt to bypass the local monopolies, but exclusive local franchises, embodied in existing statutory frameworks, preclude competition.[47] Regulatory reform has attempted to introduce competition in certain markets of a regulated business, through unbundling of services and allowing the local franchises to compete in so-called noncore activities.[48] Also, the trend in public utility companies toward diversification, especially into nonregulated markets, represents a substantial challenge to regulatory agencies which must grapple with regulating diversified companies.[49]

Reforms in state regulation have been both institutional and procedural. The institutional reforms include expanded legislative oversight of regulatory agencies and a broader participation of the public interest in regulatory review through public counsels and intervenors, which are frequently public interest advocates.[50] Procedural reforms include centralizing and codifying regulations in state registers, and most states have adopted an administrative procedure act.[51] Many states' legislatures specify the types of analysis that must be conducted on proposed regulation.

The question ultimately to be addressed here is whether a state can use its regulatory responsibility for purposes of economic development. This role depends on the ability of the state to create a competitive advantage through its regulatory activities and thus attract investment or create the conditions by which new wealth can be generated from resources internal to the state. Although this potential exists, there are several limitations on its use. Competition among states may produce "Gresham's Law of State Regulation," whereby less stringent regulations in one state drive out tougher ones in competing states.[52] As a result, a single state is not likely to be successful in establishing a competitive advantage because other states will likely replicate the action, thus eliminating any advantage.

Taking electric utility regulation as a potential instrument for economic development, the regulatory objective would be to establish commercial and industrial electricity rates lower than those in other states. The Indiana Utility Regulatory Commission, for example, allowed the Hoosier Energy Rural Electric Cooperative to offer discounted electric rates in order to attract new large industrial customers or to encourage expansion by existing customers.[53] In addition to the issue of discriminatory pricing which led to utility regulation in the first place, there are potential problems with this strategy. Though regulation of utility companies—justified because they are natural monopolies—was first established to curb abuse by utility companies, the regulatory process must also insure the economic vitality of the companies. Pursuit of the economic development goal, through low energy prices, may well result in insufficient investment in the utility companies and, subsequently, decline in bond prices and higher costs of capital. In the long run, energy prices may have to rise, thus defeating the objective of maintaining low energy prices.

Another potential constraint on the use of regulation as a development tool is found in environmental regulation.[54] This case is complicated by the fact that the federal government, not state governments, sets minimum environmental standards, though states can adopt stricter standards and are frequently responsible for enforcement. Because environmental regulation places additional costs on firms, one might assume that, in order to achieve an economic development goal, the state would not impose stricter standards since such action would place the state at a competitive disadvantage vis-à-vis other states. While a state cannot gain an advantage in this context, it can avoid incurring a disadvantage. This scenario might be used for creating a comparative advantage in a state for pollution-intense industries, but it is likely to be inconsequential for most firms. In fact, firms and industries that place high value on quality of life factors may be attracted to the very states that protect their natural environment through enacting higher than minimum standards. Furthermore, at a political level, the population of a state may place a high priority on environmental quality. In sum, a state has relatively limited ability to use its environmental regulatory capacity to promote economic development through acquiring advantages over other states.

Substantial state discretion in the intergovernmental regulatory system can produce substantial diversity among the states as noted in Chapter 3. To the extent such diversity impedes interstate commerce, the federal government, consumers, and companies have standing to intervene and have done so frequently. The federal courts and federal agencies both have acted on this basis and reduced diversity in state regulation of specific products, thus diminishing the potential competitive advantage an individual state attempts to create.[55]

Public Utility Commissions and Energy Regulation

The regulation of energy companies, especially electric power companies, and of local exchange telephone companies is one of the most politically visible regulatory activities of state governments. While other regulatory activities also affect many citizens, none have a more visible effect than those that determine residents' monthly energy and telephone bills. Energy and telecommunications expenses are also critical for many types of businesses. Given the importance of these industries to state development, it is useful to examine closely public utility commissions, especially with respect to the politics of policymaking and the extent to which policy can be used by a state to promote development.

Regulation of power companies, in the form of state public utility commissions, emerged as part of the reform movement early in this century (see Chapter 3). The contribution of the progressive movement to regulation was the belief that the politics of regulation could be separated from the administration of regulation. That is to say, in an independent regulatory body, fair and effective regulatory decisions could be reached by relying on objective analysis.

The ideal of the progressive movement has not bee achieved in practice. Little doubt exists that value judgments and interests are not separable from technical analysis in decision making. Thus, the environment in which regulatory decisions are made are better characterized as arenas of organized conflict; conflict is inherent in the regulatory process and fairness depends to a significant extent on procedural issues. Who is represented? With what access to information and resources? And what oversight provisions are provided?

Public utility commissions are responsible for controlling entry into local markets (awarding franchises), setting rates, and insuring quality of service in regulated firms. In terms of rate setting, decisions by commissions result from a regulated firm's request to modify an existing rate structure—that is, the price that the firm charges consumers. Utility commissions have used the rate of return basis for regulating local power utility companies and telephone companies. This approach attempts to establish rate structures that will insure a rate of return on investment sufficient to attract investment required by the utility company to guarantee its viability. Under rate of return regulation, a rate base for the firm is estimated—depreciation allowances on capital investments plus taxes—by the utility commission. This involves assigning the various costs incurred by the company to either its rate base or to operating costs. The commission must also determine what investments are necessary to maintain system quality and to meet future demand. Resolving these issues involves highly technical decision making which must heavily rely on data and information provided by the company being regulated.

Staffs of utility commissions are responsible for evaluating proposals of regulated companies, and this requires professional expertise of various types, including highly trained engineers, economists, accountants, and lawyers.[56] As firms have diversified and entered competitive, deregulated lines of business, issues of cross-subsidization and projections of future demand have become increasingly complex. For example, the revenues generated in a regulated line of business, which are produced by utility commission rate setting, should not be used to subsidize the company's operations in competitive lines of business. The expertise required to evaluate proposals has been developed by interest groups, which places additional pressure on utility commission staffs for even-handedness in their recommendations. The quality of staffs has improved and their size increased, although many commissions are unable to retain the services of their staff because of inadequate salaries.

Commission members, elected in 11 states and appointed by governors in other states, are key actors.[57] They are responsible for insuring that the regulated companies continue to be healthy enterprises and for fairness in rates for consumers. Although these objectives are not diametrically opposed, there is substantial room for conflict. Commission members must assess competing and general conflicting evaluations of proposals, interpret inadequately articulated policies from state legislatures, and reach decisions that affect virtually everyone in a state.

The political dynamics of utility regulation are well known. On one side are huge companies that are directly and significantly affected by commission decisions. Consumers, on the other hand, are directly affected, but in a relatively minor way, and it is difficult to organize consumers for purposes of affecting commission decisions. Individual consumers have limited interests in issues and may not be able to sustain their interests over a long period. Consumers are relatively weak and underdeveloped politically. However, quite a number of consumer groups, developed over the last 15 years, have been significant actors in utility regulation. National groups such as Consumers Union and Public Citizen, community groups like ACORN, associations of retired individuals, and others have focused on utility regulation. The attention of these groups may be attracted by an individual rate request by a firm or linked to issues such as licensing of nuclear reactors. Consumers have used a variety of modes to influence utility regulation, including the initiative and referendum, although these have not proven effective. Recognizing the relatively weak organizational position of consumers, legislatures have tried to represent consumers' interests by providing for a consumer advocate.[58] In addition, municipal and local governments are frequently intervenors in utility cases, not infrequently opposing the utility company's proposals.

Deregulation of Energy. The power industry is a vast industry and includes the production of energy (electricity or natural gas), the wholesaling and transportation of energy, and, finally, its sale to consumers through local distribution systems. The country has been successful in securing energy for all customers, even in hard-to-serve rural areas through such mechanisms as the Rural Electrification Administration and electrical cooperatives. Energy can be delivered either in the form of electricity or natural gas—other forms, such as fuel oil and coal, are available for industrial uses—and these compete with each other to some extent. The local service companies (that is, local distribution of electricity and gas) are regulated by state utility commissions (sometimes through local governments) through rate of return regulation and these companies are assigned exclusive local franchises. The production and transportation of electricity and natural gas are subject to other regulatory authorities, including federal agencies if interstate commerce is involved. The intergovernmental jurisdictions are quite complex.

The energy crisis of the 1970s led to various pieces of federal legislation in the late 1970s to alter national energy policy. The Public Utility Regulatory Policies Act (PURPA) in 1978 was directed at state regulation, and among its purposes was encouraging conservation and efficiency in energy and promoting cogeneration in industry and small power producers (QFs).[59] Industrial cogeneration refers to the process by which an industrial plant satisfies a portion of its own energy needs internally. Many plants require thermal energy in the form of steam. With cogeneration, the plant produces the steam and as a by-product produces electricity. Cogeneration production utilizes both oil- and gas-fired technologies. Under PURPA, electric utilities are required to purchase excess electricity produced by industrial cogeneration.

Oil and gas are common fuels for the production of electricity on both a large and a small scale. The small-scale technologies, gas and oil turbines, have been available since the end of the last century but were not used extensively by the nonpower industry because of regulatory constraints. Local distribution companies, electric and gas, were provided exclusive local franchises and thus were protected from potential competitors, but their rates were regulated and they were obligated to serve the entire community. With manufacturing firms able to produce their own power through cogeneration, under PURPA, firms purchased less electric power from the local electric company, thus reducing marginal demand. The manufacturing firm can thereby diversify energy sources and adjust its mix according to relative prices of alternative fuels. At the same time, the marginal demand reduced by cogeneration is the most expensive type of demand for electric companies to supply. In order for cogeneration to be viable for the manufacturing firm, however, the excess electricity produced by cogenerators has to be purchased by the electric utility.

California aggressively embraced the philosophy of PURPA, and the Public Utility Commission implemented a series of procedures to facilitate cogeneration and QFs.[60] In 1980, independent power sources represented less than 1 percent of capacity in California, but had expanded to 6 percent by 1988 and was predicted to reach 10 percent by 1990; this capacity made it possible to defer construction of two large coal-burning plants in the state.[61]

The increasing differential in oil and gas prices produced substantial growth in the demand for natural gas in cogeneration. The Natural Gas Policy Act of 1978 and Order No. 466 of the Federal Energy Regulatory Commission (FERC) in 1985 established a mechanism whereby natural gas interstate transportation companies could sell directly to industrial end-users, and thus bypass the local distribution company.[62] This created the potential for competition between local distribution companies and interstate transportation companies or, in other words, penetration of local franchise by the interstate gas transportation companies. The interstate companies, however, are likely not to have pipelines connected to these industrial users. Although they can construct their own facilities, another option would be to allow local distribution companies to unbundle certain services, such as the transport of the interstate companies' gas to industrial end-users, and offer these in a competitive market.[63] Other services of the local company would remain monopoly provided. State public utility commissions are given authority for determining whether the mechanism will be utilized within a state, and the legality of the mechanism is being tested in the courts.

This case demonstrates new complexity faced by utility commissions. First, state regulators have to balance several, potentially conflicting, policy objectives: to promote competitive wellhead-to-citygate prices for natural gas; to protect captive residential customers; and to protect local distribution companies which have service obligations that other firms do not. Second, the federal government initiated the policy change. It encouraged the bypass of local utility companies with technologies that had existed for many decades and encouraged decentralization of energy production, particularly through cogeneration and small power producers, as part of a national energy policy. Third, the policy strategy involved different industrial actors—electric power companies, natural gas companies, industrial cogenerators, and power users—holding divergent interests as well as environmentalists, consumers, and governments.

Problems with federal–state separation of responsibility and authority also appear. Local distribution systems may have interstate clients; thus, if a local utility is subjected to unfavorable state requirements, it may turn to federal regulatory authorities where better treatment can perhaps be found. For example, the minimum avoided cost set by the state of New York—the price a utility company pays for cogeneration electricity—was protested by Orange and Rockland Utilities, Inc., on grounds that this price restricted interstate commerce because the company's out-of-state customers would have to incur costs that would include this high avoided cost power.[64] FERC ruled in favor of the utility company, overruling the State of New York.

Public utility commissioners were established in simpler times, when clear distinctions in production, transportation, and distribution of the product could be established. The local distribution company was declared a natural monopoly, and states regulated these through rate of return regulation. The commission was an adversarial forum, where the commission rendered technically based decisions after hearing from interested parties. Reforms have improved decision making, but there are now serious complications with this forum. Technology is changing and natural monopolies are being undermined, as seen here for power generation and will be seen below for telecommunications. These very large and powerful companies may serve as natural monopolies for some products or services but operate in competitive markets for others. Many more groups now participate in the decision-making process. While the regulated industry is still the single most important actor, intervenors are better organized, more effective, and more likely to rely on extensive information and data analysis. An adversarial forum, such as the utility commissions, is not an effective one for sorting out development issues and to plan for the future strategically. Nevertheless, the link between regulatory policy and state development policy will have to be developed. The regulatory system is being pressured, by federal deregulation and technological change, but the response by the regulatory commissions and state legislatures has for the most part been ad hoc and, consequently, fragmented.

Regulation of Financial Institutions

State governments exercise substantial regulatory authority over certain financial institutions. In this section state regulation of banks, savings and loans

(S&Ls), and insurance companies is examined with particular attention to the effects of industry change, federal deregulation, and looseness of state regulation. The increasing complexity of the regulatory environment poses great challenges to states in terms of fulfilling their regulatory responsibilities and in utilizing this regulatory power as an instrument for economic development.

Banking. Regulatory mechanisms for financial institutions take various forms.[65] To prevent unwarranted competition and insure solvency, entry into the industry is controlled through charter requirements, capitalization requirements, and deposit insurance. The chartering authority must determine whether another bank is needed in the community where the bank proposes to locate. In addition, banks are regulated through portfolio restrictions. To insure financial soundness, banks are permitted to make only certain types of investments, generally involving low risk. Consumers are protected through compulsory deposit insurance.

As described in Chapter 3, the United States has used a dual banking regulatory system for most of its history and continuously since 1863. Under this system, banks and later S&Ls could choose to be chartered and supervised by either state agencies or federal agencies. Reforms early in the century included the Federal Reserve System, in 1913, which established reserve capital requirements and stabilized the entire banking system, and the Federal Deposit and Insurance Corporation (FDIC), in 1933, which established deposit insurance for banks and led to a stronger federal presence. The 1933 Banking Act included the prohibition of interest on demand deposits, the separation of commercial and investment banking, and the exemption of state nonmember banks from FDIC regulation. Although state authority had been encircled, to use Redford's term, by federal reform, state regulation was nevertheless important for specifying the types of investments that could be made by state-chartered banks and whether branch banking would be allowed in a state. The 1933 act created the structure of intergovernmental regulation that would be altered in the 1970s and 1980s in order to meet the changing conditions in the banking industry.[66]

States have fiercely guarded their regulatory prerogative over financial institutions for several reasons. First, the fear of large financial institutions dates from the colonial era and continues as a significant, though perhaps not dominant, theme in contemporary politics. Second, state-chartered banks and S&Ls are local institutions, generally controlled by local interests and as such have been protected and fostered as part of the local economy by state policy and regulation; hence the long-standing restrictions in many states, if not prohibition, against branch banking, particularly by out-of-state banks.

States have not always been successful in protecting their regulatory prerogative. The dual system of banking allows financial institutions to choose between the state or federal regulatory systems, and at various times, usually in response to major changes in regulation, financial institutions would, in large numbers, leave one system for the other. This engendered competition between states and the federal government but also allowed for creativity and innovation. Many banking innovations, such as deposit insurance and interest-bearing demand deposit accounts were first tried at the state level.

One compelling force that has affected contemporary state banking regulation is change in capital markets. Capital markets are now very diversified and provide investors a wide range of opportunities. Supported by expanding international trade as well as improved and more rapidly disseminated information, financial services are increasingly operating in world markets. The commercial banking community (and thrift industry) must compete with these many investment alternatives, including money market funds, in attracting deposits. Weakened at home by a banking crisis and abroad by the emergence of many foreign money-center banks, the banking community pressed for further deregulation in order to compete more effectively in the international marketplace.

At the state level, an interesting example of the response to this changing environment has been rapid expansion in interstate banking—the practice of allowing banks headquartered in one state to have deposit-taking operations in other states.[67] Provisions of the Federal Bank Holding Company Act of 1956 and a subsequent amendment permitted multistate banking acquisitions by holding companies if allowed under state law. In 1975, Maine became the first state to take advantage of the federal law, and in the early 1980s, Massachusetts and New York enacted laws to permit multistate acquisitions, subject to various conditions. By 1988, there were 40 states that allowed interstate banking.[68] Under reciprocal agreements, bank examination is frequently coordinated among the states' supervisory agencies. States may place conditions on interstate banks, such as examination of plans for lending to low- and moderate-income communities within a state, limits on the share of deposits that can be controlled by one institution acquired by an interstate bank, and requirements by which the incoming banks provide "net new funds" to the state.

The adoption and quick spread of interstate banking laws has been motivated by economic development goals.[69] Particularly in capital-poor states like Maine, interstate banking was perceived to be a way to augment capital supply. In addition, the regional reciprocal arrangements were justified on the grounds that large regional banks created under such arrangements would be more likely to meet the credit needs of the region than would the national, money-center banks. Some states hoped that interstate banking would result in the acquisition of troubled banks, a hope very much realized in Florida and Texas. That many states have adopted interstate banking over a relative short period was, at least in part, the result of competitive pressures under which a state believed it would be less able to attract capital by continuing the prohibition against it. In spite of the rapid adoption by states of interstate banking, pending federal legislation proposes unrestricted interstate banking which would preempt state discretion on the issue.

The proliferation of nonbank banks has also given rise to new regulatory concerns in some states. In Connecticut, corporations with nonbanking subsidiaries that engage in "banking business" must obtain permission from the commissioner of banking before initiating operations in the state. In addition, in 1988 there were 23 states that allowed state-charted banks to engage in certain types of securities activities.[70] New York, in particular, has been aggressively pursuing the relaxation of restrictions on state banks in this regard.[71] In North Carolina, banks have long been permitted to engage in insurance underwriting and in Indiana to act as insurance agents for property and casualty insurance. In 1988, there were 13 states that allowed insurance underwriting and/or acting as insurance brokers, and 23 states that allowed real estate investment.[72]

S&Ls. In 1933, federal legislation provided for chartering of S&Ls and deposit insurance was extended to them by the 1934 Federal Savings and Loan Insurance Corporation (FSLIC).[73] Similar to the dual banking system, S&Ls could choose to be chartered by states or by the federal government. As part of the New Deal strategy to revive the national economy, S&Ls were conceived as institutions to provide home mortgage loans to local area residents, thereby promoting home ownership and the housing industry. Home mortgage loans are usually repaid over several decades and, consequently, S&L funds are relatively illiquid and their earnings constrained by the fixed interest rate on home mortgage loans. To insure the viability of S&Ls, several special provisions were extended to the industry. To attract deposits, S&Ls were allowed to offer interest-bearing accounts (rates were fixed by federal legislation), unlike commercial banks which were prohibited from offering interest on demand deposits. In addition, restrictions were placed on commercial bank lending in real estate markets.

The high nominal rates of interest in the mid- to late 1970s, however, created difficulties for the S&Ls. Individual depositors could receive higher interest rates through a variety of low-risk investments, including money markets. In addition, commercial banks were permitted to offer interest-bearing demand deposit accounts as a result of the Depository Institutions Deregulation and Monetary Control Act of 1980 and the Garn–St. Germain Depository Institutions Act of 1981. Unable to increase interest rates on their deposits, S&Ls could not attract capital. In addition, the fixed interest rate on their long-term home mortgage loans fell well below the prevailing market interest rate.

In response to these difficulties and relying on federal enabling legislation, particularly the Garn–St. Germain Act, regulators in many states allowed easier entry into the S&L industry by lowering the required capital asset ratios, allowed S&Ls to undertake higher-risk investment, and permitted S&Ls to hold equity positions in commercial projects.[74] For example, in California, Florida, and Texas, S&Ls could take 100 percent equity positions in commercial buildings. In California, after a conversion of over half of the state-chartered S&Ls to federal charters between 1980 and 1982, in order to take advantage of the powers granted under federal law, the remaining state-charted S&Ls were permitted to invest in junk bonds.[75]

Many states were ill-prepared to examine and supervise the newly aggressive S&Ls. Unwise investment strategies and the declining value of real estate in the last half of the 1980s resulted in a dramatic increase in nonperforming loan portfolios in S&Ls, particularly in California, Texas, and Florida. The assets they acquired through loan defaults were frequently worth less than the value of the original loan, and as a result many S&Ls failed. The value of commercial real estate was also adversely affected by changes in the federal tax code in 1986. Several state insurance funds for S&Ls failed and the federal insurance fund, FSLIC, was also unable to deal with the extensive S&L failures. After several years of very large infusion of federal funding, the FSLIC was replaced as the insurer of thrifts by the FDIC in 1989. Although the source of the S&L debacle originated in the high rate of inflation of the 1970s, the real estate boom and bust in the 1980s, and deregulation of interest-bearing checking accounts, regulation of state-chartered S&Ls failed to insure the viability of these S&Ls. Although some states were more successful than others, the ultimate liability of federal insurance for S&L deposits created a compelling argument for federal preemption of state regulation of S&Ls.

Not all states performed poorly in regulation of financial institutions. A number of states, including Georgia, Illinois, Michigan, New York, and Virginia, appear quite effective in regulating S&Ls and banks. Contributing to their effectiveness are salaries commensurate with the market for well-trained examiners, substantial investment in training of examiners, and improved data bases.[76]

The recent history of state regulation of the thrift industry presents several interesting points. The earlier intergovernmental structure was rendered inadequate by high inflation and change in capital markets. To compensate, the federal government relaxed regulation of interest rates on deposits and of portfolio investments. Some states took advantage of this federal action and, ever sensitive to local businesses, permitted much greater flexibility on the part of state-chartered S&Ls. Federal insurance facilitated the generous and liberal action taken by some states. The states that avoided widespread S&L failures appear to have done so as a result of strong regulatory agencies which were able to exercise independent and thorough examination and supervision. Actions in certain states, however, contributed to deepening the crisis, and federal regulatory change and preemption has dramatically decreased the role of state regulation in this industry.

Insurance. Insurance regulation represents a form of state regulation quite unlike any other. The federal government to date has had a very limited regulatory role. Although Meier convincingly argues that the industry is complex and consists of many interest groups, which limits somewhat the ability of the industry to prevail on regulatory issues, the industry nevertheless has been more successful in obtaining satisfactory regulatory outcomes than other regulated industries.[77]

The industry successfully argued for exemption from federal antitrust regulation (granted under the McCarran–Ferguson Act of 1945; see Chapter 3) on the basis of the unique product of the industry. Products—that is, insurance policies—must be priced in current terms based on forecasts of future costs. Sharing of actuarial data among companies helps improve the estimate of future costs, the industry argues, but it also creates the appearance of collusion on rate-setting and thus a potential violation of antitrust regulations. Although the elimination of the antitrust exemption, through the repeal of McCarran–Ferguson, continues to be debated, states remain the principal regulatory actor for the industry. Although state regulation has improved in recent years, many insurance commissions are still underfunded, unable to manage and analyze the extensive data bases found in the industry.[78]

Like banks and S&Ls, insurance companies must effectively manage their assets—insure the value of the assets and the interest they accrue—in order to be able to meet future claims by policyholders. The high inflation rates, high nominal interest rates, the recession of the early 1980s, and the real estate boom and bust affected insurance companies in ways similar to those described above for the banking and thrift industries. These pressures led to the liability insurance crisis of the mid-1980s. The crisis was particularly visible because it affected many parts of society, including nonprofit organizations, local governments, doctors, and others.[79] The industry attributed the rapid increase in liability insurance rates to the adverse economic conditions as well as to greatly expanded litigation in commercial liability. Insurance commissions were unable to cope with the crisis, and both the industry and consumers did not find satisfactory outcomes there.

Further public and political concern developed as a result of several dramatic insurer insolvencies at the end of the 1980s.[80] In two insolvencies, Mission Insurance Company (commercial and workers' compensation insurance) and Transit Casualty Company (property/casualty insurance), blame was placed on the inadequacy of state regulation of managing general agents, on whom the insurance companies relied for sales and investments, and of reinsurance companies. The failures of California companies Executive Life Insurance Company and First Capital Life Insurance Company (both life insurance companies), the result of a heavily weighted high-risk junk bond portfolio, have placed around a million policyholders and annuity holders under jurisdiction of state regulators.[81] Mutual Benefit Life Insurance Company of New Jersey was taken over by the state insurance commission, a result of problems created by the weak real estate market and of its $13.8 billion in assets, 40 percent of which were in real estate loans.[82]

In recent history of the insurance industry has created enormous concern for policyholders and state and federal governments. Many fear that the state guaranty funds are inadequate and that if insurer insolvencies grow, a bailout and regulatory intervention by the federal government will perhaps be required.[83] Legislative action, both at the federal level, to repeal McCarran–Ferguson, and at the state level to remove the antitrust exemption became one focus.[84] Federal standards for state regulation of insurance solvency as well as direct federal regulation are both being considered.

State regulation of the insurance industry is a latecomer to reform. State regulators have had an inordinate amount of authority and independence, as compared to regulation of other industries but state agencies are viewed as relatively weak and understaffed. The revolving door, by which individuals leave regulatory agencies for employment in the regulated industry, is overworked. Although the industry's complexity creates enormous challenges for effective regulation, the regulatory process itself has tended to ignore consumer interests. One notable change in the configuration of resources of the various policy actors during the 1980s was that consumer organizations developed their own data sources and analytic capabilities and thereby became more powerful adversaries in the regulatory process. In addition, rate payers are turning to the referendum and initiative. Proposition 103 in California, approved in November 1988 (but immediately submitted for judicial review), which called for insurance rate roll-backs, generated great turmoil in the industry.[85] These interests have found other avenues for affecting the industry and as a result of expanded participation of the public, the industry appears ripe for regulatory reform, if not initiated by states themselves, then by Congress.

The crisis in the insurance industry has effectively postponed discussions of how insurance regulation can be used for development purposes. Effective regulation should produce a healthy insurance industry and fair rates, that is, rates comparable to those in other states. Although abnormally low rates may lead to a weakened industry, a variety of state and local policies, such as building codes, seat belt laws, and effective health and safety enforcement, may produce a state with lower claims and, consequently, lower rates for certain types of insurance.

State action in the insurance industry can have a very dramatic effect on development. In response to a series of hurricanes on the Gulf Coast in the 1960s, the State of Texas passed the Catastrophe Property Insurance Pool Act of 1971. The act established the Catastrophe Property Insurance Pool Association (CPIPA) for issuing wind and hail insurance policies, and all companies writing such coverage in the state are required to be members. The required premiums members pay to the CPIPA are used to cover claims; state government assumes any losses in excess of $100 million. Prior to the act, insurance for construction along the Gulf Coast was either unavailable or prohibitively expensive. The tremendous construction boom that occurred on the coast in the late seventies and eighties is in part attributable to this act. State governments do have considerable power to require cooperation among businesses and firms to overcome such market failures, particularly in the financial sector, but these powers are rarely exercised.[86]

The fact that the insurance industry is subject to only state regulation has generated a number of unique initiatives to promote the industry. As discussed in Chapter 3, early in the country's history states protected locally owned insurance companies in order to secure an important tax base. Protection was afforded through a number of mechanisms, such as discriminatory taxing against firms from other states. In addition, until the repeal of the Robertson law in 1963, life insurance firms in Texas had to invest 75 percent of their reserves set aside for future claims by Texas residents in Texas securities and properties.[87] The efforts in several states to benefit the industry by relaxing investment restrictions, especially those on real estate and junk bonds, led to drastic consequences. Although the U.S. Constitution prohibits interstate tariffs and the interstate commerce clause provides for a federal role in insuring unimpaired interstate trade, some states have used their unique regulatory position to promote development through providing protection to the local insurance industry. The severity of the insurance crisis, however, is likely to produce federal policy that will reduce the freedom of action currently enjoyed by state regulation of insurance.

Implications for Development

State regulation of utilities and of financial institutions represents intervention in the marketplace and thus holds potential as an instrument for promoting development. The principal objectives of these various forms of regulation, however, do not include development. In all cases, an agreement between the regulated industries and the public provide some benefit to the industries (for example, exclusive franchise or reduced level of competition) in return for some benefit to consumers (for example, protection of deposits or nondiscriminatory utility rates). Successful regulation should bring market stability and relatively efficient prices. Exercise of this regulatory role is no easy task. Legislatures and regulatory agencies must contend with powerful local constituencies that may well define economic development in their own narrow terms, such as increased returns to the regulated industries or lower prices to consumers. But states operate with limited control and authority in a changing intergovernmental regulatory structure in which the federal government has been moving toward deregulation. Industry change, as in the substantial expansion and segmentation in capital markets, and technological change, as in energy generation and telecommunications, further complicates state regulation. That the state record is mixed should come as no surprise.

Although a number of states are exemplary in fulfilling their regulatory responsibilities over financial institutions and state innovation has frequently been adopted by the federal government, the overall record of the last decade is rather dismal. A number of contributing factors were beyond the control of state regulators—such as the high rate of inflation in the late 1970s, the high real interest rates of the 1980s, and federal legislation that allowed for higher risk-taking by financial institutions—but the performance of state regulation left much to be desired. The issue of financial regulation has become salient and subject to further federal control, if not takeover, as in the case of S&Ls.

Several points can be drawn concerning the potential effect of state regulation on economic development. First, the ability to adapt regulatory action to promote economic development is frequently constrained by the purpose of the particular regulatory action and by the institutions that have developed around the regulatory process. Lowering prices, for utilities or insurance, might establish a comparative advantage for a state in the short run but if these weaken the industry, long-term development may be jeopardized. The regulated industry has frequently been strengthened by the regulatory process itself and the industry may be weakened or threatened by reformulating the objective of regulation to be one of economic growth.

Furthermore, the regulatory process has become an institutional setting for resolving conflict among the various interested parties. As PUCs and other regulatory bodies become more technically capable and consumers better informed and less hesitant to use the initiative and referendum, conflict is heightened and the regulated industry exerts relatively less influence.[88] As a result, significant pressures already exist to keep prices low, which is consistent with an economic development objective. However, the specific framework of regulation, either a narrow focus on rate of return pricing or restrictions on types of investment to guarantee solvency, may not be conducive for addressing the impact of technological and industry change.

With regard to regulation of financial regulation, other concerns emerge. Availability of capital is a major factor for economic development. These institutions—commercial banks, S&Ls, and insurance companies—are major sources of capital and important elements of state and local economies. These industries belong to the produce services sector, which was observed in Chapter 2 to be experiencing very rapid employment growth. State regulators must guarantee solvency to protect consumers, which generally involves restricting the ways in which capital can be used especially in limiting high-risk investments of the very type needed for nurturing new firms. Bad regulatory decisions, of which there have been a recent abundance, can have very negative and wide-ranging consequences. There are other instances, however, of wise state policy creating substantial benefits broadly shared.

Undoubtedly, some regulatory activities unduly restrict economic activity. Though state professional licensing may serve some legitimate and useful purposes, it does restrict entry in the market and consequently reduces competition. State regulatory activities, in addition, have accumulated over decades and as the economy and society evolve, it is only to be expected that traditional forms may no longer be necessary and that new forms of regulatory activities may arise. Many of the populist constraints on banking, such as prohibition of multistate banking, from the early part of the century are being dropped. When constraints are dropped, however, rarely will there be no losers. If regulation is viewed as a means to resolve conflict, it is obvious that regulation itself creates winners and losers and that deregulation will also have winners and losers irrespective of the impact on economic development. In any event, it is unlikely that the objective of economic development will be, or even should be, a decisive factor in regulatory decision making.

LABOR LAWS

The history of labor laws in the United States is one of extensive interaction of federal and state legislation, frequently based on different interpretations of state and federal responsibilities under the interstate commerce law. As labor started bringing its demands to the political arena around the turn of this century, the federal government took little action. Labor found a more receptive environment in a number of states, and laws were introduced concerning minimum wage, child labor, unemployment, and workers' compensation, although federal action was found in certain areas, such as railroad worker legislation. The federal role became more aggressive during the New Deal. The federal government, through the Department of Labor, National Emergency Council, and National Recovery Administration, actively encouraged states to adopt various labor laws.[89] In addition, the Social Security Act of 1935 provided various types of insurance coverage for workers, and the Wagner Act of 1935, which facilitated union organizing, and various laws setting national minimum labor standards substantially expanded the role of the federal government in labor matters. Limitations of the ability of federal government to regulate intrastate commerce, however, meant that state government would retain a critical role in labor law and programs.

The interplay between state and federal government, resulting in substantial variation among states, can be seen in laws affecting organized labor. The Wagner Act substantially expanded the power of organized labor in negotiations with management. The Taft–Hartley Act of 1947 curtailed the power of unions and provided a critical role for state governments in labor law.[90] The act delegated to states the power to establish union shop agreements. Under the union shop agreement, all employees are required to join a union if the local unit wins an election. States can prohibit these agreements through "right-to-work" (RTW) laws. In states with RTW laws, companies can hire nonunion workers even when the union has won an election in the company. In 1990, there were 22 states, including all of the Southern states, that had RTW laws.[91]

Much research has been conducted on the effect of RTW laws on wages, unionization, and economic development.[92] Though levels of unionization and wage rates are relatively low in RTW states, it is difficult to attribute these levels to the law itself rather than to predominating cultural attitudes which produce both the RTW law and low levels of unionization. The evidence concerning the effect on industrial location patterns of RTW laws—the question most relevant for economic development policy—is also unclear.

Many southern states experienced rapid growth after passing RTW laws in the 1950s. However, much of the postwar industrialization in the South occurred in nationally slow-growing, labor-intensive sectors, which were decentralizing from the industrial heartland of the country, as discussed in Chapter 2. These sectors were attracted to the low real-wage levels of relatively unskilled labor in the South.[93] The adoption of RTW laws coincided with these national location patterns and to the extent that such laws were significant, research suggests that they produce an initial effect that quickly diminishes with time.[94]

The rapidly growing advanced technology sectors have not demonstrated the same location patterns of traditional manufacturing industries. At one end, research and development activities are attracted to centers with highly skilled workers; wage levels are virtually unimportant. At the manufacturing end, the search is often for low-wage areas, particularly where women have been involved in the manufacturing process. When these trends are coupled with slow employment growth in traditional manufacturing, high rates of growth in the service sectors, and a broad decline in level of unionization throughout the country, the ability of states to influence rates of economic growth through RTW laws seems very limited. Their symbolic value, however, appears to remain strong.

The development and adoption of labor laws in the United States has been the result of two principal factors: (1) political action from labor itself and from aligned elements such as religious groups for expanded protection, and (2) the political struggle between labor and business on assigning the costs of this protection. These factors, which have played out in the context of a complex intergovernmental framework, have produced a system of national labor standards, but one in which variation can be found among states in terms of levels of benefits and enforcement mechanisms. The imposition of an economic development strategy by state government through labor laws is problematic, for reasons similar to those found above for regulation. A strategy to lower the costs of labor by maintaining weak labor laws and low standards may attract some firms, particularly labor-intensive, low-wage firms. However, such policies may also create an environment in which skilled labor will not be found, hence creating a disadvantage for the state in terms of attracting other types of firms. Weak standards or low levels of enforcement of safety standards may result in higher rates of work-related accidents and produce higher workers' compensation rates to cover the excessive accident claims.

The degree of involvement of labor in the elaboration of state economic development policies and programs varies among states as do their labor laws. Labor's participation in development policy formulation depends on two factors: its political strength in a state and the degree to which poor labor relations are perceived to be an impediment to growth. In a number of states, such as Pennsylvania, Michigan, Massachusetts, and Rhode Island, labor representatives have been directly involved in policy development. The MILRITE Council in Pennsylvania has been effective in a policy development role, due in no small part to the active and full participation of labor. In a quite different form of labor participation, many states have established labor-management programs with the expectation that improving labor relations will enhance the attractiveness of the state.[95] In some cases, encouraging labor participation in workplace innovation is itself the policy objective.[96] The role of labor in development policy and the specific set of labor laws in a state will, in any event, be determined by internal political outcomes and not significantly influenced by competition for out-of-state firms.

RELATIONS WITH LOCAL GOVERNMENTS

Local governments are created and empowered by state governments, and substantial variation among the states exists in their exercise of this responsibility.

Some variation can be traced to the historical development of communities. In New England, townships were given broad powers, while in the West, county governments were provided extensive powers perceived to be required in the settlement of the frontier.[97] Although the form of local government varied, powers provided to local governments were strictly limited to those explicitly prescribed by state law or implicitly required to exercise these powers as a result of Dillon's rule. In the *City of Clinton v. Cedar Rapids and Missouri Railroad Co.*, Judge John F. Dillon construed powers of local government very narrowly, and his decision set the pattern for subsequent interpretation.[98]

States have allowed local governments to proliferate. In 1987, there were some 83,000 local governmental units, including municipal governments, townships, county governments, school districts, and a multitude of special districts.[99] The relative size of these local governments can be seen in Table 4.4, which provides expenditures, in constant dollars, by type of government during recent decades. The large number of local governments creates a highly fragmented governmental system. Special districts, which include districts for roads, water and wastewater systems, health care and hospitals, parks, and airports, among others, are justified on two principal grounds. First, such districts allow local communities to determine their own level and quality of service, and, second, the community alone incurs the cost of the service. Special districts also allow states, municipalities, and counties to avoid incurring the responsibility for providing that service. Governments under fiscal stress are likely to value this aspect of special districts.

Special districts and the fragmented local government system are widely criticized, and there has been some consolidation of governmental units, especially among school districts. Potential economies of scale may not be realized when services, such as water and wastewater treatment systems, are provided on a limited scale in small special districts. In addition, abuse of special districts, particularly in developer-owned districts, is well documented, though perhaps not widespread.[100] A major problem with special districts and fragmentation in general is the potential they hold for producing inequities in service provision through the segregation of tax bases according to levels of wealth. Property-rich areas create their own governmental jurisdictions and provide levels of service substantially superior to those of property-poor districts. In an extensive study of governmental fragmentation in St. Louis, the loss of economies of scale was not detected, partly as a result of intergovernmental cooperation, but significant inequalities in service provision, linked to tax-base differences, were.[101] Delivery of services in distressed communities was not found to be equal to that in wealthier areas.

During the urban crisis of the 1960s, policy leadership for urban problems was assumed by the federal government, as discussed in Chapter 3, and the intergovernmental framework was subsequently affected. Due to the inability of states to respond to the growing problems of cities, as a result both of constitutional and governmental structure issues but, more important, to the lack of political will, the federal government implemented programs using states as

Table 4.4
Direct General Expenditures by Type of Local Government: 1955–1989 ($100 Million in Constant 1982 Dollars)

	STATE	LOCAL					
		Total	Municipal	County	School District	Townships	Special District
1955	411	828	289	170	300	38	31
1960	581	1098	379	214	408	42	55
1965	773	1432	466	296	544	56	70
1970	1161	1966	649	406	750	67	95
1971	1272	2122	710	447	788	72	105
1972	1334	2254	757	480	822	82	114
1973	1359	2299	776	497	830	82	114
1974	1369	2309	776	502	832	81	118
1975	1456	2414	809	521	881	83	120
1976	1519	2531	838	561	923	86	124
1977	1538	2518	811	576	918	88	125
1978	1558	2535	818	582	923	89	123
1979	1585	2563	812	591	920	95	145
1980	1677	2609	822	600	941	93	154
1981	1707	2607	823	605	930	91	158
1982	1707	2628	834	616	931	89	158
1983	1768	2704	845	632	960	93	173
1984	1869	2804	873	656	989	96	191
1985	2016	2963	922	695	1049	100	199
1986	2149	3163	979	748	1123	106	207
1987	2236	3331	1020	803	1173	112	223
1988	2313	3477	1065	827	1225	121	238
1989	2406	3607	1076	869	1284	129	249

Source: Advisory Commission on Intergovernmental Relations, Significant Features of Fiscal Federalism, vol. 2 (Washington, D.C., 1990), Table 40, p. 70.

administrative elements and in other cases working directly with municipal governments.[102]

The reforms in state government and the shifts in federal–state relations, described in Chapter 3, have fortunately filtered through to state–local relations.[103] Although the Dillon rule still holds in some states, many states have provided local governments greater flexibility and discretion in the exercise of their responsibilities through such mechanisms as home rule, devolution of authority, and annexation and consolidation laws.[104] States have required personnel and budgetary management reform in local government.[105] Similar to the way in which the political process allows states, through lobbying and elections, to check the power of the federal government, local governments and citizens hold a check on state government.

State governments have also attempted to compensate for the reduction in federal aid to local governments during the 1980s, especially after 1983 (see Figure 4.1). Local government's own source revenues, however, have risen even more rapidly than state aid. Contributing to this increase are the unfunded mandates imposed on local government by the federal government and by many states. As states have provided local governments more discretion and increased aid, many states have shifted financial burdens to local governments.[106] This practice, however, has caused significant problems in a number of states, and tentative steps are being taken to reduce such burdens on cities.[107] The fiscal stress in many cities is quite severe, reflected in the extreme case by the bankruptcy filing of Bridgeport, Connecticut, in 1991. In spite of additional aid from states and increasing local revenue generation, the financial obligations of cities and continuing suburbanization of jobs and population insure that fiscal crisis in cities will persist through the 1990s.

Among the discretionary power states can extend to local governments are a number of directly related to economic development issues. The use of tax incentives or abatement by local governments generally requires authorization by state governments. In addition, bonding authority and the formation of local development corporations are dependent on state action. Special economic development programs such as enterprise zones or tax increment finance districts are subject to state authorization. In the 1980s, most states adopted enabling legislation for these types of efforts.

States and local governments have many areas of shared responsibilities and concerns and relations between these two levels of government have become more complex. These relationships have become closer due both to the decline in federal involvement in several policy areas and to changes in economic conditions, especially with respect to tax capacity. States have made progress in addressing state–local relations, but many challenges remain.[108]

Targeting Distressed Communities

As the result of a complex set of historical, economic, political, and social forces, economic distress in the United States tends to be geographically con-

Figure 4.1
Local Government per Capita Revenues and Aid: 1952–1989 (Constant 1982 Dollars)

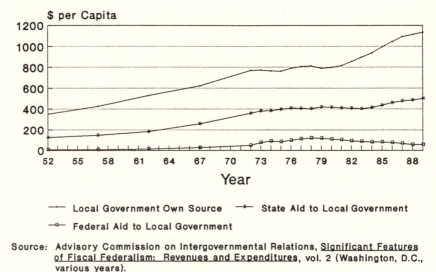

$ per Capita

Year

—— Local Government Own Source   —*— State Aid to Local Government

—□— Federal Aid to Local Government

Source: Advisory Commission on Intergovernmental Relations, <u>Significant Features</u> <u>of Fiscal Federalism: Revenues and Expenditures</u>, vol. 2 (Washington, D.C., various years).

centrated. The concentration is found in rural areas within regions, such as the Mississippi River delta and Appalachia in the South or the border area of South Texas. Small towns in formerly prospering natural resource areas such as the coal towns of Pennsylvania and the Mesabi Iron Range area of Minnesota are also examples of geographically based distressed communities. In cities, economic distress is also common. Large and mid-size cities have their ghettos and barrios. Worker displacement and plant closings during the 1980s also created severe economic distress in cities such as Gary, Indiana and Flint, Michigan.

The intergovernmental dimension of aid to distressed communities has followed a course similar to other policy areas during the 1980s. Although distressed communities in general have been politically weak, national organizations have formed for purposes of protecting service delivery systems funded by the federal government.[109] Such groups emerged during the expansion of federal programs of the Great Society period. The attempt of the Reagan administration to move toward block grants and reduce funding led to the formation of an Ad Hoc Coalition on Block Grants to resist such changes. Although the coalition met with moderate success, the fiscal stress in federal government suggests that lobbying efforts of such interest groups will be redirected toward state and local governments. The Ad Hoc Coalition, however, articulated the problem with this strategy in noting that distressed communities typically do not fare well in terms of priorities for state governments.[110] Other work has demonstrated that the higher the degree of federal involvement in social welfare programs, the less the per capita variation in aid among states.[111]

Although states may have been simply ill-prepared in terms of technical competency and political will to address economic distress in earlier decades, there are significant structural impediments to state initiatives. Given the spatial concentration of distress, inadequate local tax bases complicate efforts of local governments to provide relief themselves. In addition, residents in many distressed areas vote in relatively low proportions and tend not to be active politically, which further undermines the ability of such communities to affect policy. Some states have constitutional constraints against preferential treatment to firms, thus limiting the ability to create tax incentives for specific geographical regions.[112] Special treatment of certain geographical areas can also create a political backlash from those areas not receiving the special treatment.

The ability of states to target is constrained by the geographic representation of state legislatures. Targeting implies special treatment for some areas, and to organize coalitions to support such treatment is difficult. New York's attempt at geographic targeting was difficult to sustain because additional areas of the state secured eligibility, thus diluting the potential impact of the targeted program.[113] Hansen found that party competition and strength of the governor vis-à-vis the state legislatures were the significant factors in determining the extent of geographic targeting, but, in any event, such targeting is difficult to maintain over time.[114] Strategic planning, discussed earlier in this chapter, rarely included representatives of labor and, virtually never, representatives of distressed communities.

Although the initial phase of state activism did not focus on distressed communities, the range of efforts has broadened and the frequency of state adoption of targeted strategies has increased (see Table 4.5). One of the most widely used tools is the enterprise zone.[115] The notion of an enterprise zone was proposed in federal legislation in the early 1980s (Garcia–Kemp) and endorsed by the Reagan administration. Based on a program in England, the proposed legislation was designed to attract investment to designated distressed areas through a variety of incentives including lowered tax rates and reduced regulation. Although federal legislation was never approved, 32 states had adopted enabling legislation by 1990 (see Table 4.5). States have continued to pursue this strategy on their own, adding additional elements such as infrastructure investments and small business development efforts in the zones.

Some success in addressing the problems of distressed communities can be found in other policy areas. Significant state equalization of aid occurs for public education and to some extent for welfare, but rarely for other types of services.[116] In addition, states have experimented in a number of program areas. Workfare programs, included in the recent federal welfare reform legislation, were first tested by state governments. States and localities are developing housing programs. Many states have built on the federal Community Reinvestment Act and

Table 4.5
Growth in Targeted State Development Programs: 1980–1990

	1980		1983		1990[1]
	States	Programs	States	Programs	States
Site Development	3	4	8	9	n/a
Financial Aid	12	22	18	33	n/a
Enterprise Zone	0	0	19	21	32
Job Training	5	5	12	12	n/a
Small Business Development	7	9	8	10	35
Minority and Disadvantaged Person Business Development	21	25	26	33	35
Industrial Revenue Bonds	10	10	11	11	n/a
Support of Community-based organizations	n/a	n/a	n/a	n/a	19
Linked-Deposit Programs	n/a	n/a	n/a	n/a	8

Source: Advisory Commission on Intergovernmental Relations, The State and Distressed Communities: 1983 Update (Washington, D.C., November 1985), pp. 82, 89, 95, 98, 104, 105, and 109; Barbara Puls, "Building Communities that Work: Community Economic Development" (Denver, CO: National Conference of State Legislatures, January 1991).

[1]From National Conference of State Legislatures Survey.

require an assessment by regulators on the record of the institutions' funding to low-income communities. State governments also attempt to influence lending through linked-deposit programs which use the deposit of government funds as leverage on bank lending.

Even though distressed communities themselves have limited influence on state policy, many community-based organizations have made significant improvements to community life. Occasionally, these efforts have benefited from state aid. For the most part, however, states have not developed effective policies for distressed communities; if, however, the argument made here concerning political decentralization is correct, greater political activism of distressed communities can be expected in the future. In addition, these underdeveloped or underutilized human resources represent a substantial drag on future economic growth. As a result, there is a strong development argument for ameliorating the conditions of distressed communities in states.

CONCLUSIONS

That governors and state legislators actively engage in promoting economic development in a state should come as no surprise. State legislators are directly bound to their constituents, including economic constituents, and indirectly bound to the state's economy in that it is ultimately the source of tax revenue. The difficulty faced by state legislatures and governors is that economic and political change has rendered a number of traditional state practices and strategies inappropriate or ineffective. The search for new means of action is conducted in the midst of intensive competition among and within states for investment. Industries themselves are adapting to new economic circumstances. Not all innovation and adaptation is successful. It quickly became evident that not all states would be able to create a Silicon Valley, and imitation gave way to policies honed to the economic circumstances of individual states. On the other hand, state tax incentives, although of questionable value, continue to be politically popular and widely used. Legislative attention to the local economy and local businesses gone awry was also seen in the ill-fated deregulation of S&Ls and lax regulation of insurance companies in some states.

Strategic planning by states in the early 1980s represents one response to economic uncertainty and change. The quick diffusion of the strategic planning approach reflects not only the levels of economic distress and uncertainty found in the country, but also an element of competition in which a state undertook strategic planning so as not to fall behind other states. Although these efforts can be criticized for not leading to immediate action, it was through these exercises that the policy agenda for economic development was redefined.

The broad range of activities of state government provides ample opportunity for states to be involved in economic development; indeed, through its activities—taxation, program and infrastructure provision, regulation, and others—states play an important role in a state's economy whether or not development is part of that agenda. As seen in the historical account of state government and economic development in Chapter 3, the basic modes of intervention date from early decades of the nation. Although the broad range of activities provides states with many options, the ability of a state to use these functions to promote development, however, is conditioned by a number of factors. These include an ever-evolving system of intergovernmental relations, technological change, potentially conflicting state policy objectives, state politics, and fiscal stress.

The principal purpose of tax policy is to raise revenue. Many states have been slow to adapt tax structures to economic change. Traditional tax sources, such as property taxes and severance taxes, are not adequate revenue sources. Revision of tax structures was part of state government reform, but these structures still do not adequately cover the growing sector of the economy, the service sector, in many states. State competition has contributed to revision of tax structures and to reductions of tax rates, especially on business. Reduction in tax rates has been driven by taxpayers' revolts and hard bargaining by the business community, reinforced by competition among states for investment. These pressures on state fiscal policy are not likely to change in the foreseeable future and, consequently, guarantee continued fiscal stress in state and local governments. A substantial increase in funds for development purposes will not be available.

In terms of regulation, the historical perspective presented in the last chapter and the analysis of this chapter reflect a complex policymaking environment and suggest that state regulation can rarely be used for development purposes. There are several reasons for this conclusion. The purpose of much economic regulation is to control the actions of individual firms in order to serve some public purpose. In the case of natural monopolies—local service utilities—regulation is expected to result in fair and affordable rates for consumers but also economically viable utility firms. Such a scenario will not necessarily lead to rates so low that firms will be attracted to the state nor to utility companies earning supranormal profits.

Although state regulation may not be an effective instrument for development, it is nevertheless an important policy issue. In a simplified model of state regulation, there are two parties: the regulated industry and the consumers of that industry's product. In our historical account, we have seen that regulation of industries (economic regulation as opposed to social regulation) was susceptible to capture by industry. Regulation itself was even favored by industry in some instances. At times an industry or firm would favor state regulation and at other times federal regulation, and frequently the two were played against each other.

There is substantial variation in the effectiveness of state regulation among industries as well as among states for a given industry. The poorest record is found in state regulation of financial institutions. Although the financial institutions have suffered from forces beyond the control of state regulators, such as high rates of inflation, busts in real estate markets and others, state regulation exacerbated the S&L crisis in a number of states. The experience with banks and insurance companies may prove to be not much better. Two points are particularly important. The forms of financial regulation—regulating investment portfolios to insure solvency and regulating market entry to prevent excessive competition—are not very salient. Certainly they are much less visible than utility regulation rates confronted by consumers each month in the form of utility bills. In addition, regulatory reform at the state level for the financial industries has been slow in coming. With the increased discretion provided by federal legislation in the early 1980s, intended to enhance competitiveness in financial industries and make capital available, states provided greater flexibility to the industry. As a result of the crisis in these industries and the poor performance by states, regulatory reform is being sought both by Congress and consumers.

Change in the regulated industries, occurring for various reasons, complicates state regulation. The local exclusive utility franchise is being eroded, both by federal action and by technological change. Federal initiatives for deregulation of energy and technological change in the production of power, in cogeneration for example, have given firms substantial production flexibility, and the notion of a natural monopoly is undermined. The diversity in the structure of the regulated industries, operating in both regulated and nonregulated markets, complicates rate-setting by public utility commissions.

Vastly more public participation, especially on behalf of consumers in regulatory decision making, has tended to diminish the relative influence of the regulated industry. In some states, consumers are represented by a publicly funded counsel, and in virtually all states advocate groups are very active. The public also uses initiative and referendum as a means to express preferences in utility regulation. Although the opportunity for the regulated industry to capture the regulatory process is diminished, the regulated industry will remain a powerful force in the regulatory process.

The notion that scientific regulation could be separated entirely from value articulation and politics, the original conception for public utility commissions, has been displaced. The necessity of technical assessment in regulation, however, has clearly been established. The contemporary politics of regulation insures that extensive analysis is available for decision making. Utility commission staffs, the regulated firms, and intervenors produce their own analysis. The information base and analysis supporting various, often conflicting, positions are quite strong. The result is that the conflict is based on a broader understanding of the various interests, and this helps clarify various values inherent in regulation; it does not, however, make decision making any easier.

The relations between states and local governments have likewise been affected by economic change and political decentralization. States have generally increased the powers of local government, although not uniformly. Local governments must also address the challenges that structural change has brought, and in several respects, state governments have taken action to aid these governments. State action has been insufficient in aid to distressed communities. As in Congress, the political will to address problems of distressed populations has not been strong in most state legislatures. In spite of severe budget constraints, states are beginning to be more responsive to these communities, and the process of political decentralization and the concern for development may produce a higher priority for their complex problems.

NOTES

1. Fantus Company, *Ranking of the States by Business Climate* (Chicago, 1975).

2. Wallace W. Biermann, "The Validity of Business Climate Rankings: A Test," *Industrial Development* (March/April 1984): 17.

3. Robert P. Hartwig, "The Ratings Game: Will the Winner Please Stand Up?" *Illinois Business Review*, vol. 46, no. 1 (February 1989): 9–12; Rodney A. Erickson, "Business Climate Studies: A Critical Evaluation," *Economic Development Quarterly*, vol. 1., no. 1 (1987): 62–71; Biermann, "The Validity of Business Climate Rankings," Charles L. Skoro, "Rankings of State Business Climates," *Economic Development Quarterly*, vol. 2 (May 1988): 138–153.

4. Jurgen Schmandt and Robert H. Wilson, eds., *Promoting High-Technology Industry: Initiatives and Policies for State Governments* (Boulder, CO: Westview Press, 1987): 22–23; California Commission on Industrial Innovation, "Winning Technologies: A New Industrial Strategy for California and the Nation," Sacramento, 1981.

5. Gerald D. Nash, *State Government and Economic Development: A History of*

Administrative Policies in California, 1849–1933 (Berkeley, CA: Institute of Governmental Studies, 1964): Parts II and III.

6. Schmandt and Wilson, eds., *Promoting High-Technology Industry*, p. 24; Karen M. Padget, "State Government–University Cooperation," in *Growth Policy in the Age of High Technology: The Role of Regions and States*, edited by Jurgen Schmandt and Robert H. Wilson (Boston: Unwin-Hyman, 1990): 364–368.

7. This articulation of goals is taken from Minnesota Wellspring, "Minnesota Wellspring: A Call for Action, 1986," St. Paul, 1985; Sidney Bailey Hacker and Robert D. Sommerfeld, "Minnesota," in *Promoting High-Technology*, edited by Schmandt and Wilson, pp. 119–122.

8. Hacker and Sommerfeld, "Minnesota," p. 120.

9. Schmandt and Wilson, eds., *Promoting High-Technology Industry*, p. 107.

10. Task Force on Technology-Intensive Industries, "Report to Commissioner of Economic Development on Technology-Intensive Industry in Minnesota and Its Future," St. Paul, January 1981.

11. Harold Fischer and Amy Miriam Peck, "New York" in *Promoting High-Technology Industry*, edited by Schmandt and Wilson, Chapter 6; Frank, J. Mauro and Glen Yago, "State Government Targeting in Economic Development: The New York Experience," *Publius: The Journal of Federalism*, vol. 19 (Spring 1989): 65–74.

12. Batelle Columbus Division, *Final Report: A Strategy for the Development of High-Technology Activities in New York State* (Columbus, OH: Batelle Institute, 1982).

13. Mark Howard and Mary Kragie, "North Carolina," in *Promoting High-Technology Industry*, edited by Schmandt and Wilson, pp. 170–175.

14. Brian Muller, "Texas," in *Promoting High-Technology Industry*, edited by Schmandt and Wilson, pp. 242–243.

15. State of Texas, Office of the Governor, "Texas 2000 Commission Report and Recommendations," Austin, March 1982.

16. Hilary Silver and Dudley Burton, "The Politics of State-Level Industrial Policy: Lessons from Rhode Island's Greenhouse Compact," *American Planning Association Journal*, vol. 52, no. 3 (Summer 1986): 277–289.

17. Mark S. Hyde and William E. Hudson, "Business and State Economic Development," *Western Political Quarterly*, vol. 41, no. 1 (March 1988): 181–191.

18. Silver and Burton, "The Politics of State-Level Industrial Policy," pp. 284–286.

19. Andre Brunel and Michael Burke, "Pennsylvania," in *Promoting High-Technology Industry*, edited by Schmandt and Wilson, pp. 200–203, 213–215.

20. John E. Jackson, "Michigan," in *The New Economic Role of American States: Strategies in a Competitive World Economy*, edited by R. Scott Fosler (New York: Oxford University Press, 1988): 115–121.

21. David Osborne, *Laboratories of Democracy* (Boston, MA: Harvard Business School Press, 1988): 151–153.

22. Marianne K. Clarke, *Revitalizing State Economies: A Review of State Economic Development Policies and Programs* (Washington, D.C.: National Governors' Association, 1986): 29–33.

23. Steven D. Gold, "Taxation of Business by American State and Local Governments," Legislative Finance Paper no. 53 (Denver, CO: National Conference of State Legislatures, March 1986): 5.

24. This type of strategy is by no means a new one. See Advisory Commission on

Intergovernmental Relations (ACIR), *State–Local Taxation and Industrial Location* (Washington, D.C., 1967).

25. Clarke, *Revitalizing States' Economies*, p. 18.

26. Ronald F. Ferguson and Helen F. Ladd, "Massachusetts," in *The New Economic Role of American States*, edited by Fosler, pp. 55–56.

27. Ibid., Chapters 3, 4 and 5.

28. Surveys of the literature can be found in Michael Wasylenko, "Business Climate, Industry and Employment Growth: A Review of the Evidence," Occasional Paper no. 98 (Syracuse, NY: Maxwell School of Citizenship and Public Affairs, Syracuse University, October 1985); Robert J. Newman and Dennis H. Sullivan, "Econometric Analysis of Business Tax Impacts on Industrial Location: What Do We Know, and How Do We Know It," *Journal of Urban Economics*, vol. 23 (1988): 215–234; Timothy J. Bartik, *Who Benefits from State and Local Economic Development Policies?* (Kalamazoo, MI: W. E. Upjohn Institute for Employment Research, 1991): 36–44; Michael Kieschnick, *Taxes and Growth: Business Incentives and Economic Development* (Washington, D.C.: The Council of State Planning Agencies, 1981); ACIR, *Interjurisdictional Tax and Policy Competition: Good or Bad for the Federal System?* (Washington, D.C., April 1991).

29. See Newman and Sullivan, "Tax Impacts on Industrial Location," pp. 224–232; Timothy J. Bartik, "Business Location Decisions in the United States," *Journal of Business and Statistics*, vol. 3 (January 1985): 14–22.

30. Michael Wasylenko and Therese McGuire, "Jobs and Taxes: The Effects of Business Climate on States' Employment Growth Rates," *National Tax Journal*, vol. 38, no. 4 (December 1985): 497–511.

31. See William C. Wheaton, "Interstate Differences in the Level of Business Taxation," *National Tax Journal*, vol. 36, no. 1 (March 1983): 83–94.

32. R. J. Newman, "Industry Migration and Growth in the South," *Review of Economics and Statistics*, vol. 65, no. 1 (February 1983): 76–86; Wasylenko and McGuire, "Jobs and Taxes: The Effects of Business Climate on State's Employment Growth Rates."

33. L. J. Helmes, "The Effect of State and Local Taxes on Economic Growth: A Time-Series Approach," *Review of Economics and Statistics*, vol. 67 (1985): 574–582.

34. Charles Bartsch, Marian Barber, and Margaret Quan, eds., *The Guide to State and Federal Resources for Economic Development* (Washington, D.C.: Northeast-Midwest Institute, 1988): Chapter 8.

35. Larry C. Ledebur and William W. Hamilton, "The Great Tax-Break Sweepstakes," *State Legislatures* (September 1986): 12–15; Nancy Lind and Ann H. Elder, "The Implications of Uncertainty in Economic Development: Diamond-Star Motors," *Economic Development Quarterly*, vol. 1, no. 1 (February 1987): 30–40.

36. Dennis Farney, "Nebraska, Hungry for Jobs, Grants Big Business Big Tax Breaks Despite Charges of 'Blackmail'," *Wall Street Journal* (June 23, 1987): 70.

37. John E. Moes, "The Subsidization of Industry by Local Communities in the South," *Southern Economic Journal*, vol. 28 (October 1961): 187–193; Irving Goffman, "Local Subsidies for Industry: Comment," *Southern Economic Journal*, vol. 29 (October 1962): 111–114; Harold I. Purcell, "State and Local Taxes: A Significant Site Selection Variable," *Industrial Development*, vol. 137, no. 6 (November/December 1968): 31–33; Benjamin Bridges, Jr., "State and Local Inducements for Industry," *National Tax Journal*, vol. 18, no. 1, (March 1965): 1–14.

38. See Kieschnick, *Taxes and Growth*, Chapter 4; Richard D. Pomp, "The Role of State Tax Incentives in Attracting and Retaining Business," *Economic Development*

Review (Spring 1988): 53–62; Steven R. Kale, "U.S. Industrial Development Incentives and Manufacturing Growth During the 1970s," *Growth and Change*, vol. 15 (January 1984): 26–34.

39. For a general critique of tax incentive efforts, see Ledebur and Hamilton, "The Great Tax-Break Sweepstakes," pp. 12–15.

40. ACIR, *Regulatory Federalism: Policy, Process, Impact and Reform* (Washington, D.C., 1984).

41. For a discussion of the development of regulation in the railroad industry, see Elmer E. Smead, *Governmental Promotion and Regulation of Business* (New York: Appleton-Century-Crofts, 1969): 202–206.

42. Ibid., pp. 438–439.

43. Michael D. Reagan, *Regulation: The Politics of Policy* (Boston: Little, Brown and Co., 1987): 20–22.

44. Smead, *Governmental Promotion and Regulation of Business*, pp. 412–417.

45. Reagan, *Regulation*, Chapter 4.

46. John T. Scholz, "State Regulatory Reform and Federal Regulation," *Policy Studies Review*, vol. 1, no. 2 (1982): 347–359. For reform efforts involving public utility commissions, see William T. Gormley, Jr., *The Politics of Public Utility Regulation* (Pittsburgh: University of Pittsburgh Press, 1983): Chapter 7; Val R. Jensen and Gregory A. Wagener, "Reforming Regulatory Reform," *Public Utility Fortnightly* (June 12, 1986): 15–22.

47. Samuel H. Porter and John R. Burton, "Legal and Regulatory Constraints on Competition in Electric Power Supply," *Public Utility Fortnightly* (May 25, 1989): 24–36.

48. Louis R. Monacell, "Unbundling Natural Gas Service: Lessons from Virginia," *Public Utility Fortnightly* (May 11, 1989): 9–15.

49. Harry M. Trebing, "The Impact of Diversification on Economic Regulation," *Journal of Economic Issues*, vol. 19, no. 2 (June 1985): 463–474.

50. For a discussion of institutional reforms in the 1970s, see Scholz, "State Regulatory Reform," pp. 349–352. For an analysis of participation in public utility commission processes, see Gormley, *The Politics of Public Utility Regulation*, Chapter 2.

51. Scholz, "State Regulatory Reform," p. 352.

52. Ibid., p. 355; C. K. Rowland and Roger Marz, "Gresham's Law: The Regulatory Analogy," *Policy Studies Review*, vol. 1, no. 3 (1982): 572–80.

53. "New Economic Development Rates Adopted for Hoosier Energy," *Public Utility Fortnightly* (February 16, 1989): 50.

54. Steven Kelman, "Economic Incentives and Environmental Policy: Politics, Ideology and Philosophy," in *Incentives for Environmental Protection*, edited by Thomas Schelling (Cambridge, MA: MIT Press, 1983): 291–331.

55. Scholz, "State Regulatory Reform," p. 357.

56. Gormley, *The Politics of Public Utility Regulation*, pp. 28–30, 189–95.

57. Ibid., pp. 26–28.

58. In a survey conducted in 1979, Gormley found that a public advocate appeared in over two-thirds on the electric and telephone cases and in around half of the gas cases before public utility commissions. See Gormley, *The Politics of Public Utility Regulation*, pp. 41–42.

59. Richard Gordon, *Reforming the Regulation of Electric Utilities* (Lexington, MA: Lexington Books, 1982): 155–158; Michael J. Zimmer and Beverly E. Jones, "Co-

generation: Boon or Bane to Consumers?" *Public Utility Fortnightly* (June 12, 1986): 23–31.

60. Stanley W. Hulett, "Promoting Independent Power: The California Experience," *Public Utilities Fortnightly* (February 16, 1989): 13–17.

61. Ibid., pp. 14–15.

62. Jeremiah D. Lambert, "Bypass in the Natural Gas Industry: The Fruit of Regulatory Change," *Public Utility Fortnightly* (April 3, 1986): 11–17.

63. Ibid., p. 16; James E. Norris, "Bypass and Reverse Bypass: A Gas Industry Update," *Public Utility Fortnightly* (March 30, 1989): 43–45.

64. Diane Sponseller, "The New FERC Policy on Avoided Cost Rates," *Public Utilities Fortnightly* (February 16, 1989): 52–55.

65. ACIR, *State Regulation of Banks in an Era of Deregulation* (Washington, D.C., 1988): 13. For a general discussion of the state and federal regulatory system, see Harrison Young, "Banking Regulation Ain't Broke," *Harvard Business Review* (September/October 1986): 106–112.

66. ACIR, *State Regulation of Banks in an Era of Deregulation*.

67. Donald T. Savage, "Interstate Banking Developments," *Federal Reserve Bulletin* (February 1987): 79–82; Rich Jones and Barbara Puls, "Interstate Banking: A Summary of State Laws" (Denver, CO: National Conference of State Legislatures, March 1987); ACIR, *State Regulation of Banks*, pp. 17–19.

68. ACIR, *State Regulation of Banks*, pp. 17–18.

69. Savage, "Interstate Banking Developments," pp. 80–81.

70. ACIR, *State Regulation of Banks*, p. 23.

71. Ibid., pp. 19–20.

72. William T. Warren, "Fingerpointing: Who's to Blame for the Bank Crisis?" *Governing* (April 1991): 26.

73. Ross M. Robertson, *History of the American Economy*, 4th ed. (New York: Harcourt Brace Jovanovich, Inc., 1973): 641.

74. Bill Bancroft, "Banking on Deregulation Can Be Hazardous to your State's Financial Institutions," *Governing* (January 1988): 44–49.

75. Warren, "Fingerpointing: Who's to Blame for the Bank Crisis?" p. 26.

76. Bancroft, "Banking of Deregulation," p. 49.

77. Kenneth J. Meier, *The Political Economy of Regulation: The Case of Insurance* (Albany, NY: State University Press, 1988): Chapter 5.

78. Ibid., pp. 172–173.

79. Ibid., Chapter 5.

80. William T. Warren, "The Gathering Storm: Insurance Company Insolvencies," *State Legislatures* (January 1991): 14–19.

81. Richard W. Stevenson, "California Regulator Takes Top Role in Insurance Crisis," *New York Times* (May 20, 1991): C1, C5.

82. Wayne King, "Mutual Benefit Seized by New Jersey Officials," *New York Times* (July 17, 1991): C2.

83. "State Insurer Funds Called Weak," *New York Times* (June 24, 1991): A1, C8.

84. Margaret E. Kirz, "The Insurers in Their Sights," *National Journal* (October 15, 1988): 2595–2599.

85. "Who Really Won the California Insurance Row?" *Journal of American Insurance* (First Quarter 1989): 1–4.

86. In Chapter 4, an example of a state securing the participation of private insurance

companies in forming a venture capital fund, Massachusetts Capital Resource Company, in discussed.

87. Glen Cope and Robert H. Wilson, eds., *The Effects of the State Government on Economic Development in Texas Cities*, Policy Research Project Report Series, no. 63 (Austin, TX: LBJ School of Public Affairs, University of Texas at Austin, 1985): 25.

88. Gormley, *The Politics of Public Utility Regulation*, p. 34; Reagan, *Regulation*, pp. 204–205.

89. James T. Patterson, *The New Deal and the States: Federalism in Transition* (Princeton, NJ: Princeton University Press, 1969): 121–128.

90. Robertson, *History of the American Economy*, pp. 689–695.

91. *Site Selection*, vol. 35, no. 5 (October, 1990): 1094.

92. William J. Moore and Robert J. Newman, "The Effects of Right-to-Work Laws: A Review of the Literature," *Industrial and Labor Relations Review*, vol. 38, no. 4 (July 1985): 571–585; Cope and Wilson, eds., *The Effects of State Government on Economic Development in Texas Cities*, pp. 18–20 and footnote 21, p. 38.

93. John Rees, "Regional Industrial Shifts in the U.S. and the Internal Generation of Manufacturing in Growth Centers of the Southwest," in *Interregional Movements and Regional Growth*, edited by William Wheaton (Washington, D.C.: Urban Institute, 1979): 51–73.

94. Moore and Newman, "The Effects of Right-to-Work Laws," pp. 582–583.

95. John R. Stepp reports that programs have been established in Pennsylvania, West Virginia, Tennessee, Ohio, Illinois, Minnesota, Michigan, Iowa, New York, Massachusetts, Delaware, and Connecticut. John R. Stepp, "Labor–Management Cooperation: A Framework for Economic Development," *Economic Development Review*, vol. 6 (Winter 1988): 37.

96. John R. Stepp and John L. Bonner, "States Tie Economic Development to Improved Labor Relations Climates," *Journal of State Government*, v vol. 60, no. 1 (January/February 1987): 40–43.

97. Charles Press and Kenneth VerBurg, *State and Community Governments in a Dynamic Federal System*, 3rd ed. (New York: HarperCollins Publishers Inc., 1991): 361–363; W. B. Stouffer, Cynthia Opheim, and Susan Bland Day, *State and Local Politics: The Individual and the Governments* (New York: HarperCollins Publishers Inc., 1991): 128–130.

98. *City of Clinton v. Cedar Rapids and Missouri Railroad Co.*, 24 Iowa 455, 462, 463 (1868).

99. U.S. Department of Commerce, Bureau of the Census, *1987 Census of Governments, vol. 1: Governmental Organization* (Washington, D.C., 1988): 3,042 counties; 19,200 municipal governments; 16,691 townships; 14,721 school districts; 29,523 special districts.

100. Stouffer et al., *State and Local Politics*, pp. 147–149.

101. ACIR, *Metropolitan Organization: The St. Louis Case* (Washington, D.C., 1988).

102. Alan K. Campbell, ed., *The States and the Urban Crisis* (Englewood Cliffs, NJ: Prentice-Hall, Inc., 1970); Deil S. Wright, *Understanding Intergovernmental Relations*, 2nd ed. (Monterey, CA: Brooks/Cole Publishing Company, 1982): 376–380.

103. E. Blaine Liner, ed., *A Decade of Devolution: Perspectives on State–Local Relations* (Washington, D.C.: Urban Institute Press, 1989).

104. ACIR, *The Question of State Government Capability* (Washington, D.C., 1985): 294–296.

105. Ibid., pp. 288–290 and Chapter 14.

106. Jack A. Brizius, "An Overview of State–Local Fiscal Landscape," in *A Decade of Devolution*, edited by Liner, pp. 51–79; ACIR, *The Question of State Government Capability*, pp. 296–303.

107. ACIR, *Mandates: Cases in State–Local Relations* (Washington, D.C., 1990).

108. Steven D. Gold, *Reforming State–Local Relations: A Practical Guide* (Denver, CO: National Conference of State Legislatures, 1989).

109. Claude E. Barfield, *Rethinking Federalism: Block Grants and Federal, State and Local Responsibilities* (Washington, D.C.: American Enterprise Institute for Public Policy, 1981): 47–49.

110. Ad Hoc Coalition on Block Grants, "Block Grants Briefing Book," as reported in Barfield, *Rethinking Federalism*, p. 49.

111. Robert B. Albritton, "The Impacts of Intergovernmental Financial Incentives on State Welfare Policymaking and Interstate Equity," *Publius: The Journal of Federalism*, vol. 19 (Spring 1989): 127–141.

112. ACIR, *The States and Distressed Communities: 1983 Update* (Washington, D.C., November 1985): 74.

113. Frank J. Mauro and Glen Yago, "State Government Targeting in Economic Development: The New York Experience," *Publius: The Journal of Federalism*, vol. 19 (Spring 1989): 63–82.

114. Susan B. Hansen, "Targeting in Economic Development: Comparative State Perspectives," *Publius: The Journal of Federalism*, vol. 19 (Spring 1989): 57.

115. Michael Brintell and Roy E. Green, "Comparing State Enterprise Zones," *Economic Development Quarterly*, vol. 2 (February 1988): 50–68.

116. Brizius, "An Overview of State–Local Fiscal Landscape," pp. 70–72.

5

Development and
Technology Policy

The most prominent response of state government to the economic challenges
of the late 1970s and early 1980s was the creation of new programs designed
specifically for promoting economic development. These programs comple-
mented, rather than replaced, earlier state efforts to attract investment, using tax
or other incentives. Although precursors of these new efforts can be found, the
rapid adoption of a wide variety of programs, including the promotion of technological innovation, entrepreneurialism, and exports, revealed active state governments prepared to intervene in the economy in order to promote development.

The initial array of development programs in the traditional industrial states
attempted to slow rampant deindustrialization. In many southern and western
states, the objective was to capture manufacturing investment adopting a more
spatially decentralized location pattern. Most states attempted to attract the
emerging advanced technology industry with hopes of creating another Silicon
Valley. As time passed, a more complete understanding of economic change
emerged, and more realistic expectations of economic development programs
established. This learning and the politics of goal formulation reshaped development strategies. In particular, the diffusion of technological innovation
throughout the economy has been eliminating the distinction between policies
for advanced technology and traditional manufacturing, as noted in Chapter 2;
furthermore, attention has shifted from an exclusive concern with industrial
recruitment to new firm generation and retention of existing firms.

The first section of this chapter will identify the origins of state technology
and development programs, describe the growth of funding of such efforts, and
explain the intergovernmental context of technology policy. The next two sec-

tions will analyze two sets of programs—technology innovation and business assistance programs—that have played prominent roles in state efforts during the 1980s and early 1990s. The focus on technology policy results from the central role technological change plays in the economy, whereas the business assistance focus recognizes that the rapidly growing innovative firms face special challenges and require particular types of support. The chapter identifies the nature of the economic development programs as well as their rationale and effectiveness in coping with economic change. The final section of this chapter contrasts three types of state development strategies—requirement, retention, and new firm formation—that build on these programs.

ORIGINS, FUNDING, AND INTERGOVERNMENTAL CONTEXT

The involvement of state government in economic development, through infrastructure investments, attracting federal resources, regulatory activity, and boosterism, dates from the earliest years of the nation. However, the adoption of programs that explicitly promote economic development has a more limited history. In technology policy, state government involvement began with the formation of land grant colleges and agricultural extension activities. Initiated and supported by federal acts, including the Morrill Act (1862), the Hatch Act (1887), and the Smith Lever Act (1914), the Cooperative Extension Service (CES) of the United States Department of Agriculture was funded, operated, and administered with state assistance.[1] The CES was extremely successful in diffusing technological innovation in rural America throughout the early part of this century. Much of the agricultural research was conducted in state land grant colleges, where CES offices are located. Although the CES model has limited application in diffusing innovation in manufacturing activities, due to differing technological and information needs, it is nevertheless frequently cited as a very effective technology transfer effort involving state government.

A second instance of state involvement in technology policy again resulted from a federal initiative.[2] In 1965, Congress adopted the State Technical Services Act to promote the diffusion of new technology throughout the country, and, as a result, many states adopted science advisory boards. These boards were found to be largely ineffective and states were unable to articulate useful roles for science advisors in public policy.[3] Boards suffered from lack of funds, authority, and continuity, and only in New York and North Carolina did boards survive to participate in the current state activities in technology policy and economic development.[4] Based on a 1977 congressional authorization, the National Science Foundation created the State Science, Engineering and Technology (SSET) program to encourage states again to use science and technology to meet their various economic needs. This effort also disappeared as a result of the lack of federal funding.[5]

Another form of state economic development programs of long standing is industrial recruitment. Four states established economic development bureaus in the 1920s for that purpose.[6] As a condition for receiving federal public works funds during the 1930s, states had to form comprehensive planning agencies, but these did not survive the elimination of the National Resources Planning Board in 1943.[7] A more lasting form of state development efforts, noted above, was established in the Balance Agriculture with Industry Program in 1936 in Mississippi.[8] The program used advertising, tax abatement, and tax-exempt financing to attract manufacturing investment to the then predominately rural state.[9] Following World War II, many southern and western states adopted such programs. State government was not alone; utility companies, chambers of commerce, and local governments often engaged in these efforts as well.

State economic development programs proliferated in the 1980s (see Table 5.1).[10] Finance, technology, export promotion, and training programs were adopted by virtually all states. Particularly prominent was the widespread use of mechanisms to help finance industrial development. Loans and loan guarantees for construction and the purchase of equipment were broadly used. General obligation bonds (bonds requiring the backing of general state revenues) were not used extensively, but revenue bonds have become a very important source of funds, especially after the federal tax exemption for Industrial Development Bonds was sharply curtailed in the mid-1980s. State support for training of the hardcore unemployed was widely adopted. State programs for export promotion and research and development were virtually universal.

As the number of programs grew, the level of state funding also increased. In terms of state expenditures, *explicit* economic development programs absorb a growing but still small proportion of state budgets. The National Association of State Development Agencies reported that the average state appropriations for state development agencies increased from $5.1 million in 1982 to $32.5 million in 1990.[11] A few states invest heavily in development programs. In Illinois and Pennsylvania, the state development agency received state appropriations of $414 million and $182 million, respectively, in 1990.[12] The average budget of state agencies in 1990 was $74.1 million, reflecting the fact that these agencies may administer federal programs, such as the Job Training Partnership Act and the Small Cities Community Development Program, in addition to expending state appropriations. Many state programs operate with funds generated through bond issues or tax expenditures (resulting from tax abatements) and, consequently, are not fully reflected in these budget figures. State legislatures rapidly increased appropriations for economic development in the 1980s in spite of fiscal constraints faced by states; nevertheless, the level of state expenditures for economic development is small when compared with the level for other state functions.

The level of state development expenditures compares poorly with federal spending for development (see Table 5.2). Federal agencies and programs with development missions have existed for many years—such as the Economic Development Administration, the Small Business Administration, or those housed

Table 5.1
State Economic Development Programs: 1974–1990

Financial Programs	1974	1979	1980	1981	1982	1983	1984	1985	1986	1987	1988	1989	1990
Industrial Development Authority	31	32	32	32	31	33	35	38	38	38	38	38	40
Revenue Bond Financing	17	25	24	25	25	28	32	41	42	44	44	44	44
General Obligation Bond Financing	8	8	9	9	10	10	11	13	12	14	15	15	18
Loans for Building Construction	15	20	23	23	23	26	27	34	35	36	38	40	40
Loans for Equipment, Machinery	11	15	17	18	19	24	24	33	34	35	37	39	42
Loan Guarantees for Building Construction	12	16	19	19	18	20	17	21	22	22	25	25	28
Loan Guarantees for Equipment, Machinery	10	15	17	17	19	21	18	21	23	23	26	25	29
Industrial Expansion	25	29	31	31	31	31	34	39	38	41	42	43	44
Industrial Expansion in Areas of High Unemployment	12	17	17	18	17	20	24	25	27	31	31	33	36
Industrial Parks (State owned)	n/a	8	8	9	9	12	12	11	10	13	11	15	15
Technology Programs													
State Science and Technology Advisory Council	n/a	n/a	41	41	41	42	44	45	45	43	44	45	45
Promotion of R&D	n/a	33	35	35	38	39	41	43	43	46	46	47	47
Available to University R&D	n/a	49	50	50	50	50	50	50	50	50	50	50	50
Export Promotion	n/a	47	49	49	50	50	50	50	50	50	50	50	50
Training Programs													
State Training of Hardcore unemployed	n/a	38	39	40	39	39	42	43	43	46	47	48	49
State Incentive for Industry for Hardcore	n/a	25	28	28	30	30	34	34	35	36	36	38	41

Source: <u>Site Selection Handbook</u> (Norcross, GA: Conway Data, Inc.), various years.

Table 5.2
Intergovernmental Funding for Economic Development Programs: 1983 (in $ millions)

	State Programs	Federal Programs	
Type		Federal Administered	State Administered
Direct Expenditures[1]	280.0	18,260.2	8,604.0
Major Expenditure Functions			
Small Business Assistance[2]	5.4	1,152.0	61.0
Training, Employment, and			
Other Labor Services	121.4	1,892.0	4,002.0
Research and Development[3]	67.4	13,936.0	18.0
International Trade Promotion	36.0	608.0	0.0
Direct Loans	114.8	2,872.6	0.0
Loan Guarantees	23.2	12,095.9	0.0
Venture Capital Corporations	9.7	0.0	0.0

Source: Congressional Budget Office, Congress of United States, The Federal Role in State Industrial Development Programs, July 1984, p. 4.

[1]Excluding promotions for agriculture and energy.
[2]Includes only grants, not state technical assistance to small businesses.
[3]Civilian research and development.

in the Department of Housing and Urban Development (Community Development Block Grants) and Department of Labor (Job Training Partnership Act). These federal programs continue to provide substantial funding even though they were frequently targets for budget reductions during the 1980s. As noted earlier, states play a substantial role in the administration of two programs, Small Cities CDBG and JTPA, a result of the effort to decentralize the administration of federal programs during the Reagan administration.[13]

Investment in research and development (R&D) is now widely recognized as a critical element to the future growth of the U.S. economy.[14] States have responded with an impressive array of technology initiatives, to be discussed below, but these efforts operate in an intergovernment structure with a very important federal presence. The federal government is the principal source of public funding for R&D (see Table 5.2). National R&D funding compares well with that of such competitors as Japan and Germany, although the federal share in the United States is heavily weighted toward defense-related research, and comparisons of nondefense related research is significantly less favorable.[15] However, the rate of increase in total R&D expenditures increased in inflation adjusted dollars by 6.9 percent a year from 1980 through 1985 but declined to a 1.2 percent annual increase in the second half of the decade.[16] A preliminary estimate shows an actual decline in real spending for R&D in 1991, a decline likely to be related to the national recession. In 1990, R&D expenditures from all sources

Table 5.3

Sources of Funding and Performers of Research and Development: 1990

A. Source of Funds (in $ millions)

Research Performer

Source of Fund	Federal Government	Industry	University and Colleges	Associated FFRDCs[1]	Others	Total	Percent Distribution Source
Federal Government	16,700	35,650	9,200	5,250	2,400	69,200	46.1
Industry		72,500	1,150		600	74,250	49.5
University and Colleges			4,300			4,300	2.9
Others			1,150		1,100	2,250	1.5
Total Dollars	16,700	108,150	15,800	5,250	4,100	150,000	100.0
Percent	11.1	72.1	10.5	3.5	2.7	100.0	

B. Type of Research (%)

Type of Research	Federal Government	Industry	University and Colleges	Associated FFRDCs	Others	Total	Total Funding ($ million)
Basic	11.2	19.5	49.2	12.8	7.3	100.0	21,490
Applied	10.5	70.4	13.2	2.2	3.7	100.0	33,785
Development	11.3	84.6	.8	1.9	1.4	100.0	94,725

Source: National Science Foundation, National Patterns of R&D Resources: 1990, Surveys of Science Resources Series (NSF 90-316) (Washington, D.C., May 1990), p. 18, Table 2.

[1]Federally funded research and development centers associated with universities.

was $150 billion, 49.0 percent of which originated in the federal government and 47.6 percent in industry (see Table 5.3). Around 62 percent of the federal expenditures went to defense-related research in 1990, up from around 47 percent in 1980.[17]

Although the federal government provides the largest share of funding for R&D, it performs, in its own facilities, only a relatively small share of this research (see Table 5.3). Industry performs the largest share by far, 72.9 percent, and universities and colleges and federal research facilities associated with universities perform about 14.0 percent of the total. There is a distinct specialization by type of research performed; universities and associated federal research facilities perform almost 62 percent of basic research and industry performs 85 percent of the development research. The majority of applied research is also performed by industry, although over a quarter of such research is performed in the federal government and universities. It is applied research that has been the principal focus of state technology programs. University funding of applied research, which largely originates in state government, nearly doubled in real terms between 1980 and 1990, whereas the share of total applied research performed in universities increased during the same period from 8.1 percent to 13.1 percent.[18]

New England, the Mid-Atlantic region, and especially the Pacific Region perform relatively large shares of total research and development (see Table 5.4), which is not surprising given that these regions have relatively high shares of advanced technology manufacturing employment (see Table 2.10). The high levels of research in these regions is driven principally by industry R&D. Almost half of federal R&D is performed in the South Atlantic region, particularly in Maryland, Washington, D.C., Florida, and Virginia. From 1975 to 1987, the West South Central and Mountain regions increased their share of R&D and relied heavily on academic R&D, probably a result of their historically low levels of manufacturing. The East North Central has lost some of its share of national R&D, although industry R&D remains dominant in the traditional industrial heartland.

Federally funded research activities have historically been mission-oriented, and economic development has not been one of the missions. An underlying presumption, especially in terms of the federal funding of basic research, was that the application of new basic knowledge and spin-off commercialization would follow as a result of market forces.[19] This presumption became increasingly difficult to sustain and as the relationship between research and economic development became more broadly understood during the 1980s, greater attention was paid to the development dimension of these expenditures.

The Steven–Wydler Technology Innovation Act of 1980, the Federal Technology Transfer Act of 1986, and the 1987 Executive Order 12591 ("Facilitating Access to Science and Technology") attempted to expedite technology transfer from federal agencies and laboratories to the private sector and to state and local government. Under the Small Business Innovation Research Program (SBIR), created in 1982, federal agencies with external research budgets were required to allocate a portion of these funds to small businesses.[20] Expanding on earlier experience with university–industry centers, the National Science Foundation created the Engineering Research Center program in 1985. The Omnibus Trade and Competitiveness Act of 1988 strengthened the federal institutional base on technology issues, creating the National Institute of Standards and Technology, an Undersecretary of Technology, and the Technology Administration, all within the Department of Commerce.[21] The federal government remained a dominant actor in the funding of national R&D, but many of the new efforts were relatively decentralized in their implementation and thus created opportunities for cooperation with state and local governments, universities, and development agencies.

States have been particularly concerned with capturing a fair share of federal research and development expenditures. In a number of well-publicized cases, such as the superconducting supercollider contract, competition among states has been fierce. The federal government has been able to extract substantial

Table 5.4

Regional Distribution of Research and Development Expenditures: 1975 and 1987 (in percent)

	New England	Middle Atlantic	East North Central	West North Central	South Atlantic	East South Central	West South Central	Mountain	Pacific
1975									
Total R&D	8.9	20.0	18.3	4.2	14.3	2.6	4.2	4.8	22.7
Total Employment	5.8	17.0	19.5	8.0	16.1	6.3	9.4	4.8	13.2
1987									
Total R&D	9.0	16.6	17.5	5.5	13.7	3.1	5.2	5.6	23.8
Total Employment	5.8	15.3	17.4	7.4	17.8	5.8	10.4	5.3	14.8
Federal R&D ($13.4 billion)	6.4	5.2	9.2	1.1	41.9	6.4	3.2	6.4	16.6
Industry R&D ($94.2 billion)	8.8	18.4	19.5	6.1	9.8	2.7	5.2	4.7	24.3
Academic R&D ($16.1 billion)	9.1	14.2	13.3	5.1	12.8	2.8	6.8	10.0	25.4

Source: National Science Foundation, Geographic Patterns: R&D in the United States, Surveys of Science Resources Series Special Report, NSF-89-317 (Washington, D.C., July 1989), p. 40, Table B-12; and National Patterns of R&D Resources: 1990, Surveys of Science Resources Series (NSF 90-316) (Washington, D.C., May 1990), pp. 57, Table B-16. For source of employment data, see Table 2.2.

Note: In 1975, 7.7 percent of total R&D was unallocated to states; in 1987, 1.8 percent was unallocated.

Table 5.5
Formation of State Technology Offices: 1981–1988

Date Formed	Number of States
Prior to 1981	3
1981–1982	2
1983–1984	8
1985–1986	7
1987–1988	5

Source: Marianne K. Clarke, "Recent State Initiatives: An Overview of State Science and
Technology Policies and Programs," in Growth Policy in the Age of High
Technology, edited by Schmandt and Wilson, p. 152.

subsidies for these installations, much as firms have benefited from interstate
competition in business recruitment.

States have substantially expanded their economic development efforts during
the 1980s, in terms of the number of programs and the level of funding. These
efforts do not represent, however, a change in kind; precedents for contemporary
state development programs were established earlier in this century. In addition,
the state funding efforts, especially in the area of science and technology, are
relatively modest elements in an intergovernmental system dominated by federal
funding, although state institutions do have important roles in the implementation
of many programs.

TECHNOLOGY INNOVATION

By the early 1980s, most states demonstrated a clear interest in technology
policy. Building on science and technology advisory councils (see Table 5.1),
states expanded their efforts during the decade to create offices for technology
policy and a variety of programs (see Table 5.5). A 1988 survey by the National
Governors Association reported that 38 states had such offices, with about half
of these located in larger state offices and the other half organized as independent
agencies or as quasi-public or private nonprofit corporations.[22]

Given the diverse organizational and funding structures of state technology
offices, reliable data on funding, spending, and program priorities are elusive.
The principal sources to date are two surveys published in 1988, one conducted
by the Office of Science and Technology of the Minnesota Department of Trade
and Economic Development and the other by Robert D. Atkinson in conjunction
with the Society of Research Administrators.[23] Atkinson found total state expenditures on technology programs in 1987 to be $397.6 million, and the Min-
nesota study found state expenditures in 1988 to be $563.7 million. The latter
survey also found substantial variation among states in spending, with a high of
$76 million in New Jersey, and several states reporting no expenditures.

The differential growth potential of manufacturing sectors, an outcome of the
ongoing technological revolution and international competition, led many states

to target specific kinds of firms and industries, particularly advanced technology firms. Firms with high levels of research and development or advanced manufacturing processes are more likely recruitment targets than low-wage, standardized production firms, although a state's degree of economic distress has been a second factor affecting its targeting strategy. Although state recruitment incentives do not necessarily encourage technological innovation, the recruitment sweepstakes have frequently attempted to attract innovative, or cutting-edge, firms. In addition, the focus on the recruitment of innovative industries and firms have led states to consider a broader range of development issues.

The product or industry lifecycle model has frequently been used to explore development policy issues in the context of technological change. The lifecycle model identifies four phases through which individual products or clusters of products pass:[24]

Phase I: Research and development—preproduction phase, development of new ideas and products. This phase has become increasingly science–technology based during the twentieth century, and as a result is highly dependent on scientific and technically trained, highly skilled workers.

Phase II: Process development—experimentation with production technology and testing of market. This is generally a period of rapid growth and high profits, thus attracting new firms. The development of production processes requires highly skilled labor. The firm that originates a product will not necessarily be the firm that develops the most efficient production and marketing technology.

Phase III: Market phase—standardization of production technology and saturation of market. According to the original product cycle model, many firms engage in production during this phase, producing a highly competitive and low-profit sector. With standardized production, firms require low-skilled workers and tend to decentralize their production to low-wage areas. However, during this phase another trend is possible: the sector may become oligopolistic, with few firms controlling the market and realizing above-normal rates of profits. The large size of these firms and their relatively high profits provide more options for market strategy than those found in highly competitive sectors. The oligopolistic firms, for example, may be better able to invest in research and development for new products or for improving production technology for existing product lines.

Phase IV: Obsolescence and displacement—displacement of product from market and its eventual abandonment.

At any point in time, the national economy will have some slow-growth sectors and some rapid-growth sectors, a result of industries being in different phases of the product/industry lifecycle. Extending this model to Schumpeter's conception of technological revolutions, a clustering of many products in the early phases of the product cycle occur as new technologies are developed. These new products displace many traditional products from Phase III to Phase IV, thus creating rapid change in the composition of industrial production and employment.[25] The new technologies—such as electricity or computer chips—are eventually adopted in all sectors of the economy.

The product/industry lifecycle holds a number of implications for firms as well as for development policies and programs. Although the United States has generally excelled in basic science and research, other countries, particularly Japan, seem to have been more adept at the commercialization of innovative technology in recent decades. States and the federal government, consequently, have developed policies to nurture and facilitate the early phases of the product/industry lifecycle.

One concern has focused on a perceived tendency for firms to underinvest in R&D. Investment in R&D incurs risks, and small firms or firms in highly competitive sectors may not have the financing capabilities for taking such risks. Public policy has attempted to draw the resources of universities and research centers to the applied research requirements of the early phase of the product cycle and to special needs of innovative production technology for industries in the mature stage.

Problems faced by inventors, entrepreneurs, and new firms have also received much attention. The individual inventor must bring the new product into production and to market.[26] Entrepreneurship becomes a critical element in small firms. The early phases of the product cycle also require capital, but little revenue is being generated. Sources of seed and venture capital, in addition to entrepreneurial skills, are required in this period. (State programs to provide capital and other types of business assistance are discussed in the following section.)

Many of the new economic development programs of the early 1980s focused on technological change and emerging industries, particularly the advanced technology sectors. The early rationale for these programs was the mistaken notion that states could create their own Silicon Valley or Route 128. Policymakers eventually recognized that the unique circumstances—particularly federal defense expenditures on research—that produced the extraordinary growth in these two areas would be difficult to replicate elsewhere; but they also understood that firms in innovative and growing sectors have requirements much different from those in mature sectors such as traditional manufacturing. The result has been the creation of programs dealing with product and process innovation through direct funding of university research, technology transfers between universities and industries, and research parks.[27]

As states began to appreciate the role of science and technology in contemporary development, state universities and affiliated research institutes were identified as very important resources and then utilized as instruments for development policy. State-supported university systems have at times been given a development mission, as in agricultural extension, discussed above. In addition, of the 184 research universities in the U.S., where virtually all university R&D is conducted, 119 are public institutions, supported by state and local government, and many of the others receive state support of some type.[28] States adopted a series of measures, with an enormous variety of institutional arrangements, to expand the role of universities in the industrial innovation process.

State funding for higher education, although several times the magnitude of federal research spending, has largely supported the teaching function (see Chapter 7). Support for research is modest in most states and well below the level of federal research funding provided to universities noted above. In the 1980s, direct state funding of basic and especially applied university research was expanded, justified on the grounds that it would lead to economic growth. Strong research programs are believed to attract superior faculty and graduate students and hold the potential to generate new businesses as innovations developed at universities are commercialized. New York's Research and Development Grants Program and Texas Advanced Technologies Research Program are competitive, peer-reviewed grant programs for university-based research proposals. Other efforts, such as the Engineering School Equipment grant program, part of the Ben Franklin Partnership in Pennsylvania, attempt to acquire state-of-the-art research equipment.

A more common effort among states encourages the direct interaction of universities and the private sector in order to facilitate the transfer of research results from universities to businesses. This type of effort generally involves the creation of research centers where firms participate directly in applied research in some specified field, such as biotechnology, materials science, microelectronics, and telecommunications.[29] These joint university–industry R&D centers include the Thomas Edison Program in Ohio, the MICRO program in California, the Centers of Excellence Program in Massachusetts, the Centers for Advanced Technology in New York, Advanced Technology Centers in Pennsylvania, the Advanced Technology Development Center at Georgia Institute of Technology, and many others. Universities may provide initial funding for facilities, equipment, professorships, and graduate student scholarships. Firms participate in a variety of ways, including the funding of research, contributions in personnel and equipment, and participation in conferences and seminars. In many states, the targeted research areas have been chosen on the basis of an evaluation of the state's economic resources, needs, and perceived competitive advantage and thus are frequently tied to existing industries in the state.

Science/research parks are a special type of business park, where the majority of establishments are primarily engaged in research or product development.[30] The most well known are Stanford Research Park in California and Research Triangle Park in North Carolina. There were 32 such parks in 1981 and 116 in 1989.[31] In 1989, Luger and Goldstein found parks in 44 states, containing more than 1,500 businesses and employing over 150,000 workers.[32] About 85 percent of the parks had some type of relationship with a university (25 percent were units of a university and 21 percent were university–private joint ventures) and 65 percent with state government (7 percent were a unit of state government).[33] Although such parks are found in cities of all sizes, the greatest growth has occurred in nonmetropolitan areas. The science/research park attempts to take

Table 5.6

Funding of Technology Programs by Program Type and Region: 1987 (in percent)

	Northeast	Midwest	South	West	Total
Research	65.5	56.5	73.6	65.2	62.0
Unversity Centers	54.0	36.0	49.9	28.3	41.9
University Grants	4.9	13.6	18.8	18.1	12.9
Business Grants	6.6	2.4	2.2	10.8	4.2
Research Parks	0.0	4.5	2.7	8.0	3.0
Business Extension Services	15.9	13.7	11.0	2.3	11.6
Diffusion of Technology	12.4	0.7	1.7	0.0	3.8
Technology Transfer	1.9	3.7	4.6	1.6	3.1
Technical Assistance	0.0	5.9	2.0	0.2	2.4
Management Assistance	1.6	3.4	2.7	0.5	2.3
Capital Programs	7.7	21.4	11.0	29.1	22.9
Equity	6.2	21.3	11.0	23.8	21.4
Loan Programs	1.5	0.1	0.0	5.3	1.0
Incubators	5.0	7.0	1.5	1.4	3.9
Training	5.5	0.9	1.8	0.0	2.2
Other	0.2	0.5	0.7	1.7	0.6

Source: Robert D. Atkinson, "State Programs for Technology Development: A Summary and State-by-State Listing" (Washington, D.C.: National Association of State Development Agencies, April 1988), p. 9.

advantage of the tendency for R&D activities to cluster. The sharing of a technically trained labor pool and of specialized business services is believed to strengthen and expand the local economy, especially in terms of manufacturing activity. Only about one-half of the science/research parks have been able to generate employment that would not have occurred anyway.[34] The older parks had a higher probability of success, and the presence of a major university was a very important element. The external economies generated by major research universities may be more important than the research parks themselves.

The Atkinson survey of states in 1987 obtained expenditure data on different types of technology programs. The largest share of expenditures was devoted to support of research, particularly in the university research centers (see Table 5.6). The Northeast and South in particular relied heavily on university centers. Business extension services and new firm generation are especially important in the Northeast and Midwest, and equity capital programs have been a priority in the West. In terms of sectoral targeting, the Northeast is broad-based, with a fairly balanced range of funding, and the Midwest has specialized in biotechnology, computer technologies, and, especially, advanced manufacturing (see Table 5.7). The South is also specialized in advanced manufacturing and the West invests heavily in computer technology. This pattern suggests that regions are building on existing strengths—advanced production technology in the Midwest and South, where traditional manufacturing has been severely affected by

Table 5.7
Regional Distribution of Targeted Technology Policy: 1987 (in percent)

	Northeast	Midwest	South	West	Total
Technology					
Biotechnology	13	22	10	19	16.2
Computers	18	22	17	28	19.3
Advanced Manufacturing	18	23	25	11	18.2
Materials	11	9	10	9	9.9
Medical Technologies	11	3	15	5	8.6
Natural Resources	13	9	8	26	13.5
Miscellaneous	16	12	15	11	14.1

Source: Robert D. Atkinson, "State Programs for Technology Development: A Summary
and State-by-State Listing" (Washington, D.C.: National Association of State
Development Agencies, April 1988), pp. 5–7.

economic change; computer technology in the West—or using existing university
facilities to develop research competencies. Almost 70 percent of funding is
allocated to universities in the South, where industry R&D has traditionally been
weak (see Table 5.4). In terms of both absolute levels of funding and of per
capita expenditures, the Northeast provides the greatest support for technology
programs with the Midwest following closely behind; these are both regions of
traditional strength in R&D.

What accounts for the rapid expansion of technology programs and who are
their constituencies? Universities themselves are the most interested party. At
least for public universities, cooperation on economic development issues may
mean increased funding and greater public support. Businesses involved in these
programs appear satisfied, but relatively few participate and no broad-based
support by the business community for expansion of these programs has emerged.
Support appears to be industry specific, in that a particular industry seeks support
for research relevant to the problems faced by that industry. In Michigan, the
formation of a robotics institute was clearly tied to large and politically powerful
industries in the state. The successful adaptation of these industries is largely
dependent on innovation in process technology and the institute attempts to
address this need. But firms explore a wide range of research strategies, including
industry consortia such as MCC and Sematech.[35] University–industry centers
are unlikely to displace other mechanisms for obtaining the results of applied
research; consequently, it is unlikely that industry will be prepared to provide
significant political support for their continuation. These centers may become,
however, a useful mechanism for commercializing university research, reinforcing universities' interest in this type of program.

BUSINESS ASSISTANCE PROGRAMS

The product/industry lifecycle places emphasis on technological innovation,
either in terms of new products or improved production processes. Innovation,

however, is also highly dependent on the institutional context in which it is to be developed. A viable business establishment is a necessary condition for the adoption of technological innovation. Innovation occurs in many large firms, which have the resources to invest in research and development for new products and to experiment with production processes even though the benefits of such investment may not be realized for many years. For new and small businesses, sustaining such investments is much more problematic, even though new products and processes are often created by individuals or in small firms. Particularly in small business, the basic need may not even be technological innovation but rather the adoption of existing off-the-shelf technology.[36] States have responded to the perceived needs of these small firms by creating new programs and adopting existing industrial extension programs. In addition, all states are engaged in export promotion on behalf of local businesses.

Entrepreneurialism and Small Business

The shift from a single-minded focus on industrial recruitment to broader strategies is nowhere more evident than in the increased concern for new firm formation and support of small business. The importance of small businesses in the job creation process has been observed by a number of scholars.[37] The National Commission on Jobs and Small Business found that firms with fewer than 100 employees account for 38 percent of all private-sector employment in urban areas, 56 percent of rural, nonfarm employment, and almost one-third of the gross national product.[38] About half of the major industrial innovations of the last 30 years started in small companies.[39] In addition, the startling success of many young companies, such as Apple, Lotus, Compaq, and Federal Express, and the proliferation of journals devoted to entrepreneurship, such as *Inc.*, have further focused attention on small growing firms. Even though not all small businesses grow rapidly and in fact, about one-half fail within five years, innovation in both the formation of new firms and the expansion in young firms has been identified as a key factor in employment generation.[40]

State small business assistance programs, frequently conducted in cooperation with the federal Small Business Administration, have existed for many decades, but recent initiatives have tended to focus on innovative businesses. One form of assistance is the incubator, in which new firms are provided an array of services critical to the survival of young firms. Incubators have been formed by the private sector, state and local governments, and universities and may be oriented toward technology-based development, economic diversification, or community revitalization.[41] Firms participating in an incubator receive benefits such as low rents, low-interest loans, or a wide variety of technical assistance. A 1988 study found 300 incubators nationwide. States started adopting incubators in 1983, and by 1988 one-half the states had programs in support of incubators.[42] Pennsylvania has used the incubator approach most extensively; in 1987, there were 31 incubators, 28 of which received state assistance, serving 220 businesses.[43]

A second approach taken by states is the promotion of entrepreneurship. Although much studied, entrepreneurship is not well understood.[44] Policies have nevertheless been devised to promote it, based in part on the close relationship between the spatial incidence of technological innovation and the presence of entrepreneurs.[45] The regional characteristics associated with high levels of entrepreneurship include a favorable industrial mix (the presence of rapidly growing industrial sectors), an economy not dominated by large firms, and high levels of innovative research and development activities. Social characteristics of an area, such as high education levels, high income, favorable occupational structure, and a history of entrepreneurship, have also been correlated with high levels of entrepreneurship.

Some states have attempted to nurture an entrepreneurial environment by promoting formal and informal networks of inventors, investors, and entrepreneurs.[46] In one of the few empirical evaluations of entrepreneurial promotion policies, Morkey found that entrepreneurial policy had little effect on the birthrate of new firms in four counties in New York.[47] In the evaluation of 12 incubators in Pennsylvania, however, the prospects for survival of the firms assisted seemed to have been improved. These results are easily reconciled. Firms directly assisted by these programs do benefit, but so few firms receive assistance that the effect of such programs on the broader economy are negligible or difficult to measure; a demonstration effect, which could produce a higher rate of new firm formation, does not appear to be present.

Although entrepreneurialism is recognized as a key factor in employment growth, the ability of governments to affect this factor may be severely limited. Concentrations of research and development activities are necessary but not sufficient conditions for an entrepreneurial environment. Attempting to change local business culture through public policy is likely to be difficult if not misguided, at least in the short term. On the other hand, there are instances, generally developed over a 20- to 30-year period, where high levels of entrepreneurship emerged in areas without such a tradition (Ottawa in Canada, Silicon Glen in Scotland).[48] In the long term, public policy regarding education, R&D, and environment quality may be the critical elements in creating environments in which entrepreneurial activity can emerge.

The promoters of small business and new business programs are usually tied to the local sector; they are predominantly members of small business organizations, academics, and development practitioners. Although a state's size appears to be important in determining the appropriate division of responsibilities between state and local governments, the latter appears to have a decided advantage to implementing these programs as a result of better proximity and access to local entrepreneurial networks. Consequently, a state role that enables or facilitates local programs is more likely to succeed than one that attempts to operate such programs. The limited ability of potential constituencies to organize,

Table 5.8
Distribution of Capital by States: 1989 (in percent)

	Commercial and Industrial Loans		Disbursement of Venture Capital
Top 5	55	Top 5	63
New York	26	California	37
California	12	Massachusetts	10
Illinois	7	Texas	6
Pennsylvania	6	Pennsylvania	5
Texas	4	Tennessee	5
Next 5	14	Next 5	16
Massachusetts	4	New York	4
Ohio	3	New Jersey	4
Michigan	3	Colorado	3
Florida	2	Illinois	3
North Carolina	2	Michigan	2
Other 40 states	31	Other 40 states	21

Source: Economic Development Tomorrow: A Report from the Profession (Rosemont, IL: American Economic Development Council, July 1991), pp. 20–21, Figures 1-11 and 1-12.

the small number of firms actually helped, and the relatively weak policy instruments available suggest that these efforts, at least in terms of firm-specific, client-oriented program, will not expand significantly.

Capital Programs

Capital availability is another critical element in the early phases of the product/ industry lifestyle. In Phases I and II, firms are not generating revenue, but the costs incurred in these phases are small compared with the third phase when production is initiated.[49] The early phases can be funded from internal funds in large corporations, but small firms must look elsewhere. Given the relatively high risks associated with new firms, commercial banks are reluctant to make such loans, thus leaving this venture capital market to other investors. A number of studies have demonstrated capital shortage for small firms, especially for new and high-risk firms.[50] In Massachusetts, inadequate markets for seed, venture, and loan capital for small businesses were identified.[51] Substantial spatial inequality in venture capital investments exists: in 1989, over half of the investments were made in only three states and 79 percent of the nation's private venture capital investments was made in just ten states (see Table 5.8). The distribution of venture capital is significantly more concentrated among states than commercial and industrial lending.[52]

Recognizing these problems in capital markets, states have adopted a variety of business finance programs, including grants, loans and loan guarantees, interest subsidies, equity financing, and venture capital programs (see Table 5.1).[53] Although government-sponsored capital programs have existed for decades, the

Table 5.9
State High-Risk Capital Programs: 1990

Type of Program	Number of States
Pre-Startup Capital	23
Venture Capital	27
Finance of Product Development	19
Long-Term, Secured Debt Financing	47
Unsecrured of subordianted Debt	37

Source: Corporation for Enterprise Development, The 1991 Development Report Card for the States (Washington, D.C., 1991), p. 91.

programs of recent vintage are attempting to address the specific finance problems of small and growing firms, particularly with regard to possible failures or inadequacies in capital markets (see Table 5.9).

The variety of programs is substantial, varying with respect to purpose, form of assistance, institutional format, and source of funds. Programs exist for each stage of the product cycle. Seed programs fund the earliest phase where product prototypes are developed. Venture capital programs generally fund the following stage where the production and marketing strategies are initiated. The product development programs fund existing firms in their development of new products, generally through unsecured loans but with a share of royalties returning to the program when and if the product goes to market.[54]

The form of assistance can be a grant, tax incentive, loan, or equity position in the firm. Grants are most frequently used in the R&D phase, and the firm receiving the grant may have no obligation for repayment. Tax incentives or credits are very common forms of assistance and can be linked to R&D or new job creation, but are less appropriate in very small firms with limited tax liabilities. Loan programs can be tailored for any phase of the product cycle. The most intensive form of assistance occurs in those programs that take an equity position in a firm and thus become partners in the ownership of the enterprise.

The institutional arrangement for these programs varies. Some are administered by traditional state agencies and others are placed in institutions that are semi-independent or autonomous. The latter institutional form is adopted in order to isolate decision making or business finance from possible political influence found in some regular line agencies of state government. Many programs, if not administering agencies, are operated as a public–private partnership. Because these programs involve lending and investment decisions, the direct participation of private-sector representatives is often perceived to be necessary. A number of state efforts are structured with no state government involvement in program administration. For example, development credit corporations are private, for-profit corporations, but investors may be eligible for a state tax credit.[55] In forming the Massachusetts Capital Resource Company, the state secured the cooperation of insurance companies to provide funds to eligible technology firms in return for favorable tax treatment.

The source of funding for state business finance efforts also varies. The traditional sources—capitalization through state bonds, state appropriations, and tax expenditures—are widely used. But states have turned to other sources, particularly pension funds. Public-sector pension funds, in particular, have accumulated enormous amounts of capital, and many feel some portion of this capital should be invested in economic revitalization. Michigan, Ohio, Iowa, New York, California, and other states are using or considering the use of pension funds for economic development purposes.[56] The popular strategic investment funds frequently draw on pension funds for capitalization. Even when new institutions, such as business and industrial development corporations are established, they frequently involve private sector investment as well.[57] As another funding strategy, a few states encourage financial institutions to participate in the creation of capital pools that can be used for development.[58]

The risk-taking nature of the state business finance programs constitutes one of their weaknesses. Even if market failures indeed exist, what is the likelihood that a public-sector program will succeed? Will public-sector programs be more successful that private institutions and investors in choosing successful ventures? If private markets are operating properly, the public programs may displace private investment, an undesirable outcome. As experience accumulates, evaluation of existing efforts will help answer these questions.

The effectiveness of the programs, however, may not determine their long-term survivability. It is fairly clear that capital programs and other actions affecting capital markets are unlikely to make a major difference in growth rates in a state since they benefit a small number of firms.[59] Cost–benefit analysis, although important, has limited usefulness in evaluating these programs because some benefits are difficult to measure.[60] Programs have a symbolic importance. They reflect an aggressive state government that is willing to mobilize resources for purposes of development. The state business finance programs demonstrate Eisinger's characterization of state and local governments as increasingly entrepreneurial. That is, state and local governments are engaging in risk-taking behavior in order to promote development. By adopting an aggressive posture, states focus public attention on the problems of development.

International Trade

The changing role of the United States in the world economy—reflected in a decline of U.S. exports as a share of total world trade, deterioration in the U.S. trade deficit, and the internationalization of the U.S. economy—has significantly contributed to structural change (see Chapter 2). With growth in the world economy, however, the absolute value of U.S. exports has nevertheless continued to increase. In addition, foreign firms, sensitive to protectionist pressures in the United States and searching for investment opportunities, expanded investment in the United States. Despite intense competition in many markets, ample opportunities, as well as a compelling imperative, for increasing U.S. exports and attracting investment to the country exist.[61] Efforts to attract foreign manufacturing investment, particularly investments by Japanese firms,[62] and the promotion of exports became important elements of state development activities by the mid-1980s.[63] The federal government encourages states to promote exports, and in this policy area states and the federal government cooperate extensively.[64]

A modest state presence in export promotion began in the 1960s, and a few states opened trade offices in foreign countries. By the mid-1970s, an expanding state role became evident. In 1975, there were 28 states that had international departments and 17 states that had foreign trade offices abroad.[65] Governors have also been leaders in recent decades in promoting trade and attracting foreign investment. The activities of the International Trade and Foreign Relations Committee of the National Governors' Association, formed during the Carter administration, reflect this commitment.[66] By 1980, virtually all states had a presence in export promotion (see Table 5.1). In 1982, there were 40 states that maintained 66 offices abroad, but by 1991, 42 states maintained 146 offices.[67] The 1980s also brought a substantial expansion in the level of state appropriations for such efforts. In 1982, the average state appropriation for international trade was just over $500,000, but by 1990 the average was over $1.5 million.[68] By 1989, 36 governors made seventy trips abroad to promote exports and attract foreign investment.[69]

The dramatic increase in export promotion programs since the late 1970s is closely tied to the internationalization of the U.S. economy. Although U.S. multinational corporations have long been active in world markets, most small and mid-size firms have sold exclusively to domestic markets. The increasingly competitive environment both in the United States and abroad has placed great importance on the search for new markets. The resources required to export to foreign markets, however, are substantial and frequently beyond the means of small and mid-size firms. Exporting requires extensive legal, marketing, accounting, and engineering (concerning industrial standards) expertise about foreign countries as well as knowledge of international transportation and communications systems. Specialized financial institutions participate in international exports. Few large firms, much less small size and mid-size firms, have the resources necessary to export, and state governments and the federal government have created programs to aid them. The range of programs is wide, covering export finance, export trading companies, marketing analyses, counseling, overseas offices, and trade missions, among others.[70]

The cooperation between state and federal governments is based on a common mission—expansion of U.S. exports—and mutually reinforcing capabilities. As the party responsible for international trade relations and manager of the macroeconomy, the federal government, through various agencies, is responsible for trade performance. On the other hand, state governments have better direct access to firms in the country's highly decentralized economy. The federal government has provided export finance, through the Eximbank, for many decades, but it expanded its role substantially in the 1980s. In 1980, the Small Business Export Expansion Act provided funding to facilitate export activities. The Export Trading Company Act of 1982 encouraged the establishment of trading companies, which serve as trade intermediaries, and a number of states and localities have taken advantage of this program to good effect. Also, the International Trade Administration of the U.S. Department of Commerce provides assistance to states for trade missions and their export programs.[71] An experiment is being conducted in which states are allowed to commit Eximbank loan guarantees.

The growth in state government support of exports is interesting in several respects. It reflects a growing recognition of the internationalization of the U.S. economy and a pressing national need for U.S. firms to compete abroad. Export promotion serves firms already located in a state. States may adopt an export policy without an organized constituency, but supporters emerge if the efforts succeed. There are questions, however, about how useful and significant a state role in international trade may be.[72] Private-sector export intermediaries exist for the full range of export functions. Although there are compelling policy reasons to expand the country's export performance, public-sector programs and organizations must find a place, presumably a complementary function, among the range of existing private-sector institutions. Certainly the provision of information on foreign markets and other services can be offered by a public-sector program without competing with private-sector firms.[73] But in an area like export finance, private-sector firms may likely be the most efficient providers, though loan guarantees through public-sector programs may be very useful. Perhaps the most important function of these state programs is the attention and publicity focused on export opportunities; small and mid-size companies without experience in foreign markets may be attracted to exporting as a result.

EVOLUTION OF STATE DEVELOPMENT STRATEGIES

Economic development strategies can be classified according to three objectives: (1) to attract firms and investment to a state; (2) to retain and encourage expansion of existing firms; and (3) to nurture new firms. Technology and business assistance programs, discussed in the previous sections of this chapter, and the tax-based incentive programs discussed in Chapter 4 are the means by which these strategies are implemented. Several programs can be adopted in pursuit of each strategy, and some programs may be used for all three strategies. States may adopt all three strategies because they are not mutually exclusive. This categorization of strategies is particularly helpful in analyzing the evolution of recent state development activities and in identifying constituents of development strategies.[74]

Recruitment Strategies

Recruitment strategies have been used for decades and have been most popular in southern states as they attempted to capture a share of manufacturing firms decentralizing from the industrial heartland.[75] The programs adopted to implement this strategy usually focus on individual firms and extend tax abatement, infrastructure, loans, and training programs at subsidized rates. As applied in the post–World War II South, the strategy targeted firms in Phase III of the product cycle, during which the process technology has become standardized and the firm attempts to reduce production costs rather than to pursue further technological innovation. The industrial recruitment programs found a receptive audience among many firms searching for low production costs, such as the low land costs, low taxes, and low wages found in the South. Some states were relatively successful in attracting manufacturing investment, even though many multinational corporations frequently found that locating overseas resulted in even lower production costs.

Recruitment strategies have not been abandoned in recent state efforts. There has, however, been a change in their focus. A more discriminating attitude toward firms exists; not all jobs are created equal. Firms in growing industries tend to offer better prospects than firms in declining industries; advanced technology firms probably offer better prospects than standardized production firms. Attracting foreign firms has become a high recruitment priority for many states.[76] In deciding where to locate, foreign firms act much like domestic firms; they encourage states or cities to compete with each other for the investment. This competition obviously benefits the companies, but the benefits to the community are often much more uncertain.[77]

States have made an enormous effort to recruit certain firms and projects. Extensive and costly incentives have been offered for the large automobile plants and for airline production and maintenance facilities. The competition for private sector research installations such as MCC and Sematech and, in the public arena, for Department of Defense contracts and federally funded research facilities, such as the proposed superconducting supercollider, has been fierce. States and cities are prepared to provide these incentives because of their potential economic impact.

Support for recruitment strategies lies principally in the local-demand sector of a state or city. Rarely will benefits accrue to the existing export sector. The export sector may well adopt the position that firm-specific subsidies for relocating firms are inherently inequitable. Because recruitment rarely produces major increases in employment, there may be few benefits to labor, and support from labor is frequently weak. Hence, political support for recruitment may be narrow, but it includes some powerful stakeholders, such as utility companies and local chambers of commerce. The restrictions placed on industrial revenue bonds by federal legislation in the mid-1980s eliminated a tool that many believed was being abused in recruitment efforts.

Recruitment strategies continue to be widely used even though it is recognized that firm relocation generates relatively little employment.[78] Under conditions of structural change, lasting benefits from recruitment will most likely accrue when a state can capture a piece of the industrial innovation process. Therefore, many states have redirected their attention to incentives relevant for research and development, innovative manufacturing, and other factors important in structural change.[79]

Retention

The retention strategy attempts to improve the prospects of firms, particularly firms in the export sector, already operating in an area. The basic rationale is that traditional industries can again become competitive, either through the lowering of the costs of production, through technological innovation or entering new markets. Support for retention programs developed slowly. In some states it emerged upon the recognition that the so-called high-tech programs reached a very small part of a state's economy and might never affect traditional sectors. In other states it developed after traditional sectors, such as the automobile industry in Michigan, discovered little response to their circumstances from the federal government and redirected their attention to state and local governments. For state and local political leaders, policies that aid traditional sectors can be quite attractive. This development strategy has become increasingly prominent during the 1980s, and many of the innovative state programs have been directed toward existing firms in a state.

Programs for implementing a retention strategy can take many forms, some firm- or industry-specific and others broader. Perhaps the most exciting form evolved from the recognition that technology policy could reach traditional industry, by encouraging innovation in process technology and the use of new materials.[80] States and regions with historically high levels of manufacturing have devoted significant shares of technology policy resources to advanced manufacturing (see Table 5.7).[81] The export promotion programs are also important elements of retention strategies. The increasing popularity of the retention strategy results from its ability to associate improvement of resources in the local economy—for example, increased R&D or advances in production technology—with existing political constituencies.

Support for a retention strategy is likely to be found in the export sector and in sectors tied to the production of innovation, such as training, research, and education institutions. Support from the local-demand sector is uncertain. Successful programs may not lead to increased employment, although earnings in a city or state will be enhanced if the effort is successful. However, if the alternative to a retention effort is plant closings and increasing unemployment, the local sector may well lend its support. Although the strategy is a defensive one, at least compared with recruitment, in a period of economic change any attempt to protect one's competitive position by supporting firms that are already elements of the local economy holds substantial appeal.

New Firm Generation

The third strategy promotes new firm formation. The role of small business and new firm formation became more fully understood in the 1980s, as discussed above. High rates of new firm formation reflect risk-taking and innovation, and economies with these characteristics will likely fare better during the current period of economic change. Many of the innovative programs of the 1980s, such as incubation and business assistance programs, contribute to a new firm generation strategy. However, given that these programs reach relatively few individuals, they lack broad-based political support of retention strategies and will probably never receive major financial support. Moreover, there is little evidence that public programs of this type can be a significant force in generating new firms. The programs supporting a new firm generation strategy may be more important for their symbolic value than for their practical value. The strategy, however, may benefit indirectly from a successful retention strategy whereby improvement in existing economic and technological resources may lead to an improved entrepreneurial environment.

Two notable changes in the array of state development strategies could be noted by 1990. The predominate strategy of the pre–1980 period, recruitment, had evolved to become more consistent with the changing of the U.S. economy. In other words, targeting of recruitment was more sophisticated in that the dynamic elements of the economy tended to be chosen. The second change was that more substantial attention was provided to retention and new firm generation strategies. With the limitations of the new firm generation policies becoming clearer, greater attention to retention strategies emerged, in no small part a response to pressures from local economic constituencies.

CONCLUSIONS

The efforts of state government in technology and development policy are impressive in several respects. The wide range of initiatives, approaches, and variation in institutional frameworks very much reflect the states as experimental if not entrepreneurial. While the effectiveness of these efforts remains to be determined, an evolution of state policy—once focused on industrial recruitment, but now addressing the implications of technological change and the internationalization of the U.S. economy—has nevertheless occurred.

The competitive framework of state policy—the result of both the multiple points of access in the intergovernmental framework and the uneven spatial impact of economic change—helps explain this burst of state activism. The framework itself is not new, though constitutional and federal actions, through restrictions on interstate tariffs, for example, attempt to limit the range of competition.[82] One contemporary form of competition, a reaction to desperate economic conditions in recent decades, utilizes tax and social wage reductions in the so-called "get poor" strategy.[83]

This type of action, believed to lower the cost of production for all firms in the state and make the business climate more attractive, received substantial support from business communities, though it obviously does little to make an economy more productive. In Massachusetts, tax reduction has been viewed as an important factor—though just one of many—in the state's revival in the early 1980s,[84] but in California, tax limitations and subsequent reductions in expenditures on infrastructure and, especially, education, are blamed for weakening the state's economic base.[85]

Although firm-specific subsidies offered by state and local governments have become part of the American landscape, similar subsidies offered by countries have become a source of contention in international trade arrangements. In fact, some even argue that the "Buy America" programs violate the spirit of free trade.[86] Regardless of questions about economic efficiency concerning such subsidies, the competitive framework in which states function suggests that these types of subsidies will not disappear.

Recent technology and development policy, however, suggests that the form in which competition expresses itself has broadened to include more productive avenues. The technological needs of firms and the economy and the specific forms of assistance needed by growing firms are now better understood and have found expression in a wide variety of state programs. Although funding for state technology programs has increased rapidly, it remains a small fraction of both state budgets and of total R&D in the United States.

The R&D effort in the United States is highly segmented and decentralized. The federal government remains the principal source of funds for research conducted in universities, but state governments are encouraging universities to become more engaged in applied research and to interact more intensively with the private sector. Particularly in regions which have historically had limited industry R&D, states are using universities to develop a research base for economic development. In a similar fashion, the federal government is attempting to broaden its mission-oriented research in the direction of technology transfer to the private sector. The expansion of state technology programs has attracted great attention, but federal R&D funding remains the central source of funds for university research, and university–industry centers are fairly small endeavors. As political institutions in a society experiencing economic change, universities have been encouraged to redirect their resources and broaden their research mission. As large and mature institutions with many diverse constituencies and multiple missions, universities, however, cannot easily redefine their roles or change priorities among missions.

A striking feature of state efforts in economic development is the great variation in institutional format. Some programs are operated in traditional line agencies, some in quasi-public institutions, and others in private institutions. This variety of institutional formats represents a commitment to experimentation on the part of states as well as a recognition that large public expenditures for development programs will not occur in the near future. In fact, many state efforts represent an attempt to undertake specific roles or functions that are currently not being performed properly in the economy. These programs significantly expand the range of professional expertise needed in the public sector and may serve a demonstration effect like that identified in state strategic planning in the previous chapter.

Much as technology policy represented a break in state development policy formerly dominated by traditional industrial recruitment, the firm- or industry-specified technology programs have themselves been unable to change the rate of economic growth in a state simply because they affect relatively few firms. Thus, attention has turned toward more broad-based efforts. In the next two chapters, two state policy areas, telecommunications and education, which hold potential for affecting a broad range of development efforts activities and most sectors of the economy, will be examined.

NOTES

1. V. O. Key, Jr., *The Administration of Federal Grants to States* (Chicago, IL: Public Administration Services, 1937): 5–9.

2. Jurgen Schmandt and Robert H. Wilson, "State Science and Technology Policies: An Assessment," *Economic Development Quarterly*, vol. 2, no. 2 (May 1988): 124–137.

3. Harvey M. Sapolsky, "Science Policy in American Government," *Minerva*, vol. 9, no. 3 (July 1971): 322–348.

4. Schmandt and Wilson, "State Science and Technology Policy," p. 127. Created as the federal initiative, two industrial extension agencies—New York's Science and Technology Foundation and the Pennsylvania Technical Assistance Program (PENN-TAP)—still operate. See Marianne K. Clarke, "Recent State Initiatives: An Overview of State Science and Technology Policies and Programs," in *Growth Policy in the Age of High Technology: The Role of Regions and States*, edited by Jurgen Schmandt and Robert H. Wilson (Boston: Unwin Hyman, 1990): 150.

5. Clarke, "Recent State Initiatives," p. 150.

6. Peter K. Eisinger, *The Rise of the Entrepreneurial State: State and Local Development Policy in the United States* (Madison, WI: University of Wisconsin Press, 1988): 16.

7. Eisinger, *The Rise of the Entrepreneurial State*, p. 18.

8. James C. Cobb, *The Selling of the South: The Southern Crusade for Industrial Development, 1936–1980* (Baton Rouge, LA: Louisiana State University Press, 1982): Chapter 1.

9. John E. Moes, "The Subsidization of Industry by Local Communities in the South," *Southern Economic Journal* (October 1961): 187–193; Bruce J. Schulman, *Federal Policy, Economic Development, and the Transformation of the South, 1938–1980* (New York: Oxford University Press, 1991): 47–49; Neal R. Peirce and Jerry Hagstrom,

The Book of America: Inside the 50 States Today (New York: W. W. Norton, 1983): 468.

10. Marianne K. Clarke, *Revitalizing State Economies: A Review of State Economic Development Policies and Programs* (Washington, D.C.: National Governors' Association, 1986); National Association of State Development Agencies (NASDA), *Directory of Incentives for Business Investment and Development in the United States* (Washington, D.C.: The Urban Institute, 1983); Charles Bartsch, Marian Barber, and Margaret Quan, eds., *The Guide to State and Federal Resources for Economic Development*, 4th ed. (Washington, D.C.: Northeast-Midwest Institute, 1988); U.S. Department of Commerce, *Directory of Federal and State Business Assistance, 1986–1987: A Guide for New and Growing Companies* (Washington, D.C., May 1986).

11. NASDA, *1990 State Development Agency Expenditure and Salary Survey* (Washington, D.C., 1990). Not all economic development programs of a state are implemented by the state's development agency, so these figures underestimate total state expenditures for economic development.

12. Ibid., summary table (unnumbered).

13. For a discussion of the Small Cities CDBG program, see Eisinger, *The Rise of the Entrepreneurial State*, pp. 106–113.

14. Although the importance of R&D in growth is broadly accepted, empirical verification of the specific role and its relative importance remains the subject of a good deal of attention. For a summary of the state of knowledge, see Linda R. Cohen and Roger G. Noll, *The Technology Pork Barrel* (Washington, D.C.: Brookings Institution, 1991): 7–11.

15. National Science Foundation (NSF), *National Patterns of R&D Resources: 1990*, Survey of Science Series (NSF 90–316) (Washington, D.C., 1990): Tables B–18 and B–19, p. 59.

16. William J. Broad, "Research Spending Is Declining in U.S. as It Rises Abroad," *New York Times* (February 21, 1991): A–1, A–11.

17. NSF, *National Patterns of R&D Resources: 1990*, Table B–13, p. 55.

18. Ibid., Tables B–9 and B–10, pp. 51–52.

19. Science and Public Policy Program, University of Oklahoma, *Innovation Through Technical and Scientific Information: Government and Industry Cooperation* (New York: Quorum Books, 1989): 113–124.

20. Lois S. Peters and Patricia A. Wheeler, "Technology-Based Regional Economic Development: An Overview" (Troy, NY: Center for Science and Technology Policy, Rensselaer Polytechnic Institute, February 1988), p. 38.

21. Louis Mogavero, Kenneth R. Susskind, and Achmand M. Chadran, "Federal Technology Transfer: Critical Perspectives," in Advisory Commission on Intergovernmental Relations (ACIR), *State and Local Initiatives on Productivity, Technology, and Innovation: Enhancing a National Resource for International Competitiveness* (Washington, D.C., 1990): 37.

22. National Governors' Association, *Capital Ideas*, September 1988, as reported in ACIR, *State and Local Initiatives on Productivity, Technology and Innovation*, p. 128.

23. Office of Science and Technology, *State Technology Programs in the United States, 1988* (St. Paul: Minnesota Department of Trade and Economic Development, July 1988); Robert D. Atkinson, "State Programs for Technology Development: A State-by-State Listing" (Washington, D.C.: National Association of State Development Agencies, April 1988).

24. The original formulation of the product lifecycle is generally traced to Kuznets and Burns. The concept has been revisited many times and has been subject to broad disagreement. Some argue that rather than products, the appropriate object of analysis is profits and this allows for several different outcomes during the maturation phase of the cycle. See Ann Markusen, *Profit Cycles, Oligopoly, and Regional Development* (Cambridge, MA: MIT Press, 1985). Another point of contention concerns the role research and development. Kline and Rosenberg have convincingly argued that the role of research is not limited to the early phase of the cycle but in fact is intensively utilized during all phases. In addition, problems at the later stages may require new basic research, thus creating a nonlinear, multiple feedback role for research and development; see Stephen J. Kline and Nathan Rosenberg, "An Overview of Innovation," in *The Positive Sum Strategy*, edited by R. Landau and Nathan Rosenberg (Washington, D.C.: National Academy Press, 1986), pp. 275–305. Despite the validity of these criticisms, our intent here is to provide a means to categorize state activities and the phases in the original formulation of the product cycle serves this purpose well.

25. As noted in Chapter 2, technological change was only one of two factors contributing to structural change. Foreign competition and investment of U.S. firms abroad also significantly affected the U.S. economy.

26. Cohen and Noll, *The Technology Pork Barrel*, pp. 20–21.

27. A number of inventories of state science and technology programs for promoting economic development programs have been developed. Jurgen Schmandt and Robert Wilson, eds., *Promoting High-Technology Industries: Initiatives and Policies of State Governments* (Boulder, CO: Westview Press, 1987); Clarke, "Recent State Initiatives"; Peters and Wheeler, "Technology-Based Regional Economic Development"; Clarke, *Revitalizing State Economies*, Chapter 5.

28. Quentin W. Lindsey, "University–Industry Research Cooperation: The State Government Role," *Journal of the Society of Research Administrators*, vol. 17, no. 2 (Fall 1985): 89.

29. In Michigan an applied research center was established outside a university environment. See Osborne, *Laboratories of Democracy*, pp. 162–164.

30. Michael I. Luger and Harvey A. Goldstein. *Technology in the Garden: Research Parks and Regional Economic Development* (Chapel Hill, NC: The University of North Carolina Press, 1991): 5.

31. Ibid., p. 2.

32. Ibid., p. 175.

33. Ibid., p. 53.

34. Ibid., p. 74.

35. Feller, "University–Industry Research and Development Relationships," pp. 318–323.

36. Marianne K. Clarke and Eric W. Dobson, *Promoting Technological Excellence: The Role of State and Federal Extension Activities* (Washington, D.C.: National Governors' Association, 1989): 47.

37. David Birch, *Job Creation in America: How Our Smallest Companies Put the Most People to Work* (New York: The Free Press, 1987); Benjamin W. Morky, *Entrepreneurship and Public Policy: Can Government Stimulate Business Startups?* (New York: Quorum Books, 1988): 3–5.

38. National Commission on Jobs and Small Business, *Making America Work Again: Jobs, Small Business, and the International Challenge* (Washington, D.C., 1987): 38.

39. Ibid.

40. David Birch, *Job Creation in America*, Chapters 2 and 3; Roger Vaughn, Robert Pollard, and Barbara Dyer, "The Wealth of States: Policies for a Dynamic Economy" (Washington, D.C.: Council of State Planning Agencies, 1985): Chapters 2 and 4.

41. David N. Allen, "Creating Jobs by Creating New Businesses: The Role of Business Incubators" (Washington, D.C.: National Council of Urban Economic Development, 1985): 4–5.

42. Clarke and Dobson, *Promoting Technological Excellence*, pp. 18–19.

43. Bartsch, Barber, and Quan, *The Guide to State and Federal Resources for Economic Development*, pp. 35–36; The Pennsylvania strategy is discussed in David N. Allen and Victor Levine, *Nurturing Advanced Technology Enterprises: Emerging Issues in State and Local Economic Development Policy* (New York: Praeger, 1986), Chapter 8.

44. Morky, *Entrepreneurship and Public Policy*, Chapter 2.

45. Edward Malecki, "Technological Innovation and Paths to Regional Economic Growth," in *Growth Policy*, edited by Schmandt and Wilson, pp. 112–115.

46. Roger J. Vaughn and Robert Pollard, "Small Business and Economic Development," in *Financing Economic Development in the 1980s: Issues and Trends*, edited by Norman Walzer and David L. Chicoine (New York: Praeger, 1986): 130–137.

47. Morky, *Entrepreneurialism and Public Policy*, Chapters 5–7.

48. Malecki, "Technological Innovation and Growth," p. 116.

49. Eisinger, *The Rise of the Entrepreneurial State*, pp. 243–245.

50. Lawrence Litvak and Belden Daniels, *Innovations in Development Finance* (Washington, D.C.: Council of State Planning Agencies, 1979): Chapters 1 and 3.

51. Osborne, "Economic Competitiveness," pp. 9–12; Ronald F. Ferguson and Helen F. Ladd, "Pioneering State Economic Strategy," in *The New Economic Role of American States: Strategies in a Competitive World Economy*, edited by R. Scott Fosler (New York: Oxford, 1988): 36–46.

52. Venture Economics, Inc., as reported in Ronald J. Swagger, ed., *Economic Development Tomorrow: A Report from the Profession* (Rosemont, IL: American Economic Development Council, 1991): 20.

53. Gary Bettger, "State Venture Capital Initiatives," *State Legislative Reports*, vol. 11, no. 2 (February 1986); Lawrence Litvak and Belden Daniels, "Innovations in Development Finance" (Washington, D.C.: Council of State Planning Agencies, 1979): Chapters 4, 5, 6, and 8; Larry C. Ledebur and David W. Rasmussen, "State Development Incentives" (Washington, D.C.: The Urban Institute, 1983): Chapters 1, 2, and 3; Elinor W. Edmunds, "Montana Science and Technology Alliance: An Innovative Funding Approach," *The Journal of State Government*, vol. 61, no. 4 (July/August 1988): 144–147; Keon S. Chi, "The States and Business Incentives: An Inventory of Tax and Financial Incentive Programs" (Council of State Governments, 1989); Paul R. Brockman and Paul B. Phelps, "State-Funded Seed Capital Programs Available for New-Technology-Based Ventures" (Alexandria, VA: LFW Management Associates, June 1989).

54. Peter Fisher, "Product Development Corporations and State Economic Development," *Economic Development Quarterly*, vol. 2, no. 4 (November 1988): 303.

55. Eisinger, *The Rise of the Entrepreneurial State*, pp. 251–252.

56. John Sower, "Using Pension Funds for Business Financing Programs," *Economic Development Review*, vol. 5, no. 1 (Winter 1987): 20–22; for Michigan and its Venture Capital Fund, one of the country's largest pension-backed funds, see Osborne, *Laboratories of Democracy*, pp. 154–156.

57. Mark, Halper, "BIDCOs Part II: Now It's Public," *Venture*, vol. 10, no. 2 (February 1988): 70–73. For Michigan's Strategic Fund and its various programs, see Osborne, *Laboratories of Democracy*, pp. 158–161.

58. Thomas P. Doud suggests that capital programs can be classified as regulatory or as direct intervention. The action of the state can be passive or active. Encouraging these new forms of cooperation would be classified as an active, regulatory approach. See Thomas P. Doud, "Directing Capital to Small Young Firms," *Economic Development Review*, vol. 5, no. 1 (Winter 1987): 14–19.

59. There are a number of other concerns as well for the venture capital programs. Even if private capital is not displaced, are not the potential goals of a satisfactory rate of return and social objectives, such as targeting small firms, disadvantaged workers or regions, likely to be in conflict? See Peter S. Fisher, "State Venture Capital Funds as an Economic Development Strategy," *Journal of the American Planning Association*, vol. 54, no. 2 (Spring 1988): 166–177.

60. Timothy J. Bartik, "Product Development Corporations and State Economic Development: The Importance of R&D Spillovers," *Economic Development Quarterly*, vol. 3, no. 4 (November 1989): 327–328.

61. John M. Kline, "The International Economic Interests of U.S. States," *Publius: The Journal of Federalism*, vol. 14 (Fall 1984): 83–85; Alan R. Posner, *State Government and Exportation Promotion* (Westport, CT: Quorum Books, 1984): Chapter 2.

62. Norman J. Glickman and Douglas P. Woodward, *The New Competitors: How Foreign Investors Are Changing the U.S. Economy* (New York: Basic Books, 1989): Chapter 8.

63. Eisinger, *The Rise of the Entrepreneurial State*, pp. 294–295.

64. Ibid., pp. 299–302.

65. James Harwell, "The States' Growing International Role," *State Government* (Winter 1975): 1–5.

66. John Kincaid, "The American Governors in International Affairs," *Publius: The Journal of Federalism*, vol. 14 (Fall 1984): 95–113.

67. Kincaid, "American Governors," p. 107; Corporation for Enterprise Development, *The 1991 Development Report Card for the States* (Washington, D.C., April 1991): 90.

68. NASDA, *1990 State Economic Development Expenditure Survey*. This includes funding for both promotion of exports and for the attraction of foreign investment. The Congressional Budget Office reported in 1984 that about two-thirds of state expenditures on international trade were devoted to export promotion. See Congressional Budget Office, *The Federal Role in State Development Programs* (Washington, D.C., 1984): 25.

69. Ann O'M. Bowman and Michael A. Pagano, "The State of American Federalism: 1989–1990," *Publius: The Journal of Federalism*, vol. 20 (Summer 1990): 2; Earl H. Fry, "State and Local Governments in the International Arena," *Annals of American Academy of Political and Social Science*, vol. 509 (May 1990): 118–127.

70. Daniel E. Pilcher and Lanny Proffer, "The States and International Trade: New Roles in Export Development" (Washington, D.C.: National Conference of State Legislatures, December 1985); National Governors' Association, Committee on International Trade and Foreign Relations, "States in the International Economy" (Washington, D.C., 1985); John Kline, "The Expanding International Agenda for State Government," *State Government*, vol. 57, no. 1 (1984): 2–6; Posner, *State Government Export Promotion*, Appendix II.

71. Pilcher and Proffer, "The States and International Trade," pp. 22–24 and Chapter 2; Marci Levin, "Minnesota and the Commerce Department Form a Winning Team to Promote Development and Exports," *Business America*, vol. 10, no. 23 (November 9, 1987): 14–15; Eisinger, *The Rise of the Entrepreneurial State*, pp. 299–301.

72. For a discussion of the difficulties in evaluating these programs, see Robert Thomas Kurdle and Cynthia Marie Kite, "The Evaluation of State Programs for International Business Development," *Economic Development Quarterly*, vol. 3, no. 4 (November 1989): 288–300.

73. In a study of four export trading companies, the public sector programs, formed by port authorities, were careful to identify needs not provided by existing private sector firms. They attempted to fill information gaps and were small in scale. Mary Lou Egan, "The State and Economic Development: The Role of Port-Based Export Trading Companies in Public Sector Export Promotion," *State and Local Government* (Winter 1987): 29–35.

74. A similar use of these categories is made by John E. Jackson, "The Political Economy of Development in a Mature Economy," in *The New Economic Role*, edited by Fosler, Chapter 6.

75. Cobb, *The Selling of the South*, Chapter 1.

76. Glickman and Woodward, *The New Competitors*, Chapter 7; Blaine Liner and Larry Ledebur, "Foreign Direct Investment in the United States: A Governor's Guide," paper prepared for the 79th Annual Meeting of the National Governors' Association, July 26–28, 1987; William J. Donovan, "Economic Development: Bay State Discovers the Joys of Snaring Foreign Investment," *New England Business*, vol. 7, no. 9 (May 20, 1985): 40–41.

77. Liner and Ledebur, "Foreign Direct Investment," pp. 8–11. After a rigorous cost benefit evaluation, the state of Michigan offered a bid to attract Mazda but withdrew a bid to attract Mitsubishi. See Osborne, *Laboratories of Democracy*, pp. 167–168.

78. Birch, *Job Creation in America*, pp. 135–139.

79. David R. Allardice and Robert H. Schnorbus, "The Ordeal of Change: Working It out in the Midwest," *Chicago Fed Letter* (September 1, 1987): 1–3.

80. Birch, *Job Creation in America*, p. 66.

81. Osborne, *Laboratories of Democracy*, pp. 152–153.

82. ACIR, *Interjurisdictional Tax and Policy Competition: Good or Bad for the Federal System* (Washington, D.C., April 1991), Chapter 3.

83. John E. Jackson, "Initiation and Implementation of a Creation Strategy," in *The New Economic Role*, edited by Fosler, pp. 113–114.

84. Ferguson and Ladd, "Massachusetts," in *The New Economic Role*, edited by Fosler, pp. 21–87.

85. Henton and Waldhorn, "The Megastate Economy," in *The New Economic Role*, edited by Fosler, pp. 214–220.

86. Kline, "The International Economic Interests," pp 88–90.

6

The State as Regulator of Infrastructure: Telecommunications Policy

Until recent years, the state role in telecommunications amounted to a fairly narrow one, that of determining fair rates of basic services provided by a regulated telephone monopoly, principally the AT&T-affiliated local exchange companies. The state utility commissions, with a subordinated role in a federally dominated regulatory structure, and the telephone industry operated successfully, in terms of creating an excellent quality, widely accessible, telephone system, but did so with relatively little public attention and innovative spirit. Three interrelated changes have thrust state governments, especially state utility commissions, onto center stage in regulating and deregulating, a rapidly changing, yet vitally important industry and infrastructure.

First, the telecommunications industry has experienced dramatic technological innovation for several decades, and the prospect of further innovation stretches to the foreseeable future. The resulting increases in productivity and innovative applications of these new technologies are spreading through all sectors of the economy. Second, as a result of the divestiture of AT&T in 1984 and the subsequent proactive federal deregulatory posture, the states face a broader range of regulatory issues. But given the increasing segmentation in the industry, that is, the proliferation in the number and types of firms providing telecommunications services and equipment, and the critical importance of this infrastructure, the regulatory role is becoming one increasingly concerned with economic development. Not only must states address a complex and changing intergovernmental regulatory structure, telecommunications systems themselves are quickly becoming the most significant infrastructure for many segments of the economy. If a state, or city, is not able to obtain an adequate telecommunications infrastructure, it may become a less desirable site for many types of business activities. States have demonstrated significantly different responses as they wrestle with these new challenges in telecommunications policy.

The treatment of state telecommunications policy will follow a format somewhat different from that for the other state policy areas. First, since the telecommunications industry has received relatively little attention in the development literature and has been directly affected by technological innovation during the last two decades, a brief industry study and its spatial characteristics will first be presented. The structure of the industry has direct implications for the regulatory role of states. In addition, the extensive and fundamental changes in the intergovernmental regulatory structure, affected both by the forces of technological change and by aggressive deregulation by the federal government, require an examination of the formation and evolution of the telephone regulation that led to the divestiture of AT&T in 1984. The third section explores the policy responses of state government to their evolving regulatory responsibilities. The potential that states hold for affecting economic development through their role in securing telecommunications infrastructure is examined in the last section of the chapter.

THE TECHNOLOGY AND THE INDUSTRY

In 1990, more than 2,000 companies provided public telecommunications services on the public network,[1] which consisted of 243 million telephones on 135 million local access lines. The more than 450 billion calls that are placed on the network each year must be switched by the 15,689 central office switches. This enormous system has benefitted from technological changes, which have led to innovative applications that can improve productivity of firms and organizations and contribute to rapid growth and diversification in the telecommunications industry itself.

The Technology

Simply stated, telecommunications means to communicate over a distance. The way such communication can be accomplished, however, has changed dramatically in recent decades.[2] A wide array of technological advances have contributed to the rapid pace of change. In addition, as discussed in Chapter 2, the informational needs of the changing national economy have created a new set of demands for telecommunications services, provoking further innovation in the applications of these technologies. The most prominent technological innovation has actually been the merging of two technologies, communications and computers.[3] Computers can now communicate with each other over a great distance, and the telecommunications networks, particularly the public telephone network, are themselves becoming computer-intensive. The modern electronic switch is a computer.

The evolution of telephony is well documented, and only a few advances need to be presented here.[4] First, telecommunications systems are rapidly converting from traditional analog signals to digital signals for transmissions. Text, sound, and even video signals can be digitized in the same binary code used by computers. Moving from analog to digital signals facilitates transmission and, more importantly, replaces the electromechanical technology required by analog switching with electronic switching. With computerized switching, the capacity of the network is dramatically expanded. Because computers act as switches, the introduction of new services is driven by software rather than changes in hardware, making the system extremely flexible. Digital switching led to decentralization of the switching function as switches move closer to users.[5] In addition, the network can be expanded—more users can be attached—without increased centralization. The early hierarchical structure of the telephone network, with a central office switch at the top of the pyramid, is being replaced by a more decentralized structure, sometimes called a geodesic network. This decentralizing trend in telecommunications will contribute to declining differences in economic geography.[6]

Telecommunications systems involve a wide range of transmission technologies, including cable systems, satellites, microwave systems, cellular telephone, broadcast radio and television as well as telephone systems. Each technology has its own unique attributes and will remain appropriate in certain applications. The introduction of fiber optic cables, however, has been the most important recent advance in transmission technology.[7] Digital signals are transmitted on these cables using laser-produced light waves. Fiber optic cables have enormous capacity for high-speed transmission, compared with the traditional copper wiring, and further capacity-enhancing development is underway. For example, the ability to multiplex (send simultaneously) light of different colors (that is, different wave lengths) through a fiber optic cable is being explored. The transmission capacity of fiber optic cables is largely determined by the optoelectronic equipment which converts light signals to electronic signals at the ends of the fiber, making possible the further expansion of transmission capacity using existing optical fiber cable.

These advances in switching and transmission technologies have also facilitated the development of private telecommunications systems that partially or totally bypass public telephone networks. Many companies with multiple locations have found it advantageous, for reasons of cost or security, to develop their own telecommunications systems.[8] Some of the private systems are enormous.[9] General Motors' private network links 250,000 telephone sets and computer terminals located throughout the world.[10] Ford Motor Company's private system spans five continents.[11] In addition, local area networks (LANs) are linking communications-intensive firms or institutions in a specific geographical area, such as in a downtown, and similar wide area networks (WANs) are stretching these private systems over an ever larger area. Although the proliferation of various systems is likely to continue, the switched public network will remain the backbone of the country's telecommunications system, providing the means by which these private networks can be interconnected. The result will be a more segmented and specialized complex of integrated networks.[12]

This greatly expanded switching and transmission capacity has created the base for new types of telecommunications networks, including broad-band networks capable of transmitting enormous amounts of information. The integrated services digital network (ISDN) permits the simultaneous transmission of voice, video, and data over the same system. Such systems are even able to transmit information-intensive television signals. ISDN systems were deployed to around 150 corporate customers in 1990. Critical to the development of ISDN systems is the establishment of standards for protocol and transmission, especially at the interface of telecommunications networks and customer premises equipment (CPE).[13]

The rapidly changing technology is creating competition among alternative communications media. The capabilities of an ISDN system duplicate those of coaxial cable systems, but provide two-way communications instead of the unswitched one-way communications of existing cable systems. In addition, technological changes are expanding the opportunities for radio telephony and mobile communications. Cellular systems and the emerging personal communications systems, using digital radio technology and more efficient use of the radio spectrum, provide new means for accessing the public network and new configurations for local area networks.[14]

Applications

Although plain-old-telephone service (POTS) is used by almost all firms, a wide range of new telecommunications applications in business has emerged.[15] In mid-size and large firms of the 1960s, internal communications systems were not needed, because applications in accounting, manufacturing control, or data entry and retrieval were free-standing, independent support systems.[16] In the following decade there was a move toward integrated management information systems. The expansion in the number of multiplant or multifacility firms created additional demand for communications for internal management systems. Advances in telecommunications have allowed more centralized management structure over the far-flung locations of multiplant firms.

Telecommunications systems are now being extended externally and employed in innovative ways by firms in their relations with suppliers and customers.[17] Automated ordering, telemarketing, interactive video conference calls, WATS lines, and 1–800 and 1–900 numbers are but a few examples of the use of telecommunications for external relations. By connecting external communications with internal management systems, a firm can achieve dramatic increases in productivity. The effective and dramatic impact of telecommunications advances can be seen in the retailing giant Wal-Mart.[18] Wal-Mart uses a state-of-the-art satellite system for communications among its more than 1,500 stores, largely bypassing the public network. Wal-Mart has had great success in its inventory management system, and the nightly reporting of inventories, by satellite, is a central feature of this system.

Extensive innovation in the applications of telecommunications is found in the nonprofit and public sectors as well. Governments, themselves information-intensive, create an enormous demand for telecommunications systems and frequently find that establishing their own systems may be advantageous.[19] Public and private education systems are discovering extremely useful applications is such areas as distributed education. Universities, research institutes, and government agencies are rapidly developing networks to link computer facilities and research units. Networks, such as NYSERNet in New York[20] and PRP Net in Pennsylvania,[21] may eventually be linked to private research and business concerns as well. The federal government is considering the upgrade of existing national research networks, such as NSFnet and Internet. The proposed network, National Education and Research Network (NERN), would expand substantially the high-speed data transmission capabilities among the universities and other research institutions prepared to invest in the network.[22]

Industry Structure

The telecommunications industry, consisting of service and equipment providers, accounted for an estimated $175.8 billion in sales in 1990.[23] Providers of services can be divided into three segments: local exchange companies that provide local telephone service; interexchange companies that provide long-distance service; and providers of enhanced services.

The local exchange companies consist of the seven regional Bell companies that were created in the divestiture of AT&T, GTE, and many smaller local exchange companies that frequently provide service in rural areas and small towns (see Table 6.1). These local exchange companies had total revenues of $75 billion and total capital investment of $246 billion in 1990.[24] The Bell companies are independent and each has adopted a unique corporate posture.[25] Almost all have acquired new business ventures, a number outside the telecommunications industry and others even outside the United States.

Even after divestiture in 1984 and the deregulation of interexchange markets, AT&T remains the dominant firm, but others, such as MCI and US Sprint, are obtaining increasing shares of the market (see Table 6.2). The volume of long-distance calls, in terms of access minutes, has grown on an average of 13 percent a year between 1984 and 1990, and prices have substantially declined.[26] These interexchange companies have made substantial investments in their equipment, and in 1990 US Sprint's network was 100 percent digital and AT&T's network was 90 percent digital.[27] Other companies serve as wholesalers and resell interexchange capacity.

The markets for both local and interexchange companies are being affected by the development of private telecommunications systems that totally or partially bypass the public network. Although bypass represents a loss of customer base,

Table 6.1
Local Exchange Companies—Access Lines and Revenues: 1984 and 1988

	Equipped Lines (in millions) 1988	Revenues (in $ billions) 1984	1988
Regional Bell Operating Companies (RBOCs)			
Ameritech	15.6	8.3	9.9
Bell Atlantic	16.5	8.1	10.9
Bell South	16.4	9.5	13.6
NYNEX	14.9	9.5	12.7
Pacific Telesis	13.1	7.8	9.5
Southwestern Bell	11.3	7.2	8.5
US West	11.9	7.3	9.2
Independent Telephone Companies			
GTE	12.2	12.9	16.5
United Telecom	3.7	2.9	6.5
Contel	2.5	2.3	3.0
SNET	1.8	1.3	1.6
Centel	1.5	1.4	1.1
Alltel	1.1	0.6	1.1
Cincinnati Bell	0.8	0.4	0.7
Rochester Tel	0.6	0.4	0.5
Others	5.8	n/a	n/a

Sources: United States Telephone Association, Statistics of the Local Exchange Carriers for the Year 1988 (Washington, D.C., 1989), pp. 2 and 6; Standard and Poor's Industry Surveys, Telecommunications Basic Analysis, October 5, 1989, vol. 157, no. 40, Sec. 1, p. 47.

most telephone companies actively participate in bypass through leasing or selling circuits or even creating virtual private networks. In 1990, about 15 percent of network usage went to private lines and another 15 percent went to virtual private networks.[28] With high-capacity, high-speed lines and software-defined systems in advanced switches, customized telephone systems can be developed for individual businesses. Although very large users of telecommunications may wish to build and control a complete end-to-end bypass system—utilizing satellites,[29]

Table 6.2
Market Shares of Interexchange Revenues: 1985 and 1989 (in percent)

	1985		1989	
Carrier	Total	Non-LEC Share	Total	Non-LEC Share
AT&T	67.1	86.3	51.9	67.4
Local Exchange Carriers	22.2		23.0	
MCI	4.3	5.5	9.3	12.1
US Sprint	2.7	3.5	6.5	8.5
Others	3.7	4.7	9.3	12.0

Source: U.S. Department of Commerce, International Trade Administration, 1991 U.S. Industrial Outlook (Washington, D.C., January 1991), p. 29-3.

microwave, and other technologies—many businesses have found it attractive to work with local and interexchange companies in designing systems that partially bypass the public network.

A new and increasingly important factor in telecommunications is radio communications.[30] Cellular systems and the emerging personal communications systems are generally used for mobile communications, vehicle or pedestrian, and provide a means to access the local exchange system. Since its inauguration in 1983, cellular telephone services have shown extraordinary growth, from 3.9 million subscribers in 1989 to a projected 7 million in 1991; revenues totaled $5.2 billion in 1990, representing a 50 percent increase over 1989.[31] The deployment of digital cellular in the near future will substantially expand capacity of cellular systems, which should further contribute to high rates of growth in the industry.[32] Radio telephone is regulated by the FCC, but states are interested parties in that many local exchange companies are attempting to acquire cellular companies outside their franchise areas and these systems require access to the public, local exchange network.

Value-added services are among the most rapidly growing segment of the telecommunications service industries. Sometimes referred to as advanced or enhanced services, this market segment includes packet-switching, public data services, gateway services, protocol services, electronic and voice mail, data processing, electronic funds transfers, point-of-sale transactions, videotext services, and others. Although interexchange companies are permitted to offer these services, the MFJ restricted the regional Bell companies from participating in such service markets in hope of generating competition. The market for these services is growing at around 10 percent annually.[33] In 1990, public data networks providing enhanced services had sales of $670 million; data processing services had sales of $30 billion; and on-line database services were about $4 billion.

Videotext services, provided by such companies as CompuServe, had 1.7 million subscribers in 1990, which was a 20 percent increase over 1988. Local area networks, which are part of this market segment, had around 18 million nodes worldwide, increasingly connected to the public network, and represent a major potential for enhanced services.

The location pattern of the telecommunications service providers (defined as the employment share within a state of Standard Industrial Classification code 48) reflects a number of points suggested in Chapter 2 (see Map 6.1). Telecommunications employment should be associated with firms and occupations that are intensive users of information. Indeed, the pattern for telecommunications follows very closely the spatial distribution of producer services (producer services consists of financial, insurance, real estate, and the business services sector; see Map 2.4).

The state of New York has the largest employment share, 1.34 percent, exceeding by a third the national average. California, Connecticut, and Rhode Island are also states with high levels of producer services and Texas, Florida, and Georgia, although ranking moderately high in producer services, all have very active international export cities, which is another source of demand for communications.[34] Although the relatively high levels of telecommunications levels in Nebraska may seem unusual, the state has made a significant effort to develop a comparative advantage in telecommunications, which will be discussed below.[35] The moderately high levels of telecommunications workers in many states in the Mountain and East North Central regions are likely the result of the inability of areas with low population density to achieve economies of scale. In addition, given that many nontelecommunications services firms have established their own telephone systems, this pattern of employment in telecommunications firms no doubt underestimates actual levels of employment in telecommunications activities in intensive-use states.

The telecommunications service providers are greatly benefitting from technological change. Nestor Terleckyi has empirically investigated the telephone and telegraph service industries and found that R&D in communications, including an important government-funded R&D component, has had a significant effect on the productivity of industry.[36] Productivity in the industry has been relatively high and has contributed to the dramatic decline in the price of telecommunications services. Growth in demand for the sector's product has been rapid, linked especially to declining relative prices and to growth in GNP.[37]

Another important segment of the telecommunications industry is equipment manufacturers. The International Trade Administration estimates that in 1990 sales of domestically produced U.S. communications systems and equipment (including cellular, microwave, fiber optics, and satellite) and telephone and telegraph equipment was around $33 billion, up from $28 billion in 1987 (see Table 6.3). The communications systems segment, especially the cellular system and fiber optic cable industries, reflects in part the decentralization and increasing

Map 6.1
Employment Share of the Communications Sector by State[1]: 1988 (in percent)

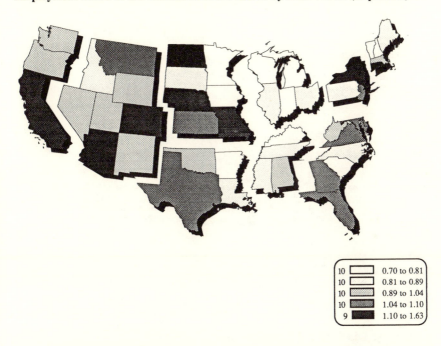

10	0.70 to 0.81
10	0.81 to 0.89
10	0.89 to 1.04
10	1.04 to 1.10
9	1.10 to 1.63

Source: U.S. Department of Commerce, Bureau of the Census, County Business Patterns, 1989, CBP89-2/50 (Washington, D.C., 1991), Table 1a; and source for Table 2.2.

[1]Standard Industrial Classification code 48.

segmentation in the telecommunications industry.[38] Communications systems equipment is frequently sold to businesses developing their own communications facilities. In contrast, the telephone and telegraph equipment segment has grown more slowly (see Table 6.3). Although domestically produced customer premises equipment sales, including private branch exchanges, modems, facsimile machines, and others, have not shown growth during the period 1987–1990, the import of foreign-produced customer equipment remained strong and helped satisfy the increasing demand for this equipment. Foreign production is increasingly shifting to the United States itself, in response to a new protectionist attitude in the country.[39]

This profile of telecommunications shows a robust and technologically driven industry. Until recently, the industry consisted largely of a single company, AT&T, which was regulated as a natural monopoly. In the following section we turn to the regulatory structure for telecommunications in order to understand

Table 6.3
Sales of Telecommunications Equipment in the United States: 1987 and 1990 (in $ billions)

	1987	1990
Communications Systems		
and Equipment, Except Broadcast	$11.0	$15.0
Cellular Radiotelephone System	0.950	2.75–3.00
Fiber Optic Systems	0.568	0.500
Optical Fiber	n/a	0.975
Telephone and Telegraph	17.0	17.9
Central Office Switches	5.1	5.2
Consumer Premises Equipment	4.9	4.4

Source: U.S. Department of Commerce, International Trade Administration, <u>1988 U.S. Industrial Outlook: With Expanded Coverage of the Services Sector, Construction, High-Tech, and Emerging Industries</u> (Washington, D.C., January 1988) pp. 31-2, 31-5, 31-6, 32-2; <u>1991 U.S. Industrial Outlook</u> (January 1991), pp. 30-1, 31-1.

how contemporary regulatory change has been in part induced by changing technology and how deregulation and divestiture are affecting states in their regulatory responsibilities.

THE REGULATORY FRAMEWORK

AT&T and Regulation of Telecommunications

The history of telecommunications regulation in the United States is largely one of public policy toward the dominant company in the industry, AT&T; the history is frequently marked by governmental reaction to a growing and aggressive company. As AT&T captured extraordinary powers at the turn of the century over independent (that is, non-AT&T-affiliated) local exchange companies through its long-distance monopoly and over its own licensed companies through the sale of equipment—produced by its subsidiary, Western Electric— resistance to its growing power emerged. To avoid potential antitrust action, in the Kingsbury Commitment of 1913—an agreement reached between AT&T Vice-President Kingsbury and Attorney General J. C. Reynolds—AT&T agreed to provide interconnection to all local exchange companies and to divest itself of Western Union stock.[40] The president of AT&T during this period, Theodore Vail, endorsed the concept of a regulated monopoly as the most efficient means of obtaining a telephone system that would allow subscribers from any local exchange to speak with subscribers from other exchanges and that would promote universal service. The Mann–Elkin Act of 1910 brought the regulation of interstate telephone rates, and the 1921 Willis–Graham Act brought the consolidation of telephone companies under the purview of the Interstate Commerce Commission (ICC). The same dual-regulatory framework that had evolved in other industries—with states regulating intrastate commerce and the ICC regulating interstate commerce—was applied to telephone companies.

The ineffectiveness of the ICC in regulating telephony and the emerging wireless communications industry led to the Communications Act of 1934, which consolidated federal regulatory activities in the Federal Communications Commission (FCC). The Act reconfirmed early agreements that prohibited competition between wire-based communications (telegraph and telephone) and non-wire-based communications (radio and TV). For wire-based communications, separate monopoly franchises were awarded, for record communications to Western Union and for voice communication to AT&T. The Communications Act ratified the existing industry structure; local exchange companies—consisting of both small, independent exchanges serving mainly rural areas as well as large, AT&T license holders serving most urban areas—were connected by AT&T for interexchange calls. The Act also ratified AT&T as a vertical monopoly; AT&T determined which equipment could be placed on the telephone system and relied on Western Electric to supply equipment.

The telephone system was regulated as a common carrier, which meant that the system had to carry all traffic, on a nondiscriminatory basis, and could not constrain or regulate in any fashion the use made of the system.[41] In addition to this commerce function of the telephone system, AT&T was obligated to provide universal service (that is, telephone service to all potential users at a responsible price). Universal service was particularly important in rural areas where the cost of service was relatively high.

Under the Communications Act, states continued to award monopoly franchises to local exchange companies and to prevent abuse by these monopolies; the rates the companies could charge were regulated, generally through the rate-of-return method. Under rate-of-return regulation, the financial soundness of the utility—a requirement necessary to attract investment—was assured by allowing the utilities to generate a level of revenue sufficient to achieve a predetermined rate of return on its investment in the physical plant, its so-called rate base. After this level of revenue was determined, rates for various types of customers would be set at levels that would generate the total revenue target.

Determining a company's rate base, however, was problematic with respect to allocating the cost of the physical plant to local exchange companies and to long-distance companies. Long-distance calls, or toll calls, require the use of local exchange company equipment on both ends of the call, and a method to allocate costs, which would become part of the rate base of companies, had to be determined. The issue of separation of costs between local and interexchange companies was resolved in the 1950s with the adoption of the station-to-station method of allocation, which shifted costs to the long-distance companies and helped maintain low local service rates.[42]

A second issue arose in the setting of telephone rates in remote, high-cost areas. The solution to the so-called "settlement" problem was to average the cost of long-distance calls according to distance instead of the cost incurred for completing the call. Cost-averaging provided a subsidy to those areas, especially rural areas, where cost of service was high. In conjunction with long depreciation periods for local exchange companies' physical plants, set by state utility commissions, separations and settlements were conducted in such a way as to maintain low basic service rates, cross-subsidized by above-cost interexchange rates.

As a vertical monopoly of enormous power, AT&T has been surrounded by antitrust concerns since its early days. Although AT&T agreed at various points to forgo certain lines of business, such as telegraphy in the Kingsbury Agreement and broadcast communications in an accord reached with RCA in 1926,[43] avoiding antitrust suits appears to have been one factor guiding AT&T's strategy. Several investigations of pricing practices of AT&T's equipment subsidiary, Western Electric, identified potential problems of abuse, but AT&T was successful, generally with support from the FCC, in avoiding any substantial limitation on its monopoly position.[44] Even the Consent Decree of 1956, the result of an antitrust suit filed by the Department of Justice under the Sherman Act, did not significantly affect its vertical monopoly status, although it did restrict AT&T's participation in the computer information market. In this case, the defense of AT&T's status was argued by the secretary of defense, among others.[45]

Regardless of the merits of the antitrust arguments, the regulatory framework has worked well; the country has produced the most advanced telephone system in the world and great strides have been made in achieving universal service, even in high-cost rural areas. Technological advances and demands from large telecommunications users, however, started eroding AT&T's protective barrier. During and immediately after World War II substantial research on all types of communications technology was supported by the federal government. Microwave technology, a wireless technology, was found to be particularly useful for point-to-point communication. In the 1959 *Above 890* case, the FCC responded to demands from an association of large private users and equipment producers and determined that microwave technology could be used for private, point-to-point communication, thus permitting bypass of the public telephone system.[46]

In spite of AT&T's argument that this technology should be considered another element in its regulated market, the FCC expanded its earlier ruling in 1969 by giving Microwave Communications, Inc. (MCI), permission to operate microwave links between St. Louis and Chicago and sell these services to businesses. High levels of business communications occurred in this corridor and AT&T was not able to meet the growing demand. The MCI service was found by the FCC to be a new service that did not compete with AT&T's traditional monopoly service. Although this particular instance did not severely affect AT&T, it established a preceded that would soon be applied broadly to other new markets, such as satellites, for telecommunications services. Steadily, AT&T lost its monopoly hold on new markets.

The impact of computer technology on the telecommunications industry has been repeatedly addressed by the FCC. Three inquiries explored the boundaries between communications markets and computer processing. In Computer Inquiry I, initiated in 1966, the FCC attempted to redefine the boundary established in the 1956 Consent Decree between the transmission of information—a communications activity—and the processing or enhancing of information—a computer processing activity.[47] The result was an agreement with AT&T to preserve its monopoly status for communications but to prohibit participation in computer equipment and processing markets. By the time of Computer Inquiry II, in 1976, it was commonly recognized that this separation was unworkable.[48] A mainframe computer connected to a network of terminals created a communications network. In addition, the new generations of switching equipment in the telephone networks were computers. The FCC, however, attempted to separate basic telephone service, which would remain a monopoly service, from enhanced telecommunications services. For the enhanced services, ''which combine basic service with computer processing applications that act on the format, content, code, [and] protocol of a subscriber's transmitted information,''[49] the Communications Act of 1934 did not apply and, consequently, these markets were not subject to regulation. To prevent AT&T from using its regulated market to cross-subsidize its nonregulated business, the FCC instituted a policy of structural separation, under which AT&T would have to establish subsidiaries for competitive markets. In Computer Inquiry III, the structural separation was found to be too costly— it required duplication of facilities and personnel—and other measures to insure competition were adopted.[50] This policy was later overturned in federal courts, but the FCC revised its approach to integrated services and ceased attempting to preempt the regulation of intrastate enhanced services by state governments.[51]

The AT&T monopoly control over equipment on the public telephone network was also eroded through several court cases. The Hush-A-Phone was a nonelectronic piece of equipment attached to a telephone to facilitate conversations. Although AT&T was initially able to prevent, through an FCC ruling, this equipment from being added to its system, a court order eventually permitted the use of Hush-A-Phones.[52] A further erosion of AT&T's control of equipment occurred in the Carterphone case. Oil companies opposed the AT&T prohibition against their adding a radio phone, needed to service oil wells, to AT&T's system, but this time the FCC ruled against AT&T. These relatively minor cases set a precedent, and in 1980 the FCC ordered that all customer premises equipment be deregulated.

A similar process opened the market for telephone network equipment as electronic switches replaced the earlier switching technology. Because these electronic switches are computers, barring computer companies from building equipment for the telephone system was not tenable. As a result, the number of firms producing switching and customer premises equipment has expanded substantially, as noted above, and these equipment providers have been significant actors in telecommunications policy.

Yet another pressure on AT&T and the traditional regulatory framework developed with regard to the pricing mechanism. The pricing structure, with its

relatively high interexchange rates, led large users to search for alternative communications strategies that would be cost-based, without the cross-subsidization
found on the public network. One strategy was to obtain private lines for exclusive
use of the firm. Telephone companies themselves can provide these lines. Much
of the U.S. Department of Defense domestic communications system relied on
private lines provided by AT&T. AT&T argued that such private line systems
represented new services and, consequently, the company should not be regulated
in that market; rather, AT&T should be subject to competitive market forces
and services priced at cost, without the cross-subsidy.

Divestiture of AT&T

Although the FCC was relatively slow to endorse competition, the Department
of Justice, through its antitrust division and a number of national political leaders
from both the conservative and liberal end of the spectrum, began to push
aggressively for deregulation.[53] An antitrust case initiated in 1974 was resolved
in an out-of-court settlement in 1982. The Modification of Final Judgement (MFJ)
ratified the various trends that undermined the monopoly status of AT&T. AT&T
had to divest its local exchange service, in the form of seven regional Bell
operating companies, but could eventually compete, without regulation, in interexchange and advanced services markets. The Bell companies remained monopolies, subject to the regulation of state utility commissions, but were forbidden
to engage in the production of equipment and the provision of value-added
telecommunications services.

Although the regulatory role of the FCC was substantially diminished, state
governments accrued new regulatory responsibilities under the MFJ.[54] The FCC,
in fact, has attempted to impose its deregulatory philosophy on state governments
in a series of preemptive regulatory positions.[55] As discussed in Chapter 3, the
federal government started using in the mid-1970s a variety of regulatory devices
to induce states to take desired actions. One such mechanism is preemptive
regulation: federal regulation preempts state policy. The FCC adopted policies
that would prevent states from (1) imposing structural separations on AT&T and
the regional Bell companies or requiring structural safeguards inconsistent with
the Computer Inquiry III order; (2) requiring Bell companies to provide customer
premises equipment on an unseparated basis; (3) regulating the communications
wiring inside buildings; and (4) regulating interstate billing. In *Louisiana Public
Service Commission v. FCC,* the FCC's attempt to preempt state decisions on
depreciation schedules of local exchange companies was overturned by the Supreme Court in 1986.[56] In 1990, the U.S. Ninth Circuit Court of Appeals vacated
the FCC rulings on federal preemptive authority on separations of regulated and
unregulated businesses and on regulation of enhanced services, discussed
above.[57] These cases have established some limits on federal preemptive powers,
limited the effects on states of the recent deregulation thrust of the FCC, and
given states a wider range of discretion in policy formulation. A major unresolved

area of potential state–federal conflict surrounds the implementation of open network architecture, a proposal for setting standards for interconnection and definitions for basic service elements on the public network that would facilitate access by all users. Although the FCC has clear authority in resolving these matters for interstate communications, states have the authority for intrastate regulation; thus, differing sets of decisions among the states could create substantial problems for interstate connectivity.[58] A Joint Conference Process, called by the FCC with representation of the state utility commissions, has been established to facilitate federal–state cooperation on open network architecture issues.[59]

The divestiture of AT&T and the attempt to make telephone rates reflect the true cost of providing services, that is, eliminating any cross-subsidy, has important implications for the goal of universal service. Under deregulation, the subsidy provided for local service by long-distance service fell. Although an access charge—for access of interexchange service to the local exchange network—replaced the separations approach to shared costs and helped to pay for the local exchange facilities, there was nevertheless to be an increase in local rates that could potentially force low-income customers off the system. To address this possibility, the FCC proposed a lifeline program in 1983.[60] Under one provision, the flat-rate charge for local telephone service could be reduced for qualifying individuals. The second provision, known as "Link Up America," subsidized the cost of connection and installation for qualifying individuals. In 1990, there were 22 states participating in the first program and 38 states in the second.

Although factors other than these programs are important in affecting the telephone penetration rate—that is, the percentage of households subscribing to some form of telephone service—the share of all households with telephone service increased from 91.2 percent in 1983 to 93.3 percent in 1990.[61] These figures suggest that the goal of universal service has not been undermined by divestiture, but troubling and significant differences in telephone penetration for young racial and ethnic groups and in some rural areas continue to exist. Furthermore, there is a growing recognition that the traditional notion of universal access to basic telephone service is no longer appropriate for our information society. The services available on systems with party lines, mechanical switches, and older equipment are extremely limited (to only voice communication). Residential customers, small businesses, and especially the poor may not be provided access to the full range of information services on the public network, increasing inequality in the distribution of information. Thus, many argue, universal service should be redefined and made consistent with access to information and advanced services.[62]

The broad impact of this new regulatory structure and divestiture has become clear. Although AT&T retains the largest share of the long-distance service market, its share has been declining as that of other firms has increased (see Table 6.2). Progress on the goal of achieving cost-based pricing for long-distance telephone traffic, the result of a more competitive environment, can be noted. The average annual real (that is, adjusted for inflation) decline in interstate long-distance prices was 5 percent between 1977 and 1983 (pre-MFJ), whereas the decline was nearly 10 percent between 1983 and 1989.[63] The decline in intrastate long-distance prices, a market still subject to state regulation, was considerably less in the post-MFJ period, declining 4.2 percent annually from 1983 through 1989.[64] Equal access, necessary for competition to exist in long-distance markets, only reached 80 percent of customers in regional Bell companies' territories in 1988.[65] The prices for basic telephone service, however, increased between 1983 and 1989 at a rate of 3.1 percent a year in real terms.[66] These increases in local rates have been even higher among the small independent telephone companies that serve predominately rural areas, as would be expected given the traditional pricing scheme effectively subsidized rural service. Differences in price changes for local and long-distance rates suggest that the new regulatory structure is having some success in shifting more network costs to local service and end users.[67]

THE STATE RESPONSE TO THE DIVESTITURE

Under the MFJ, AT&T was forced to divest its local exchange companies, the regional Bell companies, and its remaining interstate business remained subject to supervision of the FCC. Regulation of these regional companies and other independent local exchange companies as well as regulation of intrastate long-distance service remained the responsibility of state public utility commissions. The initial response of state regulatory officials to the MFJ was not favorable.[68] Commissioners were concerned that divestiture would dramatically increase basic telephone rates—the regional Bell companies did file for many rate increases—and worried that they were not adequately prepared for their new responsibilities. One challenge was to develop new methods of price regulation. Another challenge for commissions revolves around determining the best method for allowing or encouraging competition among telecommunications service providers in specific markets. Assuring high-quality basic phone service at a reasonable price, the responsibility of utility commissions, is increasingly problematic with the decline in the subsidy to basic service generated by long-distance traffic.

Policy Issues

Not only have the number and complexity of issues before public utility commissions and state legislatures increased but also the range of interests participating in policy discussions has expanded. Industry segmentation, described earlier, creates differentiated sets of interests. On some issues the Bell companies may have interests in common with the small local exchange companies, but on others they may hold different positions. The pattern in the interexchange market is similar although somewhat more regular; the smaller interexchange companies generally argue for continued regulation of AT&T in order to prevent what they perceive to be unfair competition. The providers of enhanced telecommunications services generally want to insure reasonable cost access to the public network but argue that the local exchange companies should not be allowed to compete in these service markets.

The range of users of telecommunications services is also diverse.[69] Large intensive users, such as producer service firms and large manufacturing companies, have played a significant role in federal regulatory matters. These large user groups may bypass the public network, thus creating a competitive threat to local exchange companies outside the purview of state regulators. Residential and small business representatives are also present. Organizations such as American Association of Retired Persons, Consumers Federation of America, Consumers Union, and some public research organizations are active participants not only at the federal level but also at the state level. Many states have established offices of public counsel to represent consumers in telecommunications issues. Yet other interest groups are becoming involved in telecommunications policy as the technology creates threats to other types of media. Cable TV companies and the print media have become very involved in certain types of issues. As the basic nature of state regulation of telecommunications evolves, issues not infrequently spill over from utility commissions into state legislatures.

Under traditional, predivestiture regulation, the price of basic telephone service was derived through the rate-of-return method, as discussed above. Public utility commissions determined the appropriate rate base and an acceptable rate of return on investments made by telephone companies. This form of price regulation has been found to be inadequate in contemporary telecommunications markets where competition and technological upgrading of networks are increasingly important. By 1991, only 10 states maintained rate-of-return regulation.[70] Three other forms of pricing are now being used by states: price caps, social contract, and incentive regulation.[71] Each method attempts to address the shortcomings of rate-of-return regulation in an industry experiencing technological change, which has led to cost reductions in the provision of services, increasing competition in certain markets, and ultimately to the loss of customer base as firms bypass the public network.

Price cap regulation represents a fairly substantial departure from the rate-of-return method. With price caps, a price index is constructed for a company that incorporates and weights the prices for the range of services provided. A target for the change in the price index is established, and the firm can then modify the prices for individual services as it chooses; but the overall index must fall below the prespecified price cap. This approach emphasizes pricing flexibility, which allows the company to respond more aggressively in markets where competition exists. Price caps also provide an incentive for the company to operate efficiently because cost savings can be retained by the firm or shared.

Under the social contract method, a state formally contracts with a telephone company for services on behalf of users in a state. The contract includes provisions for service requirements, and may place constraints on the price ceilings for some specific services, especially basic service, as well as providing substantial flexibility for the pricing of others. Although extending flexibility to the telephone company, the state also specifies obligations, such as network modernization or universal service issues, that are deemed important. At the end of the contract period, a new one can be negotiated.

Incentive regulation is becoming the most common form of price regulation. Under incentive regulation, a rate of return is specified by regulators and prices are established, but any cost savings generated by the local exchange company can be partially or totally retained by the company. Under rate-of-return regulation, such savings would be used in adjusting future prices downward, thus reducing the incentive for the company to achieve efficiency and reduce costs. Under the incentive regulation plan, the savings generated by the company may be allocated to profits for the company, savings for the customer, or an investment fund for network modernization (see the discussion of Michigan below). This form of price regulation is popular among states because it brings broad-based benefits—price stability for residential consumers, pricing flexibility for large customers, potential earnings for stockholders, incentives for the company to increase efficiency, and retention of regulatory oversight for the utility commission. Incentive regulation appears to work less well during recessions, when demand for services grows slowly and there appears to be a tension between the use of savings for short-term earnings for investors on the one hand and network modernization on the other.[72]

A second issue faced by states is the degree of competition to be allowed or encouraged in the intrastate long-distance market. Although long-distance service is provided principally by AT&T and other interexchange carriers, local exchange companies offer limited long-distance service within broad service areas. The MFJ established 160 local access and transport areas (LATAs), which are telephone service regions organized roughly around metropolitan service areas and generally incorporating several local exchanges. Most states have more than a single LATA. Calls between LATAs are long-distance calls and service is provided by interexchange companies. Calls between local exchanges within a single LATA are also long-distance calls and are frequently provided by the local exchange companies, especially the regional Bell companies. Virtually all states allow interLATA competition, although the degree of pricing flexibility extended to AT&T and other long-distance carriers varies substantially among the states.[73] At present, utility commissions are giving greater attention to intraLATA competition. As of 1991, only five states prohibited any intraLATA competition.[74] Even though most states do not allow full competition—easy entry and no price regulation—the trend is clearly toward opening the intraLATA market. This competition will likely place further pressure on rates for local service to increase as the cross-subsidies from intraLATA long-distance service disappear.

Competition with local exchange companies is also occurring in local markets, the so-called local loop.[75] Cellular telephones and soon-to-be-deployed personal communications networks provide alternative means for a customer to have access to the public network and consequently represent competition to the local exchange company. Twenty-five states currently regulate entry of cellular companies and nineteen regulate prices.[76] New York was the first state to adopt price regulation of the personal communications services.[77] As described above, the proliferation of private networks in businesses represents competition through the provision of alternative means of access to the public network or the bypass of it altogether.[78] Cable TV companies have the capabilities of providing high-speed data transmission to firms and thus also represent potential competitors. This competition in the local loop is foreseen in the open network architecture requirements of Computer Inquiry III, which calls for local exchange companies to unbundle their services. For example, the local exchange company may sell only switching capabilities to a customer, whereas the customer can use an alternative provider to gain access to the public network. This competition, which will develop more quickly in the large lucrative markets of major cities, creates new variations of the old problem: how to price a service—for example, access to switching facilities, which is provided by a firm with great market power, the local exchange company.

A related issue is what the long-distance company should be charged for access to the local exchange network. Although there is little disagreement that some charge is appropriate—the FCC allocates 25 percent of the cost of the local physical plant, the so-called non-traffic-sensitive costs, to interstate traffic—states must determine who will pay, users or interexchange companies, and how much. If the charge is too high, firms with substantial interexchange traffic may bypass the local exchange company; if priced too low, local exchange companies will have inadequate revenues for network investment. There is substantial variation among states on setting access charges. This problem will become increasingly complex as open network architecture offers the possibility of interconnecting with the public network for a variety of services, as discussed above.[79] These elements must be defined, and prices must be established in some fashion.

Yet another difficult issue before utility commissions is determining the degree of competition for enhanced services. If competition exists in a market, for example, an information services market, the local exchange company should be granted some pricing flexibility in order to compete. However, alternative service providers argue that the local exchange companies can use basic service to subsidize their enhanced services and can thereby offer services at below cost, creating an unfair advantage. An example of this problem is found in Centrex, a service widely available through local exchange companies which provides subscribers with a switch with advanced capabilities, such as direct inward dialing. This type of service can also be obtained through the purchase of a private branch exchange (PBX). Flexible pricing on the Centrex service, a decision under the jurisdiction of the utility commission, would allow the local exchange company to compete with private branch exchanges more effectively. State authorizing legislation generally requires that the utility commission make a determination with respect to the degree of existing competition or latent competition before deregulating specific markets.[80]

Utility commissions have traditionally set long depreciation periods for network equipment in an attempt to maintain low basic service rates. This policy becomes problematic because technological innovation makes telephone equipment obsolete relatively quickly. Telephone companies may continue to use outdated equipment because it is not yet fully depreciated. The purchase of new equipment may be postponed if the equipment's useful life is likely to be shorter than its depreciation schedule. On the other hand, a state-of-the-art system is necessary for many of the advanced telecommunications services.

One question that regulators face in relation to local exchange companies is whether the increased flexibility for telephone companies to invest and set rates undermine the universal service objective. Specifically, the major network investments that a local operating company must make to remain competitive with other service providers can result in increased rates for basic service even though consumers of basic services do not utilize the new services. A related question is that, as services are unbundled and more are offered through competitive markets, a smaller base of services with which to subsidize local rates remain, possibly undermining the universal service goal. Competitors worry that the local exchange companies will create an unfair advantage by using basic rates to subsidize investments for network modernization and advanced services. On the other hand, decisions taken by state regulators, with regard to rates and determination of competitive markets, may provoke further bypass of local exchange companies and undermine the public network.

A Cautious Response

The initial response in California, Florida, and Texas to this rapidly changing regulatory environment has been a relatively slow move from traditional rate-of-return regulation. In California, a substantial commitment to a redefinition of universal service has been balanced with a commitment to network modernization and efficiency in markets.[81] The nature of the information society implies that citizens without access to all types of information—education, emergency services, security healthcare, and even employment—will not be able to participate effectively in the society. One solution to this new context is to redefine universal service to mean not only access to a dial tone at a reasonable rate, but also access to information on the public telephone network. The balancing of a commitment to universal service and to network modernization has been attempted through maintenance of the state's relatively low basic service rates and a slow but deliberate move to competition. Initially intraLATA competition was not allowed, providing local exchange companies a means to subsidize local rates, except for high-speed private line services, but these markets were partially deregulated later. InterLATA markets have been deregulated, but AT&T's rates are controlled on a cost-of-service basis. Where competition for new services can be demonstrated, great pricing flexibility is extended to AT&T. In terms of the provision of advanced services by the local exchange companies, such as private lines, Centrex, and special access services, pricing flexibility has been adopted. Although the trend toward flexible pricing and encouragement of competitive markets is clear, California has adopted a fairly cautious approach.

Although Florida has left traditional regulation of local exchange companies relatively unchanged and local rates have changed little, the utility commission has nevertheless been innovative. Distinctive features of regulation in the state include the very strong consumer lobby, a well-respected public utility commission and Office of Public Counsel. A long period of economic and population growth has permitted the local operating companies to invest in modernization while maintaining low basic rates, a situation not present in many states. The state implemented 22 equal access exchange areas—the state has 10 LATAs—which has encouraged more interstate long-distance competition and secured equal access to long-distance companies for the state. The result has been a substantial expansion in the number of long-distance companies serving the state, which is a very important result given that much of the state's economy is information-intensive. IntraLATA competition is also permitted. Although telecommunications rates have been kept relatively low as a result of the rapid growth in the state, issues of bypass by large users, cross-subsidies, and the provision of advanced services will inevitably be faced by the state. The utility commission appears to be moving in the direction of incentive regulation.

Telecommunications regulation in Texas is adversarial and contentious. The state did not establish a public utility commission until 1975, when ineffective regulation of telephone companies by cities and large rate increases created significant public controversy. The utility commission has generally ruled in favor of low local rates, through imposing high access rates on the long-distance carriers and preserving the monopoly status of most local exchange company services. Keeping local rates low has been a particularly important issue in the state, given the relatively low residential density in many areas of the state and thus high costs in providing service.

Many rural areas are served by small, independent local exchange companies. In response to the commission's unfavorable decisions in the mid–1980s, the telephone companies attempted to avoid the utility commission and achieve their objectives through state legislation. In the long-distance markets, AT&T sought deregulation, but the other long-distance companies argued that AT&T remained dominant and therefore warranted continued regulation. The small independent exchange companies had a set of concerns different from that of the largest local exchange company, Southwestern Bell, although all wanted a more streamlined regulatory process in order to compete more effectively in competitive markets.

Although the telephone companies, especially AT&T, were not entirely successful, this legislative activity reflected the aggressive stance of companies faced with what is perceived to be an uncooperative utility commission.

By 1989, however, the major telecommunications issues had returned to the utility commission. In the context of the commission's review of Southwestern Bell's services and rates, the company proposed a plan for incentive regulation, called the Texas First Plan.[82] Soon thereafter, the commission staff found excess earnings by the company and proposed a plan to return these to customers. In 1990, the commission adopted a settlement that combined features of both plans—a cap on basic rates with no change for four years, the upgrading of all switches to digital capability, reductions in intraLATA rates, and incentive regulation—with many but not all intervenors concurring. In particular, a number of consumer organizations did not agree with the terms. In 1992, the issue of telecommunications policy returned to the state legislature as a result of the sunset review of the commission.

Promoting Competition

In contrast to these three states, the state of Illinois has adopted an aggressive policy of regulatory flexibility with a goal of inducing efficiency in pricing and competition.[83] The Universal Telephone Service Protection Act (UTSPA) of 1985, developed in the context of a sunset review of the Illinois Commerce Commission (ICC), found that it was no longer accurate to characterize the telephone business as a natural monopoly and that competition in the industry would most benefit the state's information-intensive economy. The UTSPA's definition of ''competitive market'' is less strict than that found in most other states. Entry of new firms into interexchange markets is eased and carriers can declare a service competitive and therefore unregulated. Demonstrating that a competitive market exists is the responsibility of the ICC; hence, a major regulatory burden is removed from the telephone companies. The findings that justified the UTSPA stated that competition can be substituted for regulation in many markets and that competition will ensure penetration into residential markets, thus promoting universal service. The UTSPA certainly encourages competition, but it can best be characterized as one endorsing regulatory flexibility rather than deregulation in that an oversight role for the utility commission is maintained. The utility commission has itself taken two types of actions that attempt to drive rates closer to costs. The commission deaveraged access charges which eliminated the subsidy provided to rural rate payers when a single, averaged access rate was charged to all customers.

In 1987, intraLATA competition was permitted in Illinois. In 1991, the chairman of the utility commission argued that deregulation of the local exchange market (that is, the local loop) should be permitted in Chicago.[84] Noting that several special access companies in effect compete with the local exchange company, the proposal is to test competition in the local market by creating a "free trade zone" in which the franchise for the local monopoly would be ended, as would service obligations, and prices deregulated.[85] Illinois has been very aggressive in forcing prices of services to reflect the cost of services, even when it means increases in basic service rates and encouraging competition in all phases of the telecommunications business. An innovative utility commission with a long tradition of procompetition positions, a very strong and innovative regional Bell company, Illinois Bell Telephone, and a strong organization of large users, the Information Industry Council of Metropolitan Chicago, have created an exceptional telecommunications policymaking environment in which aggressive and innovative policies are being examined and adopted.

Telecommunications policy in Michigan has involved a wide range of actors and has evolved rapidly in recent years. In 1988, Governor James Blanchard formed an interagency task force, with broad representation, to develop "Connections: A Strategy for Michigan's Future Through Telecommunications."[86] Much like the strategic planning efforts for economic development discussed in Chapter 4, this task force attempted to establish a far-reaching agenda for telecommunications, involving not only the role of telecommunications in development, but also its role in education, delivery of public services and information, and an improved quality of life.

On the regulatory front, the utility commission adopted a very innovative incentive regulation plan in 1990. Unlike most incentive programs in other states, which divide excess earnings between rate payers and the company, the Michigan plan allocated a proportion of earnings to a construction fund to be used for upgrading the network.[87] In 1991, Michigan Bell, the principal local exchange in the state, with support of the communications union in the state, proposed a plan for radical deregulation of telecommunications. That was opposed by a broad range of interests, including large and small telecommunications users, competitors such as cable companies, and various consumer organizations.[88] The legislation adopted in December of 1991 did not incorporate the major deregulatory features proposed in the Bell plan, but nevertheless substantially modified the previous regulatory framework.[89] In particular the innovative incentive program was replaced by price cap regulation. The utility commission was given broad authority to deregulate competitive services, and the innovative use of telecommunications in education was encouraged.

Rural Concerns

In Washington and Vermont, the large proportion of rural residents makes basic telephone rates and universal service an important concern, and this concern is embedded in their telecommunications policy. Vermont enacted social contract legislation in 1987, the result of negotiations between the state and the various telephone companies, business trade groups, and consumer interest groups.[90] This legislation authorizes the Department of Public Service to negotiate a five-year contract with the local exchange company. Under this contract, implemented in 1989, a firm and clear commitment toward universal service is maintained, but rate-of-return regulation of telephone companies is eliminated and the companies are provided substantial pricing flexibility on the belief that it nurtures competition by allowing providers to respond quickly to changes in the market, a response not possible with the cumbersome rate-of-return regulation. The first contract was sufficiently successful that a second five-year contract was negotiated.[91] The proposed contract raises basic rates but also institutes a pricing system that will result in low rates for intrastate long-distance service. Other provisions of the proposal are the completion of network upgrading for the state by 1995, increases in prices dependent on performance standards, and obligations to provide technical assistance in meeting educational and business needs in the state.

Similar to Vermont, telecommunications policy in Washington is the result of broad debate and participation of many actors. The Regulatory Flexibility Act of 1985 went through nine iterations before adoption and represented a compromise in which the interests of many different policy actors were incorporated. The distinctive features of the Act were a commitment to universal service, especially in the form of low rates for rural customers, deregulation in competitive markets, and an incentive system whereby a relatively high rate-of-return could be earned by local exchange companies if they met certain performance requirements. The utility commission was authorized to examine and classify services provided by monopoly companies as competitive and thus not subject to regulation. Provisions were also established to prevent such unbundling from being subsidized by the regulated portion of the firm's businesses.

The Deregulation Option

Two states, Virginia and Nebraska, have embraced deregulation. In 1984, Virginia became the first state to deregulate AT&T (for intrastate long-distance service).[92] At the same time, it eased entry requirements for interexchange companies in an attempt to encourage competition. This step was taken by the state assembly and was based on a finding that AT&T was losing its market dominance. The state's utility commission has also acted to reduce the extent of regulation of the local exchange companies, first for the small companies and eventually with a streamlined process for regulating large companies. Under this process, local exchange companies are no longer required to file rate change cases; they are to provide public notification 30 days in advance of a rate increase, and the utility commission becomes involved only if protests are filed.

Nebraska aspires to be the "800 capital" of the United States, so attracting telemarketers is a high priority and Map 6.1 indicated the state had a relatively large employment share in the communications sector, suggesting it may be achieving this goal.[93] Prompted principally by the length of time required to gain approval from the state's utility commission for a rate-change request, two bills, with different degrees of deregulation and support from different elements of the telephone industry, were introduced to the state legislature in 1986. With opposition from the utility commission, active support from Governor Robert Kerrey, and very aggressive support from U.S. West,[94] the legislature passed the Telecommunications Act of 1986, which adopted a more radical deregulation posture than either of the two other proposed bills. Economic development and competitiveness concerns were frequently used to justify deregulation. Although the act maintains exclusive geographical franchises for the local exchange companies, rate-setting for all telephone companies is virtually deregulated; the utility commission retains an oversight role when a rate increases by more than 10 percent or when customers petition for review. The act also included provisions to deaverage costs which will eventually reduce the subsidy that long distance provides to basic service.

An assessment of the impact of deregulation in Nebraska was released in 1992.[95] It found no significant deviations between the change in local rates in Nebraska and changes in four other nonderegulated states. However, the lack of change in U.S. West's rates may reflect an informal social contract between the company and the state and an arrangement necessary to maintain political support for deregulation. On the other hand, intrastate long-distance rates have risen. New services have been relatively quickly introduced in the state by U.S. West, perhaps reflecting the deregulated environment. Network modernization has proceeded at a good pace, but may not necessarily be the result of deregulation. A number of small telecommunications companies have successfully taken advantage of the flexibility in line of business opportunities and have diversified and grown very rapidly.

The Cutting Edge

The state of New York has fully recognized the importance of telecommunications in its economy and has invested substantial resources in attempting to design an appropriate telecommunications policy. A sophisticated telecommunications infrastructure is credited for maintaining New York City's comparative advantage in financial and other producer services, and the state has the highest share of communications sector employment in the country (see Map 6.1).[96] However, telecommunications advances also represent a potential threat in that certain activities can become more footloose and leave New York, such as the backoffice operations of Citicorp that moved from Long Island to South Dakota. But complicating policymaking in New York is the extraordinarily diverse telecommunications community, involving not only many local and interexchange carriers, but many firms providing advanced services, large and powerful users of telecommunications, including the country's largest concentration of Fortune 500 corporate headquarters, and powerful rural interests in upstate New York. Consensus among these diverse interests is required for any successful policy initiative. The public utility commission has been successful in maintaining a nonpartisan environment, and commissioners are frequently individuals with

substantial expertise in telecommunications.[97] As a result, the analysis and discussion of the broader importance of telecommunications in the state economy
are frequently conducted in the commission, a situation unlike that in most other
states. A cautious but deliberate process of deregulation was initiated even before
the divestiture of AT&T.

Unlike Virginia, New York's public utility commission found that in the 1980s
AT&T remained a dominant actor in many markets and thus has been slow to
deregulate the company. But in its commitment to provide efficient regulation,
the commission has attempted to develop generic proceedings, as distinct from
case-by-case hearings. By establishing general principles for assessing market
dominance, proceedings will be more efficient and provide greater predictability
in rapidly changing markets. The commission has also negotiated with AT&T
a move from the traditional rate-of-return regulation—which was prejudicial to
AT&T given its relatively small postdivestiture rate base—to price caps.

The state has been extensively exploring the regulatory implications of technological change in telecommunications networks.[98] In response to the FCC's
Computer Inquiry III, which required the regional Bell companies to present
plans for open network architecture, the state utility commission instituted its
own order in an effort to insure fair competition in the competitive advanced
services markets. The purpose of open network architecture is to design the
public network, so as to secure unfettered access to it for advanced service
providers. With such a network, the regional Bell companies can unbundle
services required by advanced service providers—for example, switching services—but must guarantee equal treatment of all private providers wishing to
interconnect to the public system. New York State has provided a vision of a
futuristic modular network that emphasizes interconnection of the multitude of
networks and services that will be available. The state took its first step in the
application of this thinking when it authorized the direct connection of private
telephone lines to the switching offices of New York Telephone; this authorization
brings direct competition to New York Telephone in its local loop, a major
precedent fracturing the local exchange's natural monopoly. New York Telephone has requested permission to negotiate contract prices with the private
companies wishing to have access to the public network's switching function—
that is, switching is being unbundled from the range of services purchased by a
user.[99] The state utility commission also required New York Telephone to conduct
an ISDN trial on the public network.

The Policymaking Environment

The considerable variation in policy outcomes among the states relates to the
institutional context of telecommunications policy, especially the relative power
and prestige of the utility commission, the legislature, and in a few cases the
governor. In some cases leadership in addressing these challenges is found in
utility commissions, as in New York, Illinois, and Florida. In other instances,

state legislatures either overrule the utility commission's policy, as in the case of Nebraska, or delegate substantial authority to the utility commission for policy development, as in Illinois. In Florida and California, public interest groups are effective and low basic service rates have been maintained. However, in states with urban centers that depend greatly on telecommunications services for their economy, such as Chicago and New York City, the large intensive users of telecommunications appear to have played an important role, if not in policy design, certainly in helping to create the need for a competitive market. The regional Bell companies remain significant actors and are frequently the source of policy proposals. Although some continue to emphasize universal service issues and quality of the public network, all appear to be adapting their strategies for a competitive environment. States with relatively strong economies, such as Florida and California, appear to have had less intense pressure from the business community and perhaps from the local exchange companies to pursue deregulation policies; the growing economy facilitates network investment and helps maintain low basic rates.

Significant changes have come to public utility commissions, although the extent of change varies among the states. Some utility commissions, sensitive to traditional mandates of low basic service rates and strong local exchange companies, have been overridden by state legislatures. In most utility commissions, the method of price regulation has been substantially reformed. Much more discretion is provided to many commissions, especially with respect to determining degree of competition in existing and emerging advanced service markets.[100] A 1988 study concluded that utility commissions, because of their traditional legislative mandate to regulate monopoly providers, were inappropriate forums for developing a future-oriented telecommunications policy for the rapidly evolving industry.[101] It is now clear that in a number of states utility commissions are serving this role quite well.

The speed and direction of change in telecommunications policy in a state are clearly affected by the composition of forces and institutional traditions unique to each state, although virtually all states are moving toward a more flexible regulatory framework and allowing competition in many telecommunications markets. In an empirically based study, Teske assessed the relative strength of various factors—interest group representation and institution variables—in determining the extent of deregulation of prices and competitive entry among states.[102] In spite of difficulties with defining appropriate variables for this type of analysis, his results are quite helpful in clarifying the relative importance of various factors. Interest group involvement has a positive effect on competitive entry. Large users and, to a lesser extent, government-sponsored advocates successfully encourage greater competition in markets. However, with regard to price regulation, Teske finds that the institutional variables, particularly the level of funding for the public utility commission, have far greater influence in predicting deregulation. The sophistication of the commission, roughly estimated by the size of its budget, is positively related to deregulation of prices. States with a general deregulatory environment also tend to deregulate price and entry. One interpretation of these findings is that when strong interest representation is found on various sides of an issue, the utility commission becomes more critical in policy outcomes.

TELECOMMUNICATIONS AND ECONOMIC DEVELOPMENT

The movement toward regulatory flexibility and deregulation in telecommunications markets is widespread. The principal arguments supporting this strategy are that the natural monopoly characteristics of the telephone industry no longer hold and, as a result, competition will produce more efficient investment decisions and prices. In particular, the technologically driven declining cost of production for long-distance service will be reinforced by deregulation of prices for long-distance service as a result of the elimination of cross-subsidy of local service. A secondary argument is that deregulation of telecommunications markets will lead to economic development. The economic development dimension of telecommunications, however, cannot simply be reduced to an issue of the price of telecommunications services. Price is obviously important but certainly not the only consideration in formulating development policy. We will begin the discussion with the case where price and competition most closely fit theory—in long-distance and advanced services for large telecommunications-intensive businesses—then examine external economies of networks, and conclude with a reexamination of development strategies.

Pricing and Competition

The provision of long-distance telecommunications services is no longer a natural monopoly and has not been one for quite some time. Given a fair number of options for intensive users of long-distance services, a deregulated market is an appropriate strategy. Not only will intensive users be able to acquire similar services under competition at lower prices, but more important for economic development, the range of options allows for more creativity and innovation in the use of telecommunications, both by the multitude of telecommunications service and equipment vendors and by users themselves. Large telecommunications users and AT&T's competitors have been influential in developing current policy at the federal level and in a number of states.

Businesses that serve local or intrastate markets are obviously less affected by interstate telecommunications rates. Particularly for businesses that serve only local markets, and thus incur limited intrastate long-distance telephone expenses, the traditional regulatory scheme with its low local service rates probably worked in their favor. Deregulation of long-distance rates may well lead to increased expenses for these firms through higher local rates. The critical factor, however, in terms of economic development is whether these local demand firms can increase their productivity through new telecommunications applications or even become exporting firms through easier access to nonlocal markets. The innovative use of telecommunications by a firm depends only partially on price of services; it also depends on the availability of systems appropriate for small and mid-size businesses and the innovative capacity of firms.

Even a competitive telecommunications market will not necessarily lead to innovative uses of telecommunications for these types of firms. When questioned about services for small businesses, the National Manufacturers Association replied that it has not expanded its bulletin board for small business because owners say that they do not have the time to use such services. The American Small Business Association, based in Grapevine, Texas, however, has created an electronic bulletin board, offered through CompuServe, for its 155,000 members[103] and offers on-line databases and other marketing services.

The availability of advanced services to small and mid-size businesses will continue to depend on services available on the public network for the foreseeable future. These businesses tend not to have the internal resources for developing their own systems, and advanced service providers tend to serve the large, more lucrative telecommunications users. Only the local exchange companies and AT&T have obligations to provide services to all customers. The other inter-exchange carriers and advanced service providers have no such obligations, but rather serve only these markets expected to be lucrative. This issue is particularly acute in rural areas, where demand is sparse and alternative providers may be absent.

Economywide Effects

There is substantial agreement on the importance of telecommunications to economic growth and development. However, the specific nature of this rela-tionship is uncertain. For example, is there a direct relationship between the level of telecommunications expenditures in an area and its rate of economic development? Or is the relationship an indirect one, dependent on the pace of innovation diffusion? Is the critical element total telecommunications expendi-tures, the price of telecommunications services, or the range of services available? The answers to these questions are very important for developing telecommun-ications policy in the states.

Determining the precise impact of infrastructure investments has always been a difficult empirical question. There is little doubt that the construction of canals, railroads, and highways has historically been critical for economic growth. Es-timates of the short-term impacts of construction are easily obtainable, and even the savings to individual firms resulting from improved infrastructure systems can plausibly be estimated. But the impact of the infrastructure on future in-vestment decisions, which generates new economic activity, cannot be estimated with any reliability. This problem, however, does not impede infrastructure development, which can be justified on more narrow grounds such as existing or future demand for the service and the rate of return for either public or private investment in projects.

Kenneth Arrow notes an interesting relationship between the costs associated with the production of information and rapid expansion in telecommunications capacity in the intelligent network: the cost of producing information is independent of the scale on which it is used.[104] This finding holds importance for estimating future demand because advanced telecommunications systems permit rapid expansion in scale of use, to the benefit of both the information producers and consumers. In other words, as the telephone network expands, the potential market reached by the network expands but the increase in the cost of distribution of information is relatively insignificant. In addition, telecommunications advances can actually reduce market transaction costs.

The public telephone network has characteristics of a public good as do other infrastructure systems. Access to a public good is usually available to all, although some cost may be assigned to users. Technological innovation and change in industry structure, however, may undermine public access to a state-of-the-art telecommunications system. Bypass of the public system, by firms building their own networks or acquiring services through private networks, means less telecommunications traffic on the public network. This loss of revenue may lead to underinvestment in the public network and, consequently, inhibit its upgrading. The result could be one telecommunications system for residential consumers and businesses unable to build their own systems and a second, superior, privately owned system. Hence, investment in private systems will likely bring benefits to individual firms and enhance their growth prospects but may not provide the broader benefits to the local economy that telecommunications investment in a regulated monopoly did in the past.

An uneven spatial distribution of telecommunications infrastructure can already be seen. The most sophisticated infrastructures, in terms of the quality of the networks and array of services, including multiple long-distance providers, are found in large cities, where the greatest demand exists (that is, demand generated by producer services). But access to advanced services is not available to all firms even in large cities. Such services will eventually reach mid-size and small businesses as providers search for clients in an increasingly competitive environment, but this search will largely rely on the public network for delivery of services and on decisions concerning open network architecture and interconnection with the public network.

In addressing economic development through telecommunications, states are faced with potentially conflicting goals. An advanced telecommunications network has become a necessity for many types of firms. Areas with inferior networks—with older switches or low transmission capacity—will be at a competitive disadvantage vis-à-vis areas with advanced systems and may not be able to support a whole range of businesses. In regulating local exchange companies, states help determine the quality and capacity of the system available to the public. The goal of providing an advanced system may conflict with the goal of universal service and low telephone rates because the capital required for building an advanced system may have to be raised through increases in local rates. Another revenue source for local exchange companies is advanced services. Advanced services providers oppose the deregulation of local exchange companies in these markets. However, if local exchange companies are not allowed into these service markets and this source of revenue is not available, the local network may become distinctively inferior, with those on the public network unable to access needed telecommunications advances.

Although this discussion has focused on state telecommunications policy and economic development, the issue of universal service and public access to information services should not be forgotten. Just as telecommunications has the potential for improving productivity in the private sector, it holds enormous potential for the public sector as well. Most governmental activities rely heavily on information management and diffusion, and as a result, telecommunications advances offer the potential for substantial improvement in the delivery of virtually all public services.[105] There are also important political issues regarding the public's access to information services and public telecommunications systems. Unless the definition of universal service is expanded to include access to information services, we risk the potential for new sources of social inequality.

For many types of business, especially small, mid-size, and rural businesses, telecommunications services will be limited to those available on the public network. The economic development strategy with respect to state regulation, therefore, must be to insure that a sophisticated network with advanced services is available. This means that the private networks of advanced services must be allowed to connect to the public network and that local exchange companies must be deregulated in these service markets. To insure fairness, the transition to full interconnection and deregulation of services must be carefully planned and monitored. At the same time the long-term goal should be clear: to provide all firms access to telecommunications systems and to a market of providers responsive to user needs.

Industrialized countries have adopted significantly different policy approaches to the development of national telecommunications systems. The United States has adopted a highly decentralized approach, in contrast to Japan, which is implementing a centralized system that will provide capacity well into the next century.[106] In the United States, federal policy in recent years has been one of deregulation and reliance on private sector decision making on investment and service provision. However, the issue of a national system has again arisen, in the context of broad-band systems. Broad-band systems are distinct from current telephone systems in that they are able to provide switched transmission capacity for voice, data and video image simultaneously. Cable TV systems, while not offering the switching capability, have similar capacity. The creation of a national broad-band network is being advocated by a number of policy actors with the justification that the United States is losing its edge to those countries that are deploying national, centralized systems.[107] The financing and ownership of a national system, the pace of modernization, the role of the states—some of which are considering the construction of their own broad-band networks—and control of and access to the network are highly contested issues. In any event, states will remain actors as a result of their jurisdiction over intrastate telephone communications, and their policy decisions will affect, to some degree, the competitiveness of firms within their boundaries.

Development Strategies

In terms of the provision of economic development programs by states, telecommunications is too rarely part of the development effort. Yet each category of state development strategies—recruitment, retention, and new firm formation—could and should include a telecommunications component. In industrial recruitment, telephone companies and utility companies have a long tradition of working with state and local governments and chambers of commerce in attempting to attract firms. Rarely, however, are the telecommunications capabilities of a city or state an important part of the promotion effort. To a certain extent, this simply reflects the fact that most state and local governments have yet to develop significant expertise in telecommunications. Many telecommunications services are relatively easy to extend to new firms or customers, at least to firms locating in large cities; consequently, they may not be a critical factor in determining location. Even so, it is imperative that industrial recruiters develop an understanding of the role telecommunications plays in the local economy and, in particular, in telecommunications-intensive firms.

As discussed earlier in this chapter, providers of telecommunications equipment and services are among the most rapidly growing industries. States may well wish to consider placing such firms as high priorities in their recruitment efforts, particularly the manufacturing firms. Recruitment strategies might also be targeted toward telecommunications research facilities. An untapped segment for recruitment is producer services and information and telecommunications service providers. States and localities need to assess the location patterns of such firms and their own locational advantages so that they can design strategies for attracting these types of companies. Because most of these firms are relatively small, success will not be as notable as when a large manufacturing firm comes to a state. However, these firms represent the future and will be critical in the realization of the full potential of telecommunications in a state's economy.

In terms of a retention strategy, the argument concerning telecommunications has already been made. Telecommunications represents a promising means of improving productivity in many different types of firms. In fact, the industry has grown in response to the telecommunications needs of large firms, and these firms have been very innovative in developing new applications. Firms that do not adopt these innovations are, consequently, less competitive. Some firms may adopt innovation more slowly than others not because of the lack of access to an advanced telecommunications system but rather because of inadequate information or risk-averse behavior. In this respect, telecommunications represents an enabling technology but the use of the technology will depend on the innovative capacity of firms. The ability to incorporate this new technology is certainly not the only dimension in which large firms have advantages over smaller firms, but it is a dimension that is rarely addressed in small business programs. State and local governments should incorporate telecommunications expertise in all small business assistance programs. New-firm generation strategies, such as incubator facilities and venture capital funds, should also place a priority on telecommunications and information service and equipment manufacturing firms.

States can also adapt technology and education and training policies to take advantage of the telecommunications industry. A number of states have established research centers or other institutions to consider telecommunications issues. Research centers typically involve industry, academia, and government and generally focus on specific subject areas, as discussed in Chapter 5. New York's Center of Advanced Technology at Polytechnic University and Virginia's Center for Innovative Technologies have chosen telecommunications as one of their research areas. These centers will help train personnel for the industry and may spur technology transfer and new-firm formation. Such centers may become an important national resource given the more proprietary focus of the preeminent telecommunications research center, Bell Laboratory, following divestiture.

Telecommunications can also be used to facilitate the research effort in a state and connect research institutions with the private sector. High-speed, high-capacity data networks like NYSERNet in New York and PRP Net in Pennsylvania can improve cooperative research and technology transfer as well as demonstrate the innovative uses of telecommunications systems. For such networks, and the proposed national network, NREN, to realize their full potential, access to the networks must be made available to potential users.

Another potential tool for promoting the telecommunications industry is human resource development. The skills required of telecommunications workers are unique, and the number of workers with the necessary skills is limited. States and cities, through their educational systems, can help create a comparative advantage by developing programs for telecommunications workers. In New York City, for example, telecommunications courses are available in high schools, trade schools, and universities.[108] An interesting example of a telecommunications strategy for development in a rural community is found in Kearney, Nebraska, where the local college has established a telecommunications management degree program.[109]

There is little doubt that telecommunications is a central feature in the emerging national and international economy. The production of information is becoming increasingly important in the economy, and telecommunications is the key infrastructure for transporting information. The technology itself may spatially reconfigure our cities and regions in addition to affecting the competitiveness of their economies. State governments are making progress with the challenges presented by this infrastructure. Altogether new strategies are likely to evolve given that this infrastructure is provided principally by the private sector. Economic change has presented a new array of challenges to state governments, but none may be as significant as that presented by telecommunications.

NOTES

1. U.S. Department of Commerce, *1991 U.S. Industrial Outlook* (Washington, D.C., January 1991): 29–1.

2. See Wilson P. Dizard, *The Coming Information Age: An Overview of Technology, Economics and Politics*, 2nd ed. (New York: Longman, 1985): Chapters 3 and 4.

3. Howard R. Turtle, "The Telephone System," in *Telecommunications for Management*, edited by C. T. Meadow and A. S. Tedesco (New York: McGraw-Hill, 1985): 91–113.

4. John Brooks, *Telephone: The First Hundred Years* (New York: Harper & Row, 1975); Turtle, "The Telephone System," pp. 91–113.

5. P.W. Huber, *The Geodesic Network: 1987 Report on Competition in the Telephone Industry* (Washington, D.C.: U.S. Department of Justice, 1987): 1.2–1.6.

6. Hepworth argues that another form of decentralization is found in the disintegration of large, hierarchical organizations, especially in the private sector. Vertical integration is being replaced by markets, hence economic decentralization. This phenomenon, in Hepworth's terms, may produce a more dispersed "information space." Mark Hepworth, *Geography of the Information Economy* (New York: The Guildford Press, 1990): 36.

7. Lars Ramqvist, "Information Technologies in Industry and Society," in *Globalization of Technology*, edited by Janet H. Muroyama and H. Guyford Stever (Washington, D.C.: National Academy Press, 1988): 51—53; Dizard, *The Coming Information Age*, pp. 45–46.

8. For a discussion of various networks and their technologies, see Hepworth, *The Geography of the Information Economy*, Chapter 3; Francois Bar, "Information and Communications Technologies for Economic Development," BRIE Working Paper no. 25 (Berkeley, CA: University of California at Berkeley, May 1987): 12–13.

9. Hepworth, *The Geography of the Information Economy*, Chapter 5.

10. "Telecommunications Survey," *The Economist* (October 17, 1987): 13.

11. U.S. Department of Commerce, *1991 Industrial Outlook*, pp. 29–2.

12. Eli M. Noam, "Network Pluralism and Regulatory Pluralism," in *New Directions in Telecommunications Policy, Volume 1: Regulatory Policy: Telephony and Mass Media*, edited by Paula R. Newberg (Durham, NC: Duke University Press, 1989): 69–71.

13. Christopher Tamarin, "Telecommunications Technology Applications and Standards: A New Role for the User," *Telecommunications Policy* (December 1988): 323–331.

14. Roger P. Newell, "When Communications Comes Out of the Comics," *Rural Telecommunications* (March/April 1991): 24–31; Anthony Ramirez, "Coming: Telephone Calls That Follow You Around," *New York Times* (January 5, 1992): E–5.

15. Frederick Williams, *The New Telecommunication: The Infrastructure for the Information Age* (New York: The Free Press, 1991): Chapters 4 and 5; Charles Jonscher, "Assessing the Benefits of Telecommunications," *Intermedia*, vol. 13, no. 1 (January 1985): 23–24.

16. Fredrick Williams, "Telecommunications as Strategic Investment," (Center for Research Communication, Technology and Society, University of Texas at Austin, March 1988): pp. 8–10.

17. Herb S. Dordick and Frederick Williams, *Innovative Management Using Telecommunications: A Guide to Opportunities, Strategies, and Applications* (New York: John Wiley & Sons, 1986).

18. Martin S. Bernal, Joan Stuller, and Liching Sung, "Doing Business in Rural America," in *Telecommunications and Rural Development: A Study of Private and Public Sector Innovation,* edited by Jurgen Schmandt, Frederick Williams, Robert H. Wilson, and Sharon Strover (New York: Praeger, 1991): 36–43.

19. Jurgen Schmandt, Frederick Williams, and Robert H. Wilson, eds., *Telecommunications and Economic Development: The New State Role* (New York: Praeger, 1989).

20. Larkin Jennings and Harmeet S. Sawhney, "New York," in *Telecommunications and Economic Development,* edited by Schmandt et al., pp. 130–131.

21. C.A. Cariappa, "Pittsburgh," in *The New Urban Infrastructure: Cities and Telecommunications,* edited by Schmandt et al. (New York: Praeger, 1990): 249–250.

22. The projected capacity for NERN would be the transmission of a gigabit of information (about 31,000 pages of single-spaced text) per second; David L. Wilson, "High Cost Could Deny Big Computer Advance at Some Colleges," *Chronicle of Higher Education,* vol. 38, no. 15 (December 4, 1991): 1, 32.

23. This includes revenues from local and long-distance service, value-added network, database services, cellular and satellite services, telephone and telegraph services, and communications systems. U.S. Department of Commerce, *1991 Industrial Outlook,* pp. 29–2, 29–6, 29–7, 29–8, 30–1, and 31–1.

24. Ibid., p. 29–2.

25. "Regional Telephone Firms Are Becoming Poles Apart," *Wall Street Journal* (February 9, 1990): A4.

26. U.S. Department of Commerce, *1991 Industrial Outlook,* pp. 29–2 to 29–3.

27. Ibid., p. 29–3.

28. Ibid., p. 29–3.

29. Morgan Guaranty Trust Bank of New York City adopted an all-digital, high-speed satellite system for its international communications needs in 1986. See "Bank Speeds Its International Transaction, Cuts Telecom Costs with IBS Satellite Service," *Communications News,* vol. 23, no. 7 (July 1986): 54–56.

30. Satellite services is another wireless technology and an important and growing segment of the telecommunications industry. Although satellite technology can be used to bypass local and long-distance telephone service, state governments play virtually no regulatory role, and thus the industry will not be discussed here. For a discussion of the industry, see U.S. Department of Commerce, *1991 U.S. Industrial Outlook,* pp. 29–8 to 29–9.

31. Ibid., p. 29–7.

32. Newell, "When Telecommunications Comes Out of the Comics," p. 25.

33. U.S. Department of Commerce, *1991 U.S. Industrial Outlook,* p. 29–6.

34. Case studies of telecommunications in Atlanta, Houston, Miami, and New York can be found in Schmandt et al., eds. *The New Urban Infrastructure,* Chapters 2, 5, 7 and 9.

35. Also see Joellen M. Harper and Benet Younger, "Nebraska," in *Telecommunications and Economic Development,* edited by Schmandt et al., pp. 83–110.

36. Nestor E. Terleckyi, "A Growth Model of the U.S. Communication Industry, 1948–80," in *Communication and Information Economics,* edited by Meheroo Jussawalla

and Helene Ebenfield (Amsterdam: North-Holland, 1984): 119–145. This work was up-
dated and expanded in Nestor E. Terleckyi, "Growth of the Telecommunications and
Computer Industries," in *Changing the Rules: Technological Change, International Competition, and Regulation in Communications,* edited by Robert W. Crandall and Kenneth
Flamm (Washington, D.C.: The Brookings Institution, 1989): 328–370.

37. The GNP elasticity was 0.59 the period between 1964 and 1985, and the price
elasticity for the period was −1.80.

38. Robert W. Crandall, *After the Breakup: U.S. Telecommunications in a More
Competitive Era* (Washington, D.C.: The Brookings Institution, 1991): Chapter 4.

39. U.S. Department of Commerce, *1991 U.S. Industrial Outlook,* p. 30–3.

40. Robert Britt Horwitz, *The Irony of Regulatory Reform: The Deregulation of
American Telecommunications* (New York: Oxford University Press, 1989): 97–103;
Advisory Commission on Intergovernmental Relations (ACIR), *Intergovernmental Reg-
ulation of Telecommunications* (Washington, D.C., July 1990): 5–6.

41. For a history of common carrier status in telegraphy and its application to the
telephone industry, see Horwitz, *The Irony of Regulatory Reform,* Chapter 4.

42. ACIR, *Intergovernmental Regulation of Telecommunications,* p. 8; Horwitz, *The
Irony of Regulatory Reform,* pp. 132–135.

43. Horwitz, *The Irony of Regulatory Reform,* pp. 116–117.

44. For a discussion of the 1935 Walker Report, see Horwitz, *The Irony of Regulatory
Reform,* pp. 137–138.

45. Ibid., pp. 141–142.

46. Ibid., pp. 225–230.

47. Ibid., p. 236. Matter of Regulatory and Policy Problems Presented by the Interdependence of Computer and Communications Services and Facilities, First Computer
Inquiry, FCC Docket No. 16979 (notice of inquiry, November 10, 1966).

48. In the Matter of Amendment of Section 64.702 of the Commission's Rules and
Regulations, Second Computer Inquiry, Docket 20828 (notice of inquiry and proposed
rulemaking, 1976).

49. Computer II Final Decision, p. 55.

50. ACIR, *Intergovernmental Regulation of Telecommunications,* p. 28. For a critique of structural separations in the telecommunications industry, see William J. Baumol
and Robert D. Willig, "Telephones and Computers: The Costs of Artificial Separation,"
Regulation: AEI Journal on Government and Society (March/April 1985): 23–32.

51. U.S. Circuit Court of Appeals for the Ninth Circuit, Nos. 87–7230, 87–7233,
87–7362, 87–7441, 87–7451; June 6, 1990, 1990 U.S. App. Lexis 8930, p. 77; "FCC
Treads Carefully Around States as It Reinstates Computer III," *State Telephone Regulation Report,* vol. 9, no. 24 (November 28, 1991): 1.

52. ACIR, *The Intergovernmental Regulation of Telecommunications,* pp. 9–10.

53. Horwitz places the push for telecommunications deregulation in the broader
national context of regulatory reform initiated in the mid-1970s and continuing through
the Reagan years. Horwitz, *The Irony of Regulatory Reform,* Chapter 7 and pp. 237–
244.

54. A number of unresolved issues resulting from the MFJ remain. Here we will
examine only a few directly related to state economic development policy.

55. ACIR, *Intergovernmental Regulation of Telecommunications,* pp. 26–30.

56. 106 S. Ct. 1890 (1986), discussed in ACIR, *Intergovernmental Regulation of
Telecommunications,* pp. 26–27.

57. U.S. Circuit Court of Appeals for the Ninth Circuit, Nos. 87–7230, 87–7631, 87–7362, 87–7441, 87–7451; June 6, 1990, 1990 U.S. App., Lexis 8930, p. 77.

58. Robert M. Entman, "State Telecommunications Regulation: Developing Consensus and Illuminating Conflicts" (Communications and Society Forum Report, Aspen Institute Conference, July 30–August 3, 1988): 29–40.

59. ACIR, *The Intergovernmental Regulation of Telecommunications*, p. 35.

60. Ibid., pp. 21–22.

61. Herbert S. Dordick, "Towards a Universal Definition of Universal Service," in Institute for Information Studies, *Universal Telephone Service: Ready for the 21st Century?* (Queenston, MD: 1991): 120.

62. A very interesting broad-based study of this issue can be found in the Intelligent Network Task Force, "The Intelligent Network: Task Force Report October, 1987" (Pacific Bell, 1987); see also Institute for Information Studies, *Universal Telephone Service*.

63. Crandall, *After the Breakup*, p. 61.

64. Robert W. Crandall, "Fragmentation of the Telephone Network," in *New Directions in Telecommunications Policy*, edited by Newberg, pp. 54–55.

65. Roger G. Noll, "Telecommunications Regulation," in *New Directions in Telecommunications Policy*, edited by Newberg, p. 33.

66. Crandall, "Fragmentation of the Telephone Network," pp. 54–55.

67. Crandall, *After Divestiture*, pp. 30–33.

68. Robert M. Entman, "Issues in Telecommunications Regulation and Competition: Early Perspectives from the States" (Cambridge, MA: Program on Information Resources and Policy, Harvard University, March 1985).

69. An estimate of the stakes for various users of services is made in Paul Eric Teske, *After Divestiture: The Political Economy of State Telecommunications Regulation* (Albany: State University of New York Press, 1990): Chapter 4.

70. "Fifteen Eastern States Implement Major Telephone Reforms," *State Telephone Regulation Report*, vol. 9, no. 3 (February 7, 1991): 1; "Reform Well Along in Western States," *State Telephone Regulation Report*, vol. 9, no. 4 (February 21, 1991): 1.

71. Noll, "Telecommunications Regulation in the 1990s," pp. 36–42.

72. Joseph S. Kraemer, "Improving LEC Incentive Regulation Plans," *Public Utility Fortnightly* (February 1, 1991): 27–30.

73. Although interLATA competition is allowed in most states, competition has not emerged in all areas. Because of service obligations, AT&T must serve all areas desiring services, but other interexchange companies can choose to provide service in selected markets. As a result, many rural areas in the U.S. are provided service by only AT&T.

74. "IntraLATA Competition Nearly Universal in Eastern States," *State Telephone Regulation Report*, vol. 9, no. 17 (August 22, 1991): 1–9; "IntraLATA Competition Widespread in Western States," *State Telephone Regulation Report*, vol. 9, no. 18 (September 5, 1991): 1–7.

75. "Competition in Local Loops Seen in at Least Nine States," *State Telephone Regulation Report*, vol. 9, no. 26 (December 26, 1991): 1, 5–10.

76. "PCs Regulation Unlikely in at Least Half the States," *State Telephone Regulation Report*, vol. 9, no. 19 (September 19, 1991): 3.

77. "New York Commission Approves Nation's First State PCS Tariff," *State Telephone Regulation Report*, vol. 9, no. 21 (October 17, 1991): 1.

78. Paul Teske and John Gebosky, "Local Telecommunications Competitors," *Telecommunications Policy* (October 1990): 429–436.

79. Noam, "Network Pluralism," pp. 80–87.

80. For a discussion of definitions and alternative methods for determining market dominance, see Donald C. Eberle and Lyle Williamson, "Deregulation of Telecommunications at the State Level: Managing a Transition," *Public Utility Fortnightly* (September 1, 1988): 20–21.

81. Danny B. Garcia III and Mahmoud Watad, "California," in *Telecommunications and Economic Development*, edited by Schmandt et al., pp. 22–25.

82. For a summary of the Public Utility Commission's actions, see "Status of Competition in Long-Distance and Local Telecommunications Markets in Texas" (Public Utility Commission of Texas, Austin, January 14, 1991): 24–26.

83. John Horigan and Darren Rudloff, "Illinois," in *Telecommunications and Economic Development*, edited by Schmandt et al., Chapter 4.

84. Terrence L. Barnich, Craig M. Clausen, and Calvin S. Monson, "A Telecommunications Free Trade Zone: Chicago As the Model for Open Competition—A Proposal and Issues Paper" (Illinois Commerce Commission, August 15, 1991).

85. The proposal attracted the support of alternative service providers. John Keller, "Teleport Plans Tough Assault on Illinois Bell," *Wall Street Journal* (November 22, 1991); B1; Edmund L. Andrews, "Regulators Moving to Break Local Telephone Monopolies," *New York Times* (December 27, 1991): A1, C3.

86. Governor's Telecommunication Task Force, "Connections: A Strategy for Michigan's Future Through Telecommunications," May 1990.

87. Michigan Public Service Commission, *Public Utilities Reports*, 114th (March 13, 1990): pp. 1–27.

88. "Lobbying Heavy Over Michigan Law to Restructure Regulation," *State Telephone Regulation Report*, vol. 9, no. 9 (May 2, 1991): 6–8; "Big Users See Long Michigan Deregulation Bill Battle," *State Telephone Regulation Report*, vol. 9, no. 12 (June 13, 1991): 2–3; Peter Luke, "Ma Bell Ringing Up a Big Bill in Major Deregulation Effort," Grand Rapids Press News Service, April 9, 1991.

89. "Michigan Finally Passes Telecommunications Reform Bill," *State Telephone Regulation Report*, vol. 9, no. 25 (December 12, 1991): 1–3.

90. Janee Briesemeister and Philip Treuer, "Vermont," in *Telecommunications and Economic Development*, edited by Schmandt et al., Chapter 8.

91. "Vermont, Florida Address Reforms," *State Telephone Regulation Report*, vol. 9, no. 21 (October 17, 1991): 1–3.

92. Amy M. Korzick and Sehba Sarwar, "Virginia," in *Telecommunications Policy and Economic Development*, edited by Schmandt et al., Chapter 9.

93. Harper and Younger, "Nebraska," Chapter 5.

94. U.S. West has been the most aggressive of the regional Bell companies in promoting deregulation of local exchange companies. The company did not meet with the same success in Utah, Washington, and Minnesota where states did not adopt the Nebraska approach. See Eberle and Williamson, "Deregulation of Telecommunications," pp. 23–24; Teske, *After Divestiture*, Chapter 8.

95. Milton Mueller, "Telecommunications Rate Deregulation in Nebraska: A Five-Year Review—Executive Summary" (International Center for Telecommunications Management, University of Nebraska, Omaha, January 8, 1992).

96. Thierry Noyelle and Penny Peace, *The Information Industries: New York's New*

Export Base (New York: Conservation of Human Resources, Columbia University, November 1988); Jennings and Sawhney, "New York," Chapter 6.

97. Teske, *After Divestiture*, pp. 93–96.

98. ACIR, *Intergovernmental Regulation of Telecommunications*, pp. 32–33.

99. Edmund L. Andrews, "Regulators Moving to Break Local Telephone Monopoly," *New York Times* (December 27, 1991): A1, C3; "The Local Call Goes Up for Grabs," *New York Times* (December 29, 1991): Section 3, pp. 1 and 6.

100. Eberle and Williamson, "Deregulation of Telecommunications," pp. 26–27.

101. Schmandt et al., eds., *Telecommunications and Economic Development*, Chapter 11.

102. Teske, *After Divestiture*, Chapter 5.

103. "Small Firms Are Linked by Electronic Network," *Wall Street Journal* (December 31, 1991): B1.

104. Kenneth Arrow, "The Economics of Information," in *The Computer Age: A Twenty Year Review*, edited by Michael L. Destorzos and Joel Moses (Cambridge, MA: MIT Press, 1980): 306–317.

105. For public sector applications of telecommunications, such as in distance learning, telemedicine, and information management, see Schmandt et al., *Telecommunications and Economic Development, The New Urban Infrastructure,* and *Telecommunications and Rural Development.*

106. Williams, *The New Telecommunications*, pp. 45–48.

107. Leonard S. Greenberger, "Telecommunications: Toward the Twenty-First Century," *Public Utilities Fortnightly* (July 15, 1991): 33; Charles Mason, "LECs, Regulators Confront Infrastructure Issues," *Telephony*, vol. 221, no. 20 (November 11, 1991): 8–9; Charles Mason, "NTIA: U.S. Must Move Telecom Policy Debate to National Forefront," *Telephony*, vol. 221, no. 18 (October 28, 1991): 8–9; "States Divided on Need for National Broadband Development Act, *State Telephone Regulation Report*, vol. 9, no. 16 (August 8, 1991): 1–2; William Page Montgomery et al., "The Telephones Infrastructure in Perspective," a report prepared for the Consumer Federation of America and International Communications Association (Boston: Economics and Technology, Inc., March 1990); "Telecommunications Modernization: Who Pays?" *Trends in Communications Policy*, vol. 14, no. 1 (January 1989): 5—8; Henry Geller, "Fiber Optics: An Opportunity for a New Policy," A Report of the Anneberg Washington Program in Communications Policy Studies of Northwestern University, 1991.

108. Dalianis and Daniels, "New York," pp. 204–205.

109. Lane Darnell Bahl et al., "Telecommunications and Community Development," in *Telecommunications and Rural Development*, edited by Schmandt et al., pp. 198–201.

7

The State as Social Infrastructure Provider: Education and Training

State governments hold a primary role in the provision of education and training in the United States. Around 40 percent of state government revenues are expended on education through public schools, community colleges and state university systems, and work-related training. The provision of education is a responsibility states share with other levels of government, especially local school districts and the federal government. As economic change affects the types and numbers of jobs in the economy, the training requirements for the labor force also change. This creates a new set of demands on the education and training systems, and these demands, in the form of public policy issues, fall principally to state governments.

Education, as most public policy concerns, incorporates a number of different missions. A justification of public provision of education can be made on grounds that a well-educated citizenry is required to maintain democratic institutions; that education—that is, the development of reason—is crucial for the realization of human potential; and that education and training prepare individuals for employment and thus improve the productivity of the country's economy. Although these various missions are not necessarily in conflict, decisions about types of training—general education or occupational training—types of institutions, and levels of funding reflect social priorities among these alternative missions. Establishing priorities and reforming educational systems, for which state governments hold principal responsibility, is further complicated by changing work force requirements.

That the country's educational systems, especially primary and secondary education, are failing is a widely held perception. The academic abilities of high school graduates do not compare well to those of other advanced countries. Businesses are not finding workers with the right types of skills. Demographic trends, especially the aging of the baby boom population, may lead to inadequate numbers of young people entering the labor force in the future. And, finally, the persistently elevated high school dropout rate in the country is creating an ever-growing segment of the population that may not become part of the economic mainstream. Many worry that the racial and ethnic composition of the dropout population will produce a drag on the society, if not the ingredients for an explosive social problem.

To determine how state education policy has responded to these forces, the multiple roles education and training serve and the specific work force requirements of economic change will first be discussed. This discussion will help clarify the link between education and training systems and economic development. The second section consists of an empirical examination of educational levels, the earnings, and geographical distribution of the labor force. These two sections provide the context in which states are adapting educational systems. The following sections describe the institutions, funding, and missions of public education, higher education, and work-related training systems. The chapter concludes with a discussion of the performance of state policymaking in education and training given the labor force requirements of a changing economy.

EDUCATION AND ECONOMIC DEVELOPMENT

Education serves a multitude of functions in any society, and public policy and educational systems must reflect the relative priority society places on these various missions. From the first years of the republic, education was recognized as an important requirement for citizenship and democratic institutions. This Jeffersonian and Jacksonian tradition argued for public education in order to nurture and stabilize the democratic political system; education was necessary for creating a civic-oriented population capable of good decision making. This argument was used early in the country's history to disenfranchise uneducated populations but eventually justified the expansion of public education as the electoral franchise was extended to greater segments of the population. The view has also become intertwined over time with the desire to transmit a common culture and values among generations and to new immigrant groups.

A related, yet distinct, attitude identified education as necessary for the realization of human potential. This view belonged to the humanist tradition that viewed society as a means for improving an individual's capacity to experience and enjoy life. This position was frequently adopted by various religious denominations and led to active church involvement in the formation of schools. Schools for freed slaves immediately following the Civil War—run by freed slaves themselves, religious organizations from the North, and the Freedman's Bureau—were established on these grounds.[1]

The view of education as a necessary factor for the realization of human potential was applied in broader scale by the reform movement in the early part of the twentieth century. In part a response to an increasingly complex society in the throes of rapid industrialization, Thomas Dewey advocated education as an instrument for social change and progress.[2] This tradition emphasized " . . . the extension of schooling to all levels, expansion and differentiation of curricula, individualization of school programs, and the socializing of school purposes."[3] In the 1960s, this tradition justified the use of education as the means to create equal opportunity for all members of the society, especially for those who had suffered discrimination.

Yet another important rationale for the public provision of education is to prepare individuals for the labor market. As early as the 1830s, Horace Mann, who advocated universal public education on several grounds, argued that education contributes to the generation of wealth, or as we say today, to economic development.[4] This linkage can occur in two ways. First, an education system can help sort individuals into various segments of the labor market and produce an efficient deployment of human resources throughout the economy. This function of the education system became evident at the end of last century when vocational education programs were developed to steer individuals into and prepare them for manufacturing occupations. In addition, an education system represents an investment in human capital and thus increases the productivity of individuals, the second type of linkage between an educational system and economic development.

The economic development rationale has dominated the discussions of state policy concerning education and training in the 1980s. The slow improvement in productivity, relative decline in the size of the manufacturing sector, and increasing inequality in earnings in the U.S. economy, identified in Chapter 2, have led to an examination of the labor force, particularly with respect to education and skills levels. Growing public concern about education was galvanized with the publication of *A Nation at Risk* in 1983.[5] The study, produced by a blue-ribbon commission chartered by the secretary of education, found a pronounced deterioration in educational performance in the country in recent decades and levels of performance substantially below chief competitors in Europe and Japan. Poor educational performance was linked to poor performance of the U.S. economy in the international arena and a weakening of the social fabric of the country.

The current and future skills and education levels needed by the labor force were examined in several important reports later in the decade. In 1987, the Hudson Institute published *Workforce 2000: Work and Workers for the 21st Century*.[6] Based on the same trends in occupational structure identified in Chapter 2 (see Table 2.5), the report projected skill requirements for the labor force and found that skill requirements are increasing: the median number of years of education required for jobs created between 1984 and 2000 is expected to be 13.5 years, compared with 12.8 years for the jobs that existed in 1984.[7] The skill requirements for new jobs will be higher, particularly for the higher-end occupations. Although large numbers of jobs for medium-skilled and low-skilled workers will be created, the number of jobs for unskilled workers will decline. The implications for minorities, which make up a large share of unskilled workers, are distressing.

The report *America's Choice: High Skills or Low Wages!* examined the ability of the education and training system in the United States to meet the requirements of the changing labor force.[8] This report formulated the issue of the education and skill requirements of the changing economy as a question: Will the American labor force continue along its present trend of slow deterioration in labor force skills, attempting to compete internationally on the basis of low wages, or will the skills of the labor force be raised to the point that the country can compete in terms of highly productive and efficient workers? The latter approach, the report argued, would require a major restructuring of the country's training systems. The report focuses specifically on the inadequate training opportunities for the noncollege labor force. In 1989, one-third of the labor force was employed in jobs not requiring a high school degree and another third required some noncollege training beyond high school.[9] The training available to individuals in these types of jobs was found to be woefully inadequate. Although this report finds more "de-skilling" in the labor force than *Labor Force 2000,* and thus views the skills gap not as a new phenomenon but rather a continuation of past trends, it formulates the nature of skills distribution as a policy issue: a large segment of the labor force will be confined to low wages unless the training system is substantially restructured and the nature of jobs available fundamentally changed.

Carnevale, in *America and the New Economy,* notes that during the long period of very slow growth in average earnings that started in the early 1970s, individuals with greater education and access to learning on the job fared best.[10] In other words, the economic returns to education and training have remained relatively high, and increased substantially in the 1980s. Carnevale argues that the ongoing technological and organizational changes in the economy are reinforcing the need for higher-level skills in the labor force. This phenomenon is particularly important in the service sectors, where routine functions such as backoffice operations and transportation are increasingly automated—computer processing and telecommunications are central to this process—and workers must increasingly rely on higher-order and problem-solving skills on the job. Formal education is not, however, the only source of learning. On-the-job training is very important, but such training, as currently provided by the private sector, is heavily skewed to the higher-level managerial and technical positions.

EDUCATIONAL LEVELS AND REGIONAL LABOR FORCES

The attention to skill requirements of the labor force and the performance of the educational system has occurred during a period of fairly dramatic improvement in the educational levels of the U.S. labor force (see Table 7.1). In 1976,

26.3 percent of the labor force had less than a high school education, whereas in 1988 only 16.7 percent did. During the same period, the share of labor force with a college degree increased from 16.6 percent to 22.4 percent. These dramatic changes in the overall composition of the work force suggest an even more favorable distribution of education among new entrants to the labor force (that is, younger workers).

The change in the educational composition of the labor force is significant for a number of reasons, but particularly with respect to relative earnings for individuals with different educational levels. Relative wages for those without a high school degree was low in 1976 but had fallen even further by 1988, when such workers earned a little more than one-half of the average earnings of all workers (see Table 7.1). Even the relative earnings for high school graduates declined, and only workers with college degrees earned, on average, significantly more than the national average. In other words, the level of average earnings was becoming increasingly associated with education levels, confirming the Carnevale finding noted above and thus warranting the concern with skills requirements and training.[11]

The spatial distribution of the labor force, by educational level, demonstrates interesting yet troubling patterns. Application of the Theil measure, used in Chapter 2 to capture the spatial distribution for industrial and occupational structure, reveals that the overall spatial distribution of the labor force according to educational levels changed little between 1976 and 1988. However, the period ended with the highest level of inequality; that is, the labor force, by educational levels, had become somewhat less evenly distributed. The distribution of individual education levels, however, reveals quite distinct patterns (see Map 7.1). The higher levels are more spatially concentrated, and by the end of the period workers with no more than an elementary school education had become the most spatially concentrated group.

Although the national trends in educational composition appear in all regions, there are significant differences in education levels among regions (See Table 7.2). At the upper levels, New England, the Mid-Atlantic, and the Pacific hold considerable advantages over other regions. The North Central regions have less polarization in structure than most regions (low shares of both very poorly and very highly educated workers), and the southern regions demonstrate relatively large shares of lower education levels even though these levels dramatically decreased between 1976 and 1988. As one might expect, the relative shares of various education levels are clearly associated with average earnings. The two regions with the highest average earnings in 1988, New England and the Mid-Atlantic regions, have the largest shares of workers with at least a college education. In contrast, the regions with the lowest average earnings, the East South Central and West South Central regions, have relatively large shares of workers with either elementary school or some high school training.

The increasing differences in state and regional earnings were noted in Chapter 2 in the context of industry and occupational change. These data on educational

Table 7.1

Education Levels: Composition of Labor Force, Earnings Ratios, and Spatial Structure: 1976–1988

	National	Elementary School	Some High School	High School	Some College	College Graduate	Post College
A. Proportion of Workers							
1976	100.0	9.89	16.41	39.74	17.41	9.96	6.60
1977	100.0	9.62	16.06	39.77	17.95	9.90	6.69
1978	100.0	8.75	15.15	40.13	18.68	10.15	7.15
1979	100.0	8.22	14.92	40.36	18.79	10.35	7.37
1980	100.0	7.75	14.32	41.05	18.88	10.70	7.30
1981	100.0	7.28	13.92	41.09	18.93	10.90	7.88
1982	100.0	6.69	12.81	40.53	19.81	11.60	8.56
1983	100.0	6.37	12.29	40.76	19.95	11.90	8.73
1984	100.0	6.16	12.34	40.40	20.48	12.16	8.46
1985	100.0	5.74	11.88	40.55	20.77	12.65	8.41
1986	100.0	5.59	11.87	40.13	20.99	12.75	8.67
1987	100.0	5.35	11.97	40.03	20.82	13.00	8.82
1988	100.0	5.26	11.54	39.63	21.08	13.37	9.12
B. Earnings Ratio							
1976	1.0	0.76	0.69	0.94	0.98	1.46	1.84
1977	1.0	0.74	0.66	0.94	1.00	1.47	1.82
1978	1.0	0.73	0.66	0.94	0.99	1.45	1.79
1979	1.0	0.73	0.66	0.93	0.99	1.43	1.78
1980	1.0	0.71	0.64	0.92	1.00	1.45	1.78
1981	1.0	0.71	0.62	0.92	0.99	1.42	1.82
1982	1.0	0.66	0.60	0.90	0.96	1.44	1.85
1983	1.0	0.67	0.59	0.88	0.96	1.45	1.83
1984	1.0	0.65	0.58	0.88	0.94	1.48	1.88
1985	1.0	0.63	0.57	0.86	0.97	1.47	1.89
1986	1.0	0.62	0.56	0.86	0.96	1.49	1.89
1987	1.0	0.62	0.56	0.86	0.97	1.44	1.88
1988	1.0	0.61	0.55	0.86	0.97	1.45	1.83
C. Index of Inequality in Spatial Structure—Theil Index							
1976	0.395	0.396	0.355	0.364	0.453	0.420	0.493
1977	0.400	0.385	0.366	0.370	0.460	0.426	0.489
1978	0.399	0.408	0.361	0.377	0.438	0.409	0.478
1979	0.390	0.410	0.351	0.370	0.415	0.412	0.466
1980	0.394	0.440	0.362	0.359	0.434	0.426	0.449
1981	0.400	0.473	0.361	0.360	0.446	0.423	0.463
1982	0.396	0.453	0.360	0.351	0.430	0.439	0.481
1983	0.391	0.464	0.355	0.345	0.436	0.421	0.455
1984	0.391	0.495	0.358	0.343	0.416	0.439	0.469
1985	0.398	0.542	0.365	0.350	0.421	0.441	0.460
1986	0.403	0.560	0.377	0.352	0.424	0.439	0.470
1987	0.406	0.593	0.364	0.351	0.425	0.460	0.470
1988	0.401	0.631	0.355	0.347	0.414	0.445	0.467

Source: See source for Table 2.2.

Map 7.1
Educational Levels by State: 1988

a. Share of Labor Force with Less than High School Education

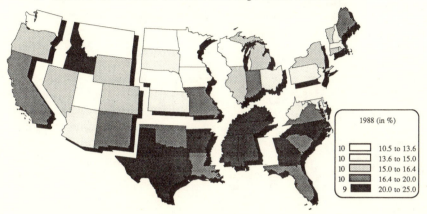

b. Share of Labor Force with College Degree

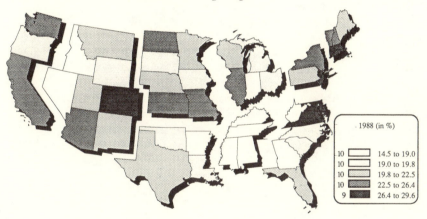

Source: See source for Table 2.2.

levels now suggest that the educational levels of the labor force are also significant determinants of earnings. But the relationship is a complex one, especially in terms of national economic change.[12] In 1976, New England had a relatively favorable educational composition in its labor force, but average earnings were relatively low. However, the region appeared to be well positioned as a result of its occupational and educational structure, which allowed it to take advantage of national trends; thus, in 1988 it had high average earnings. In contrast, the

Table 7.2

Educational Levels by Region: 1976 and 1988 (in percent)

	Elementary School	Some High School	High School	Some College	College Graduate	Post College	Average Earnings ($)
New England							
1976	9.4	15.3	39.0	17.8	11.4	7.1	8,656
1988	4.7	10.6	37.9	19.4	15.9	11.5	21,653
Mid-Atlantic							
1976	9.3	16.0	42.2	15.9	10.1	6.5	9,334
1988	4.1	10.2	42.2	18.8	14.3	10.4	21,618
E N Central							
1976	8.5	16.9	43.0	16.1	9.5	6.0	9,455
1988	3.3	12.3	43.5	21.0	11.7	8.2	19,444
W N Central							
1976	7.8	14.3	44.0	17.0	10.1	6.8	8,369
1988	3.4	9.9	43.9	20.4	13.7	8.7	17,565
S Atlantic							
1976	12.6	18.5	37.4	15.4	9.8	6.2	8,253
1988	5.4	13.2	39.2	20.0	13.5	8.6	19,133
E S Central							
1976	15.2	19.9	39.0	14.2	7.3	4.4	7,563
1988	7.9	15.0	42.2	17.8	9.6	7.5	15,911
W S Central							
1976	13.8	17.4	36.2	16.3	10.3	6.0	8,071
1988	8.2	11.9	37.8	21.3	13.5	7.3	17,458
Mountain							
1976	6.4	14.6	39.6	21.3	10.7	7.4	8,261
1988	3.9	11.5	37.3	25.2	13.1	9.0	17,828
Pacific							
1976	6.8	13.6	35.2	24.8	10.7	8.9	9,368
1988	7.1	9.6	32.5	25.4	14.7	10.7	20,948
National							
1976	9.9	16.4	39.7	17.4	10.0	6.6	8,791
1988	5.2	11.5	39.6	21.1	13.4	9.1	19,442

Source: See source for Table 2.2.

relatively strong educational composition of the labor force in the West North Central region has not been able to compensate for the difficulties of its agriculture and traditional manufacturing economy.

The changing racial and ethnic composition of the labor force and the associated educational characteristics present very troubling trends. Minority populations, especially African-Americans and Latinos, are growing rapidly, and the majority of the student-age population in several states are members of minority groups. The high school dropout rate for minorities is substantially higher than that for the white population (Table 7.3). The spatial incidence of minority

Table 7.3

Dropout Rates by Race/Ethnicity and Region[1]: 1986–1988 (in percent)

a. Event Dropout Rate (three-year avearge, 1986–1988)

| | Total | Race/Ethnicity | | |
		White	Black	Hispanic[2]
Total U.S.	4.40	4.20	5.78	9.27
Region				
Northeast	3.17	2.83	6.12	8.17
Midwest	4.19	3.87	7.10	7.75
South	5.04	4.86	5.44	9.62
West	4.86	5.09	4.33	9.96

b. Status Dropout Rate, 1988

| | Total | Race/Ethnicity | | |
		White	Black	Hispanic[2]
Total U.S.	12.86	12.66	14.87	35.78
Region				
Northeast	10.63	9.62	16.94	37.43
Midwest	9.27	8.71	14.20	28.19
South	14.99	14.82	15.82	28.59
West	16.03	17.62	7.20	41.58

Source: Mary J. Frase, Dropout Rates in the United States: 1988, National Center for
Education Statistics Analysis Report, NCES 89-609 (Washington, D.C.: U.S.
Department of Education, Office of Educational Research and Improvement,
September 1989), pp. 8 and 21, Tables 3 and 7.

[1]There are several different ways of thinking about dropouts. First, the transition of a
student from being in school to not being in school (without graduating in the meantime)
indicates the event of dropping out. The number and rate of these transitions or events can
be measured over a period of time, such as a school or calendar year. Second, the number of
persons who have ever dropped out and not subsequently completed school can be counted
at a given time. This reflects the status of persons in the population with respect to being a
dropout at that point in time.

[2]Hispanics may be of any race.

populations (that is, relatively large Latino populations in the Southwest and in
some large cities, and African-American populations in the South and in some
large cities) contributes to the substantial variation among states and regions of
high school dropout rates.[13]

The distribution of labor force by educational levels reflects in part the level
of commitment to education found among states. As individuals educated in one
state can move their residence to another state, there is not a perfect correlation

Table 7.4
Enrollments in Educational Institutions: 1959–1989 (in thousands)

	Total	Elementary and Secondary Education			Higher Education		
Year	All Levels	Total	Share of School-Age Population	Public	Private	Total	Public	Private
1959	44,497	40,857	93.1%	35,182	5,675	3,640	2,181	1,459
1969	59,124	51,119	97.6%	45,619	5,500	8,005	5,897	2,108
1979	58,215	46,645	97.1%	41,645	5,000	11,570	9,037	2,533
1989[1]	59,339	45,881	99.9%	40,526	5,355	13,458	10,515	2,943

Source: U.S. Department of Education, National Center for Education Statistics, Digest of
Education Statistics (Washington, D.C., 1991), Table 3.

[1]Preliminary data.

between education systems and educational levels of the labor force. Nevertheless, clear regional and state variations in historical commitment to educational
systems are revealed in the educational levels of the labor force.

THE CURRENT ROLE OF STATES IN THE PROVISION OF EDUCATION: AN OVERVIEW

Education and training is an enormous enterprise. In just the formal educational
institutions—primary, secondary, and higher education—almost 69 million individuals were enrolled in 1989 (see Table 7.4). According to 1986 estimates,
the $238 billion dollars expended in these formal institutions were virtually
equalled by expenditures for work-base employee training; about one in eight
workers participated in a formal training course and many times that number
participated in informal training.[14] The education and training system in the
United States is highly fragmented and decentralized, although state government
plays a pervasive role in funding and administration of the endeavor in formal
educational institutions. Around 43 percent of all state expenditures are for
education (see Table 3.3).

Enrollment trends in educational institutions in recent decades reflect the
changing educational composition of the labor force (see Table 7.4). Although
the absolute level of enrollments in elementary and secondary education has
declined since 1969, the share of the school-age population enrolled in school
has remained in the high nineties. The share of the adult population enrolled in
higher education has continued to increase throughout the period. The great
majority of students enrolled in educational institutions, 88.3 percent in elementary and secondary schools and 78.1 percent in higher education, attend
public institutions. These institutions are largely supported and controlled by
state governments.

State government expenditures on education vary considerably. Direct expenditures per capita on education, including elementary, secondary, and higher education, ranged in 1988 from $1,667 (in Wyoming) to $651 (in Tennessee). While considerable variation in expenditures exists within regions, states in the South and South Atlantic spend relatively less than states in other regions (see Map 7.2). Between 1980 and 1988, however, many of the states in the South and South Atlantic raised their per capita spending substantially, as did states in the Mid-Atlantic and Northeast. The increase in spending in states in the South was motivated by the recognition that their relatively undereducated population represented an impediment to economic development.

State expenditures per capita on elementary and secondary education are roughly twice their expenditures for higher education (see Map 7.2). Some states, especially those in the Mid-Atlantic and Northeast, spend considerably more on elementary and secondary education than on higher education, a result of a well-developed system of private higher education institutions. In contrast, several states in the South, particularly in the East South Central region, spend relatively more on higher education than on elementary and secondary education.

The education and training system can be characterized along several dimensions, such as the institutional framework, type of education or training, and funding structure. In order to emphasize the role of state government in this complex system, the discussion will be structured around two major institutional elements, public education (including primary and secondary education) and higher education (two-year and four-year institutions), and a third element, work-related education and training, which occurs in a wide variety of settings (including public schools, institutions of higher education, proprietary schools, and private-sector businesses). The discussion of this third element will focus principally on vocational education.

PRIMARY AND SECONDARY EDUCATION

The provision of primary and secondary education in the United States by public sector began in earnest during the decades of rapid industrialization following the Civil War. Although universal education had been advocated by a number of individuals and institutions since the early 1800s, as noted above, the rapid expansion of public education following the Civil War was one expression of the earlier extension of political suffrage.[15] Expanded suffrage for males, combined with the very substantial flood of immigrants needed for the growing economy, severely limited outright opposition to public education, at least in cities. Although progress was difficult, even in the South there was substantial support for universal education at the end of the nineteenth century; "redemption" for the South was sought through education.[16] A factor further contributing to rapid expansion of public education was the success of labor reformers in securing the passage of child labor laws in many state legislatures during the

Map 7.2
Direct Educational Expenditures per Capita by State: 1988

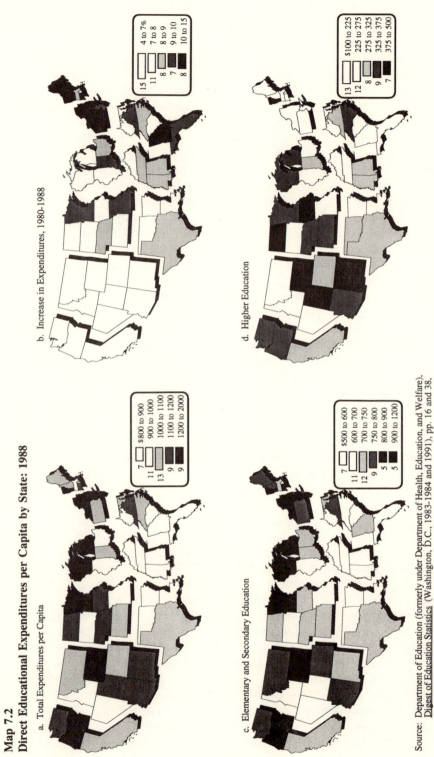

a. Total Expenditures per Capita

7	$800 to 900
11	900 to 1000
13	1000 to 1100
9	1100 to 1200
9	1200 to 2000

b. Increase in Expenditures, 1980-1988

15	4 to 7%
11	7 to 8
8	8 to 9
7	9 to 10
8	10 to 15

c. Elementary and Secondary Education

7	$500 to 600
11	600 to 700
12	700 to 750
9	750 to 800
5	800 to 900
5	900 to 1200

d. Higher Education

13	$100 to 225
12	225 to 275
8	275 to 325
9	325 to 375
7	375 to 500

Source: Department of Education (formerly under Department of Health, Education, and Welfare),
Digest of Education Statistics (Washington, D.C., 1983-1984 and 1991), pp. 16 and 38,
respective years.

early decades of the twentieth century.[17] Combined with compulsory education laws passed by state and local governments, the population eligible for schooling increased substantially.

Public education in this formative period needed to acquire a stable financial base which, in turn, depended on political support for education because budgets for schools were raised almost entirely from local tax revenues. Public schools, or common schools as they were called during that period, were one of several alternatives for educating children, and public school systems and local taxpayers had to be convinced that public schools were a worthwhile enterprise. One strategy of educators was to introduce primary and secondary schools simultaneously and thus minimize the perception that public education was intended principally to provide immigrants with primary education.[18] The availability of high schools made the public school system more attractive to the growing middle class.

Rapid industrialization, in the decades following the Civil War, and the associated labor force training requirements directly affected public school systems. Vocational education—to be discussed in more detail later—became a concern among elements of the business community, especially the rapidly growing manufacturing sector as well as organized labor, which advocated apprenticeship programs and access to skilled employment.[19] Public high schools were only one of several institutional settings in which vocational education could be provided, but through a carefully crafted strategy of institutional development, public school systems were able, with the support of the business community and labor, to largely capture this type of education.

A final feature important in this history of the formation of public education was a phase of administrative reform. Although local politics influenced specific outcomes of reform, the size of the undertaking and the success of the progressive movement led to the eventual adoption of a corporate form of professional management in centralized school systems and professionalization of teaching.[20] The progressive school movement advocated a system in which politics and policy, concerns of school boards, were to be separated from the efficient, scientific management of school systems. The purported strengths of such large bureaucracies were that they were particularly adept at managing very large numbers of students, they could assure equal treatment of all students, and they could allocate resources efficiently and effectively.

Before turning to contemporary education issues, the role of the federal government needs consideration. The U.S. Constitution does not provide a role for the federal government and its role historically has been modest. The federal government's attempt to end racial and ethnic discrimination in school systems, which started in the 1950s and continues today, was a very significant endeavor.[21] Spurred by action in the federal judiciary, especially the *Brown vs. Board of Education* decision in 1954, federal laws and enforcement policies were established to insure the equal treatment of all public school students. In addition, through a variety of Great Society programs, the federal government assumed funding responsibilities for compensatory education provided to disadvantaged students through public schools. An additional role, of substantial proportion, was established in the 1960s in work-related training, and this will be discussed below. In all these federal activities, local education training systems were utilized in implementation, and as a result very few federal institutions provide education and training.

The widespread criticism of public education and calls for reform in the 1980s were based on a dissatisfaction first articulated in the 1970s. Although research in the 1960s argued that academic achievement was related not to quality of schools[22] but rather to the family's socioeconomic status, subsequent research in the 1970s reestablished the importance of the school. Unfortunately, much of the research indicated schools were not working very well. Student achievement scores were in decline, desegregation efforts were fraying the consensus around public schools, and school finance systems were frequently inequitable. The responses of states in the 1970s were modest; the most prominent of these were the imposition of accountability measures, an attempt to encourage local school districts to perform better, and some court-mandated school finance reform.[23]

The criticism and calls for reform exploded in the 1980s, and state government was the principal forum for these debates. The capabilities of state education policymaking, especially in terms of competence and resources in state education agencies, had improved along with the other elements of state government discussed in Chapter 3. [24] Initiated by a number of southern governors in the late 1970s, including Bob Graham of Florida, Charles Robb of Virginia, William Winter of Mississippi, Bill Clinton of Arkansas, James Hunt of North Carolina, and Lamar Alexander of Tennessee, calls for improvement in public education were frequently based in part on a concern for economic development. Although southern states were attempting to compensate for long-standing differentials in educational expenditures, the increased spending and school reforms were also based on the recognition that educational levels were critical elements in the changing economy and that the South was poorly situated for this change.

Public education quickly became an issue throughout the country after the publication of *A Nation at Risk* in 1983.[25] The response was a flood of school reform legislation in the states on a wide range of issues such as upgrading of teachers, increased pay for teachers, curriculum reform, accountability, school governance, and performance standards.[26] The reforms of the early 1980s tended to be top-down policies, formulated by state legislatures and imposed on local school districts by state boards of education. A variety of factors, not the least of which is the enormous size of the public education enterprise, contributed to the ineffectiveness of these measures. As the decade passed, more emphasis was placed on decentralized strategies, especially placing more discretion and decision making in the hands of local actors, including teachers, principals, and parents. Although decision making has been decentralized, oversight of school performance, in terms of improvement in student learning, remains a prominent feature of policy discussions. Some argue that the federal government should play a role in establishing national tests for assessing school performance.

The country has witnessed many short periods of anxiety over education. One reason that public attention and state policymaking have remained focused on schools for more than a decade is that the current economic development imperative has reinforced and partially shaped the drive for enhanced educational systems. In addition, the dynamics of policymaking, although increasingly complex in all states, varies substantially among the states.[27] But evidence that many states have undertaken fundamental shifts in their attitudes about their role in economic development is nowhere clearer than in education reform and school finance.

Funding for public schools originally relied largely on local property taxes. This source of funding reinforced local control of public schools, but also contributed to a later expanded role of state government in schools. In the 1930s, the dramatic decline in property values resulting from the Depression pushed school districts to financial bankruptcy. State governments, in response, substantially increased their share of school funding: In 1929, state governments provided 16.9 percent of school revenues; this share rose to 30.2 percent by 1939.[28] The baby boom following World War II led to rapid expansion in elementary schools, particularly the construction of new schools, and further expansion of state support; by 1949, state government was the source of 39.8 percent of school revenues.

The structure of school funding remained relatively unchanged during the 1950s, but in the 1960s, federal funding of primary and secondary schools increased (see Figure 7.1). The education programs of the Great Society increased the federal share of school revenues to just under 10 percent of the total in the 1970s; this had fallen to just over 6 percent of the total by the end of the 1980s. State government's share steadily increased from 1971, reaching 50 percent of total revenues, until 1986, when it declined somewhat. The taxpayer revolt of the late 1970s centered on property taxes, the principal source of revenues the school districts themselves raise. States have frequently helped support school districts in fiscal distress, but by the end of the 1980s, the ability of state governments to do so was severely limited, and the share of revenues originating within school districts themselves rose.

The state role in education expanded in response to reductions in federal support and taxpayer revolt, but there was substantial variation among states (see Map 7.3). States in the Mid-Atlantic, Northeast, and North Central regions invest most heavily in primary and secondary education. Major increases in funding for education, in states with traditionally low expenditures, such as in Arkansas, Florida, Texas, and other states, reflect in no small part the belief that a well-educated labor force is an investment for the future economic well-being of the state.[29]

Although adequacy of revenues for public education has provided one justi-

Figure 7.1
Sources of Revenue for Public Elementary and Secondary Education: 1955–1988

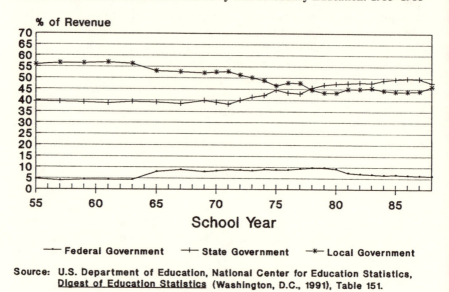

% of Revenue

School Year

— Federal Government   —+— State Government   —*— Local Government

Source: U.S. Department of Education, National Center for Education Statistics, *Digest of Education Statistics* (Washington, D.C., 1991), Table 151.

fication for the increased role of state government in school finance, a second basis for an expanded role has revolved around equity in school finance. The multitude of local school districts in the United States, 12,000 in 1990, and the dependence of school district funding on property taxes have aggravated the spatial disparities in property wealth in the country. Suburban school districts generally have relatively high property values and, consequently, can raise substantial revenues for school districts with relatively low tax rates. In the 1970s, a number of court cases were filed against school finance systems under the equal protection clause of the Fourteenth Amendment of the U.S. Constitution. Although this action was not sustained in the federal courts, a number of state courts and state governments reformed school finance with the intent of reducing the disparities in educational expenditures per student resulting from differences in property wealth among school districts.[30] Although judicial action was frequently the decisive factor, many state legislatures have acted to reduce inequities in school finance systems to the benefit of low-wealth school districts.

HIGHER EDUCATION

In 1988, some 3,400 colleges and universities in the United States enrolled 13.5 million students (see Table 7.5), employed 700,000 faculty members, and generated income of $108.8 billion.[31] The system is comprised of many different types of both private and public institutions, ranging from the two-year junior college and community college to the comprehensive research university. The

Map 7.3
Expenditures per Student in Public Elementary and Secondary Education by State: 1979–1988 (1988–1989 Constant $)

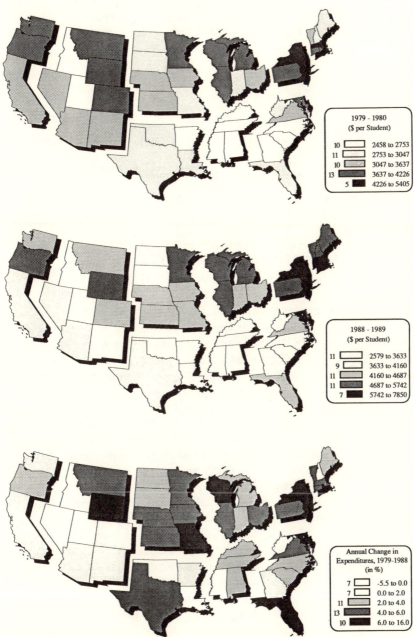

Source: U.S. Department of Education, National Center for Education Statistics,
<u>Digest of Education Statistics</u> (Washington, D.C., 1991), p. 157, Table 159.

Table 7.5
Enrollments in Institutions of Higher Education: 1970–1989 (in thousands)

Year	All Institutions			Four-Year Institutions			Two-Year Institutions		
	Total	Public	Private	Total	Public	Private	Total	Public	Private
1970	8,581	6,428	2,153	6,262	4,233	2,029	2,319	2,195	124
1975	11,185	8,834	2,351	7,215	4,998	2,217	3,970	3,836	134
1980	12,097	9,458	2,639	7,571	5,129	2,442	4,526	4,329	197[1]
1985	12,247	9,480	2,767	7,716	5,210	2,506 •	4,531	4,270	261
1989[2]	13,458	10,515	2,943	8,374	5,694	2,680	5,084	4,820	263

Source: U.S. Department of Education, National Center for Education Statistics, Digest of Education Statistics (Washington, D.C., 1991), Table 167.

[1]Large increase is due to the addition of schools accredited by the National Association of Trade and Technical Schools.

[2]Preliminary data.

various components serve varying missions, ranging from postsecondary occupational training to liberal arts and professional education to the production of new knowledge. The research function of universities, particularly as it relates to science and technology, was examined in Chapter 6. This discussion will focus principally on the education and training functions of higher education.

The relative share of funding for higher education in the United States, including public and private universities, has changed significantly over recent decades (see Figure 7.2). The federal share has declined steadily, from about 25 percent in 1955 to 12.5 percent in 1988. The share provided by state governments increased fairly rapidly from 1965 to 1975 and has represented roughly 30 percent since then. In the 1980s, tuition and other sources of funding increased their relative share. Among public universities, which enroll about 80 percent of all college students, the trends are similar. The federal share of university revenue has declined from roughly 18 percent in 1961 to around 10 percent from 1982 through 1987. The state share of public higher education reached about 46 percent in the late 1970s and declined somewhat during the 1980s to roughly 43 percent by the end of the decade. In the 1980s, additional revenues were generated by tuition and other sources of revenue.

Given their distinct differences in mission, the community colleges will be examined separately from the four-year colleges and universities.

Figure 7.2
Sources of Funding for Higher Education: 1955–1987

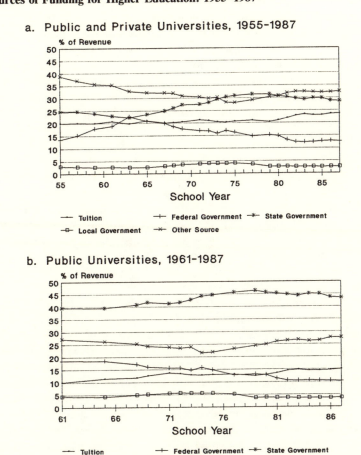

a. **Public and Private Universities, 1955-1987**

b. **Public Universities, 1961-1987**

Source: U.S. Department of Education, National Center for Education Statistics, Digest of Education Statistics (Washington, D.C., various years).

Community Colleges

Enrollment in two-year schools of higher education, including junior colleges, community colleges, and technical institutes, has grown substantially in recent decades (see Table 7.5). The emergence of community colleges as a very significant institution is all the more remarkable given their lack of a clear identity and mission for most of this century. The initial proposal for junior colleges originated in the discussions for reform of higher education soon after the Civil War.[32] Adopting the German model of higher education, leaders such as William Rainey Harper at the University of Chicago, Alexis F. Lange at Berkeley, and David Starr Jordan at Stanford endorsed the creation of junior colleges for the purpose of providing lower-division general education courses. Universities could dispense with teaching such courses and focus on upper-division and professional education. (Higher education reform during this period will be discussed below.) Such junior colleges were to be extensions of public high schools. Although preparing some students for transfer to universities, junior colleges were principally to serve the function of diverting a large number of students from universities.

A number of states, including California, Illinois, Iowa, Michigan, Missouri, and Texas, enthusiastically embraced the model and created junior college systems, frequently with the support of local communities which welcomed the prospect of further educating young people in local institutions. The Populist movement, attracted to the prospect of bringing a liberal arts education to a broad spectrum of the population, provided public support in many states. This impulse saw in junior colleges the democratization of higher education, and a substantial expansion of enrollment in junior colleges occurred in the 1920s.

A small but vocal group of educators in the junior college community started articulating and promoting the vocational training mission in the 1920s. Under this mission, junior colleges would offer a two-year associate degree. This degree, which included liberal arts coursework requirements, was a terminal degree which prepared students for employment in semiprofessional occupations.[33] The vocationalism approach of the community college broadened its number of adherents through the 1930s. In 1932, the Carnegie Foundation for the Advancement of Teaching issued "State Higher Education in California," which attempted to rationalize the state's system of higher education.[34] The initial framework for what became the three-tier system was presented in this report. The third tier of this system was to be the junior colleges, and their principal function was to provide vocational training in two-year terminal programs rather than to prepare students for transfer to universities. The second tier of the system, the state colleges, was assigned the function of training for mid-level occupations such as teaching and social work, and the first tier, the universities, would be research oriented and provide professional training.

Junior colleges continued to experience rapid enrollment growth following World War II, largely as a result of the G.I. Bill, which provided funds for education to returning veterans. The tension between vocational training and liberal arts training remained. The 1948 Truman Commission report, "Higher Education in American Democracy," however, endorsed the vocational training emphasis and recommended that these institutions be renamed community colleges. The name junior college suggested that training would have to be completed at a senior institution. The community college, however, could more readily be construed as an institution offering terminal programs and, more importantly, one that would fit into community life in the same way that high schools were community institutions.[35] Community colleges were to be, and later became, comprehensive institutions that provided a range of training and services in addition to serving their traditional university transfer function.

The extraordinary growth of enrollment in community colleges continued in the two decades following World War II. In the 1950s, enrollment doubled and in the 1960s, fueled by the baby boom, a more than threefold increase occurred.[36] This growth and the continued preference of students for general education and college transfer courses over vocational education programs led to further efforts at differentiation of functions in the higher education system. California again provided the blueprint in its 1960 Master Plan for Higher Education. The diversion of substantial numbers of lower-division students from state colleges and universities to community colleges was a crucial element in the system. Although this three-tier tracking system was largely intended to prevent overcrowding in the other institutions, especially the universities, the effort proved to be consistent with the vocationalization advocates found in community colleges.

Community colleges finally began to receive the attention of the business community, which eventually endorsed their vocational education programs. In the 1960s, grants for curriculum development in vocational education were provided by business associations, foundations, and the federal government.[37] In addition, during the 1970s, the long-held belief that a college education would bring financial rewards began to be seriously questioned and student interest in vocational education increased. The widely reported difficulties of college graduates in finding employment or being underemployed—the Ph.D. student driving a taxi—were widely reported in the press and had a detectable effect on program enrollment in community colleges. By the 1980s, the vocationalization of community colleges was complete. In 1970, 42.6 percent of all two-year associate degrees conferred in institutions of higher education were for occupational curricula—as distinct from arts and science or general education curricula—but in 1980, the share was 62.5 percent.[38]

Although the 1980s saw a consolidation of support for vocationalism in community colleges, the array of forces operating on higher education continue to evolve. The fiscal stress experienced by state government in the late 1980s and early 1990s was also felt in community colleges. The upgrading of community colleges to four-year institutions, a long-standing ambition of some community college advocates, has again been proposed as a relatively inexpensive way for the public sector to respond to the continued demand for higher education, given the overcrowding in four-year universities.[39] Another strategy, being contemplated in California, is to have entering freshman in universities and state colleges complete their first two years in community colleges, thereby relieving overcrowding in the four-year institutions and making a college degree less costly for the student.

The demand for postsecondary education and training in the labor market has increased, as discussed earlier in this chapter. Although the share of workers with at least a baccalaureate degree has demonstrated the greatest growth, the share of workers with less than four years of postsecondary education has also increased substantially (see Table 7.3). This training occurs largely in community or junior colleges and accounts for the very substantial growth in enrollment, which doubled during the 1970s and increased another 12 percent in the 1980s, ending the decade with over 5 million students (see Table 7.5). In addition to the two-year associate degree programs that provide training for specific occupations, are the shorter-term, nondegree skills development courses. The latter have become increasingly common as community colleges establish closer relations with local businesses and labor.[40] This relationship can take the form of customized training, discussed below,[41] or a business service function tied to state or local development initiatives.

The Colorado Training Network (CTN) provides an example of the extensive use of community colleges for state development efforts.[42] The CTN, which consists of the state's community college system, the Department of Labor and Employment, the Division of Commerce and Development, and other state agencies, attempts to package state training programs in order to encourage firms to locate or expand in Colorado. CTN has been involved in a number of collaborative projects in which community colleges develop specialized programs for firms, especially programs for retraining existing work forces.

Other states are also exploring ways of targeting community college activities for specific types of businesses. Community colleges in Oregon have established Business Assistance Centers targeted specifically to the needs of small business.[43] Established by the state legislature, Iowa's area community colleges offer an Industrial New Jobs Training Program, which provides not only training assistance to new firms, but also such services as testing and evaluation for prospective employees. The Des Moines Community College created a business incubator. The Ohio Technology Transfer Organization (OTTO), established to promote the transfer of technological innovation to firms in the state, is implemented through field agents located principally in the state's two-year technical colleges.[44] Eight centers of technology transfer have been created in the state's community colleges to provide access to local business communities.

In Tyler, Texas, a customized retraining program for computerized production of radial tires, developed by Tyler Junior College, was recognized as critical in preventing the closing of a Goodyear Tire plant which employed 1,400 workers.[45] Public-sector funding, from state and local sources, amounted to around $1 million, and Goodyear provided $8 million. The Illinois Community College Board reported in that in fiscal year 1987, it spent $3.73 million on business center–economic development offices, located in community colleges, throughout the state.[46] In support of these functions, an additional $24 million was raised, including $5 million from fees paid by firms, $10 million from the federal Job Training Partnership Act (JTPA) funds, and $4.5 million from other state agencies. The total budget for the state's community colleges during that year was $554.2 million, indicating that the business service function was quite a small share of its total activities. Although the firms benefitting from such services provided some funding, the community and technical colleges incurred substantial expenses; these expenditures were justified, however, on the grounds that subsequent development will be more than sufficient to recover these public-sector costs.

A 1985 survey of the Association of Community and Junior Colleges reported that nearly three-fourths of two-year colleges offer customized training for the private sector and that 83 percent are involved in state and local development initiatives.[47] Among the community colleges most heavily involved in customized training, however, only 10 to 12 percent of the students are enrolled in such training. The great majority are enrolled in degree programs, both college transfer and associate degree, or vocational training courses. The dropout rate in community colleges, however, is quite high.[48]

The expansion of customized training and nondegree programs in community colleges is not endorsed by all. The private sector competes in the training business, and some fear that this competition is forcing community colleges and other institutions to focus too much on short-term objectives like firm-specific, customized training, thus undermining efforts that would contribute to long-term development of transferable skills and human resources.[49]

The actions of community colleges can be characterized as a search for an institutional niche. During certain periods, community college leaders have tried to create their niche in higher education, but during other periods they focused on establishing a role in the vocational training sequence initiated in high schools. Most recently, community colleges have shown entrepreneurial spirit and effectively consolidated a niche through a fairly quick response, in terms of expansion of vocational education and short-term training programs to economic development concerns. Both high schools and higher education have adapted to economic change, but not as quickly as community colleges.[50] Community colleges, however, will remain comprehensive in nature and even occupational training programs will include a liberal arts curriculum.

The advocates for redefinition of the mission of community colleges have for the most part been members of the educational community.[51] These advocates have responded to opportunities originating in the competition among institutions for particular types of training. The business community has historically not been a major participant in this evolution. Only in recent years, after community colleges established an institutional base, has the private sector demonstrated any significant interest in the community college curriculum. Although the closeness of the relationship of community colleges and the business community may remain controversial, community colleges have become important elements of economic development strategies in many states and cities. The expected growth in jobs requiring some postsecondary education suggests that community colleges will retain an important development role in the future.

Four-Year Institutions

The four-year colleges and universities have played a crucial role in insuring that large numbers of individuals receive levels of education necessary for the increasing number of high-skilled occupations. In terms of occupational structure, as discussed in Chapter 2, and in terms of wage levels associated with education, discussed earlier in this chapter, the importance of a college or postcollege education for high-wage occupations is clear. And the higher education system in the country has been successful at graduating large numbers of individuals in response to their increasing demand in the labor force. But four-year institutions, like community colleges, serve multiple missions and there is a great diversity in the types of colleges and universities in the country. To understand the principal roles, and how state governments became the principal source of funding for higher education, a brief historical sketch is useful.

The colleges of the eighteenth and nineteenth centuries frequently adopted the liberal education curriculum which prevailed in Europe during the period, although the American outlook was more sectarian than that found in Europe. The purpose of such education was to develop the character and judgment of students who would later become social and political leaders.[52] Most were linked to religious denominations and were only open to males.

Following the Civil War, three new educational missions were introduced to higher education and each had relevance to the economy. The Morrill Land Grant Act of 1862 and other pieces of federal legislation during the following decades induced states to establish and expand state colleges.[53] These colleges tended to be more heavily oriented toward technical education—especially the fields of agriculture and mechanics—than toward liberal education.[54] The training offered by these colleges was not, however, vocational or manually oriented but rather intellectual and scientific. A secondary objective of this effort was to extend a liberal education to a much greater share of the population.

Another mission of colleges—service to society—was articulated by Charles R. Van Hise, president of the University of Wisconsin from 1903 to 1918.[55] University professors were obligated to undertake research in all areas of human knowledge, but they were similarly obligated to apply their scientific expertise to the improvement of agriculture and manufacturing activities through collaboration with government officials. In addition, Hise argued that the university has an obligation to instruct all members of the public, not just students enrolled in the university. The success of this new model at the University of Wisconsin was widely studied and adopted in other states.

The third new mission of this period was research and the creation of the research universities, represented by Johns Hopkins University under the leadership of Daniel Coit Gilman.[56] To the extent that science was practiced in the United States prior to this time, it was conducted through scholarly societies, based on the model in England. Drawing substantially on the German university model, in which scientific research and graduate education were the university's principal missions, Gilman instituted a focus on pure or basic research at Johns Hopkins University which would later be replicated in other universities.

Although these elements of American higher education were introduced at the end of the nineteenth century, the end of World War II brought their full and dramatic development. An extraordinary expansion in higher education, largely in public colleges and universities, occurred with a focus on professional, practical education. The federal government, through scholarships available in the G.I. Bill of Rights and loans and grants under the National Defense Education Act of 1958, the Higher Education Act of 1965, and the Higher Education Amendments of 1972 helped fund this expanded enrollment.[57] The federal government played a central role in changing the composition of the student population through securing racial integration of universities and equal opportunities for women. In addition, the federal government induced the dramatic expansion of university research, especially related to and justified as an expense associated with the national defense. This research support provided a crucial element in the development and proliferation of research universities.

The enormous expansion in enrollment and the expanded research mission led to organizational changes in higher education. State higher education systems were created with specialization and differentiation among the various types of institutions. Building on its long-term commitment to higher education dating from the 1920s, the State of California implemented a three-tier system for higher education, mentioned above, in the Donahoe Higher Education Act of 1960 that became a model for many other states.[58] The third tier, consisting of nearly one hundred institutions in the California Community College system, specialized in technical curricula leading to the Associate in Arts degree. The second tier consisted of the nineteen institutions in the California State University system, which were predominantly teaching colleges offering liberal arts and occupational curricula and awarding bachelor's and master's degrees. The first tier, the University of California system, was oriented toward professional and graduate training, and faculty members were expected to engage in state-of-the-art research. Although students might advance from one tier to the next, the principal impact of the system was increased structural differentiation among the tiers and distinct educational experiences and opportunities for students in the various tiers.

Higher education became a higher priority for governors after 1981, a change induced by economic development concerns.[59] Although applied research in universities, discussed in Chapter 5, was a principal element, substantial attention was given to human resource development as well.[60] States in the South Atlantic, East South Central, and Mountain regions showed substantial increases in funding in the 1980s (see Map 7.4). Some states have recognized a need to improve science and engineering education in order to increase the number and quality of scientists and engineers available to advanced technology firms.[61]

In recognition of the human resource requirements of an advanced technology economy, Florida adopted a number of programs to increase the number and

Map 7.4
Increase in State Appropriations for Higher Education: 1981–1991

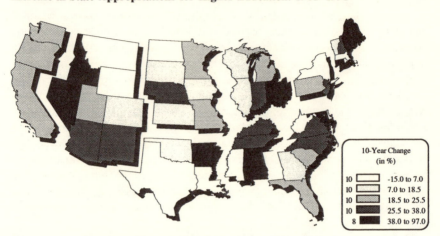

Source: "State Appropriations for Higher Education, 1991-1992,"
Chronicle of Higher Education (November 6, 1991), p. A39.

improve the quality of technically trained individuals in the state.[62] The 1980 Task Force on Science, Engineering, and Technology Service to Industry, created by the State's Board of Regents, identified three important needs: increase in the number of scientists and engineers; improvement in the quality of engineers and scientists; and expansion of the continuing education opportunities for employees in advanced technology industries. Based on this effort and further studies, the state appropriated $54 million, for 1982 through 1987, in the Special University Funding category for investment in facilities and equipment for university-based engineering programs. Enrollment in these programs increased 30 percent over the five-year period ending in 1986.

The legislature also created the Florida Engineering Education Delivery System (FEEDS), an off-campus graduate engineering program. Relying on an educational TV network with interactive audio capability and with videotaped instruction provided by engineering school faculty in the state universities, students can enroll in graduate courses without being present on a campus. The sites used for instruction are frequently businesses, and programs are made available for engineering employees wishing to obtain a graduate degree. In 1984, FEEDS enrolled 2,500 students on a budget of only $1.4 million. As a means to improve the quality of curricula, Florida introduced Postsecondary Programs of Excellence in Mathematics, Science, and Computer Education in 1983. This competitive grant program encourages innovation in the teaching of technical subjects in community colleges and universities. Although Governor Bob Graham, the State Board of Education, and the Florida High Technology and Industry Council, established in 1983, played important roles in articulating development goals, the higher education system itself brought forth most of the specific proposals for higher education.

The expansion of Arizona State University's College of Engineering and Applied Sciences originated in a study of the state's human resources needs.[63] A number of firms indicated that adequate human resources could not be found in the state. In collaboration with supportive business interests, Arizona State proposed to the governor and legislature diversification and expansion of its programs, with a particular focus on graduate education and a new specialization in telecommunications; additional funding was acquired.

At George Mason University in Virginia, a study of its relationship with industry produced new priorities.[64] One of the three priorities established for the university was in human resource development for advanced technology industries. Working closely with an advisory board of local business executives, the university created a new School of Information Technology and Engineering. The school received $3 million from the private sector for establishing endowed faculty positions, and the state legislature created 50 new faculty positions, in spite of severe fiscal constraints.

Universities, like community colleges, serve diverse functions, and these occasionally result in conflicts and tensions. Liberal arts education vs. professional education, teaching vs. research, popularization of knowledge vs. training of experts are long-standing tensions that have not been reconciled during the recent expansion and diversification in higher education. Rather, a number of functions have been given additional weight as a result of economic change. The increasingly information- and research-based economy places a premium on the research mission of universities. In addition, good number of the high-growth occupations, especially managerial, professional, and technical, require a college degree, and the human resource development function of universities is crucial for supplying this demand. As noted above, there is significant variation among states in terms of high-skilled employment and opportunities for higher education, and many states have attempted to improve quality at the higher end of their labor forces. Furthermore, new fields are emerging, frequently interdisciplinary fields, such as computer sciences, information management, bio-engineering, foreign area studies, telecommunications, and environmental studies, and universities target these fields through research centers and new academic programs to satisfy the human resource development need.

Higher education policymaking is unique among state policy issues. Great deference is extended to public managers—that is, to higher education officials and planners—by policymakers. This is the result of several factors. The importance of higher education to a state's economy and prospects for economic development is not questioned by policymakers nor by the public. State university systems also have quite large constituencies, drawing from the graduates of these systems. State legislators involved in establishing policies and determining funding levels may be doing so for their alma maters. As a result, higher education is fairly autonomous, and strategies and programs more often than not originate within state agencies and institutions of higher education. In admissions policy, particularly with respect to enrollment of adequate members of minority students, and tuition policy, higher education is subject to close scrutiny by state officials. But otherwise, university systems manage themselves. Public higher education is certainly not immune to state budget crises, but compared with other state functions, it has fared relatively well.

WORK-RELATED EDUCATION AND TRAINING

Of the various education policy areas, it is in work-related training that states and the federal government most extensively share responsibility. Although states administer federal programs, they also provide funding through school districts, community colleges, and other institutions for vocational education and training. As a result of funding and administering vocational education programs, state and local governments have placed them in a critical position given the changing labor force training requirements. In addition, states have utilized training programs in their economic development efforts.

Although vocational training had received attention from Benjamin Franklin and others in an earlier period, the Russian exhibit of the Moscow Imperial Technical School in the 1876 Philadelphia Centennial Exposition marked the introduction of a new approach.[65] Prior to that time, technical education consisted of classroom instruction combined with on-the-job training in construction shops. The new approach substituted the classroom with an instruction shop. The curricula for the instruction shop, which represented the major innovation in technical training, broke down the skills required in various trades to a sequence of increasing difficult tasks. The students mastered each of these increasingly challenging tasks until obtaining a prescribed level of skill. This approach to manual training was widely viewed as a means of adapting schools to the needs of a rapidly industrializing economy.

The National Society for the Promotion of Industrial Education, organized in 1906 by a group of businessmen, labor leaders, farmer representatives, and academics sought federal legislation for its cause.[66] Fear of competition from Germany, with its highly developed vocational education system, provided further incentive for the vocational education movement and in 1917 the Smith–Hughes Act was adopted by Congress.[67] This landmark legislation provided financial assistance for the teaching of agriculture, the trades and industries, and home economics in high schools and led to the rapid expansion of professional schools in colleges and universities.[68]

The Smith–Hughes Act established an important federal role in training, maintained through the rest of the century, that was not found in public education. In terms of policy design and funding, federal leadership has prevailed, although state and local institutions have been used in providing the training. The Manpower and Training Act of 1962, an important element of the Great Society programs, provided very substantial funds for the training of the disadvantaged.[69]

This program was relatively centralized, and its successor, the Comprehensive Employment and Training Act (CETA) of 1973, was administratively more decentralized, consistent with other Nixon efforts. Under CETA, states and especially local governments had substantial program design and goal-setting authority, and greater attention to linking training and employment was mandated. The institutional mechanism to provide this linkage was the local Private Industry Council (PIC), whose task was to analyze labor markets and to use training as an economic development incentive. The Job Training Partnership Act (JTPA) of 1982 maintained a highly decentralized training system, but increased the private-sector role through enhancing the importance of the PICs. In addition, restrictions were placed on the types of individuals and of employment that could qualify for training, and a range of federal performance requirements were instituted. Even though the federal role in training has been substantially reduced, the federal government has attempted to force states to coordinate and improve services for disadvantaged workers by placing certain requirements on their administration of JTPA.

The institutional framework for the provision of vocational education and training for the disadvantaged is quite complex and ever changing. Vocational education is offered in high schools, proprietary schools, community colleges, and technical institutes. Although the debate has raged for many years and will no doubt continue in the future, there appears to be a trend for less vocational training in high school as a result of the lack of responsiveness in high schools to rapidly changing training needs in the economy. Introducing new courses in high schools, such as courses for preparing workers for employment in the advanced technology industries, is a cumbersome and prolonged process. In addition, as discussed above, there appears to be a consensus emerging that high schools need to prepare students better for lifelong learning, which means more general education requirements and, consequently, less time for job-specific vocational education. The exception to the general decline in enrollments in high school vocational education is the specialized vocational high school, which effectively operates as a magnet school in some designated areas, such as allied health sciences or electronics and computing.[70]

One specific response of states to the changing training needs of employers has been the development of programs that provide customized training for employers.[71] These programs frequently serve as a type of incentive for recruiting firms. In Florida, the Industry Services Training Program (ISTP), created in 1968 and funded in 1974, trains individuals for firms considering locating or expanding in Florida.[72] By the mid-1980s the state appropriation for ITPS surpassed $1 million. After a firm chooses a location for a new facility or expansion, ITPS helps the firm identify its specific training needs and secures customized training programs through local providers such as community colleges. Although the firms do not incur any training costs, they are expected to hire individuals completing the training programs.

Massachusetts established the Bay State Skills Corporation (BSSC) in 1980 in response to advanced technology firms that argued the state was not developing sufficient numbers of high-skilled workers.[73] The board of BSSC consists of members with experience in business, the training industry, state government, labor organizations, and minority employment. With a budget of around $13 million by the mid-1980s, BSSC designs customized training programs in cooperation with employers. Employers provide a financial match for the training efforts and a priority is placed on firms and individuals in economically distressed areas of the state. The training occurs in two- and four-year universities, community-based organizations, vocational/technical schools, and business trade groups. The BSSC model has met with broad support and has been replicated in other states.

North and South Carolina have a 25-year-old record of using the training services of community and technical colleges in their industrial recruitment and expansion programs.[74] Between 1982 and 1987, some 400 manufacturing companies in North Carolina utilized such training services. The Customized Job Training Program in North Carolina pursues two objectives: to train dislocated and unemployed workers, and to attract firms to the state.[75] Similar to other customized training, the program develops training activities in consultation with firms either locating or expanding in the state. In North Carolina, however, the extensive community college system is the primary provider of the customized programs. The program, which had reached a $5 million budget by the mid-1980s, had expanded its traditional focus on textiles to include advanced technology manufacturing. In South Carolina, customized programs for automated production have been established to upgrade workers' skills needed for advanced technology manufacturing.

Many states attempt to coordinate labor force programs and other economic development efforts.[76] This linkage can take the form of joint administration or planning, formal liaison between departments, development officials, participation of JTPA boards and shared databases. The linkages, in this 1985 study, were strongest in states with declining economies and with governors less constrained to reorganize state agencies. The complementarity between work-related training and development initiatives, especially recruitment and retention strategies, has led to greater coordination of programs in most states.

Many states are extending coordination beyond training programs and attempting to link their broad range of human resource initiatives with their economic development programs. Coordination among state and local agencies providing work force training and other services is an important element of the JTPA, through its required coordinating council,[77] and of the Job Opportunities and Basic Skills (JOBS) program of the 1988 Family Support Act. Federal program requirements have forced states to study possible linkages between training, welfare, and economic development and to design human resource investment strategies. Although collaborative planning among agencies is fairly widespread, collaborative service delivery is less common. Nevertheless, these federal requirements have reinforced the efforts of states to coordinate their human service delivery systems.

Formal human resource investment planning bodies responsible for establishing policy guidelines and benchmarks for education, training, and economic development are increasingly common among states.[78] Oregon, in its Progress Board, has pursued most aggressively and comprehensively a human investment strategy.[79] This board, chaired by the governor and consisting of leaders from the public and private sectors, identifies goals and standards for assessing progress in primary and secondary education reform, professional and technical education reform, adult education, apprenticeship programs, youth services, and vocational education. The goals are reviewed, and those adopted by the state legislature become the long-term measures for evaluating the state's progress.

Indiana uses a "superagency" approach to workforce development.[80] The Department of Employment and Training Services, the Commission on Vocational and Technical Education, and the Office of Workforce Literacy were consolidated into the Department of Workforce Development. This new department, created in 1990, will take the lead in implementing Governor Evan Bayh's initiative in workforce training, which includes basic skills mastery, advanced science and math programs, among others. In New York, the Human Resource Investment Subcabinet, consisting of representatives from the State Job Training Partnership Council, the Departments of Education, Social Services, and Labor Economic Development, the state and city university systems, and other agencies, are developing an integrated human resource investment system. This approach to training requires the mobilization of the full range of public services for each individual client in order to ensure the client acquires the training and support necessary to obtain gainful employment. MASSJOBS in Massachusetts, the Washington Work Force Training and Education Coordinating Board, the New Jersey State Employment and Training Commission, and California's Workforce Education and Skills Training (CALWEST), all created in recent years, are strategic planning efforts similar to the economic development strategic planning efforts of the early 1980s described in Chapter 4. They are intended to reform and restructure existing training systems in order to respond to the evolving work force requirements. These efforts frequently place attention on areas, such as the transition for school to work for non-college-bound youth, which have been neglected in the earlier fragmented service delivery structures.

CONCLUSIONS

The development of human resources has become a central theme in discussions of the country's economic future. The emerging economy will require better-trained and higher-skilled workers, and most workers will be retrained several times during their working careers. Private-sector training, conducted in firms, has expanded tremendously in recent years, and the level of spending for this training is estimated to be comparable to the level of public-sector expenditures on education and training. The focus on human resource development has affected all parts of the country's education system, including primary and secondary education, vocational education, community colleges, and universities.

These state efforts in education and training bring together a number of interesting elements. First, states have made very substantial financial commitments even during a period of fiscal austerity. Even though state resources are limited, additional funding is being found for education. One fairly important explanation for this public support is related to the issue of economic development. Investment in human capital is believed to increase the opportunities for individuals and lead to stronger economies. There is, however, substantial skepticism about the effectiveness of the educational systems, and further increases in funding will likely be dependent on improvement in the performance of these various educational systems.

The foundation of the educational system and of the quality of a state's labor force is the public school system. Many states with historically low levels of funding for public education have substantially increased funding. The link between poor public schools, high dropout rates, and the extremely poor prospects for those individuals who do not finish high school is clear. States and local governments that do not satisfactorily redress this situation will be at a clear disadvantage with respect to the ability of their labor forces to meet the requirements of the more promising sectors of the economy.

The increased requirements for high school graduation common throughout the states appear to meet the changing skill requirements of the economy. Strong general education is essential for the lifelong learning required for success in the changing economy. On this point there appears to be a convergence in thinking. Education should be practical but the best preparation in today's economy is not job-specific training but rather generic training. A sound general education provides the basis for quickly assimilating the specific training obtained on the job.

A number of the education and training initiatives are directly linked to business development. The business assistance centers in community colleges and universities, customized training efforts, science and engineering education, and the prominent role of the private sector in JTPA all constitute strategies that are directly attuned to the needs of businesses. Although these initiatives have provided further evidence that states are responding aggressively to economic change, these efforts are relatively small in the context of education's primary task, which is to prepare millions of individuals each year, through terminal programs or continuing education, for an enormous range of occupations. The challenge to the educational systems is made more difficult given that the range of occupations and the numbers of individuals required in each occupation have been changing fairly dramatically and that the racial/ethnic composition of the student population is becoming increasingly diverse.

State government leadership in education and training results from several factors. First and foremost, state government has the major governmental responsibility for the provision of education. When the public voices concern about education, state government provides a principal forum for developing new policies. The dynamics of change, however, vary among the three types of institutions, public schools, community colleges, and institutions of higher education.

Citizen fears and concerns about public schools are directly expressed and felt in school boards. Local control, even when it is eroded by state legislatures and boards of education, makes school reform and finance very salient issues. Although many reform proposals originate with educators themselves, the process of debating and deciding on reforms incorporates broad public participation, and structural reforms are most often adopted at the state, not the local, level. In contrast, community colleges have for much of their history been attempting to garner public and business interest and only recently have they consolidated a sound institutional base and mission. They did so by identifying an unfilled need—expanded vocational education—produced by economic change.

University systems, in contrast, hold a privileged position among public institutions of education and rely much more heavily on internal planning than external forces to shape their activities. Universities have responded to the human resource needs of the more technologically oriented sectors of the economy in many states and have proven to be crucial elements in several states with historically small, technically and scientifically trained labor forces. However, the continuing fiscal crises of states even threaten the independence long enjoyed by universities.

NOTES

1. Eric Foner, *Reconstruction: America's Unfinished Revolution, 1963–1877* (New York: Harper & Row, 1988): 96–100.

2. Lawrence A Cremin, *American Education: The Metropolitan Experience, 1876–1980* (New York: Harper & Row, 1988): Chapter 5.

3. Cremin, *American Education*, p. 242.

4. Louis Filler, ed., *Horace Mann on the Crisis of Education* (Lanham, MD: University Press of America, 1983).

5. National Commission on Excellence in Education (NCEE), *A Nation at Risk* (Washington, D.C., 1983).

6. William B. Johnston and Arnold H. Packer, *Workforce 2000: Work and Workers for the 21st Century* (Indianapolis, IN: Hudson Institute, 1987).

7. Ibid., p. 97.

8. Commission on the Skills of the American Workforce, *America's Choice: High Skills or Low Wages!* (Rochester, NY: National Center on Education and the Economy, 1990).

9. Ibid., p. 27.

10. Anthony Patrick Carnevale, *America and the New Economy* (Washington, D.C.:

The American Society for Training and Development and U.S. Department of Labor, Employment and Training Administration, 1991): 87.

11. There are well-known problems with associating educational attainment and earnings. More reliable determinants of earnings would include skills, quality of training, experience, and others. Even though a causal relationship between educational attainment and earnings is not being argued here, the striking pattern found in Table 7.1 nevertheless identifies attainment as an important factor. See W. Norton Grubb, "Simple Faiths, Complex Facts: Vocational Education As an Economic Development Strategy," in *Growth Policy in the Age of High Technology: The Role of Regions and States*, edited by Jurgen Schmandt and Robert H. Wilson (Boston: Unwin Hyman, 1990): 255–256.

12. Stephen F. Seninger, *Labor Force Policies for Regional Economic Development: The Role of Employment and Training Programs* (New York: Praeger, 1989): 44–45.

13. Peggy Siegel, *Education and Economic Growth: A Legislator's Guide* (Denver, CO: National Conference of State Legislatures, January 1988): Chapter 4.

14. Anthony Patrick Carnevale, "The Learning Enterprise," *Training and Development Journal*, vol. 40, no. 1 (January 1986): 18–26.

15. Paul E. Peterson, *The Politics of School Reform, 1870–1940* (Chicago: University of Chicago Press, 1985): 6–9.

16. Cremin, *American Education*, pp. 216–220.

17. Peterson, *The Politics of School Reform*, pp. 36–37.

18. Ibid, pp. 11–12.

19. Ibid, pp. 65–70, 199–201.

20. Peterson, *The Politics of School Reform, 1870–1940*, pp. 204–207; Cremin, *American Education*, pp. 226–239.

21. Cremin, *American Education*, pp. 196–204.

22. James S. Coleman, *Equality of Educational Opportunity* (Washington, D.C.: U.S. Department of Health, Education, and Welfare, Office of Education, 1966).

23. Denis P. Doyle and Terry W. Hartle, *Excellence in Education: The States Take Charge* (Washington, D.C.: The American Enterprise Institute, 1985): 7–13.

24. Jerome T. Murphy, "Progress and Problems: The Paradox of State Reform," in *Policy Making in Education: Eighty-First Yearbook of the National Society for the Study of Education*, edited by Milbrey W. McLaughlin (Chicago, IL: University of Chicago Press, 1982): 95–202.

25. NCEE, *A Nation at Risk*.

26. Doyle and Hartle, *Excellence in Education*; Dennis P. Doyle et al., *Taking Charge: State Action on School Reform in the 1980s* (Indianapolis, IN: Hudson Institute, 1991).

27. Richard F. Elmore, "The Political Economy of State Influence," *Education and Urban Society*, vol. 16, no. 2 (February 1984): 125–144; Murphy, "Progress and Problems."

28. Michael W. Kirst, *Who Controls Our Schools? American Values in Conflict* (New York: W. H. Freeman and Company, 1984): 98.

29. A special issue on the long-term economic challenges for southeastern states was published in the *Economic Review* (Federal Reserve Bank of Atlanta), vol. 73, no. 1 (January/February 1988). The story was similar in all states. The natural resource–based, low-wage economy and the prevailing low education levels in the region are a poor foundation for future growth. Improved education systems were proposed as an important policy for reducing unemployment, raising wage levels and stabilizing the vulnerable economy of the region. For the case of Arkansas and the role of Governor Bill Clinton

see David Osborne, *Laboratories of Democracy* (Boston: Harvard Business School Press, 1988): Chapter 3. For a general discussion of the issues involved see Ray Marshall, "The Impact of Elementary and Secondary Education on State Economic Development," in *Growth Policy in the Age of High Technology,* edited by Schmandt and Wilson, pp. 211–253.

30. Kirst, *Who Controls Our Schools?*, pp. 99–102.

31. Modesto A. Maidique, "Universities: A Focal Point for Economic Development," *National Forum,* vol. 68, no. 4 (Fall 1988): 38–39.

32. Steven Brint and Jerome Karabel, *The Diverted Dream: Community Colleges and the Promise of Educational Opportunity in America, 1900–1985* (New York: Oxford University Press, 1989): Chapters 1 and 2.

33. Brint and Karabel, *The Diverted Dream,* pp. 32–46.

34. Carnegie Foundation for the Advancement of Teaching, "State Higher Education in California" (Sacramento, CA: California State Printing Office, 1932).

35. Brint and Karabel, *The Diverted Dream,* p. 70.

36. Ibid., p. 84.

37. Ibid., pp. 94–101.

38. Arthur M. Cohen and Florence Brawer, *The American Community College* (San Francisco: Jossey-Bass, 1982): 203; W. Norton Grubb, "The Decline of Community College Transfer Rates: Evidence from National Longitudinal Surveys," *Journal of Higher Education,* vol. 62 (March/April 1991): 194–227.

39. Joye Mercer, "States Turn to Community Colleges as Route to Bachelor's Degree as 4-Year Campuses Face Tight Budgets and Overcrowding," *The Chronicle of Higher Education,* vol. 38, no. 39 (May 6, 1992): A1, A28.

40. Cary A. Israel, James F. McKenney, and Jerome F. Wartgow, "Community Colleges: A Competitive Edge for Economic Development," *Economic Development Review,* vol. 5, no. 2 (Summer 1987): 19–23.

41. William L. Deegan and R. Drisko, "Contract Training: Progress and Policy Issues," *Community and Junior College Journal,* vol. 55, no. 6 (March 1985): 14–17.

42. Israel et al., "Community Colleges," p. 20.

43. Ibid, pp. 19–20.

44. Ibid, pp. 21–22; Cheryl Fields, "Community Colleges Discover They Are at the Right Place at the Right Time," *Governing* (February 1988): 33.

45. Ibid, pp. 33–34.

46. Ibid, p. 33.

47. Ibid, p. 32.

48. W. Norton Grubb, "Dropouts, Spells of Time, and Credits in Postsecondary Education: Evidence from Longitudinal Surveys," *Economics of Education Review,* vol. 8 (1989): 49–67.

49. For a discussion of the issues involved, see Grubb, "Simple Faiths," pp. 276–277.

50. Grubb, "Simple Faiths," pp. 273–274.

51. Brint and Karabel, *The Diverted Dream,* Chapter 8.

52. Sheldon Rothblatt, "Standing Antogonisms: The Relationship of Undergraduate to Graduate Education," in *The Future of State Universities: Issues in Teaching, Research, and Public Service,* edited by Leslie W. Koepplin and David A. Wilson (New Brunswick, NJ: Rutgers University Press, 1985): 42–43.

53. Clark Kerr, *The Uses of the University, With a Postscript—1972* (Cambridge, MA: Harvard University Press, 1972): 46–52.

54. Rothblatt, "Standing Antagonism," pp. 43–44.

55. Cremin, *American Education*, pp. 246–247.

56. Ibid, pp. 386, 557–558; Kerr, *The Uses of the University*, pp. 11–15.

57. Cremin, *American Education*, p. 555.

58. Lance Silbert and Michael P. Burke, "California," in *Promoting High-Technology Industry: Initiatives and Policies for State Governments*, edited by Jurgen Schmandt and Robert H. Wilson (Boulder, CO: Westview Press, 1987): 26–28. Cremin, *American Education*, pp. 252–253.

59. Eric B. Herzik, "The Governors' State-of-the-State Addresses: A Focus on Higher Education," *State Government*, vol. 58, no. 2 (Summer 1985): 65–66.

60. Public Policy Center of SRI International (SRI International), "The Higher Education–Economic Development Connection: Emerging Roles for Public Colleges and Universities in a Changing Economy" (Washington, D.C.: American Association of State Colleges and Universities, 1985).

61. Stuart Rosenfeld and Robert D. Atkinson, "Engineering Regional Growth," in *Growth Policy*, edited by Schmandt and Wilson, pp. 283–312.

62. Michael Freudenberg and Tracy L. Henderson, "Florida," in *Promoting High-Technology Industry*, edited by Schmandt and Wilson, pp. 52–62.

63. SRI International, "The Higher Education–Economic Development Connection," pp. 12–13.

64. Ibid, pp. 13–14.

65. Cremin, *American Education*, pp. 223–224.

66. Cremin, *American Education*, p. 228.

67. Marvin Lazerson and W. Norton Grubb, *American Education and Vocationalism: A Documentary History, 1870–1970* (New York: Teachers College Press, Columbia University, 1974): 17–30; W. Norton Grubb, The Bandwagon Once More: Vocational Preparation for High-Tech Occupations," *Harvard Educational Review*, vol. 54, no. 4 (November 1984): 444.

68. Cremin, *American Education*, p. 8.

69. Stephen F. Seninger, *Labor Force Policies for Regional Development: The Role of Employment and Training* (New York: Praeger, 1989): 63–69.

70. W. Norton Grubb and Lorraine M. McDonnell, "Local Systems of Vocational Education and Job Training: Diversity, Interdependence, and Effectiveness," National Center for Research in Vocational Education, University of California at Berkeley (July 1991).

71. Beverly Geber, "Supply-Side Schooling," *Training*, vol. 24, no. 4 (April 1987): 24–30.

72. Michael Freudenberg and Tracy L. Henderson, "Florida," in *Promoting High-Technology Industry*, edited by Schmandt and Wilson, pp. 56–58.

73. Kathleen A. Merrigan and Suzanne E. Smith, "Massachusetts," in *Promoting High-Technology Industry*, edited by Schmandt and Wilson, pp. 80–84.

74. Israel et al., "Community Colleges," p. 22.

75. Mark Howard and Mary Kragie, "North Carolina," in *Promoting High-Technology Industry*, edited by Schmandt and Wilson, pp. 179–181.

76. Susan A. MacManus, "Linking State Employment and Training and Economic Development Programs: A 20-State Analysis," *Public Administration Review* (November/December 1986): 640–648.

77. Rodney Riffel, "Job Training: A Legislator's Guide" (Denver, CO: National Conference of State Legislature, September 1986).

78. Lawrence N. Gold, "States and Communities on the Move: Policy Initiatives to Create a World-Class Workforce" (Washington, D.C.: William T. Grant Commission on Work, Family, and Citizenship, 1991).

79. Gold, "States and Communities on the Move," pp. 11–12.

80. Ibid., pp. 12–14.

8

State Policymaking and Economic Change

The old formula for American economic prosperity no longer works, and the dominance of American industry in the world economy has ended. Not only has a more competitive environment emerged, but the underpinnings of this new economy—in terms of R&D requirements, industrial organization, skill and education requirements, and other infrastructure requirements—have substantially changed.

The federal role in adapting institutions to this new reality has been to attempt to remove barriers to the market, including deregulating markets, weakening labor, reducing the size of government, and increasing the returns to capital. A divided and fiscally weak federal government has limited further action. States have been thrust into this new policy environment with institutions and programs designed for a different era. Although states have taken a subordinate role in economic development issues for most of the century, current economic stress has forced a range of issues onto their policy agenda.

In this chapter, several elements of state policymaking, related to the context of economic and political decentralization, will be analyzed, drawing on the findings of this study. First, the emerging economic geography and the stakes for the states will be presented. The following section discusses the nature of intergovernmental change and its effects on certain types of state policymaking; this change has encouraged state activism. Conclusions are drawn about the process of state policymaking itself, as revealed principally in the three case studies. Areas of inadequate state response to existing problems will then be identified. The final section argues that states provide a very appropriate forum for addressing many development issues as a result of both economic and political decentralization.

ECONOMIC GEOGRAPHY AND THE STAKES FOR STATES

The effect of economic change on state economics in the 1980s, defined in terms of changes of average earning in a state, has become clear (see Map 8.1). The three regions with the highest average earnings—New England, the Mid-Atlantic, and the Pacific—had several elements in common.

In terms of their industrial structure, each had large employment shares of advanced technology manufacturing, producer services, telecommunications, and, in New England and the Mid-Atlantic, health and education (Table 2.10). These employment sectors were identified as high-wage, spatially concentrated sectors with good, if not strong, growth potential. These three regions also had large shares of the upper-end occupations and of well-educated workers (see Map 7.1). They were also found to have high levels of research and development activity, especially in the important industrial R&D. Many states in these three regions make relatively high investments in education, although California has been unable to maintain its long-standing support for education for a variety of reasons. New England, in particular, has dramatically improved its relative position, as defined by average earning during the period, and all three regions are well positioned to take advantage of trends in economic change.

The East North Central region has fallen in its relative standing, although in 1990 it still maintained average earnings equal to that of the nation (see Figure 2.1). This region suffered the most from the downsizing and decline in relative wages of the machinery, metallurgy, and transportation equipment sectors. States in these regions have been the most active in economic development strategies and hold substantial shares of industrial R&D. The technology policy in the region is weighted toward advanced manufacturing, and the region now appears to have stabilized the slide in manufacturing and, in fact, has benefitted from increased manufacturing activity in recent years. In education, the region has relatively few poorly educated workers and invests relatively more in primary and elementary education than in higher education.

The South Atlantic region has substantially improved its standing, in terms of average earnings, and ended the period only slightly below the average for the nation. The dynamics of change within the region have varied. Virginia, Delaware, and Maryland lead the region in terms of average earnings, and these economies are heavily weighted to producer services and telecommunications employment, the result of their proximity to Washington, D.C. The region has a well-educated labor force and benefits from a very large share of federal R&D. Virginia, in particular, invests heavily in education. States farther to the South— North Carolina, South Carolina, Georgia, and Florida—have engaged in sub-stantial development efforts. These states, especially Georgia and South Carolina, are having moderate success in moving from low-wage, traditional manufacturing

Map 8.1
Average Earnings by State: 1988; and Rate of Increase in Average Earnings:
1976–1988

a. Average Earnings in 1988

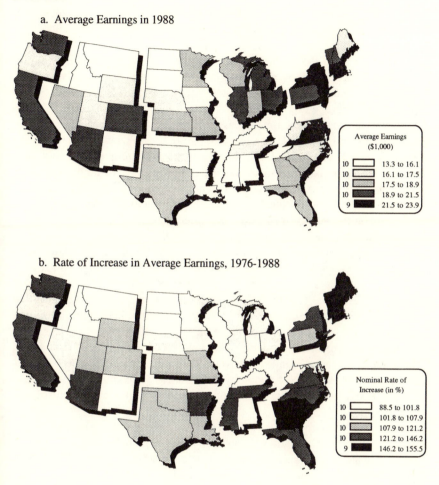

b. Rate of Increase in Average Earnings, 1976-1988

Source: See source for Table 2.2.

and agricultural economies and have captured a fair share of the more dynamic
sectors. These states are increasing their spending on education from a traditionally low base.

Three regions—Mountain, West North Central, and West South Central—
have not maintained the same rate of increase in average earnings as the nation
as a whole, and all ended the period below the national level. The economies
of these regions have diversified, especially in terms of manufacturing, and some

states, including Arizona, Colorado, Texas, and Minnesota, have large employment shares of the important producer services sector. These regions, however,
have large shares of several low-paying sectors, including agricultural, retail
trade, and consumer services. Although the industrial structure, though improved, remains unfavorable and R&D funding is low, the Mountain and West
North Central have labor forces with quite good education levels and invest
heavily in education. Nebraska has taken an interesting initiative, taking advantage of this labor force, by attempting to capture a comparative advantage in
telecommunications services, and its state policy reflects this priority.

The East South Central region has become the region most specialized in
manufacturing. At the same time, its average earnings, relative to other regions,
has declined (see Figure 2.1), the result in part of specializing in manufacturing
industries with lower wage levels. R&D expenditures are quite low, but most
states in the region have substantially increased spending for higher education
and for research centers. The educational composition of the labor force is poor,
with high levels of poorly educated workers, but again most states in this region
are attempting to enhance their public school systems with increased funding.

A principal feature of this new geography is the diminishing importance of
manufacturing; that is, an economy based on manufacturing is no longer a
guarantee for economic well-being. Manufacturing is diverse both with respect
to location patterns and wage levels, and growth of blue-collar employment
will be well below the growth of the labor force as a whole. With the exception
of advanced technology manufacturing, other manufacturing sectors are either
too slow-growing or too low-wage to be the driving force of economic growth
in a state, as demonstrated in both the East North Central and East South
Central regions. An economically diverse economy, especially one with significant levels of advanced technology manufacturing, producer services, and,
to a lesser extent, health and education, appears to be a prerequisite for
economic prosperity.

An important feature of this new economic geography is an increased specialization in occupational structure and education. Significant shares of higher-
skilled occupations and higher education levels appear to be critical elements to
future prosperity. Regions with larger proportions of lower skills and education
levels are falling further behind in terms of average earnings. The occupational
and educational characteristics appear to be the source of increasing income
inequality among states, lending credence to the argument that human capital,
the skills embodied in the work force, is becoming the decisive factor in economic
development.

To what extent can state government influence this new geography? The
requirements of the new economy—including R&D, a more sophisticated labor
force, access to international markets, information infrastructure, and others—
have placed new demands on the public sector, creating new opportunities for
states and cities to attempt to establish comparative advantages. Attempts by

states to create such advantages date from the colonial period. Constitutional provisions and a need for national (that is, federal) action to establish a national market restricted the range of actions states could use in creating comparative advantages, but the principle nevertheless survived. A good number of state-sponsored promotion efforts had extraordinary impact, but others revealed bad judgment, and a number even led to political backlash and actions for reform. In our contemporary setting, the politics of economic distress has focused on state capitols, but economic change has redefined the mechanics of comparative advantage. One challenge to states has been to adjust their policy instruments accordingly.

States have at their disposal policy instruments—such as infrastructure investment, regulation of business, and many others—whose effects are significant for at least some sectors of their economies. Specific policy actions will depend on political circumstances in a state; the number of affected constituents can be few or many, and certainly not all interests are successful in obtaining desired results. But policy actions will also impinge on the comparative advantage of states, and in this respect states compete with one another on numerous fronts. The competition has become even more intense in recent years because economic change has created many opportunities for a more spatially dispersed investment pattern. As a result of the increased mobility of capital, firms seeking new investment locations are less tied to old patterns, thereby creating more opportunities for states. But the location factors underlying these new patterns are not completely understood; consequently, states have had to experiment with a wide range of policy instruments. Some location factors, such as the existence of an entrepreneurial climate, may be largely beyond the control of states or may take a long time to develop in a state.

Here we find one of the dilemmas faced by state policymakers. Diverse economic constituencies look to state government for actions consistent with their interests. Support for policies consistent with economic change, such as technology policy or capital formation programs, may be relatively weak, particularly in terms of sustaining certain policy initiatives over time. But without reform and adaptation, a state will not be well positioned for the future. Policymaking in the states must contend with these potentially conflicting interests, but the broad pattern is clear: states are adopting, at different speeds, programs and policies consistent with the forces of economic change.

Openness of state economies means that success must be determined in an increasingly competitive environment. Local producers cannot be effectively protected from imports, either from other states or from other countries, through policies adopted by states. Local markets receive some protection as a result of geography, at least in large states, but economic geography is being stretched and formerly local markets are being subjected to competition. Hence, competitiveness and productivity of all firms are critical for the long-term economic growth prospects of a state.

THE INTERGOVERNMENTAL CONTEXT

In the historical treatment of intergovernmental relations in Chapter 3, it was observed that the dynamics of policy initiative in the United States and the forum in which policy is addressed have varied greatly throughout the country's history. With respect to development policy, the sources of policy initiative are of several types: pressures generated in the local economy, growth of large enterprises, structural economic change, formation of a national economy, management of a national economy, new sources of economic growth, resource mobilization, and others. The interplay between federal and state governments as the forum for addressing these issues is complex. The requirements associated with the formation of a national market have generally been provided through federal action, although a number are embodied in the Constitution. Federal roles have emerged due to specific historical circumstances, such as the banking crisis at the turn of the century and the depression of the 1930s. The shift to federal policy initiative in the early decades of the century was in part the result of the inability of states to address development issues.

During the recent period of economic change, federal leadership in addressing development issues has been less evident, in part due to the prevailing policy of recent presidential administrations of encouraging development decisions to be made in markets operating without governmental interference. Such was the justification for deregulation of several industries and a partial justification for the reductions in federal funding for a wide range of development programs. State governments, however, have been extraordinarily prolific in developing innovative policy and programs during the 1980s. The sources for this initiative are many, but a federal role is frequently present. Competition among states and the ease of information diffusion, especially through national organizations, has contributed to the rapid diffusion of ideas.

Development and Technology Policy

In technology policy, federal funding for research exceeds state funding by many magnitudes. Much of the federally funded basic research occurs in state universities, suggesting an important complementarity between the two levels of government. Both levels of government have elaborated policies to encourage commercialization of research findings. The programs of the federal Small Business Administration, with a network of offices throughout the country, are frequently used by state and local governments in their business assistance programs. The Job Training and Partnership Act relies heavily on states for administration, as does the Small Cities Community Development Block Grant. In the area of export policy, we again see an important complementarity between the states and federal efforts. Virtually all states are promoting exports, although relatively little funding is provided. The principal source of information about foreign markets is the federal government, and the federal government holds responsibility for securing access to foreign markets for U.S. goods. Although states may wish to expand funding for such efforts, fiscal constraints will prevent substantial increases in the future, suggesting that states and the federal government will remain partners in these efforts.

States have certainly seized the initiative in development and technology policy, and they continue to experiment with a wide range of approaches, but the actual funding levels for these efforts, though growing rapidly, represent only a small proportion of state budgets. Faced by fiscal constraints, states have adopted other approaches, such as adapting the missions of existing state institutions, providing greater powers to municipal governments, and mobilizing private-sector resources. Although federal policy may dictate market solutions and decentralization of policymaking as the means to adapt to economic change, states have taken a substantially more aggressive and interventionist approach to technology and development policy.

Regulation

State policy initiative in regulation is quite a different story. Here the motivating force has clearly been the federal government, and states have not simply been filling a void. The federal concern in regulatory issues is fundamentally different from that of the states. Federal government's authority rests on interstate commerce, and thus, on firms that export. Interstate commerce has been relatively easy to deregulate because many competitors have been attracted to these lucrative markets. Intrastate markets, however, which are heavily served by local-demand firms, are the focus of state concern. Local service utility companies, especially local telephone companies, are being affected by economic and technological changes. The monopoly status of local service delivery firms is being threatened by federal deregulatory decisions, and technological change and these issues must be addressed by state regulation.

Federal deregulation of interstate markets has created new issues for states, but of greatest significance to states has been the attempt of federal regulatory policy to force deregulation at the state level. The federal government has great regulatory leverage, based on the interstate commerce clause, as a result of the spatial integration of the national economy. This integration creates high levels of interstate commerce, and a history of favorable court decisions has ratified the expansion of federal authority on such matters. States, therefore, must not only address the concerns of regulated local service monopolies and their customers as the impacts of deregulation are expressed, but also respond to federal preemption on regulatory issues. Deregulation may permit competition to emerge, but the captive local service market will be the last to benefit from it. In addition, the local service companies and their customers are significant political forces in states. States are also moving toward deregulation, although the movement is slower than it is at the federal level for just these reasons.

Another force at work in regulation, especially in telecommunications, is technology. An underlying element of the antitrust case against AT&T and the justification for deregulation—related yet distinct issues—is technological change. Technology has undoubtedly weakened the argument that telecommunications is a natural monopoly. The task before the intergovernmental regulatory structure, in which states have an important role, is determining which services should continue to be provided on a regulated basis and which on a competitive basis. Again, the impact on local service markets is important and has significant development implications.

In the regulation of financial institutions states have generally performed poorly. For most of this century, and especially during the Depression, state regulatory authority over banks and savings and loans was eroded as the federal authority grew. Federal deregulation of financial institutions and adverse economic conditions in the late 1970s and 1980s created circumstances under which increased state regulatory permissiveness, especially with regard to S&Ls, had extremely adverse consequences in many states. Although a fair number of states performed their regulatory responsibilities quite successfully, the federal government was forced to take over an industry in crisis. A similar scenario in the insurance industry, where states have retained almost total regulatory autonomy and authority, may well occur in the near future. Although some forces at work were clearly beyond the control of states and certainly federal actions contributed to the problems, in many respects the contemporary federal initiatives are similar to instances in the 1930s where states were unable to resolve a crisis and federal action was then taken.

In sum, the federal government has played a dominant role in changing the intergovernmental context of regulation, and states have largely reacted to federal actions. States have been prodded by the federal government for broader and more rapid deregulation, but they have used their discretionary authority in distinct ways. Especially in telecommunications, the traditional regulatory framework has been rendered inadequate by technological change, and the federal adjustment to this change has complicated policymaking for states. As a consequence, states have adopted a variety of policy strategies. Given states' regulatory responsibility for intrastate markets and the political environment they face, their diversity of policy priorities is not surprising. The federal deregulatory thrust has, ironically, pushed states into a more activist regulatory role.

Education and Training Policy

Policy initiatives in education and training have followed yet a different pattern, largely because education is principally a state and local responsibility. Although the federal government provides high levels of funding for specific activities, such as job training, and has played a critical regulatory role in desegregation, on balance, education continues to be conceived as principally a responsibility of state and local government. The perceived inadequacies of the educational system have certainly arisen in national forums—though not necessarily federal forums—but have not resulted in significant and far-reaching federal initiatives. There has been widespread concern with education, and a principal forum for addressing this problem nationally is the National Governors' Association. This national organization of state leaders has in some respects eclipsed the prerogatives of the federal government and certainly of the federal executive branch. Although the lack of consensus may suggest that the issue is not yet sufficiently ripe for federal action, it is just as likely that divided federal government and the budget deficit will minimize federal leadership at least in terms of funding. Federal requirements for states to coordinate human services through human investment strategies is a promising development. As has been true many times in the past, the federal initiative will probably be patterned on earlier efforts in some states.

Competition and Cooperation Among States

The intergovernmental context governing relations among states is also of central importance. Under the federalist system, the federal government had the authority to prevent unfair, or what today might be called protectionist, state policies. The most notable was the prohibition against interstate tariffs. A state could not erect barriers or subject imports from other states to conditions that would provide unfair advantage to local firms. Federal regulation of interstate commerce helps moderate the provincial instincts of states.

The federal government has not been entirely successful, however. State autonomy in the regulation of insurance companies allowed states to create advantages for local companies. In addition, intense competition among states in recent years has led to similar actions by states. Targeted tax abatement programs of states and local governments are the contemporary manifestation of this inclination to give advantage to local firms. In the context of international free trade, tax reductions of this type are considered undue protection and a violation of free trade.

The politics of the so-called state bidding wars suggests that they will not disappear. With a single seller and many buyers, the relatively weak bargaining position of states and of cities results in very high bids, through incentive packages, and produce controversial, if not questionable, public policy. As long as other states continue this practice, it is difficult for a particular state or city to withdraw from the competition. The federal government may not have the authority, and likely not the will, to prevent this form of competition.

Although competition abounds, there are many examples of information exchange and coalition building among states that clearly improve public policymaking. A program in one state is seldom adopted without change by another, but a single state frequently builds on the experiences of other states. This exchange could certainly be conducted by the federal government, but national associations such as the National Association of State Legislatures, National Association of State Planning Agencies, Council of State Governments, and especially the National Governors' Association, as well as an ever-increasing number of research organizations and think tanks, serve this role. This intense exchange of ideas and experience sheds a different light on the "laboratories of democracy" idea. The process is better conceived as a learning system model, whereby a single state continually monitors and learns from other states, adapting ideas to the political context of the state. This phenomenon is particularly important in smaller states with fewer resources to apply, for example, in the regulation of financial institutions.

The ideological rationale for devolution of state powers and restitution of appropriate intergovernmental relations has contributed only modestly to the state initiatives discussed here. In each of the three policy case studies, the origin of the state initiatives varied, but in none do we find a theoretical justification for state action to be a compelling force. In development and technology policy, economic distress and nonaction of the federal government were the most significant forces. In telecommunications, deregulation, in no small part the result of new technological capabilities in a complex intergovernmental regulatory system, led to state action. No devolution of state authority occurred; in fact, the federal policy has been to impose deregulation on states. In education policy, broad public dissatisfaction with educational systems, a major responsibility of state government, was the principal motivating factor for state action, although a federal disposition to decentralized delivery system for training in the JTPA program partially accounts for state action. Although the normative discussion of what the role of government, in general, and intergovernmental relations, in particular, *should* be had been prominent in the 1980s, there is little evidence that the discussion has informed actual state policymaking.

Multiple points of access to policymaking contribute to the proliferation of state initiatives. Many participants in policymaking apparently find state government to be an increasingly appropriate forum for expressing their interests. A complementarity between federal and state governments exists, and a federal role remains essential in many areas. But the federal role has become increasingly one of establishing market institutions, such as those regulating interstate commerce, freedom of movement, industrial standards, and national infrastructure systems. Development initiative, however, and the creative mobilization of development strategies through public policy is largely being exercised by states. Diffusion of information and initiatives among states plays an important supportive role, and municipal governments are demonstrating innovative responses, though they tend to be even more constrained by fiscal pressures than states. The creativity in the policy system for development issues rests more with states than at any time since the early decades of the century.

THE DYNAMICS OF POLICY CHOICE

The policy decisions reached by states depend on the interplay of several factors—including the availability of resources, interest groups, institutional capabilities, and political leadership—and the adoption of a policy does not guarantee its effectiveness. The quality of policy adopted by states depends directly on the competency of state policymaking and resources available to states. Policymaking itself has become more problematic. Legislatures increasingly reflect a growing range of groups and interests, and reaching consensus is difficult, especially if the new course of action implies substantial funding. At the same time, a greater range of resources can be brought to bear on policy development. The legislative and executive branches have greater policy analysis capabilities. A number of state utility commissions, for example, have very successfully served a policy development role in addressing cutting-edge issues. In telecommunications and education policy many interest groups have the ability to conduct studies and obtain analyses that are later used in the legislative process. As a result, policy decisions can be better informed, even though decision making is more difficult given the competing interests and proposals.

In technology and development policy, there are relatively few significant constituencies and relatively limited funding is available. Support for this type of policy rests largely with the recognition of its importance in economic change and is not the result of strong constituency support. The university research centers and research funding do have one large and significant constituent, state university systems, but the general level of interest in applied research has been modest in contrast to the basic state appropriation for higher education. Many of the development programs, such as venture capital programs and export promotion programs, help relatively few businesses and consequently have limited constituencies. Priorities in recruitment efforts more adequately incorporate a recognition of economic change and the role of technology by focusing on advanced technology firms and prestigious research facilities. However, the more dominant appeal of recruitment remains its high visibility, and support is found in local-demand sectors, especially chambers of commerce, utilities, and labor.

Telecommunications policymaking has become extremely complex, with many actors and diverse interests. Diversification in the industry creates new trade groups and alliances. Even in a single segment, such as long-distance service, increased competition creates multiple actors and interests. Technological change has created competition among various media—wire, radio, and cable TV—and thus has created other potentially antagonistic interests. In many states, consumers are well organized and effective intervenors at utility commissions and lobbyists in legislatures. Virtually all parties use the multiple-access characteristic of the country's governmental system and take their appeals to various governmental units. Parties that do not obtain the desired results at the utility commission may turn to legislatures, and in a good number of states the utility commissions have been overruled by legislatures. Preemptive strategies of the FCC, congressional action, and Judge Green can all affect state policymaking.

Education and Training

In education and training policy, the range of interest groups may be somewhat narrower than in telecommunications, but some groups have very significant influence and have effective lobbies. Teachers, administrators, school boards, school districts, and state agencies are significant policy actors. Business organizations are increasingly involved in education issues. Large and entrenched public education bureaucracies also condition policymaking. The very substantial levels of public funds and the number of people employed make policymaking in this field unlike that of the other two cases.

Education reform has become an important political issue for several reasons. Judicial actions taken against perceived inequities in school finance systems by low-income school districts have often led to legislative action. Business leaders associated with sectors where skill requirements are critical have helped place education on the agenda of state and local government. Requests for tax increases to fund education meet with resistance from taxpayers reluctant to spend more on a system that may not be functioning properly. A number of reports by blue-ribbon commissions have made the public aware of the challenges faced by education. Education has become a core political issue for the country, and state government is the principal forum for addressing the issue.

Education policy is associated with several critical objectives. The quality and skill levels of the labor force, an increasingly important element of the economy, to a significant extent depend on the education and training systems. At the same time, education represents the principal public policy instrument for creating equal opportunity for all members of the society, an important egalitarian value of the country. For reasons of economic change and of existing inequities for many low-income groups in the educational system, education and training policy has been under intense scrutiny.

The uncertainty associated with appropriate strategies for change and the decentralized nature of education and training have produced many proposals for school reform and much experimentation by states and local school districts. Most efforts attempt to reduce the control of centralized state education bureaucracies, which have been identified as a principal source of inefficiency and which stifle creativity. Decentralization inside state education systems can be achieved through site-based management, for example, but such reforms are being accompanied by more extensive accountability measures focused on school performance. Although little systemwide improvement can yet be discerned, the breadth of reform and experimentation suggests that innovation is occurring in this large and unwieldy public sector bureaucracy.

Public higher education has benefitted in the 1980s from above-average increases in state funding, although the recession of the early 1990s has put a dramatic end to this trend in a number of states. Spending has tended to favor the science and engineering fields and thus constitutes an effort to improve the labor force characteristics of a state for the technologically oriented sectors. But perhaps most interesting are the quite substantial increases found in a number of southern states, especially Florida and Texas, which have attempted to match the educational systems of more economically advanced states. Given the importance of the educational composition of a state's labor force in establishing a comparative advantage for future prosperity, this priority is indeed warranted.

The Quality of State Economic Development Policymaking

The creation by state governments of forums to explore economic change has been a particularly notable and useful effort. In economic development policy, telecommunications, and education, strategic planning exercises or blue-ribbon panels have frequently been used to educate the public and state governments about pressing issues. The forums often consist of members from various interest groups, and consensus building may be part of their agenda. These forums have been particularly important at a time of an uncertain future. The traditional policymaking procedure in state government is not a very efficient way of exploring broad development issues and certainly not an efficient way of educating the public. Representatives of future constituencies are not represented in that process and, consequently, policy is unlikely to respond to their needs. Certainly the long-standing problems with such forums—producing reports soon forgotten or serving as a justification for postponing action—persist, but they also represent nonadversarial forums for exploring wide-ranging issues. In many instances the ideas developed in these forums have eventually found their way into legislation.

The activities and initiatives of states in these various policy areas reflect an increasingly sophisticated understanding of the future and of the role state governments can play in the economy. Both the range of efforts and the evolution of strategies adopted by states capture a knowledge of economic change. States no longer expect to shape their economies by relying only on tax incentives or low-interest loans. Retention strategies, particularly efforts to improve productivity of existing industries, as well as broad-based education reform, are the result not of firms driving a hard bargain with state governments but a broad-based commitment to improve the productivity of resources within a state. These types of efforts represent an investment in the future, not attempts to secure short-term benefits. Thus, old forms of state action are being adapted and new forms tested.

These general patterns of recent state policy should not mask variations in the specific responses of individual states. States with relatively few resources and less sophisticated industrial structures have been forced to rely on recruitment to a greater extent than other states. Some states have endorsed targeting, whereas others feel that the public sector is unable to pick winners. The role of individual leaders, particularly governors, can be very important. Here political culture—specifically, the history of overt intervention in a state's economy—and attention to consensus building seem to be important factors in the way states respond. In New York, with its long history of aggressive state involvement in economic affairs, the question is not whether the state should be involved but rather how the many governmental agencies that deal with economic development can be coordinated to achieve effective intervention. In Rhode Island, the rejection of a very elaborate and comprehensive development plan, the Greenhouse Compact, has been explained by the failure of the corporatist approach to policy development to garner broad political support.

The specific state strategies have been found to be embedded in a state's political economy. In technology policy, priorities have been attuned to the existing economic strengths of a state. Although zero sum strategies for lowering the costs for individual firms were emphasized initially, strategies focused on increasing the productivity of resources have emerged. Such strategies attempt to make existing business more competitive, nurture new firms, and secure advanced infrastructure.

An issue raised in Chapter 4, the effect of tax rates and structures on growth, can now be revisited. One response to economic distress in the North was to reduce tax rates, especially for businesses; lowering taxes was believed to be an effective means to achieve economic competitiveness. But it is also clear that budget constraints and improperly designed spending patterns can each lead both to underinvestment in critical infrastructures and to slow growth.

Budget limitations have brought into focus another development role for states, that of mobilizing nongovernmental resources for development. In strategic planning exercises, relatively little spending can inform state government and the public on pressing policy issues. Creating capital funds and imposing service obligations on regulated companies can serve development goals without increasing governmental spending. Modifying objectives of existing state institutions and programs can further develop objectives without requiring new funds. The use of telecommunications innovations represents an opportunity to increase the efficiency in the delivery of a wide array of governmental services. Fiscal constraints have forced states to be innovative not only in their development strategies but in the full range of their activities as well.

INADEQUATE POLICY RESPONSES

Although the record of state responsiveness to economic challenges has been fairly positive, a number of shortcomings can be noted. The growing problems of distressed communities are not adequately being addressed by states, nor by any other level of government. The tools available to states for distressed communities—enterprise zones, business assistance and training programs—are important, but states usually rely on municipal government for their implementation and these strategies are weak given the magnitude of the problems faced. The economic development strategies discussed here rarely address the unique problems of low-income populations. Some revenue equalization occurs for public services, but the wealth disparities, generated by socioeconomic segregation and rapid suburbanization, are significant, and inequalities in service levels continue. The fact that issues of low-income populations are not high priorities for states is linked to the problem of representation and participation in the policy process.

The movement of population, jobs, and tax base to suburban areas started in the early part of the century. The rapidly growing resource disparities, however, are of more recent vintage. Given that substate governmental structure is the creation of state government, these growing disparities in resources and service delivery in a highly fragmented local governmental system present a great political challenge to states. Although the development strategies of states tend to focus on metropolitan areas, resource disparities across jurisdictions in a single metropolitan area still abound and are troublesome. Short of cooperation of local governments, actions by states will be necessary if the resulting disparities in service delivery are to be resolved. This issue has yet to become a pressing concern of state governments with the possible exception of school finance systems.

In redistributive policy, states participate in a complex intergovernmental system in which the federal government has been the principal actor, at least since the 1930s, as discussed in Chapter 3. The fiscal constraints on states and localities have significantly limited their ability to respond to federal actions of the 1980s and 1990s, which shifted to states greater responsibility for redistributive activities. State efforts to target to distressed communities, discussed in Chapter 4, were more common and substantial than expected, and certainly a significant effort in equalization of school finance is found. However, these efforts pale in view of the extensive needs of a quite large poverty population. The lack of commitment to addressing these needs at the federal level will only partially be offset by state actions.

The problems of rural America have received scant attention in this study. Although the problems are extensive and deserving of consideration, states and the federal government are only now coherently analyzing these problems and developing strategies for solving them. Rural constituencies, with the exception of agribusiness, have not successfully placed rural development issues on the agenda of most state governments. Economic development initiatives of states have been principally concerned with urban and suburban America, partly as a result of the urban location of the advanced technology and producer services sectors. Some types of development policies, however, such as the deaveraging of telecommunications costs and the subsequent rise in prices, may well have important, and perhaps adverse effects on rural areas.

THE IMPORTANCE OF THE STATE ROLE

The basic structure of intergovernmental relations affecting the country's economy shows no signs of fundamental change. For constitutional, political, economic, and historical reasons, stability rather than change in this structure prevails. Many requirements of a national economy, increasingly competing in a world economy, can be satisfied only by federal action. A divided and fiscally stressed federal government, however, has created a permissive intergovernmental context, at least with respect to state action. And state governments have been able to respond to both the distress and opportunities presented by economic change in a way that would have seemed unimaginable two to three decades ago, though perhaps not unprecedented in American history. This result has been produced by an economic development imperative, a flexible intergovernmental system with multiple points of access, and more open, competent, and assertive state governments. The federal government has deliberately induced state action in some instances, but in a number of policy areas, state programs and efforts have replaced federal initiatives and now states exercise policymaking leadership on many development fronts.

The changing economy has provided state governments the opportunity to influence its emerging spatial pattern. States are important not only for supporting growth within a state but also for enhancing the competitiveness of the national economy. The infrastructure provision function of states—in technology, telecommunications, and education and training—requires modification if states and the nation are to prosper, and states are responding to this imperative. A number of significant inadequacies in state action and the growing problems of poverty and deteriorating income distribution may temper one's optimism about the future. However, if development strategies allow states to adapt to changing economic circumstances and create the infrastructure required, the prospects for all citizens will be improved. The pressures on state governments for action within the context of fiscal limitations create extremely difficult conditions for policymaking; however, states appear better able to struggle with these challenges than at any time since the turn of the century.

State activism in economic development has occurred in the midst of a national discussion about the appropriate role of government. Although the discussion has been cast in a normative framework—what the role of government *should* be—it has been rendered somewhat dated by changing events. The growth in federal revenues has been substantially slowed and expenditures on social programs curtailed; but overall federal spending has grown and the enormous federal debt virtually eliminates any flexibility in federal priorities. Federal policy discussions now tend to focus on what the federal government has to do, not what it should do.

As we have seen here, this national discussion has been occurring as states have been taking decisive and bold, though experimental, action on a wide range of activities. These actions have not been simply the result of aggressive state policymakers and agencies attempting to increase the size of state government, although as we have seen, the tendency for public bureaucracies to insure their own survival should not be underestimated. Because most state governments must balance their budgets, each increase in expenditures has meant higher taxes for the public. And the political power of tax rebellion has not been lost on state politicians. Although the question of what government *should* do needs to be raised continually as one of several elements of public accountability, compelling political and economic forces have led to the creation of a wide variety of new economic development initiatives, substantial adaptation in educational systems, new approaches to telecommunications policy, and significant increases in state funding for many activities.

Imperatives of the international marketplace and federal policymaking may constrain the effectiveness of state governments. Nevertheless, states are responding in innovative ways, and a new set of state institutions and expenditure patterns are evolving to meet the needs of the emerging economy. Although competition among states for external resources will not abate, the challenges presented by structural change and the politics of development policymaking have converged to force states to place greater emphasis on developing their internal resources, and this will prove useful to the states and the country.

Selected Bibliography

Advisory Commission on Intergovernmental Relations (ACIR). *Intergovernmental Regulation of Telecommunications*. Washington, D.C., July 1990.

ACIR. *Interjurisdictional Tax and Policy Competition: Good or Bad for the Federal System*. Washington, D.C., April 1991.

ACIR. *The Question of State Government Capability*. Washington, D.C., 1985.

ACIR. *Regulatory Federalism: Policy, Process, Impact, and Reform*. Washington, D.C., 1984.

ACIR. *State and Local Initiatives on Productivity, Technology, and Innovation: Enhancing a National Resource for International Competitiveness*. Washington, D.C., 1990.

ACIR. *The States and Distressed Communities: 1983 Update*. Washington, D.C., November 1985.

ACIR. *The Transformation in American Politics: Implications for Federalism*. Washington, D.C., 1986.

Allen, David N. and Victor Levine. *Nurturing Advanced Technology Enterprises: Emerging Issues in State and Local Economic Development Policy*. New York: Praeger, 1986.

Barfield, Claude E. *Rethinking Federalism: Block Grants and Federal, State, and Local Responsibilities*. Washington, D.C.: American Enterprise Institute for Public Policy Research, 1981.

Bartik, Timothy J. *Who Benefits from State and Local Economic Development Policies?* Kalamazoo, MI: W. E. Upjohn Institute for Employment Research, 1991.

Bartsch, Charles, Marian Barber, and Margaret Quan, eds. *The Guide to State and Federal Resources for Economic Development*. 4th ed. Washington, D.C.: Northeast-Midwest Institute, 1988.

Baumol, William, Sue Anne Batey Blackman, and Edward M. Wolff. *Productivity and American Leadership: The Long View*. Cambridge, MA: MIT Press, 1989.

Beer, Samuel H. "The Modernization of American Federalism." *Publius: The Journal of Federalism* 3, no. 2 (Fall 1973): 53–91.

Birch, David. *Job Creation in America: How Our Smallest Companies Put the Most People to Work*. New York: The Free Press, 1987.

Brint, Steven and Jerome Karabel. *The Diverted Dream: Community Colleges and the Promise of Educational Opportunity in America, 1900–1985*. New York: Oxford University Press, 1989.

Brooks, John. *Telephone: The First Hundred Years*. New York: Harper & Row, 1975.

Carnevale, Anthony Patrick. *America and the New Economy*. Washington, D.C.: The American Society for Training and Development and U.S. Department of Labor, Employment and Training Administration, 1991.

Clarke, Marianne K. *Revitalizing State Economies: A Review of State Economic Development Policies and Programs*. Washington, D.C.: National Governors' Association, 1986.

Cobb, James C. *The Selling of the South: The Southern Crusade for Industrial Development, 1936–1980*. Baton Rouge, LA: Louisiana State University Press, 1982.

Cohen, Arthur M. and Florence Brawer. *The American Community College*. San Francisco: Jossey-Bass, 1982.

Cohen, Linda R. and Roger G. Noll. *The Technology Pork Barrel*. Washington, D.C.: Brookings Institution, 1991.

Cohen, Stephen S. and John Zysman. *Manufacturing Matters: The Myth of the Post-Industrial Economy*. New York: Basic Books, 1987.

Commission on the Skills of the American Workforce. *America's Choice: High Skills or Low Wages!* Rochester, NY: National Center on Education and the Economy, 1990.

Conlan, Timothy. *New Federalism: Intergovernmental Reform from Nixon to Reagan*. Washington, D.C.: Brookings Institution, 1988.

Corporation for Enterprise Development. *The 1991 Development Report Card for the States*. Washington, D.C., April 1991.

Crandall, Robert W. *After the Breakup: U.S. Telecommunications in a More Competitive Era*. Washington, D.C.: The Brookings Institution, 1991.

Crandall, Robert W., and Kenneth Flamm, eds. *Changing the Rules: Technological Change, International Competition, and Regulation in Communications*. Washington, D.C.: The Brookings Institution, 1989.

Cremin, Lawrence A. *American Education: The Metropolitan Experience, 1876–1980*. New York: Harper & Row, 1988.

Denison, Edward F. *Estimates of Productivity Change by Industry: An Evaluation and an Alternative*. Washington, D.C.: The Brookings Institution, 1989.

Derthick, Martha. "American Federalism: Madison's Middle Ground in the 1980s." *Public Administration Review* (January/February 1987): 66–74.

Dizard, Wilson P. *The Coming Information Age: An Overview of Technology, Economics and Politics*. 2nd ed. New York: Longman, 1985.

Dordick, Herb S. and Frederick Williams. *Innovative Management Using Telecommunications: A Guide to Opportunities, Strategies and Applications*. New York: John Wiley & Sons, 1986.

Doyle, Denis P., and Terry W. Hartle. *Excellence in Education: The States Take Charge.* Washington, D.C.: The American Enterprise Institute, 1985.

Dresang, Dennis L. and James J. Gosling. *Politics, Policy, and Management in the American States.* New York: Longman, 1989.

Dye, Thomas R. *American Federalism: Competition Among Governments.* Lexington, MA: Lexington Books, 1990.

Dye, Thomas R. *Politics, Economics and the Public: Policy Outcomes in the American States.* Chicago: Rand McNally & Co., 1966.

Eisinger, Peter K. *The Rise of the Entrepreneurial State: State and Local Development Policy in the United States.* Madison, WI: University of Wisconsin Press, 1988.

Elazar, Daniel J. *American Federalism: A View from the States.* New York: Thomas Crowell Co., 1966.

Elazar, Daniel J. *The American Partnership: Intergovernmental Relations in Nineteenth-Century American Federalism.* Chicago: University of Chicago Press, 1962.

Foner, Eric. *Reconstruction: America's Unfinished Revolution, 1963–1877.* New York: Harper & Row, 1988.

Fosler, R. Scott, ed. *The New Economic Role of American States: Strategies in a Competitive World Economy.* New York: Oxford University Press, 1988.

Galbraith, James K. "A New Picture of the American Economy." *The American Prospect* (Fall 1991): 27–29.

Gittell, Marilyn, ed. *State Politics and the New Federalism.* New York: Longman, 1986.

Glickman, Norman J. and Douglas P. Woodward. *The New Competitors: How Foreign Investors Are Changing the U.S. Economy.* New York: Basic Books, 1989.

Goodrich, Carter. *Government Promotion of American Canals and Railroads: 1800–1890.* New York: Columbia University Press, 1960.

Gormley, William T., Jr. *The Politics of Public Utility Regulation.* Pittsburgh, PA: University of Pittsburgh Press, 1983.

Grodzin, Morton. "Centralization and Decentralization in the American Federal System." In *A Nation of States,* edited by Robert A. Goldwin. Chicago: Public Affairs Conference Center, 1964.

Grubb, W. Norton. "The Bandwagon Once More: Vocational Preparation for High-Tech Occupations." *Harvard Educational Review* 54, no. 4 (November 1984): 429–51.

Grubb, W. Norton. "Dropouts, Spells of Time, and Credits in Postsecondary Education: Evidence from Longitudinal Surveys." *Economics of Education Review* 8 (1989) 49–67.

Gulick, L. H. "Reorganization of the States." *Civil Engineering* (August 1933): 421.

Handlin, Oscar and Mary Flug Handlin. *Commonwealth, A Study of the Role of Government in the American Economy: Massachusetts, 1774–1861.* New York: New York University Press, 1947.

Hartz, Louis. *Economic Policy and Democratic Thought: Pennsylvania, 1776–1860.* Cambridge: Harvard University Press, 1948.

Hepworth, Mark. *Geography of the Information Economy.* New York: The Guildford Press, 1990.

Horwitz, Robert Britt. *The Irony of Regulatory Reform: The Deregulation of American Telecommunications.* New York: Oxford University Press, 1989.

Huber, P. W. *The Geodesic Network: 1987 Report on Competition in the Telephone Industry.* Washington, D.C.: U.S. Department of Justice, 1987.

Hughes, Jonathan R. T. *The Governmental Habit: Economic Controls from Colonial Times to the Present.* New York: Basic Books, 1977.

Israel, Cary A., James F. McKenney, and Jerome F. Wartgow. "Community Colleges: A Competitive Edge for Economic Development." *Economic Development Review* 5, no. 2 (Summer 1987): 10–23.

Johnston, William B. and Arnold H. Packer. *Workforce 2000: Work and Workers for the 21st Century.* Indianapolis, IN: Hudson Institute, 1987.

Kerr, Clark. *The Uses of the University, With a Postscript—1972.* Cambridge, MA: Harvard University Press, 1972.

Key, V. O., Jr. *The Administration of Federal Grants to States.* Chicago, IL: Public Administration Service, 1937.

Koepplin, Leslie W. and David A. Wilson, eds. *The Future of State Universities: Issues in Teaching, Research, and Public Service.* New Brunswick, NJ: Rutgers University Press, 1985.

Lazerson, Marvin and W. Norton Grubb. *American Education and Vocationalism: A Documentary History, 1870–1970.* New York: Teachers College Press, Columbia University, 1974.

Liebschutz, Sara F. "Targeting by the State: The Basic Issues." *Publius: The Journal of Federalism* 19 (Spring 1989): 12.

Liner, E. Blaine, ed. *A Decade of Devolution: Perspectives on State–Local Relations.* Washington, D.C.: Urban Institute Press, 1989.

Luger, Michael I. and Harvey A. Goldstein. *Technology in the Garden: Research Parks and Regional Economic Development.* Chapel Hill, NC: The University of North Carolina Press, 1991.

Machlup, Fritz. *The Production and Distribution of Knowledge in the United States.* Princeton, NJ: Princeton University Press, 1962.

MacManus, Susan A. "Linking State Employment and Training and Economic Development Programs: A 20-State Analysis." *Public Administration Review* (November/December 1986): 640–648.

Markusen, Ann R. and Virginia Carlson. "Deindustrialization in the American Midwest: Causes and Responses." In *Deindustrialization and Regional Economic Transformation: The Experience of the United States,* edited by Lloyd Rodwin and Hidehiko Sazanami. Boston: Unwin Hyman, 1989.

Markusen, Ann, Peter Hall, Scott Campbell, and Sabina Deitrick. *The Rise of the Sunbelt: The Military Remapping of Industrial America.* New York: Oxford University Press, 1991.

Meier, Kenneth J. *The Political Economy of Regulation: The Case of Insurance.* Albany, NY: State University of New York Press, 1988.

Moes, John E. "The Subsidization of Industry by Local Communities in the South." *Southern Economic Journal* 28 (October 1961): 187–193.

Mokry, Benjamin W. *Entrepreneurship and Public Policy: Can Government Stimulate Business Startups?* Westport, CT: Quorum Books, 1988.

Nash, Gerald D. *State Government and Economic Development: A History of Administrative Policies in California, 1849–1933.* Berkeley: Institute of Governmental Studies, 1964.

National Commission on Excellence in Education. *A Nation at Risk.* Washington, D.C., 1983.

Newberg, Paula R., ed. *New Directions in Telecommunications Policy, Volume 1: Reg-*

ulatory Policy: Telephony and Mass Media. Durham, NC: Duke University Press, 1989.

Noyelle, Thierry and Penny Peace. *The Information Industries: New York's New Export Base.* New York: Conservation of Human Resources, Columbia University, November 1988.

Osborne, David. *Laboratories of Democracy.* Boston: Harvard Business School Press, 1988.

Patterson, James T. *The New Deal and the States: Federalism in Transition.* Princeton, NJ: Princeton University Press, 1969.

Peterson, Paul E. *The Politics of School Reform, 1870–1940.* Chicago: University of Chicago Press, 1985.

Porat, Marc Uri. *The Information Economy: The Technology Matrices (1967).* Washington, D.C.: Department of Commerce, 1977.

Primm, James Neal. *Economic Policy in the Development of a Western State: Missouri, 1820–1860.* Harvard University Press, 1954.

Reagan, Michael D. *Regulation: The Politics of Policy.* Boston: Little, Brown and Co., 1987.

Redford, Emmette. "Centralized and Decentralized Political Impacts on a Developing Economy: Interpretations of American Experience." In *Spatial Dimensions of Development Administration,* ed. James J. Heaphey. Durham, N.C.: Duke University Press, 1971.

Robertson, David B. and Dennis R. Judd. *The Development of American Public Policy: The Structure of Policy Restraint.* Glenview, IL: Scott, Foresman and Co., 1989.

Robertson, Ross M. *History of the American Economy.* New York: Harcourt Brace Jovanovich, Inc., 1973.

Rosenthal, Alan. *Governors and Legislatures: Contending Powers.* Washington, D.C.: Congressional Quarterly Press, 1990.

Rosenthal, Alan. *Legislative Life: People, Process and Performance in the States.* New York: Harper & Row, 1981.

Rowland, C. K. and Roger Marz. "Gresham's Law: The Regulatory Analogy." *Policy Studies Review,* vol. 1, no. 3 (1982), pp. 572–580.

Sanford, Terry. *Storm Over the States.* New York: McGraw-Hill, 1967.

Schmandt, Jurgen and Robert H. Wilson, eds., *Growth Policy in the Age of High Technology: The Role of Regions and States.* Boston: Unwin Hyman, 1990.

Schmandt, Jurgen and Robert H. Wilson. "State Science and Technology Policies: An Assessment." *Economic Development Quarterly* 2, no. 2 (May 1988): 124–137.

Schmandt, Jurgen, Frederick Williams, and Robert H. Wilson, eds. *Telecommunications and Economic Development: The New State Role.* New York: Praeger, 1989.

Schmandt, Jurgen, Frederick Williams, Robert H. Wilson, and Sharon Strover, eds. *The New Urban Infrastructure: Cities and Telecommunications.* New York: Praeger, 1990.

Schmandt, Jurgen, Frederick Williams, Robert H. Wilson, and Sharon Strover, eds. *Telecommunications and Rural Development: A Study of Private and Public Sector Innovation.* New York: Praeger, 1991.

Scholz, John T. "State Regulatory Reform and Federal Regulation." *Policy Studies Review* 1, no. 2 (1982): 347–359.

Schulman, Bruce J. *Federal Policy, Economic Development, and Transformation of the South, 1938–1980.* New York: Oxford University Press, 1991.

Seninger, Stephen F. *Labor Force Policies for Regional Economic Development: The Role of Employment and Training Programs.* New York: Praeger, 1989.

Smead, Elmer E. *Governmental Promotion and Regulation of Business.* New York: Appleton-Century-Crofts, 1969.

Teske, Paul Eric. *After Divestiture: The Political Economy of State Telecommunications Regulation.* Albany, NY: State University of New York Press, 1990.

U.S. Department of Commerce, International Trade Administration, *1991 Industrial Outlook.* Washington, D.C., January 1991.

Welborn, David M., and Jesse Burkhead. *Intergovernmental Relations in the American Administrative State: The Johnson Presidency.* Austin, TX: University of Texas Press, 1989.

Williams, Frederick. *The New Telecommunications: The Infrastructure for the Information Age.* New York: The Free Press, 1991.

Wright, Deil. *Understanding Intergovernmental Relations.* 2nd ed. Monterey, CA: Brooks/Cole Publishing Co., 1982.

Index

About the Author

ROBERT H. WILSON is professor at the Lyndon B. Johnson School of Public Affairs of the University of Texas. He is the coeditor of *Telecommunications and Rural Development* (Praeger, 1991) and *The New Urban Infrastructure* (Praeger, 1990).